Structuring politics

This volume brings together original essays by scholars working on a diverse range of empirical issues, but whose work is in each case informed by a "historical institutional" approach to the study of politics. By bringing these pieces together, the volume highlights the methodological and theoretical foundations of this approach and illustrates the general contributions it has made to comparative politics.

The introductory essay identifies common analytic themes among these essays and within historical institutionalism generally. Institutions are defined, key precepts of historical institutionalism are explained, and the theoretical antecedents of this approach are identified. Historical institutionalism is contrasted both to earlier forms of institutional analysis and to rational choice analysis. The introductory essay also identifies key "frontier" issues, such as institutional dynamism and change, and the interaction of ideational innovation and institutional constraints.

The essays demonstrate the potential of a historical institutional approach to illuminate a broad range of issues: How and why institutions change, how political ideas are filtered through institutional structures in the formation of specific policies, and how institutional structure can have unintended effects on the shaping of policy. Through these richly detailed pieces, the reader is provided not only a thorough understanding of the method of analysis but also an overview of its theoretical underpinnings.

CAMBRIDGE STUDIES IN COMPARATIVE POLITICS

General editor
PETER LANGE   Duke University

Associate editors
ELLEN COMISSO   University of California, San Diego
PETER HALL   Harvard University
JOEL MIGDAL   University of Washington
HELEN MILNER   Columbia University
SIDNEY TARROW   Cornell University

This series publishes comparative research that seeks to explain important, cross-national domestic political phenomena. Based on a broad conception of comparative politics, it hopes to promote critical dialogue among different approaches. While encouraging contributions from diverse theoretical perspectives, the series will particularly emphasize work on domestic institutions and work that examines the relative roles of historical structures and constraints, of individual or organizational choice, and of strategic interaction in explaining political actions and outcomes. This focus includes an interest in the mechanisms through which historical factors impinge on contemporary political choices and outcomes.

Works on all parts of the world are welcomed, and priority will be given to studies that cross traditional area boundaries and that treat the United States in comparative perspective. Many of the books in the series are expected to be comparative, drawing on material from more than one national case, but studies devoted to single countries will also be considered, especially those that pose their problem and analysis in such a way that they make a direct contribution to comparative analysis and theory.

OTHER BOOKS IN THE SERIES

Allan Kornberg and Harold D. Clarke   *Citizens and Community: Political Support in a Representative Democracy*
David D. Laitin   *Language Repertoires and State Construction in Africa*

Structuring politics

Historical institutionalism in comparative analysis

Edited by

SVEN STEINMO
University of Colorado at Boulder

KATHLEEN THELEN
Princeton University

and

FRANK LONGSTRETH
University of Bath

CAMBRIDGE
UNIVERSITY PRESS

PUBLISHED BY THE PRESS SYNDICATE OF THE UNIVERSITY OF CAMBRIDGE
The Pitt Building, Trumpington Street, Cambridge CB2 1RP, United Kingdom

CAMBRIDGE UNIVERSITY PRESS
The Edinburgh Building, Cambridge CB2 2RU, UK   http: //www.cup.cam.ac.uk
40 West 20th Street, New York, NY 10011-4211, USA   http: //www.cup.org
10 Stamford Road, Oakleigh, Melbourne 3166, Australia

© Cambridge University Press 1992

First published 1992
Reprinted 1994, 1995, 1997, 1998

Typeset in Times

A catalogue record for this book is available from the British Library

Library of Congress Cataloguing-in-Publication Data is available

ISBN 0-521-41780-5 hardback
ISBN 0-521-42830-0 paperback

Transferred to digital printing 2002

To our children
Siri and Ian,
Andy,
Kimber, Rachel, Matthew, Emma, and Helen

Contents

Preface

This book grew out of a workshop held in Boulder, Colorado, in January 1990. The workshop brought together a group of scholars working on a diverse range of empirical issues, but whose work in each case was informed by a "historical institutional" approach. The purpose of the workshop was to highlight common analytic themes within historical institutionalism, to assess the contribution of this approach to comparative politics, and to identify research agendas for the future that can refine and develop it further. Our goal was to initiate a conversation among institutionalists working in different empirical fields on fundamental questions of how institutions develop and influence political outcomes. Thus, unlike similar enterprises of the past, this book is not organized around a common empirical focus.* By bringing together writings that apply institutional analysis to a variety of national contexts and policies we want to highlight the methodological and theoretical foundations of this approach and to focus attention on the general contributions it can make to comparative politics.

The book makes no pretense to encompass all strains of thought within what is more broadly referred to as the "new institutionalism." For many, new institutionalism is associated with historical sociologists such as Theda Skocpol and political scientists with predominantly "qualitative" methodologies such as Peter Katzenstein and Peter Hall. But new institutionalism comes in a rational choice variant as well (see, e.g., Popkin, Bates, North, Levi, and Lange). The introductory chapter addresses some areas of overlap and differences between rational choice institutionalism and historical institutionalism, but the primary emphasis throughout the book is on historical institutionalism.

We would like to thank all the participants in the Boulder workshop, and especially the senior participants, many of whom have provided continuing advice and guidance: Christopher Allen, Douglas Ashford, Richard Coughlin, Peter Hall,

---

*See, e.g., G. John Ikenberry, David A. Lake, and Michael Mastanduno, eds., *The State and American Foreign Policy* (Ithaca, N.Y.: Cornell University Press, 1988).

Peter Katzenstein, Peter Lange, and Theda Skocpol. For useful comments on the introductory chapter, we thank Barry Ames, Douglas Ashford, Nancy Bermeo, Henry Bienen, Frank Dobbin, David Finegold, Geoffrey Garrett, Peter Hall, John Ikenberry, Desmond King, Atul Kohli, Peter Lange, Charles Lockhart, Jonas Pontusson, Ben Schneider, David Soskice, and John Waterbury. We owe a special debt of gratitude to George Tsebelis; our discussions with him were very helpful in clarifying the differences between rational choice and historical institutionalism. We also extend special thanks to Emily Loose at Cambridge University Press. Kathleen Thelen wishes to acknowledge the support of the Wissenschaftszentrum für Sozialforschung in Berlin. Sven Steinmo thanks the Council for European Studies and the University of Colorado for sponsoring the Boulder workshop.

Contributors

COLLEEN A. DUNLAVY is an Assistant Professor of History at the University of Wisconsin, Madison. She received a Ph.D. in political science from the Massachusetts Institute of Technology in 1988. Her book, *Politics and Industrialization: Early Railroads in the United States and Prussia*, is being published by Princeton University Press. Professor Dunlavy's current research examines similarities and differences in the American and German patterns of industrialism in the late nineteenth century.

PETER A. HALL is Professor of Government and a Senior Research Associate of the Center for European Studies at Harvard University. His publications include *Governing the Economy: The Politics of State Intervention in Britain and France* (Oxford University Press, 1986), *The Political Power of Economic Ideas: Keynesianism across Nations* (Princeton University Press, 1989), and *Developments in French Politics* (St. Martins, 1990).

VICTORIA C. HATTAM is an Assistant Professor in the Department of Political Science at Yale University. Her book, *Labor Visions and State Power: The Origins of Business Unionism in the United States*, is being published by Princeton University Press. Hattam was awarded the E. E. Schattschneider prize for the best dissertation in the field of American Government and Politics in 1989. She has published articles in *Studies in American Political Development* and *Politics and Society*. Hattam's next project focuses on the origins of the Republican Party in the mid–nineteenth century.

ELLEN M. IMMERGUT is Associate Professor of Political Science at the Massachusetts Institute of Technology, where she holds the Ford International Career Development chair. She has written *Health Politics: Interests and Institutions in Western Europe* (Cambridge University Press, in press), and is now researching efforts to decentralize the welfare state in Germany and Sweden.

DESMOND S. KING is Fellow and Tutor in Politics at St. John's College, University of Oxford. His publications include *The New Right: Politics, Markets and Citizenship* (Dorsey and Macmillan, 1987) and (with Ted Robert Gurr) *The State and the City* (University of Chicago Press, 1987), and coeditorship of *Challenges to Local Government* (Sage, 1990).

FRANK LONGSTRETH is a Lecturer in the School of Social Sciences at the University of Bath, England. His main research interests lie in the area of business, labor, and government in Britain. He has published articles in *Political Studies, Economy and Society,* and *Sociology,* and his forthcoming book is entitled *The City, Industry and the State: Business and Economic Policy in Twentieth Century Britain.* Professor Longstreth received his A.B. in Social Studies at Harvard University and his Ph.D. in Sociology from the London School of Economics.

BO ROTHSTEIN is an Associate Professor in the Department of Government at Uppsala University, Sweden. Among his publications in English are "State Structure and Variations in Corporatism" in *Scandinavian Political Studies,* Vol. 14 (1991); "The Success of the Swedish Labour Market Policy: The Organizational Connection" in *European Journal of Political Research,* Vol. 13 (1985); and "Social Justice and State Capacity" forthcoming in *Politics and Society.* He has been a Visiting Scholar at Cornell University and at the Center for European Studies at Harvard University. He is currently working on English editions of his two books in Swedish – *The Social Democratic State* and *The Corporatist State.*

SVEN STEINMO is an Assistant Professor in the Department of Political Science at the University of Colorado, Boulder. He has published articles on health policy, tax policy, British politics, and Scandinavian socialism in various journals, including *World Politics* and *Politics and Society.* He has recently finished his first book, *Taxation and Democracy: British, Swedish and American Approaches to Financing the Modern State,* which will be published by Yale University Press. Professor Steinmo is the recipient of numerous honors and awards in both teaching and research. Some of these include the American Political Science Association's Gabriel Almond Award for the best doctoral dissertation in comparative politics completed in 1987 or 1988, the Social Science Research Council Dissertation Research Fellowship, and the Fulbright–Hays Dissertation Research Fellowship.

KATHLEEN THELEN is an Assistant Professor of Politics at Princeton University. She is the author of *Union of Parts: Labor Politics in Postwar Germany* (Cornell University Press, 1991) and several articles on European labor politics. Her current research is a comparative study of the historical evolution of labor relations in Sweden, Britain, Germany, and the United States. She has received grants from the Alexander von Humboldt Foundation, the American-Scandinavian Foundation, and the German Academic Exchange program, and has been a guest scholar at the Wissenschaftszentrum Berlin für Sozialforschung.

MARGARET WEIR is a Senior Fellow in the Governmental Studies program of the Brookings Institution. She is the author of *Politics and Jobs: The Boundaries of Employment Policy in the United States* (Princeton University Press, 1992); and *Schooling for All: Class, Race and the Decline of the Democratic Ideal* (Basic Books, 1985). She is currently examining the isolation of cities in American national politics during the 1980s and 1990s.

1

Historical institutionalism in comparative politics

KATHLEEN THELEN AND SVEN STEINMO

The "rediscovery" of institutions has opened up an exciting research agenda in comparative politics and comparative political economy.[1] Scholars working in different disciplines and writing on subjects as diverse as the political economy of advanced capitalism and policy-making during China's Great Leap Forward have all focused on the significance of institutional variables for explaining outcomes in their respective fields.[2] Within comparative politics, "new" institutionalism has been especially associated with leading students of comparative political economy such as Suzanne Berger, Peter Hall, Peter Katzenstein, and Theda Skocpol, among others.[3] Although it has now been around for several years, few have stepped back to analyze the distinctive features of the kind of historical institutionalism these theorists represent, nor to assess its strengths and overall contribution to comparative politics.[4] These are themes we take up in this introductory chapter.

The chapter proceeds in three steps. We begin with a brief discussion of the building blocks of this approach: how institutions are defined and how they figure into the analysis. Second, we sketch the characteristic features of historical institutionalism and the broader theoretical project that animates institutional analyses. New institutionalists draw inspiration and insights from older traditions in economics, political science, and sociology.[5] But renewed, explicit attention to institutional variables since the late 1970s grew out of a critique of the behavioral emphasis of American and comparative politics in the 1950s and 1960s, which – although it drew attention to other important and previously neglected aspects of political life – often obscured the enduring socioeconomic and political structures that mold behavior in distinctive ways in different national contexts. The historical institutional literature is diverse, but scholars in this school share a

For their comments on this introduction, we would like to thank Barry Ames, Douglas Ashford, Nancy Bermeo, Henry Bienen, Frank Dobbin, David Finegold, Geoffrey Garrett, Peter Hall, John Ikenberry, Desmond King, Atul Kohli, Peter Lange, Jonas Pontusson, Ben Schneider, David Soskice, and John Waterbury. We are especially indebted to George Tsebelis for his many conversations with us on rational choice.

theoretical project aimed at the middle range that confronts issues of both historical contingency and "path dependency" that other theoretical perspectives obscure.

Third, we turn to a discussion of the frontier issues in historical institutionalism. These frontiers are defined by the limits of the historical institutional literature to date, that is, questions on which historical institutionalists have until now been relatively silent. We focus on two such areas: the question of institutional dynamism and the interaction of institutional and ideational variables in policy formation and change. Drawing on the literature at large, and especially on the essays assembled here, we suggest the ways in which institutional analysis can be further developed to address these areas.

HISTORICAL INSTITUTIONALISM: DEFINITIONS AND APPROACH

At its broadest, historical institutionalism represents an attempt to illuminate how political struggles "are mediated by the institutional setting in which [they] take place."[6] In general, historical institutionalists work with a definition of institutions that includes both formal organizations and informal rules and procedures that structure conduct. Peter Hall's widely accepted definition, for example, includes "the formal rules, compliance procedures, and standard operating practices that structure the relationship between individuals in various units of the polity and economy."[7] John Ikenberry breaks down his definition into three distinct levels that "range from specific characteristics of government institutions, to the more overarching structures of state, to the nation's normative social order."[8]

Just where to draw the line on what counts as an institution is a matter of some controversy in the literature.[9] However, in general, institutionalists are interested in the whole range of state and societal institutions that shape how political actors define their interests and that structure their relations of power to other groups. Thus, clearly included in the definition are such features of the institutional context as the rules of electoral competition, the structure of party systems, the relations among various branches of government, and the structure and organization of economic actors like trade unions.[10] Beyond institutions of this sort, on which most historical institutionalists can agree, are a number of other factors – ranging from norms to class structure – on which they might disagree.[11]

Peter Hall is the most explicit on the question of how institutions fit into the analysis of policy-making and politics within historical institutionalism. He stresses the way institutions shape the goals political actors pursue and the way they structure power relations among them, privileging some and putting others at a disadvantage. In his words:

Institutional factors play two fundamental roles in this model. On the one hand, the organization of policy-making affects the degree of power that any one set of actors has over the policy outcomes. . . . On the other hand, organizational position also influences an actor's definition of his own interests, by establishing his institutional responsibilities and relationship to other actors. In this way, organizational factors affect both the degree of pressure an actor can bring to bear on policy and the likely direction of that pressure.[12]

What is implicit but crucial in this and most other conceptions of historical institutionalism is that institutions constrain and refract politics but they are never the sole "cause" of outcomes. Institutional analyses do not deny the broad political forces that animate various theories of politics: class structure in Marxism, group dynamics in pluralism. Instead, they point to the ways that institutions structure these battles and in so doing, influence their outcomes.

REINVENTING THE WHEEL?

"Political science *is* the study of institutions," a senior colleague once remarked. "So what's new about the New Institutionalism?" he asked.[13] This question reveals a skepticism toward the so-called new institutionalism that deserves attention. Political scientists, sociologists, and economists have studied institutions for a very long time. So what is all the fuss about?

There is certainly no gainsaying that contemporary "new" institutionalists draw inspiration from a long line of theorists in political science, economics, and sociology. Most would readily acknowledge an important intellectual debt to writers like Karl Polanyi, Thorstein Veblen, Max Weber (not to mention Montesquieu), and, more recently, to theorists like Reinhard Bendix and Harry Eckstein. To understand why so many have found the kind of institutionalism represented by writers like Katzenstein, Skocpol, and Hall new and exciting, we need to outline the theoretical project that animates the work of these and other new institutionalists and distinguishes their approach both from previous theories and contemporary contenders in comparative politics. Thus, without getting into a long exegesis on the newness of this sort of institutionalism, a subject we believe has been overemphasized in the literature to date, it is useful to summarize important junctures that led to the revival of interest in institutions today.

At one time the field of political science, particularly comparative politics, was dominated by the study of institutions. The "old" institutionalism consisted mainly, though not exclusively, of detailed configurative studies of different administrative, legal, and political structures. This work was often deeply normative, and the little comparative "analysis" then existing largely entailed juxtaposing descriptions of different institutional configurations in different countries, comparing and contrasting. This approach did not encourage the development of intermediate-level categories and concepts that would facilitate truly comparative research and advance explanatory theory.[14]

The "behavioral revolution" in political science in the 1950s and early 1960s was precisely a rejection of this old institutionalism. It was obvious that the formal laws, rules, and administrative structures did not explain actual political behavior or policy outcomes. Behavioralists argued that, in order to understand politics and explain political outcomes, analysts should focus not on the formal attributes of government institutions but instead on informal distributions of power, attitudes, and political behavior. Moreover, in contrast to what was perceived as the atheoretical work of scholars in the formal-legal tradition, the behavioralist project as a whole was explicitly theoretical.

In comparative politics, the emphasis on theory-building often took the form of "grand theorizing," and this period witnessed a dramatic increase in broad, cross-national research (some, though not all of it behavioralist). Cutting through the idiosyncratic, country-specific categories of the old institutionalism, comparativists searched for broadly applicable concepts and variables to guide cross-national research. The theories that emerged and held sway in this period highlighted similarities and trends reaching across wide ranges of nations (with very different institutions). A number of them pointed to convergence both among the advanced industrial countries[15] and between industrialized and developing countries.[16]

This is not the place for a history of the discipline. However, a couple of points are in order concerning the role of *institutional* variables in political analysis during the 1950s and 1960s. First, it is clearly not the case that institutions disappeared from the agenda. One need only think of theorists such as Samuel Huntington and Reinhard Bendix to realize that institutions continued to play a very prominent role in the work of some scholars, whether as the object of analysis or as forces molding political behavior.[17] But second, it is equally important to recall that these theorists built their analyses around a fundamental critique of the dominant tendencies in the discipline at the time which had in fact pushed institutional variables to the side. Eckstein's critique of pluralists[18] and Bendix's important rebuttal to the dominant modernization paradigm in comparative politics[19] illustrate how both fields had come to downplay the structural features of political life that shaped the behavior of interest groups or that accounted for the persistence of cross-national diversity beneath the surface of homogenizing concepts such as modernity and tradition. The work of these "dissidents" from the mainstream of their day contained important insights and, at least in embryonic form, key elements of a new institutional perspective.[20]

The point about newness is not that no one was writing about institutions in the 1950s and 1960s, for of course many were.[21] Rather, the question is how institutional variables fit into the larger theoretical project that animated research in this period. The spirit and the thrust of work within the dominant behavioralist paradigm was precisely meant to *get beyond* the formal structures of the old institutionalists and especially the reified structures of Marxist theories of capitalist domination, by looking at the actual, observable beliefs and behaviors of groups and individuals. Given this emphasis and this agenda, it seems to us no coincidence that the behavioral revolution ultimately spawned not one but two separate institutionalist critiques, one from a historical and another from the more formal "rational choice" perspective. For all the differences between the two (see subsequent remarks), many historical institutionalists would agree with Kenneth Shepsle's (rational choice) critique of behavioralism:

The price we have paid for the methodological and theoretical innovations of the post–World War II era, however, is the inordinate emphasis now placed on *behavior*. Our ability to describe (and less frequently, to explain) behavior . . . has diminished the attention once given to institutional context and actual outcomes. On net, the behavioral revolution has probably been of positive value. But along with the many scientific benefits, we have been burdened by the cost of the restricted scope in our analyses.[22]

Because mainstream behavioralist theories focused on the characteristics, attitudes, and behaviors of the individuals and groups themselves to explain political outcomes, they often missed crucial elements of the playing field and thus did not provide answers to the prior questions of why these political behaviors, attitudes, and the distribution of resources among contending groups themselves differed from one country to another. For example, interest group theories that focused on the characteristics and preferences of pressure groups themselves could not account for why interest groups with similar organizational characteristics (including measures of interest-group "strength") and similar preferences could not always influence policy in the same way or to the same extent in different national contexts. To explain these differences required more explicit attention to the institutional landscape in which interest groups sought influence.[23]

The "grand theorizing" that dominated comparative politics in this period also, in its own way, obscured the intermediate institutions that structure politics in different countries. Thus, it is also probably no coincidence that renewed and more systematic attention to institutional factors in comparative analysis corresponded with a period of upheaval in the international arena associated, among other things, with the declining hegemony of the United States and the oil crisis of 1973–4. Whereas the prosperity of the 1950s and 1960s may have masked sources of national diversity in policy-making and politics among the advanced industrial countries, the economic shocks in the early 1970s gave rise to a diversity of responses that flatly discredited the claims of the convergence theories of the 1960s.[24] These events led to the search for explanatory factors to account for these outcomes, and national-level institutional factors figured prominently in the answer.[25]

Explaining this persistence of cross-national differences despite common challenges and pressures was a central theme in the work of the early new institutionalists, and this implied a shift in emphasis on both an empirical and a theoretical level. Criticizing the ahistorical approach of traditional interest-group theories and Marxist analysis alike, these theorists wanted to know why interest groups demanded different policies in different countries and why class interests were manifested differently cross-nationally. At the same time, and related to this, new institutionalists moved away from concepts (like modernity and tradition) that tended to homogenize whole classes of nations, toward concepts that could capture diversity among them (e.g., the distinction between "strong" and "weak" states in the advanced industrial countries). Thus, the empirical challenge posed by diverse responses to common challenges drove a partial shift, away from general theorizing toward a more midlevel Weberian project that explored diversity within classes of the same phenomena. A critical body of work in the mid to late 1970s and early 1980s pointed to intermediate-level institutional factors – corporatist arrangements, policy networks linking economic groups to the state bureaucracy, party structures – and the role they play in defining the constellations of incentives and constraints faced by political actors in different national contexts.

These new institutionalists shared the behavioralists' concern for building theory. However, by focusing on intermediate institutions, they sought to explain systematic differences across countries that previous theories had obscured. The range of institutions studied depended of course on the outcomes to be explained. Katzenstein's work on foreign economic policy of the advanced industrial countries, for example, drew attention to differences in the "policy networks" linking state and society to explain divergent responses to a common economic shock.[26] Corporatist theorists focused on the structure and organization of key economic actors, especially labor and employers' associations, to draw conclusions about labor's role in adjusting to economic change and about cross-national variation in economic performance more generally.[27] Theorists such as Suzanne Berger, Theda Skocpol, and Douglas Ashford were in the forefront of recasting the study of interest-group behavior, the state, and public-policy formation in explicitly institutional terms.[28] Other authors, notably March and Olsen, Peter Hall, Stephen Skowronek, and later John Ikenberry, have built on this tradition and have helped to advance it through a self-conscious definition and application of an institutional approach. Key to their analyses was the notion that institutional factors can shape both the objectives of political actors and the distribution of power among them in a given polity.[29]

One feature typifying this new institutional perspective is its emphasis on what Hall refers to as the "relational character" of institutions.[30] More important than the formal characteristics of either state or societal institutions per se is how a given institutional configuration shapes political *interactions*. This feature of a new institutional perspective is well illustrated by Ellen Immergut's contribution to this book, Chapter 3. In her analysis of health care policy in France, Switzerland, and Sweden, Immergut argues that it is not useful to think of political power as a static attribute of certain groups or actors. Traditional interest-group theories that look at the characteristics of pressure groups themselves for clues on their relative power cannot explain why doctors in the three countries she examines – though all equally well organized and powerful in their internal organizational resources – nonetheless had very different degrees of success in achieving their policy objectives. For Immergut, the point is not to identify "veto groups'' so much as ''veto points'' in political systems. Veto points are areas of institutional vulnerability, that is, points in the policy process where the mobilization of opposition can thwart policy innovation. The location of such veto points varies cross-nationally and depends on how different parts of the national policymaking apparatus are linked. While such veto points are in general rather sticky, they are not permanent, immutable characteristics of a political system. Shifts in the overall balance of power can cause veto points to emerge, disappear, or shift their location, creating ''strategic openings'' that actors can exploit to achieve their goals. Immergut's notion of veto points thus illustrates and builds on some of the core characteristics of the historical institutional approach more generally: the emphasis on intermediate institutions that shape political strategies, the ways institutions structure relations of power among contending groups in society, and especially the focus on the *process* of politics and policy-making within given institutional parameters.

HISTORICAL INSTITUTIONALISM AND RATIONAL CHOICE

As is well known, there are in fact two different approaches that have been assigned the label ''the new institutionalism.'' Rational choice institutionalists such as Shepsle, Levi, North, and Bates share with historical-interpretive institutionalists such as Berger, Hall, Katzenstein, and Skocpol a concern with the question of how institutions shape political strategies and influence political outcomes.[31] But important differences distinguish the two. The essays assembled here come out of the historical institutional tradition, but it is worth considering briefly how they relate to the rational choice variant. The two perspectives are premised on different assumptions that in fact reflect quite different approaches to the study of politics.

For the rational choice scholar, institutions are important as features of a *strategic context,* imposing constraints on self-interested behavior. For example, in the classic prisoner's dilemma game, when the rules (institutions) are changed, the prisoner's choices (to defect, to cooperate, and so on) also change because these rules structure the choices that will maximize the prisoner's self-interest. Thus political and economic institutions are important for rational choice scholars interested in real-world politics because the institutions define (or at least constrain) the strategies that political actors adopt in the pursuit of their interests.

For historical institutionalists the idea that institutions provide the context in which political actors define their strategies and pursue their interests is unproblematical. Indeed, this is a key premise in historical institutional analysis as well. But historical institutionalists want to go further and argue that institutions play a much greater role in shaping politics, and political history more generally, than that suggested by a narrow rational choice model.

Historical institutionalists in general find strict rationality assumptions overly confining.[32] First, in contrast to some (though not all) rational choice analyses, historical institutionalists tend to see political actors not so much as all-knowing, rational maximizers, but more as rule-following "satisficers."[33] As DiMaggio and Powell argue, "The constant and repetitive quality of much organized life is explicable not simply by reference to individual, maximizing actors but rather by a view that locates the persistence of practices in both their taken-for-granted quality and their reproduction in structures that are to some extent self-sustaining."[34] In short, people don't stop at every choice they make in their lives and think to themselves, "Now what will maximize my self-interest?" Instead, most of us, most of the time, follow societally defined rules, even when so doing may not be directly in our self-interest.[35]

Second, and perhaps most centrally, rational choice and historical institutionalism diverge rather sharply on the issue of preference formation. While rational choice deals with preferences at the level of assumptions, historical institutionalists take the question of how individuals and groups define their self-interest as problematical.[36] Rational choice institutionalists in effect "bracket" the issue of preference formation theoretically (by assuming that political actors are rational and will act to maximize their self-interest), though of course in the context of specific analyses they must operationalize self-interest, and generally they do so by deducing the preferences of the actors from the structure of the situation itself.[37] This is quite different from historical institutionalists, who argue that not just the *strategies* but also the *goals* actors pursue are shaped by the institutional context.[38] For example, a historical institutionalist would emphasize how class interests are more a function of class position (mediated – reinforced or mitigated – by state and social institutions like political parties and union structure) than individual choice.

The idea of socially and politically constructed preferences that figures prominently in the work of many contemporary historical institutionalists echoes the writings of an earlier generation of economic institutionalist-historians. Earlier in this century, for example, Thorstein Veblen argued that the individualistic, competitive features of modern life must be seen as products of the particular economic institutions that we have constructed in the advanced capitalist states.[39] This point is also made in a recent essay by sociologists Roger Friedland and Robert Alford, who argue:

> The central institutions of the contemporary capitalist West – capitalist market, bureaucratic state, democracy, nuclear family, and Christian religion – shape individual preferences and organizational interests as well as the repertoire of behaviors by which they may attain them.

And because of the dense matrix of institutions in which individuals maneuver, they are motivated by a complex mix of sometimes conflicting preferences. Friedland and Alford argue that conflicts between preferences and behaviors evoked by these institutions contribute to the dynamism of the system:

These institutions are potentially contradictory and hence make multiple logics available to individuals and organizations. Individuals and organizations transform the institutional relations of society by exploiting these contradictions.[40]

By taking the goals, strategies, and preferences as something to be explained, historical institutionalists show that, unless something is known about the context, broad assumptions about "self-interested behavior" are empty. As we pointed out earlier, historical institutionalists would not have trouble with the rational choice idea that political actors are acting strategically to achieve their ends. But clearly it is not very useful simply to leave it at that. We need a historically based analysis to tell us what they are trying to maximize and why they emphasize certain goals over others.[41]

Taking preference formation as problematical rather than given, it then also follows that alliance formation is more than a lining up of groups with compatible (preexisting and unambiguous) self-interests. Where groups have multiple, often conflicting interests, it is necessary to examine the political processes out of which particular coalitions are formed. As Margaret Weir points out in Chapter 7, new ideas can cause groups to rethink their interests; consequently, the way in which various policies are "packaged" can facilitate the formation of certain coalitions and hinder others. As Bo Rothstein's analysis (Chapter 2) makes clear, leadership can play a key role in this process. The historical analysis of how these processes occur (what Katzenstein calls "process tracing") is thus central to a historical institutional approach.

Thus one, perhaps *the,* core difference between rational choice institutionalism and historical institutionalism lies in the question of preference formation, whether treated as exogenous (rational choice) or endogenous (historical institutionalism). But beyond this, and on the "output side," it seems that there is more than one way to achieve one's ends, even assuming self-interested, maximizing behavior. Recent game theory has shown that there is more than one efficient solution to certain kinds of games.[42] If there is no single political choice or outcome that maximizes the individual's self-interest, then clearly game-theoretic tools need to be supplemented with other methods to understand which solutions will be or were chosen.[43]

In sum, institutions are not just another variable, and the institutionalist claim is more than just that "institutions matter too." By shaping not just actors' strategies (as in rational choice), but their goals as well, and by mediating their relations of cooperation and conflict, institutions structure political situations and leave their own imprint on political outcomes.[44] Political actors of course are not unaware of the deep and fundamental impact of institutions, which is why battles over institutions are so hard fought. Reconfiguring institutions can save political actors the trouble of fighting the same battle over and over again. For example (and as a number of rational choice theorists have pointed out) this explains why congressional battles over district boundaries are so tenacious. The central importance of institutions in "mobilizing bias" in political processes also accounts for why such formidable political leaders as Charles DeGaulle have been willing to stake their careers not on particular policy outcomes, but on institutional ones. This view is especially at odds with the "transaction costs" school within rational choice that sees institutions as efficient solutions to collective action problems, reducing transaction costs among individuals and groups in order to enhance efficiency.[45] But to view institutions in these terms is to beg the important questions about how political power figures into the creation and maintenance of these institutions, as well as to deny the possibility of unexpected outcomes.[46]

THE HISTORICAL INSTITUTIONALIST PROJECT

The historical institutional literature is diverse, to say the least. This approach has been applied in a wide range of empirical settings, but in each case what has made this approach so attractive is the theoretical leverage it has provided for understanding policy continuities over time within countries and policy variation across countries. Working at the level of midrange theory, institutionalists have constructed important analytic bridges: between state-centered and society-centered analyses by looking at the institutional arrangements that structure relations between the two,[47] and between grand theories that highlight broad cross-national regularities and narrower accounts of particular national cases, by focusing on intermediate-level variables that illuminate sources of "variation on a common theme."[48]

Beyond these more well-known analytic bridges, institutional analysis also allows us to examine the relationship between political actors as objects and as agents of history. The institutions that are at the center of historical institutional analyses – from party systems to the structure of economic interests such as business associations – can shape and constrain political strategies in important ways, but they are themselves also the outcome (conscious or unintended) of deliberate political strategies, of political conflict, and of choice. As Bo Rothstein puts it in the next chapter, by focusing on these intermediate institutional features of political life, institutionalism provides the theoretical "bridge between 'men [who] make history' and the 'circumstances' under which they are able to do so."

Macro theories such as Marxism focus on the broad socioeconomic structures (class structure, for example), that define the parameters of policy-making at the broadest level. But these theories often obscure the nontrivial differences between different countries with the same broad structures, for example, differences in how capitalism is organized in Sweden and the United States. Moreover, even where they do address such differences, the kinds of explanations they produce (the "requirements of capital accumulation," for example) still point to the primacy of systems-level variables and downplay the role of political agency in explaining outcomes. But to the extent that we take seriously notions of human agency as crucial to understanding political outcomes, we need to come to terms not just with political behavior as the dependent variable, influenced by these macro-socioeconomic structures, but as independent variables as well.

This brings us back to an important conceptual issue that we flagged at the beginning of this chapter concerning how broad a conceptual net to cast in defining institutions. Our definition emphasized intermediate-level institutions, such as party systems and the structure of economic interest groups like unions, that mediate between the behavior of individual political actors and national political outcomes. But couldn't more macrolevel structures – class structure, for example – also qualify as institutions? Clearly such structures can impose significant constraints on behavior.

We would argue that it is less useful to subsume such macro (systems-level) structures into the definition of institutions than it is to maintain a narrower focus and examine how these forces are mediated by the kinds of intermediate-level institutions we have cited. This does not mean that we cannot examine differences between capitalist and precapitalist or other socioeconomic systems; it only suggests a particular research strategy for doing so. Polanyi's work is in the spirit we would advocate. His analysis of the "great transformation" deals explicitly with the consequences of macrolevel changes in broad social and economic structures. But his examination of the causes and consequences of the shift to a market economy and what he calls a "market society" is anchored in an analysis of specific social and economic institutions (such as the Speenhamland system) in which battles over and within these broader forces are crystallized.

The focus on intermediate-level institutions that mediate the effects of macrolevel socioeconomic structures (like class) also provides greater analytic leverage to confront variation among capitalist countries. Class differences characterize all capitalist countries and as an analytic category can be applied to all of them. But if we want to understand differences in political behavior across these countries, what we really need to know is how and to what extent class differences figure into how groups and individuals in different capitalist countries define their goals and their relations to other actors. Arguably, class in this sense matters more in Sweden and Britain than in the United States. And we would argue that such differences in the salience of class to actual political behavior depends on the extent to which it is reinforced and reified through state and societal institutions – party competition, union structures, and the like.

In short, this focus on how macrostructures such as class are magnified or mitigated by intermediate-level institutions allows us to explore the effects of such overarching structures on political outcomes, but avoiding the structural determinism that often characterizes broader and more abstract Marxist, functionalist, and systems-theory approaches. Thus, another of the strengths of historical institutionalism is that it has carved out an important theoretical niche at the middle range that can help us integrate an understanding of general patterns of political history with an explanation of the contingent nature of political and economic development, and especially the role of political agency, conflict, and choice, in shaping that development.

The emphasis in historical institutionalism on political agency and political choice *within* institutional constraints is also a characteristic of the "other" new institutionalism. But there are still important differences in the theoretical project that informs the work of historical institutionalists and rational choice institutionalists. Rational choice theorists work with what one might call a "universal tool kit" that can be applied in virtually any political setting.[49] The kind of deductive logical system that informs rational choice analysis has important strengths, parsimony first among them, but its characteristic weaknesses, such as those imposed by the highly restrictive assumptions that make this kind of analysis possible, are also well known.

In these characteristics – its "ruthless elegance" (Hall) and the deductive logic on which it is built – rational choice theory shares something with other deductive theories such as Waltz's "systems" theory of international relations and Marxist theory. Of course, rational choice theory is clearly at odds with the substance and many aspects of the methodology of traditional Marxist theory (especially the teleology of Marxism and the denial of individual agency which is so central to rational choice theory). But at a more abstract level, both are animated by a similar theoretical project premised on deduction from a limited number of theoretical assumptions and the application of a set of concepts that are held to be universally applicable (class for Marxists; rationality and interest maximization for rational choice theorists). Rational choice shares both the strengths and weaknesses of these previous attempts to build deductive theories to explain political outcomes.

Historical institutionalists lack the kind of universal tool kit and universally applicable concepts on which these more deductive theories are based. Rather than deducing hypotheses on the basis of global assumptions and prior to the analysis, historical institutionalists generally develop their hypotheses more inductively, in the course of interpreting the empirical material itself. The more inductive approach of historical institutionalists reflects a different approach to the study of politics that essentially rejects the idea that political behavior can be analyzed with the same techniques that may be useful in economics. Rational choice theorists criticize this as inelegant and atheoretical, and sometimes even dismiss it as storytelling. As can be readily imagined, we disagree, and would argue that since each approach has characteristic strengths and weaknesses that flow rather directly from their different assumptions and logics, it may be more fruitful to explore what they have to offer each other than to decide between the two once and for all.

To conclude, for all of their diversity, historical institutionalists share a common theoretical project and a common research strategy. The emphasis on institutions as patterned relations that lies at the core of an institutional approach does not replace attention to other variables – the players, their interests and strategies, and the distribution of power among them. On the contrary, it puts these factors in context, showing how they relate to one another by drawing attention to the way political situations are structured. Institutions constrain and refract politics, but they are never the only cause of outcomes. Rather, as Hall points out, the institutionalist claim is that institutions structure political interactions and in this way affect political outcomes.

While many theories achieve elegance by pointing to particular variables that are alleged to be decisive (Marxism: class; pluralism: interest groups), institutional analyses focus on illuminating how different variables are linked. None of the contributions to this book proposes a simple, single-variable explanation. All demonstrate the relationships and interactions among a variety of variables in a way that reflects the complexity of real political situations. However, just as a particular institutional configuration gives structure to a given political situation, an institutional approach structures the *explanation* of political phenomena by providing a perspective for identifying how these different variables relate to one another. Thus, by placing the structuring factors at the center of the analysis, an institutional approach allows the theorist to capture the complexity of real political situations, but not at the expense of theoretical clarity. One of the great attractions and strengths of this approach is in how it strikes this balance between necessary complexity and desirable parsimony.

We have argued here that part of the initial appeal of the institutionalist approach to comparativists was that it offered a new angle through which to better understand policy continuities within countries and policy variation across countries. The chapters in this book go a step further, extending the logic of the institutionalist approach to build powerful explanations for variation in political behavior and outcomes *over time* as well as across countries, and a framework for understanding the sources and consequences of institutional change. We now turn to what we consider to be the crucial frontiers of this approach and to the contributions made by the authors in this book to those frontiers.

FRONTIERS OF HISTORICAL INSTITUTIONALISM

The essays in this book demonstrate the strengths of historical institutionalism as a general approach to comparative politics. In addition, however, they push at the frontiers of this approach to overcome some of the limits in its development to date. In particular, these essays confront a strong tendency toward "static" institutional analyses and, from various vantage points, all address the often neglected issue of dynamism in institutional analysis. Some chapters illustrate how the meaning and functions of institutions can change over time, producing new and sometimes unexpected outcomes. Other chapters are concerned with the political processes through which institutions themselves are created and continue to evolve. Finally, some of the chapters delve into the interaction of "ideational innovation'' and institutional constraints to illuminate distinctive patterns of policy innovation and change.

Until now, the strong focus on how institutional structure shapes politics has yielded compelling accounts of policy continuities within countries over time (see, for example, Shonfield, Skowronek) and differences in policy outcomes across countries (for example, Zysman, Hall, Steinmo). But precisely because institutionalism has proved so powerful in explaining different policy trajectories across countries, it often creates the impression that political outcomes can simply be "read off" the institutional configuration (see Chapter 2, by Colleen Dunlavy). Part of the reason, as John Ikenberry has pointed out, is that the emphasis on institutional constraints has meant that institutional approaches have often been better at explaining what is not possible in a given institutional context than what is.[50] What has been missing is more explicit theorizing on the reciprocal influence of institutional constraints and political strategies and, more broadly, on the interaction of ideas, interests, and institutions. The tendency in many existing analyses toward institutional determinism becomes clear when we consider two aspects of the literature to date: (1) the emphasis on analyzing "comparative statics" and (2) the relative underdevelopment of theories of institutional formation and change.

So far, historical institutionalism has been especially helpful in illuminating cross-national differences and the persistence of patterns or policies over time within individual countries. Cross-national studies in the new institutionalism tend toward the study of comparative statics; that is, they explain different policy outcomes in different countries with reference to their respective (stable) institutional configurations. But such argumentation invites a kind of institutional determinism. We can illustrate this critique by focusing on a recent essay by none other than one of the authors of this introduction.[51] Sven Steinmo's analysis is concerned with the way political institutions have shaped tax policy in the United States, the United Kingdom, and Sweden. He demonstrates how the electoral and constitutional structures, combined with the structure of economic interest organizations in these three countries have led rational actors (elected officials, interest-group elites, and bureaucrats) in each case to make quite different policy choices, which have in turn produced different policy outcomes. The preferences, strategies, and relative power of the relevant actors are defined by the institutional context in which the political game is played. The result is quite different taxation systems and very different (and unexpected) distributions of effective tax burdens.

Steinmo's analysis provides a compelling explanation for significant cross-national differences in tax policy, but his framework is not well suited to deal with the question of change. First, while it is empirically true that these three tax systems have undergone considerable transformations over the past several decades, Steinmo's analysis obscures changes within individual countries over time. Second, and related to this, the argument can create the impression that domestic political institutions are the only variables that matter in determining tax-policy outcomes, and that no other outcomes were possible given these institutional constraints. Such an argument highlights the thin line that institutionalists often walk between institutional constraints and institutional determinism.[52]

The relative underdevelopment of explicit theorizing about the reciprocal influence of institutions and politics is also clear when one considers the question of institutional formation and change. Although arguably one of the most important issues in comparative politics, this issue has received relatively little attention in most of the literature to date. Again, one reason for this deficit is that institutionalists generally focus on constraints and offer explanations of continuity rather than change.

Up to this point perhaps the most explicit model of institutional change in the literature is Stephen Krasner's model of "punctuated equilibrium."[53] This model appears to enjoy rather widespread acceptance among institutionalists.[54] Briefly, Krasner's model posits that institutions are characterized by long periods of stability, periodically "punctuated" by crises that bring about relatively abrupt institutional change, after which institutional stasis again sets in. Institutional arrangements help explain policy outcomes during periods of institutional stability, since these arrangements structure political conflicts in distinctive ways. In Krasner's version, institutional crises usually emanate from changes in the external environment. Such crises can cause the breakdown of the old institutions, and this breakdown precipitates intense political conflict over the shape of the new institutional arrangements.

The punctuated equilibrium model suggests a very elegant and powerful theory of institutional change. It is entirely appropriate that this model emphasizes the "stickiness" of historically evolved institutional arrangements. After all, if institutions simply respond to changes in the balance of power in society around them, then, as Krasner points out, they are epiphenomenal and we should be studying the forces that affect them. Institutionalists can scarcely take issue with this fundamental point.

But beyond this central observation, the "punctuated equilibrium" metaphor involves broader assumptions that warrant closer scrutiny. The problem with this model is that institutions explain everything until they explain nothing. Institutions are an independent variable and explain political outcomes in periods of stability, but when they break down, they become the dependent variable, whose shape is determined by the political conflicts that such institutional breakdown unleashes. Put somewhat differently, at the moment of institutional breakdown, the logic of the argument is reversed from "Institutions shape politics" to "Politics shape institutions."[55] Conceiving of the relationship in this way, however, obscures the dynamic interaction of political strategies and institutional constraints. A more dynamic model is needed to capture the interplay of the two variables over time.

Institutional dynamism

We have argued that the critical inadequacy of institutional analysis to date has been a tendency toward mechanical, static accounts that largely bracket the issue of change and sometimes lapse inadvertently into institutional determinism. The chapters in this book significantly extend institutional analysis by explicitly addressing the sources of what we will call "institutional dynamism." They do so by examining the interaction of institutions and political processes both across countries and over time. They not only look at how institutions mediate and filter politics but turn the question around to demonstrate how the impact of institutions is itself mediated by the broader political context. In short, all of them go beyond comparative statics to explore the political conditions under which particular institutions have specific consequences, and several of them also deal explicitly with the issue of institutional formation and change.

We can identify four distinct sources of institutional dynamism, by which we mean situations in which we can observe variability in the impact of institutions over time but within countries. These sources of change are often empirically intertwined, but it is useful to separate them analytically for purposes of exposition.

First, broad changes in the socioeconomic or political context can produce a situation in which previously latent institutions suddenly become salient, with implications for political outcomes.[56] For instance, the European Court of Justice has until very recently played a rather minor role in European politics, until the political events surrounding the Single European Act suddenly transformed the institution into an increasingly important locus of conflict and cooperation among the states in Europe.[57]

Second, changes in the socioeconomic context or political balance of power can produce a situation in which old institutions are put in the service of different ends, as new actors come into play who pursue their (new) goals through existing institutions. A classic example of an old institution being harnessed to new ends can be found in the system of job classifications in U.S. industrial relations. Job classifications were introduced by some large employers in the 1920s (prior to widespread unionization) as the basis for incentive systems in which foremen could reward workers for their industry or cooperation by shifting them to better jobs within the plant hierarchy. However, as unions grew in the 1930s and 1940s, they were able to capitalize on the power they gained due to changing political and labor-market conditions and to attach a number of conditions to personnel moves within the plant. They did so among other things by attaching to the job classifications rules regarding transfers and the content of individual jobs. Over time, this process through which union rights became attached to job classifications ultimately turned the logic of the system on its head: from a system of management control to one of union control.[58]

Third, exogenous changes can produce a shift in the goals or strategies being pursued within existing institutions – that is, changes in outcomes as old actors adopt new goals within the old institutions. An illustration comes out of the literature on the "crisis" of Fordism.[59] A number of authors have argued that certain features of the American political economy – notably the structure of the state and the U.S. model of the multidivisional (and often, multinational) corporation – were ideally suited for an international trade regime premised on international liberalism and mass production. But in the 1970s and 1980s, the decline of the free trade regime and the crisis of Fordism and mass production called for new, more "flexible" strategies. As capitalists moved to adapt to the new political and economic context, the very same institutions produced dramatically different results. Rather than guaranteeing the continued competitiveness of American industry, these institutions are seen as a major impediment to it under conditions in which markets are more volatile and competitiveness hinges on factors other than simply economies of scale.

These first three sources of dynamism in fact describe situations in which the very same institutions can produce different outcomes over time. But of course a fourth source of dynamism can occur when political actors adjust their strategies to accommodate changes in the institutions themselves. This can occur in moments of dramatic change (institutional breakdown or institutional formation of the sort that Krasner's model of punctuated equilibrium highlights), but it can also be the result of more piecemeal change resulting from specific political battles or ongoing strategic maneuvering within institutional constraints. The latter possibility is documented, for example, in Kathleen Thelen's study of the development of Germany's "dual system" of labor relations.[60] Thelen elaborates a model of "dynamic constraints" that differs from the punctuated equilibrium model in two important respects. First, it emphasizes that institutional breakdown is not the only source of institutional change (and that it is not just in moments of institutional breakdown that political strategies matter). Strategic maneuvering by political actors and conflict among them within institutional constraints (also short of crisis) can influence the institutional parameters within which their interactions occur. Second, while the external pressures that are central to the punctuated equilibrium model are important, the dynamic constraints model focuses more on maneuvering *within* the institutions in response to these external events. Groups and individuals are not merely spectators as conditions change to favor or penalize them in the political balance of power, but rather strategic actors capable of acting on "openings" provided by such shifting contextual conditions in order to defend or enhance their own positions. In short, Thelen's analysis illustrates a pattern in which changes in the meaning and functioning of institutions (associated with broader socioeconomic and political shifts) set in motion political struggles within but also over those institutions that in fact drive their development forward.

The following chapters of this book provide illustrations of many of these points. All of them speak not only to issues of institutional constraints, but also to questions of institutional dynamism. The vantage point adopted by each author varies, but the essays cluster around three general themes into which we can organize them for purposes of introduction. First, we examine sources of policy change under stable institutional arrangements. Here we ask the question, "How can we explain policy change if institutions remain (relatively) stable?" We turn next to the issue of institutional change itself. How and under what conditions do institutions themselves become the object of change? Finally, we explore the dynamic interaction between political institutions and political ideas to explain how ideational innovation within particular institutional constraints can produce policy change.

Policy change within stable institutions

Political institutions do not operate in a vacuum. But as we have suggested, there has not been a great deal of explicit theorizing about the ways in which institutions themselves interact with the broader socioeconomic context in which they operate. Several essays in this book take significant strides in this direction. Many institutionalist scholars have shown that institutions tend to remain "sticky" even when the political or economic conditions in which they exist have changed dramatically. But the implication of this line of analysis has generally been that institutions tend to have constant or continuous effects even while the world changes around them.[61] We take a different view. As several of the essays in this book illustrate, institutions themselves may be resistant to change, but their impact on political outcomes can change over time in subtle ways in response to shifts in the broader socioeconomic or political context.

Two of the chapters in this book provide excellent examples of how the meaning and functioning of institutions can be transformed by changes in the socioeconomic context or political balance of power. Chapter 6, by Victoria Hattam, best illustrates the first source of institutional dynamism described earlier, how a shift in the socioeconomic or political context can cause certain previously latent institutions to become salient; Chapter 5, by Colleen Dunlavy, echoes this conclusion and provides an analytic bridge to the second point, the emergence of new actors pursuing new goals through existing institutions.

In her analysis of nineteenth-century working-class politics, Hattam addresses the puzzle of why the British and American labor movements took off in very different directions in the late nineteenth century. She demonstrates how the strategies of the two union movements were closely parallel until that point, before diverging sharply as the Americans retreated from politics into an increasing focus on the industrial realm to pursue working-class goals through "business unionism." Hattam solves the puzzle of sharp strategic divergence between the two labor movements by examining the political and institutional landscape that organized labor faced in its formative years in the two countries.

. She shows that so long as workers defined themselves as producers rather than laborers, British and American political institutions seemed equally open. But in the late nineteenth century, when workers turned their attention to securing rights to collective action as workers, the role of the courts in the two countries, which had previously not been an important part of workers' institutional context, suddenly became so. In that moment, significant differences in the relationship between the legislature and the courts (previously present but latent, as it were) channeled conflicts in very different ways. In both countries, unions won significant legislation protecting their rights to organize workers and press their claims on employers. In Britain, where the judiciary is clearly subordinate to parliament, the courts upheld the spirit of these new laws, and the labor movement learned that its political lobbying could result in very tangible benefits. In the United States, in contrast, the courts enjoyed more autonomy and continued to hand down conservative rulings in spite of similar legislation. This experience reinforced a very different lesson about what labor could expect to gain through political action; organized labor's retreat from politics was a pragmatic response to repeated experiences in which legislative victories were rendered meaningless by subsequent court actions.

In sum, Hattam's argument highlights how social and political realignments (as wage earners began to organize as members of a distinct working class) led to the sudden salience of the courts as an arena of conflict. The institutional context did not change; rather, the power and autonomy of American courts was simply revealed as the goals of workers shifted. Latent institutions became salient, which accounts for why English and American labor's strategies diverged in the last part of the nineteenth century and not before.

Colleen Dunlavy's analysis of public infrastructure development in nineteenth-century Prussia and America dovetails theoretically with Hattam's, and also provides an analytical bridge to the second source of dynamism discussed earlier, namely the emergence of new actors who pursue their new goals through existing institutions. Contrary to popular conceptions that contrast Germany's "strong and interventionist" state with the United States' "weak and noninterventionist" state, Dunlavy shows how until the 1840s, it was the latter that was both more active and successful in regulating railroads, a key vehicle for industrialization. Not the federal government, but rather state governments were the main actors, actively promoting but also successfully regulating the nascent railroad industry in the United States. The relative openness of American political institutions (especially state legislatures) allowed railroad capitalists their say in policy, but it also served as a point of access for other interests who were able to impose certain restrictions on railroad development. Political liberalism in this sense brought with it a degree of economic illiberalism, in the form of state intervention and regulation.

However, as Dunlavy shows, this outcome obtained only so long as the task faced by the American government was regulating railroads on a fairly small scale. By the mid-nineteenth century, railroad development itself outgrew the regulatory framework and capacities of the individual American states. As railroads increasingly crossed state boundaries, railroad regulation became a problem of national rather than state regulation. With this shift, the fragmented authority of national institutions (federalism, but also the separation of powers) came into play, offering capitalists ways to avoid regulation (in Dunlavy's terms, "escape routes"), among other things by playing authorities in different states off against one another.

Although the empirical cases are quite different, the theoretical parallels between Hattam's and Dunlavy's analyses are clear. In Dunlavy's case, federal institutions gained new salience for railroad regulation as the industry grew beyond state bounds. In addition, however, Dunlavy emphasizes that the shift from the state to the federal level as the primary arena of conflict was not simply the logical culmination of the growth of the industry itself. She also stresses how railroad development helped to create a new group of political actors, large-scale industrial capitalists whose economic activities spanned state boundaries and who could pursue their goals by actively playing the full range of institutions at all levels (indeed, sometimes pitting them against each other). This new class of entrepreneurs (of which the great robber barons of the railroad industry are only one part) orchestrated the shift to the national level, for example, as they sought to extract more favorable outcomes from federal courts in their efforts to escape regulation at the state level.

Ellen Immergut's theory of shifting veto points (in Chapter 3) is compatible with the kind of analysis suggested by Hattam and Dunlavy. Indeed, one might recast their arguments in terms of Immergut's language to show how in both cases new veto points emerged as a result of changes in exogenous conditions. In the case Hattam examines, the changing goals of workers played a role in shifting the arena of conflict to the courts, which provided a new veto point for opponents of labor organization in the United States, though not in Britain. In the case Dunlavy presents, it was the growth of the railroads themselves that helped shift the arena to the national level, opening new veto points for U.S. capitalists to fend off regulation. The Prussian story is the "mirror image" of the United States: There similar developments had the consequence of closing certain veto points that Prussian capitalists had been able to exploit before the 1850s, which in turn allowed the Prussian government to impose more restrictions on their activities.

In sum, by viewing the institutional landscape as a whole, these studies highlight important and often neglected sources of dynamism. They pose a challenge to more static institutional analyses that imply that political outcomes can be read off the institutional map, by illustrating how the meaning and functioning of institutions are shaped by features of the socioeconomic and political context in which they are embedded.

Institutions as objects of change

Another dimension of institutional dynamism, in some ways the most obvious, concerns the question of institutional change itself. Some authors have been concerned to illuminate how institutions themselves become the object of contention, and to show how institutional change results from deliberate political strategies to transform structural parameters in order to win long-term political advantage. Others have explored related questions of more gradual institutional evolution and change, often emerging as unintended consequences of political battles fought over other issues.

Bo Rothstein's analysis of unemployment insurance systems, in Chapter 2, focuses on one particularly significant set of institutional choices that were explicitly designed to have longer-term policy impacts. Rothstein demonstrates that labor's long-term organizational strength is more firmly anchored in countries that adopted union-administered unemployment insurance schemes (the so-called Ghent system) rather than universal compulsory unemployment systems. His analysis provides a very elegant explanation for why some countries are more unionized than others.

Beyond this, however, Rothstein also makes an important theoretical contribution to our understanding of institutional formation and change. By tracing the development of the Ghent system he is able to show how "at certain moments in history . . . institutions are created with the object of giving the agent (or the interests the agent wants to further) an advantage in the future game of power." In the case of Sweden, conscious political strategies produced a system that ensured high organization levels and union power to control critical aspects of the labor market. While not optimal in the short run (and indeed despite an initially rather cool reception to the Ghent system by the unions), inspired political leadership by the Social Democratic leader Gustav Möller gave the unions an organizational advantage that entrenched their power in the long run.

Rothstein shows that in other countries either labor could not implement the system of its choice, or in some cases even where it could have, labor leaders apparently did not see the strategic advantages of the Ghent system. Rothstein thus explicitly allows for the possibility of mistaken strategies or "wrong choices." His shadow cases (outside Sweden) show that the consequence of piecemeal decisions and less inspired leadership was that these labor movements ended up with insurance schemes that did not anchor labor unions as firmly as in Sweden. Thus, while Rothstein agrees with some rational choice theorists in viewing institutions as the product of deliberate political strategies, his analysis of unintended consequences outside of Sweden also emphasizes how behaving "rationally" is not so straightforward. Where actors hold conflicting preferences, and where it is not clear to them which goals to maximize (short- or long-term) or how best to pursue their interests, other factors – such as leadership – appear to play a key role in defining goals and how to pursue them.

Immergut's analysis of health care policy in France, Switzerland, and Sweden demonstrates just how important the unintended effects of institutional structure and change can be for policy-making. In Immergut's analysis, a nation's electoral rules and constitutional structure provide the institutional "rules of the game" in which subsequent political battles are fought. She demonstrates convincingly how quite different national health systems developed in France, Switzerland, and Sweden because different institutional configurations provided different "veto points" for competing interests as each country attempted to reform the financing and delivery of medical care. "By making some courses of action more difficult, and facilitating others," she argues, "the institutions redefined the political alternatives and changed the array of relevant actors. The institutions, in other words, established a strategic context for the actions of these political actors that changed the outcome of specific policy conflicts."

Immergut makes a clear distinction, however, between "political actors and their strategies" on the one hand, and the institutional framework in which action takes place on the other. As she points out, institutions are most certainly created and changed in struggles for political power. But, she suggests, those who participated in institutional design are not necessarily the same individuals who engage in later policy struggles. She implies that the long-term policy impact of particular institutional changes is unknown or at least highly uncertain. Indeed, as she shows in the case of Sweden, constitutional reforms designed to protect the interests of Conservatives at the turn of the century in fact had the effect of insulating and entrenching Social Democratic governments and, in the area of health care, providing medical interests fewer veto points through which they could block national health insurance reforms.

In sum, people fight about both institutions and policy outcomes. Battles over institutions are important precisely because broad policy paths can follow from institutional choices. Each of these authors demonstrates how the existence of certain institutional structures shapes subsequent policy battles. In addition, these analyses provide us with important insights into the politics of institutional design and change. Rothstein devotes special attention to the Swedish case because it in fact deviates from what appears to be a broader pattern that corroborates March and Olsen's argument that

institutional change rarely satisfies the prior intentions of those who initiate it. Change cannot be controlled precisely. . . . [Moreover] understanding the transformation of political institutions requires recognizing that there are frequently multiple, not necessarily consistent, intentions, that intentions are often ambiguous, that intentions are part of a system of values, goals, and attitudes that embeds intention in a structure of other beliefs and aspirations.[62]

Ideational innovation in institutional constraints

The chapters by Peter Hall, Desmond King, and Margaret Weir all speak to a third theme and source of dynamism in institutional analysis by explicitly exploring the relationship between new policy ideas and the institutional configuration that mediates between such ideas and specific policy outcomes. They offer an important alternative to more abstract treatments of the realm of ideology or public philosophy that reify the concepts and obscure the concrete processes through which certain ideas (and not others) come to dominate political discourse. Rather than bracketing the realm of ideas, or treating ideas and material interests as separate and unrelated variables (or as competing explanatory factors), they explore how the two interact within specified institutional contexts to produce policy change.

In Chapter 4 Peter Hall explores the development of monetarist ideas in the United Kingdom, arguing that what has really occurred since the mid-1970s is a shift between two competing "policy paradigms," each deeply rooted in very different ideas about how the economy works. Understanding both the timing and source of the shift from Keynesianism to monetarism, he argues, requires an examination of how the institutional structure of British politics mediated conflicting interests and structured the flow of ideas in the 1970s and 1980s. While the Heath government had proposed many specific policies of a monetarist tone in the early 1970s, the deep entrenchment of Keynesian ideas, especially in the powerful and autonomous Treasury, and the lack of a fully articulated alternative policy paradigm with which to confront and resist these entrenched ideas prevented the prime minister from accomplishing a full shift in policy.

By the time Margaret Thatcher came to power, however, the possibilities for policy innovation looked very different. Changes in the socioeconomic balance of power, especially the waning strength of the unions, had eroded important sources of support for Keynesianism. At the same time, institutions that reflected but also reinforced the growing power and cohesion of financial markets (including newly founded economic institutes and the media) came to play an increasingly important role in policy discourse, all the more so because they represented what in the meantime had developed into an increasingly coherent alternative policy paradigm. Thatcher was able to draw on growing support from key actors in the City, universities, and the media, to fashion a new coalition premised on a now fully articulated monetarist alternative to Labour's failed policies and to effect a radical break with the entire policy paradigm on which they had been premised. Moreover, the structure of government facilitated this full-scale shift. The high degree of power and autonomy available to reigning governments in the British parliamentary system enabled Thatcher to bring about policy switches that would have been far more difficult in more decentralized decision-making systems. In short, the structure of British political institutions helps Hall explain why new ideas were sought, the process by which new ideas were filtered and cultivated, and ultimately why certain ideas and interests (and not others) prevailed when they did.

By tracing the interaction of institutions, ideas, and interests, Hall confronts a widespread characterization of institutions as biased toward policy continuity or even posing obstacles to change, and he explores the idea that some institutions may facilitate rather than impede policy change. His analysis thus forces us to rethink some of our assumptions about institutions. We tend to think of institutions as bureaucracies that are conservative and biased toward continuity. But as Hall points out, some institutional structures may establish a dynamic tension that inspires creativity and encourages innovation. In Britain the combination of two-party competition (which gives parties a "structural interest in product differentiation and incentive to initiate changes" to garner electoral support) and responsible cabinet government (which allows governments great power to implement their programs) provided the institutional parameters that enabled Thatcher to implement more thoroughgoing reforms than her conservative counterparts in many other countries.

Desmond King's comparative analysis of the adoption of work–welfare programs in the United States and Britain, in Chapter 8, drives home these basic points. For King, much like Hall, the institutional structures define the channels and mechanisms by which new ideas are translated into policy. As King puts it, "Ideas must be translated into language and slogans appropriate for political decision-making, a process that often results in metamorphosis of the original notions. Parties and elected state officials play a crucial role in this 'translation'." King's analysis shows how New Right ideas linking welfare to work requirements traversed two different institutional routes to power in the United States and Britain. In the United States, changes in federal policies (especially Reagan's "New Federalism" initiatives in the early 1980s) pushed policy-making in the area of welfare and training programs toward the state level. This shift set the stage for state governments to emerge later as important actors in the move to reform federal policy concerning unemployment, especially as particular state programs became important models for national reform. However, the approach and ideas such programs represented were compromised in their journey through the national policy-making process. In particular, Reagan was able to use the power of the office of the president to interpret the successes of these programs in a way that recast them in terms of the New Right approach to poverty, toward which the president himself tended. In addition, the institutional power of the president (especially veto power) forced compromises at the drafting phases that led to the incorporation of work requirements for welfare benefits that had been absent in many of the state programs after which the federal legislation had been modeled.

King shows why political parties were institutionally better positioned in Britain than in the United States to play the role of initiator of policy change in work–welfare programs. In Britain New Right ideas and indeed explicit imitation of the American model entered the political arena through the Conservative Party and made their way through the legislative process relatively unscathed. In the absence of checks on central government policy-making that constrain U.S. policy-makers (federalism and the separation of powers), Thatcher – borrowing ideas from Reagan – was able to bring about a more fundamental break with prevailing policy ideas rooted in the tradition of a separation of welfare from labor-market policies, and even to successfully restructure existing institutions (such as the Manpower Services Commission) that stood in the way of the policy shift she sought.

In short, King's two cases demonstrate different institutional channels for policy innovation in Britain and the United States. Beyond this, however, his analysis shows how the institutional labyrinth can affect the content of new ideas, diluting them in the United States through the need to forge compromise in the context of fragmented national authority, and magnifying them in Britain, where similar compromise was unnecessary because of greater centralization in policy initiation and legislation. Like Hall's analysis, King's study thus shows how "institutions shape the absorption and diffusion of policy ideas." For both authors the specific mechanisms for integrating or adopting new ideas into the political arena are critical in shaping the interpretation and meaning behind those ideas.

Margaret Weir (Chapter 7) also explores the dynamic relationship between ideas and political institutions, in this case to illuminate how the structure of the American state led to a narrowing of the possibilities for policy innovation in the area of employment policy from the 1930s through the 1980s. As she puts it, "Central to this narrowing was the creation of institutions whose existence channeled the flow of ideas, created incentives for political actors, and helped determine the meaning of policy choices." "Bounded innovation" is Weir's description of the process through which particular institutional arrangements "created opportunities for some kinds of innovation [but also] set boundaries on the types of innovation possible." The fragmentation of American political institutions make the U.S. government relatively open to a wide range of policy innovations. Keynesian ideas first developed "on the outskirts" of the political mainstream, but when these ideas were picked up by key presidential advisers, and when Franklin Roosevelt put the power of the presidency behind them, the United States became a leader in social Keynesianism. However, these ideas proved difficult to institutionalize in the American context. The same fragmentation of national policy made it easy for opponents to mobilize opposition, which forced innovators to rely on short-term coalitions and to pursue innovation through existing channels rather than recast the institutions themselves.

The compromises that were necessary to implement Keynesianism in turn left an imprint on the form it assumed and channeled subsequent policy debates along particular paths. For example, one of the legacies of the postwar conflicts over the implementation of Keynesianism in the American context was an institutionally anchored division between social and economic policy that made it difficult to forge a conceptual and policy link between the two later. Indeed, other programs, such as Lyndon Johnson's War on Poverty in the 1960s not only reflected but reinforced these divisions. And when this program "intersected unexpectedly'' with subsequent events – in particular the racial tensions of the 1960s – policy-makers again sought to channel answers to new questions through existing institutions. Weir shows how the racial focus assumed by the War on Poverty program shaped its political fate. In short, innovators' reliance on short-term coalitions ultimately undermined future possibilities for forging the kinds of coalitions that would have been necessary to reorient American policy toward the unemployed in a more fundamental way, and especially threw up impediments to creating the institutional foundation that would have been necessary to anchor these new conceptions. This absence of strong institutional moorings meant that the programmatic ideas behind social Keynesianism were difficult to sustain over time; ultimately the failure to institutionalize these ideas made it difficult to defend government action when it came under attack by proponents of market-oriented approaches to employment policy in the 1970s.

CONCLUSION

We close this essay with some observations about where we see the theoretical insights offered by historical institutionalists leading, and what this suggests in terms of a future theoretical and methodological agenda in the study of comparative politics and comparative political economy.

The field of comparative politics has long suffered a dilemma. The "scientific revolution" in political science inspired comparativists to search for continuing patterns of politics across nations and over time and to set these down in a limited number of propositions which could be systematically tested. Przeworski and Teune are very explicit about the core premise of comparative analysis in *The Logic of Comparative Social Inquiry,* which states that, "The pivotal assumption of this analysis is that social science research, including comparative inquiry, should and can lead to general statements about social phenomena. This assumption implies that human and social behavior can be explained in terms of general laws established by observation."[63]

At the same time, however, there has also been an enduring skepticism among many scholars of an overemphasis on science in the study of comparative politics. The suspicion here is that in modeling themselves on the physical sciences, political scientists are inviting reductionism and ignoring the inherent complexity of human political action in favor of elegant but unrealistic laws. Many comparativists would agree with Gabriel Almond when he argues: "Social scientists who – for whatever philosophical or methodological reasons . . . view human behavior as simply reactive and consequently susceptible to the same explanatory logic as 'clocklike' natural phenomena are trying to fashion a science based on empirically falsified presuppositions."[64] What distinguishes social and political from natural phenomena is that humans can and do consciously affect the environment in which they operate. This element of agency and choice does more than add analytic complexity; it also suggests that the premises of analysis are different from those of natural science, in that "a simple search for regularities and lawful relationships among variables – a strategy that has led to tremendous successes in the physical sciences – will not explain social outcomes, but only some of the conditions affecting those outcomes."[65]

There are two issues suggested here for the role of institutional analysis within the logic of more refined comparative political inquiry. First, because humans shape the constraints in which they interact through institutional choice and design, it is especially compelling to look at these moments of institutional change. Conflicts over institutions lay bare interests and power relations, and their outcomes not only reflect but magnify and reinforce the interests of the winners, since broad policy trajectories can follow from institutional choices. Without taking away from the scientific interest in the regularities, then, political scientists legitimately can and should be particularly interested in moments of institutional choice and change. In this view, political evolution is a path or branching process and the study of the points of departure from established patterns ("critical junctures" of institutional choice) becomes essential to a broader understanding of political history. The authors in this book illustrate the benefits of this approach. Each of these essays pushes well beyond the insight that "Policies create politics" (Heclo) and goes on to demonstrate how specific institutional arrangements structure particular kinds of politics. They present powerful institutional explanations that go a long way toward helping us understand not just the choice of particular policies adopted in various nations, but also sources of historical divergence and the more general paths that different countries have followed.

Second, as several authors in this book suggest, institutional choices can shape people's ideas, attitudes, and even preferences. In this view, institutional change is important not only because it alters the constraints in which actors make strategic choices but ultimately because it can reshape the very goals and ideas that animate political action. What makes political evolution different from physical evolution is that the former is influenced by the intentions of its subjects. The book's essays capture the dynamic interplay of humans both as agents and subjects of historical change. In each of these analyses political institutions directly affected political choices, but in no case does the author argue that state or societal structures are the only things that matter. Instead, each offers a sophisticated explanation of the way in which factors such as conceptions of class, public philosophies, historical contexts, and elite and public preferences intersect with institutional structures to produce particular policy outcomes. These outcomes, then, themselves become the arenas of future political and institutional struggles in which, as Weir puts it, "ideas and interests develop and institutions and strategies adapt" (Chapter 7). In addition, many of these essays also provide clues into the conditions under which both institutional and ideational innovation is possible.

To conclude, historical institutionalists have carved out an important theoretical niche at the middle range that explicitly focuses on intermediate variables in order to integrate an understanding of general patterns of political history with an explanation of the contingent nature of political and economic development. As an alternative to broad and often abstract Marxist, functionalist, and systems theory approaches, historical institutionalism provides an approach to the study of politics and public policy that is sensitive to persistent cross-national differences. As a corrective to narrow interest-group theories, the institutionalist perspective illuminates how historically evolved structures channel political battles in distinctive ways on a more enduring basis. And most important, by focusing on institutions that are the product of political conflict and choice but which at the same time constrain and shape political strategies and behaviors, historical institutionalism provides a framework for directly confronting the central question of choice and constraint in understanding political life.

NOTES

1 James March and Johan Olsen, *Rediscovering Institutions* (New York: Free Press, 1989); see also James March and Johan Olsen, "The New Institutionalism: Organizational Factors in Political Life," *American Political Science Review* 78, no. 3 (Sept. 1984):734–49.

2 Peter Hall, *Governing the Economy: The Politics of State Intervention in Britain and France* (New York: Oxford University Press, 1986); David Bachman, *Bureaucracy, Economy, and Leadership in China: The Institutional Origins of the Great Leap Forward* (Cambridge: Cambridge University Press, 1991).

3 The kind of analysis these authors have undertaken differs in important ways from another variant of new institutionalism that builds on rational choice theory. See, for example, Douglass C. North, *Institutions, Institutional Change, and Economic Performance* (Cambridge: Cambridge University Press, 1990); Margaret Levi, *Of Rule and Revenue* (Berkeley: University of California Press, 1988); Robert H. Bates, *Beyond the Miracle of the Market: The Political Economy of Agrarian Development in Rural Kenya* (Cambridge: Cambridge University Press, 1989); and the entire Cambridge University Press series edited by James Alt and Douglass North, The Political Economy of Institutions and Decisions. We will address points of divergence and convergence between the two variants as a secondary theme in this introductory chapter, though this book focuses primarily on the non–rational choice variant.

4 We borrow the term "historical institutionalism" from Theda Skocpol, to distinguish this variant of institutionalism from the alternative, rational choice variant.

5 Including Marx, Weber, Veblen, and Polanyi, among others.

6 G. John Ikenberry, "Conclusion: An Institutional Approach to American Foreign Economic Policy," in G. John Ikenberry, David A. Lake, and Michael Mastanduno, eds., *The State and American Foreign Economic Policy* (Ithaca, N.Y.: Cornell University Press, 1988), pp. 222–3.

7 Hall, *Governing the Economy*, p. 19. On its face, and at this rather abstract definitional level, Hall's definition is not very different from definitions used by some rational choice theorists. Douglass North, for example, defines institutions to include "any form of constraint that human beings devise to shape human interaction." He includes both formal constraints "such as rules" and informal constraints "such as conventions and codes of behavior." See Douglass C. North, *Institutions, Institutional Change,*

and Economic Performance (Cambridge: Cambridge University Press, 1990), p. 4. Where historical institutionalism and rational choice diverge more sharply is on the question of how institutions affect political behavior and where institutions come from. We return to these points later in the chapter.

8 Ikenberry, "Conclusion," p. 226.

9 For example, we ourselves are in full agreement with Ikenberry's first two levels of institutions, but somewhat more skeptical about whether the third, the "normative order defining relations between state and society" should be included. While norms that define the "legitimacy and illegitimacy of alternative types of policy" (p. 227) may pose constraints on behavior, these are not necessarily *institutional* constraints. Because most institutionalists readily admit that institutions cannot explain everything, there would seem to be great analytic advantage to casting a somewhat narrower definitional net and focusing on the question of how institutions interact with these other causal variables. Several of the essays in this volume pursue this strategy, focusing on the often blurred relationship between ideas and institutions.

10 And of course this list is not exhaustive.

11 We will return to this issue below, offering our own view of how broadly the institutional net should be cast.

12 Hall, *Governing the Economy*, p. 19.

13 Nelson Polsby.

14 For the best single review of the history of the discipline up to the 1960s see Harry Eckstein, "A Perspective on Comparative Politics, Past, Present and Future," in H. Eckstein and D. Apter, *Comparative Politics* (New York: The Free Press, 1963), pp. 3–32. See also Sidney Verba, "Some Dilemmas in Comparative Research," *World Politics* 20 (Oct. 1967):111–27. For another review of the development of the field from this perspective, see James Bill and Robert Hardgrave, *Comparative Politics: The Quest for Theory* (Columbus: Charles Merrill, 1973).

15 See, for example, Daniel Bell's *The End of Ideology* (New York: Free Press, 1965).

16 This applies to much of the literature associated with "modernization" theory of the 1960s.

17 And of course everyone can think of specific literatures that continued to look explicitly at the impact of different institutional arrangements on political outcomes. The literature on political parties is an important example.

18 See *Pressure Group Politics* (Stanford, Calif.: Stanford University Press, 1960), p. 8; or, for example, E. E. Schattschneider, *The Semi-Sovereign People* (New York: Holt Reinhart, 1960). Even David Truman's classic pluralist analysis *The Governmental Process* (New York: Knopf, 1951) contains oblique references that his analysis is set in an American institutional context. He does not, however, elaborate or make this point explicit, and instead falls into the classic pluralist trap that *assumes* a particular institutional structure and builds an entire model of politics based on behavior within these institutions.

19 Reinhard Bendix, "Tradition and Modernity Reconsidered" in Reinhard Bendix, *Nation-Building and Citizenship* (Berkeley: University of California Press, 1977). See also his introduction to *State and Society* (Berkeley: University of California Press, 1973), in which he criticizes those theorists who neglect the "formal" aspects of society and focus only on "informal interactions" among actors: "We, on the other hand, hold that social life is structured – not exclusively of course, but structured nonetheless – by just those formal institutional mechanisms. To disregard such structures at least implies the belief that social life is essentially amorphous. This does not mean that institutions work as they are intended to work; it does mean that they have an effect" (p. 11).

20 From a different perspective, Marxist theorists in the 1970s were coming to comple-

mentary conclusions as they began to pay closer attention to state structures and the ways these interacted with class interests in liberal democracies. Marxist theorists of the state were still primarily interested in how the same general "requirements of capital accumulation" were met in different settings, but the thrust of the analysis – focusing on how different institutions mediated class relations differently – also provided early insights into persistent differences across the advanced capitalist countries. See Hall's discussion of their contribution in *Governing the Economy* (p. 18).

21 Structural functionalists certainly were, but institutions also figure in the work of some behavioralists.

22 Shepsle, "Institutional Equilibrium and Equilibrium Institutions," in Herbert Weisberg, ed., *Political Science: The Science of Politics* (New York: Agathon Press, 1986), p. 52.

23 This is exactly what Eckstein meant when he criticized pluralists for implying that pressure group politics were fought on a "clean slate" (see Eckstein, *Pressure Group Politics*, p. 8). For another such critique in its time, see Schattschneider, *The Semi-Sovereign People*. See also Chapter 3, by Ellen Immergut, in this volume.

24 And even before that, the student rebellions and worker unrest of the late 1960s put an end to the belief in the "end of ideology."

25 In one of the most important early contributions to new institutionalism in comparative politics, this is exactly how Katzenstein frames his empirical and theoretical agenda. See his introduction to *Between Power and Plenty* (Madison: University of Wisconsin, 1978). See also Peter Gourevitch, *Politics in Hard Times* (Ithaca, N.Y.: Cornell University Press, 1986); Suzanne Berger, ed., *Organizing Interests in Western Europe* (Cambridge: Cambridge University Press, 1981); Philippe Schmitter, "Modes of Interest Intermediation and Models of Societal Change in Western Europe," *Comparative Political Studies* 10, no. 1 (April 1977):7–38; and other corporatism theorists.

26 Katzenstein's sophisticated analysis explains cross-national variation in both policy objectives and instruments. Although he places the greatest weight on the structure of domestic institutional arrangements for explaining the specific foreign economic policies in the 1970s, his analysis also pays careful attention to the position of each country in the international political economy as well as the historical policy traditions within each country *(Between Power and Plenty*, p. 297).

27 See, for example, Philippe Schmitter and Gerhard Lehmbruch, eds., *Trends toward Corporatist Intermediation* (Beverly Hills, Calif.: Sage, 1979); Peter Lange and Geoffrey Garrett, "The Politics of Growth: Strategic Interaction and Economic Performance in the Advanced Industrial Democracies, 1974–1980," *World Politics* (July 1986):792–827. See also Frank Wilson, "Interest Groups and Politics in Western Europe: The Neo-Corporatist Approach," *Comparative Politics* 16, no. 1 (1983), and Gary Freeman, "National Styles and Policy Sectors: Explaining Structured Variation," *Journal of Public Policy* 5 (1986):467–96.

28 Suzanne Berger, "Introduction," in Suzanne Berger, ed., *Organizing Interests in Western Europe* (Cambridge: Cambridge University Press, 1981); Theda Skocpol, "Bringing the State Back In: Strategies of Analysis in Current Research," in Peter B. Evans, Dietrich Rueschemeyer, and Theda Skocpol, eds., *Bringing the State Back In* (Cambridge: Cambridge University Press, 1985); Douglas Ashford "Structural Analysis of Policy or Institutions Really Do Matter" in D. Ashford, ed., *Comparing Public Policies: New Concepts and Methods* (Beverly Hills; Calif.: Sage, 1978).

29 See, for example, March and Olsen, "The New Institutionalism," pp. 734–49; Ikenberry et al., eds., *The State in American Foreign Economic Policy;* Stephen Skowronek, *Building a New American State* (Cambridge: Cambridge University Press, 1982).

30 Hall, *Governing the Economy*, p. 19.

31 For some of the best recent work in this tradition, see the excellent series edited by

Alt and North, The Political Economy of Institutions and Decisions (Cambridge University Press).

32 To be sure, many scholars who come from the rational choice tradition are also willing to relax the rationality assumption. Indeed, some of the most interesting work in rational choice theory is moving away from a narrow view of *Homo economicus* toward a more contextual view of human behavior. See, for example, Douglass North, "A Transaction Cost Theory of Politics," *Journal of Theoretical Politics* 2, no. 4 (October 1990):355–67; Douglass North, Karen Cook, and Margaret Levi, eds., *The Limits of Rationality* (Chicago: University of Chicago Press, 1990); and, from a different perspective, Jon Elster, "Social Norms and Economic Theory," *Journal of Economic Perspectives,* 3, no. 4 (Fall 1989):99–117. See also Jane Mansbridge, ed., *Beyond Self-Interest* (Chicago: University of Chicago Press, 1990).

33 Herbert Simon, "Human Nature and Politics: The Dialogue of Psychology with Political Science," *American Political Science Review* 79 (1985):293–304; March and Olsen, "The New Institutionalism," James March, "Theories of Choice and Making Decisions," *Society* 20 (Nov.–Dec. 1982):29–39.

34 Paul DiMaggio and Walter Powell "Introduction," in Powell and DiMaggio, eds., *The New Institutionalism in Organizational Analysis* (Chicago: University of Chicago Press, 1991), p. 9.

35 Rational choice theorists would not deny such rule-following behavior, but they would attempt to explain it as a rational response – for example, to complex situations or high costs of information gathering.

36 See, e.g., Sven Steinmo, "Political Institutions and Tax Policy in the United States, Sweden, and Britain, *World Politics* 41, no. 4 (July 1989):502.

37 We thank Geoffrey Garrett for this point.

38 In the present volume, Peter Hall (Chapter 4) and Margaret Weir (Chapter 7) explicitly probe this deeper impact of institutions. Other historical institutionalists – among the authors represented here, Ellen Immergut, for example – are more agnostic on the issue of how institutions shape preferences. Consequently, her analysis is in some ways more compatible with a rational choice perspective than others in this book. Immergut treats this issue briefly in Chapter 3.

39 Thorstein Veblen, *The Place of Science in Modern Civilization and Other Essays* (New York: Russell and Russell, 1961). Karl Polanyi's *The Great Transformation* is another example. Polanyi's book is about the social and political ramifications of the rise of the (meta-)institution of the market economy. See also C. E. Ayers, *The Theory of Economic Progress* (New York: Schocken Books, 1962). For a more recent account of the economic institutionalist school and its view of history, see Edyth Miller, "Institutional Economics: Philosophy, Methodology, and Theory," *Social Sciences Journal* 15, no. 1, (Jan. 1978):13–25.

40 Roger Friedland and Robert Alford, "Bringing Society Back In: Symbols, Practices, and Institutional Contradictions" in Powell and DiMaggio, *New Institutionalism,* p. 232.

41 For a very interesting essay on the difference between historical and rational choice institutionalists as it bears on preferences, see John Ferejohn, "Rationality and Interpretation: Parliamentary Elections in Early Stuart England," unpublished manuscript, Stanford University, Jan. 1990.

42 See Geoffrey Garrett and Barry Weingast, "Ideas, Interests, and Institutions: Constructing the EC's Internal Market," paper presented at the American Political Science Association Meeting, Aug. 28–Sept. 1, 1991, esp. pp. 2–3. (And there is also the difference between short-term and long-term interests.)

43 We thank Peter Katzenstein for this insight.

44 Hall, *Governing the Economy,* p. 19.

45 See especially Williamson and early North. Some rational choice theorists are also critical of this version of transaction costs theory.
46 This efficiency view of institutions also cannot explain the persistence of clearly dysfunctional or inefficient institutions. See the discussion in North, *Institutions, Institutional Change*, p. 7.
47 Katzenstein, *Between Power and Plenty*.
48 Hall, *Governing the Economy*.
49 Discussions with Geoffrey Garrett, Peter Hall, and Atul Kohli helped to sharpen the argument presented here. "Universal tool kit" is Garrett's term; "deductive logical system" is Kohli's.
50 Ikenberry, "Conclusion," p. 242.
51 Steinmo, "Political Institutions and Tax Policy," pp. 500–35.
52 See Sven Steinmo, *Taxation and Democracy: Swedish, British and American Approaches to Financing the Welfare State* (New Haven, Conn.: Yale University Press, forthcoming 1993) for a more nuanced treatment of these issues.
53 Stephen D. Krasner, "Approaches to the State: Alternative Conceptions and Historical Dynamics," *Comparative Politics* 16, no. 2 (Jan. 1984):223–46. Krasner borrows this model from the evolutionary biologists Stephen Jay Gould and Niles Eldredge.
54 See, for example, Ikenberry, "Conclusions," pp. 223–5 and 233–5; Samuel Huntington's *American Politics: The Promise of Disharmony* (Cambridge, Mass.: Harvard University Press, 1981) also seems compatible with this.
55 In addition, the "punctuated equilibrium" model tends to understate the continuities that are so key to institutional analysis in times of institutional stability. As Skocpol points out, institutions may break down in a national or international crisis, but they are never constructed entirely from scratch; successor institutions bear the stamp of their predecessors, partly because they are reconstituted out of pieces of the old. This is essentially Shonfield's point when he describes how, after being shattered in World War II, the institutions of the postwar German political economy (bank–industry links, for example) were recreated in ways that reflect the prewar institutions.
56 We owe this point to Victoria Hattam, and her essay in this book (Chapter 6) provides an excellent example of this source of change. See also our discussion of her essay later in the present chapter.
57 With the new salience of the Court has come renewed scholarly interest in this institution – its activities and its sources of legitimacy, for example. On the latter, see Garrett and Weingast, "Ideas, Interests, and Institutions."
58 See Nelson Lichtenstein, "The Union's Early Days: Shop Stewards and Seniority Rights," in Mike Parker and Jane Slaughter, eds., *Choosing Sides: Unions and the Team Concept* (Boston: South End Books, 1988). Desmond King and Bo Rothstein demonstrate a similar analytical point in their analysis of labor market policies. See Desmond S. King and Bo Rothstein, "Institutional Choice and Labour Market Policy: A British–Swedish Comparison," *Comparative Political Studies* (forthcoming).
59 See, especially, Michael Piore and Charles Sabel, *The Second Industrial Divide* (New York: Basic Books, 1984), among many others.
60 Kathleen Thelen, *Union of Parts: Labor Politics in Postwar Germany* (Ithaca, N.Y.: Cornell University Press, 1991).
61 This general idea is implicit in the work of some historical institutionalists (e.g., Skowronek) and quite explicit in that of others.
62 March and Olsen, *Rediscovering Institutions*, pp. 65–6.
63 Adam Przeworski and Henry Teune, *The Logic of Comparative Social Inquiry* (New York, John Wiley and Sons, 1970), p. 4.
64 Gabriel Almond and Stephen Genco, "Clouds, Clocks, and the Study of Politics," *World Politics* 29, no. 4 (1977):493.
65 Ibid., p. 493.

2

Labor-market institutions and working-class strength

BO ROTHSTEIN

The central question in this essay is simple yet important: Why are some working classes more organized than others? This phenomenon has since World War II shown increased variation among Western capitalist countries (von Beyme 1980; Wallerstein 1989). The latest figures show that unionization among these countries ranges from below 15% in France to 86% in Sweden (see Table 2.1). Among industrialized Western states hardly any other political variables of this kind vary to such an extent. In this essay I will equate degree of unionization with working-class strength. It can of course be argued that working-class strength is also dependent on other variables such as party organization and cultural homogeneity. But following Marxist theory, unionization may be seen as the primary organization form of the working class and can thus be considered a basis for other forms of working-class strength, such as political and cultural organization (Olofsson 1979; Offe and Wiesenthal 1980).[1]

The importance of the level of working-class organizational strength stems, inter alia, from the established positive correlation between union strength and the development of welfare-state policies. One can say that, with few exceptions, the stronger is the organization of the working class, the more developed the welfare state (Korpi 1983; Shalev 1983a, b; Amenta and Skocpol 1986; Noble 1988). But, critically, this correlation does not in itself show how the causal link between social policies and working-class formation operates. It does not show, that is, which of the two variables explains the other or in what way they are interconnected (Esping-Andersen 1985; Przeworski 1985; Skocpol 1988).

How can this great variation in workers' inclination to join unions be explained? A traditional interpretation of Marxist theory (such as that of Cohen 1978) would explain it as due to differences in the development of the productive

This essay is an outcome of a research project titled Interest Organizations and the Public Interest, financed by the Swedish Central Bank's Tercentenary Fund. I would like to thank Frank Longstreth, Jonas Pontusson, Theda Skocpol, Ulla Arnell-Gustafsson, Stefan Björklund, Charles Noble, and Michael Wallerstein for their valuable comments on earlier versions. Thanks also to Anders Westholm who helped me in computing the statistics and to Peter Mayers for checking the language.

forces. But it is obvious that this cannot explain why Swedish workers are almost
six times more organized than their French colleagues. Even if Sweden techno-
logically is a well-developed country, France, and for that matter Japan and the
United States, are not such laggards. A traditional interpretation of Marxist theory that seeks to reduce political factors to the level of economic development
obviously cannot help us here (von Beyme 1980:73–84). Nor can the timing and
pace of industrialization – that is, the formation of the working class *an sich* –
explain the variation in unionization. Nor does it seems convincing to point to
such variables as cultural factors or social norms (Elster 1989). If union membership reflects the norm – for example, of solidarity among workers – then we
still need to know why some working classes are more inclined to the norm of
collective action than others. For instance, two countries that may be said, without any deeper analysis, to be culturally and socially rather similar, such as
Belgium and the Netherlands, differ dramatically in degree of unionization (74%
and 29% respectively). The same, albeit to a lesser degree, goes for such very
similar countries as Sweden and Norway (86% and 58% respectively). Obviously, we have to look for some kind of independent variable(s) *between* socioeconomic structure and social norms.

The following section discusses theoretically the kinds of variables that can be
expected to explain differences in the degree of unionization – that is, working-
class strength – among Western capitalist countries. A comparative quantitative
description and statistical analysis of these variables follows. Then, in order to
illuminate the causal logic of the statistical analysis, a brief historical comparative overview is presented. Finally, for reasons that will be obvious, a more
detailed analysis of the Swedish case is undertaken.

INSTITUTIONAL FACTORS AND WORKING-CLASS ORGANIZATIONAL STRENGTH

The theoretical point of departure here is that differences in unionization can to
a large extent be explained by historical variation in national *political institutions*. Arguing that political institutions are important is of course not new; indeed it has been a commonplace theme in political science from Aristotle through
Tocqueville and beyond (see March and Olsen 1984; Steinmo 1989). Yet there
is a fresh insight in what has been called "new institutionalism," namely the
treatment of political institutions as important *independent* variables in explaining political behavior and social change (Douglas 1987; Thelen and Steinmo,
Chapter 1 in this volume). As against social and economic structures (such as
the productive forces), political institutions are entities that might once have been
deliberately created by rational, goal-oriented, political agents (Levi 1990;
Tsebelis 1990:9–11, 96f). While political institutions may be understood as setting limits on, as well as enabling, agents in the pursuit of their objectives (Giddens 1979), they can, because of their general "stickiness," be seen also as

political and administrative *structures* (Shepsle 1989). This takes us right into one of the basic questions in social science and history, namely whether agency or structure is primary in causing social change (Mouzelis 1988; Cerny 1990). If institutions set limits on what some agents can do, and enable other agents to do things they otherwise would not have been able to do, then we need to know under what circumstances these institutions were created. For if political agents can design or construct institutions, they may then construe an advantage in future political battles (Knight 1988:25; Levi 1990).

If we can empirically identify such moments of institutional creation in history, then we will have moved much closer to understanding the agency–structure, micro–macro problem in social science. The analysis of the creation and destruction of political institutions might thus serve as a bridge between the "men who make history" and the "circumstances" under which they are able to do so. Thus my theoretical object in this essay is not restricted to showing that institutions are important in shaping political behavior but that at certain *formative moments* in history, these institutions are created with the object of giving the agent (or the interests the agent wants to further) an advantage in the future game of power. I agree with Tsebelis's argument (1990:96–100) that the choice of institutions is the sophisticated equivalent of selecting policies. I am, however, less confident than he or other rational choice theorists that their approach can be used to explain why some actors are better suited than others in choosing institutions that maximize their future goals, or for that matter why some actors have goals different from others.

Pointing to the relation between public policies or institutions and working-class formation (or deformation) is not of course unique (see Esping-Andersen 1985; Korpi 1985:38; Przeworski 1985; Skocpol 1988). However, two problems are left unsolved in the literature relating public policy and institutions to class formation. First, as the number of political institutions and public policies is very great, one needs some sort of theory distinguishing the political institutions that are more decisive than others in influencing working-class formation. To point to public policy or government institutions in general is not very helpful. In other words, we need a theory that explains why some games (or their structuring) are more important than others. Second, one needs to show exactly how differences in the operation of these government institutions affect workers' inclination to join in collective action. By "exactly" I mean that one must specify the way in which the operational logic of a government institution changes the rationality (or ordering of preferences) of agents when deciding how to act. This is thus a *methodological* request for a "microfoundation" of institutional or structural analysis but without any hard-nosed *theoretical* restriction to methodological individualism (Callinicos 1989). Such an approach might bridge the gap between rational choice and historical approaches to institutional analysis (see Chapter 1, by Thelen and Steinmo).

As a solution to the problem of deciding which political institutions are important to study in this matter, I will argue that the organizational strength of a social class is based in its position in the *relations of production*. The latter are, however, not to be seen as a mere reflection of the productive forces but as having an explanatory force of their own (Callinicos 1989). By this I mean that while in every capitalist society, the relations of production contain capitalists and wage-workers involved in a special sort of uneven economic exchange, this is nonetheless not the whole story. It is not the whole story because the power of workers and capitalists, respectively, in the relations of production differs greatly between different capitalist societies operating more or less at the same stage of the development of the productive forces (Korpi 1983; Wright 1985:123f). In some capitalist democracies workers have been able to organize themselves to a large extent and thus confront the capitalists on a more intense and equal level than in other such countries.

Logically, if we wish to explain these differences from a Marxist standpoint, we should concentrate on *political institutions directly affecting the relations of production*. In common language this means labor-market institutions or policy taken in a broad sense, including such things as rules governing the right of labor to organize and take collective action against capitalists, unemployment policies, training programs. The argument is that of all the games to be played, this is the most important one in the explanation of working-class organizational strength. This also involves a shift of focus for Marxist social analysis from the economic to the political and organizational spheres, which implies that we should be looking at how organized class interests invest power resources when shaping and creating political institutions on the labor market (Korpi 1983:19). Marxists have sometimes argued that the only social structures that matter are the purely economic ones. Because such structures by definition are not deliberately created, but rather result from the evolutionary logic of economic and technological development (Cohen 1978), focusing solely on such structures has imparted to Marxist social science a flaw of structural determinism (Elster 1985). The rational choice variant of this involves seeing institutions solely as resulting from evolutionary processes rather than deliberate creation. Following Nicos Mouzelis (1984, 1988) I argue here that political institutions, such as bureaucracies, armies, and the complex of legal regulations, can be as constraining for agents as economic structures. If it can be shown that more or less *deliberately created* political institutions exist on the labor market that affect class formation and class organization, then we can escape the structural-determinist trap in Marxist (and other kinds of) social science (Callinicos 1989; Cerny 1990).

EXPLAINING UNIONIZATION

According to Mancur Olson (1965), workers would not join unions if acting out of individual rationality, because the benefits unions provide are collective goods. Rationally acting workers would choose to become "free-riders" – that is, to collect the benefits from the organization without contributing to the costs of reproducing it. The fact that workers historically have joined unions, sometimes on a rather large scale, Olson explains by showing that unions have been able to create *selective incentives* that lie outside their main purpose of collective bargaining. If Olson's theory is correct, then we need to know two things. First, why are unions in some countries more successful than others in creating these selective incentives? Since the degree of unionization differs to a very great extent between similar countries, it would seem that the creation of such selective incentives must be done on a nationwide scale. Second, if it is in their rational interest to create such incentives, and if the theory of rational choice is all that is needed to explain political behavior, then why are some working classes more rational than others?

Many objections have been made to Olson's famous theory about collective action, but it is fair to say that it is still at the center of efforts to explain problems of collective action. One telling criticism of Olson's theory, however, is that he neglects the uniqueness of labor power as a commodity in that it is inseparable from its individual bearer. Unions, therefore, unlike organizations of capitalists, have good reason to take the *individual* well-being of their members into account (Offe and Wiesenthal 1980). Thus, when there is no further demand for an individual worker's labor power on the labor market, there is a cost to the union if it simply abandons him or her. This is so because the main power resource unions possess is their control over the supply of labor power. If unions abandon workers when the demand for their labor power declines, the workers, now deprived of their means of existence, will be liable to start underbidding the union-set price for labor power. This leads to a situation in which capitalists are able to get labor power at a price below that which the unions have decided upon, which is to say the unions no longer control the supply of labor power. There is simply no greater threat to union strength or working-class mobilization, than this (Unga 1976; Åmark 1986; Wallerstein 1989:484f).

If the preceding line of reasoning is correct, the searchlight in our quest for important institutions should be directed at government institutions and policies influencing unions' prospects of maintaining their control over the supply of labor power. This can be done in several ways, such as by a ''closed shop,'' but one of the most common is the institutionalization of public unemployment-insurance systems. Public unemployment insurance is a direct way for governments to intervene in the labor market by supporting that portion of the labor power for which there is presently no demand. Unemployment insurance is more important in this matter than are other government social policies such as sickness, disability, and old-age insurance, because workers in any of these latter three circumstances do not usually have the possibility to start underbidding wages. Thus, in contrast to the direct link between unemployment policy and the power situation in the relations of production, social policy in general has only indirect effects, if any, on the relations of production (see Przeworski 1985).

Many analysts of labor relations have hitherto tried to explain variations in unionization (von Beyme 1980; Kjellberg 1983). Strange as it may seem, differences in government labor-market institutions have usually not been taken into account. It has recently been shown that neither the traditional business-cycle thesis, nor theories based on differences in dependency on international trade, can explain variations in unionization (Wallerstein 1989). Instead, a structural factor, the size of the national labor force, is reported to be strongly but negatively correlated to degree of unionization. The argument behind this is that the larger the number of potentially recruitable wage-earners, the more difficult and expensive the process of recruitment (Wallerstein 1989).

There are, however, a few problems with treating this correlation as an explanation.One is that it is not the national central union organization, if it exists at all, that recruits members, but rather the local, more or less branch-specific, union. Why costs for recruitment should increase with the size of the *national* labor force is thus not clear. The other problem is why there could be no such thing as a diminishing marginal cost in organizing workers. Size is certainly statistically significant, but, as will be shown subsequently, there are countries with practically the same number of wage-earners in the labor market that differ considerably in unionization (for example, Belgium and the Netherlands). The evident conclusion is that, however important, the size of the labor force can be overcome as an organizational problem by some working classes.

Second, it has been shown that the political color of governments is important in explaining national differences in the degree of unionization (Kjellberg 1983; Wallerstein 1989). The more frequent and the longer the periods of left-party government, the higher the degree of unionization. The problem with this explanation is that it is not clear which of these two variables explains the other. Having a large number of workers organized in unions is evidently an important resource for labor parties competing in national elections, and that once in government, labor parties can launch labor-market laws that facilitate unionization. But one might also claim that union strength is sometimes detrimental to the stability of labor governments, as in the British "winter of discontent" 1978–9.

It is, however, reasonable to think of the relation between level of unionization and degree of left-party government as dialectical. Theda Skocpol, for example, has argued against the existence of any unidimensional causality between working-class strength and left-party government or the development of social policies. Instead, she argues that the social policies launched in some European countries during the 1930s, such as Sweden, furthered working-class strength and that the causal link between the two variables is to be understood as a continuous "positive loop" (Skocpol 1988:9; compare Weir and Skocpol 1985). But even if we accept the hypothesis that these two variables are interdependent, we need to know how this relationship works; that is, we need a microfoundation of how, exactly, left-party government promotes unionization. In what ways can, for example, government labor-market institutions change workers' preferences as to whether or not to join unions? It has been argued that, compared to other countries, labor-market legislation in the United States imposes comparatively high costs for unions in their efforts to organize labor (Goldfield 1987). Another example is former West Germany, where the Supreme Court ruled out the legal possibility of the Bundestag passing any law that gives privileges to workers on account of their being union members (Streeck 1981). Another example is of course the fate of the British trade unions during the 1980s.

In Sweden, on the other hand, almost all legal entitlements that wage-earners possess concerning their position in the relations of production (and they are many) have been granted them in their capacity as union members – have been granted, that is, to their unions (Schmidt 1977). I would argue that, while the choice of whether or not to join a union is a free choice, the rationality in the decision can be severely affected by the operation of government labor-market institutions. If this is so, then we cannot understand national differences in unionization solely by using some sort of rational-choice or game-theoretic approach, because we need to know how preferences were established in the first place, and in what way and by whom the game of collective action has been structured. When we know all this, rational choice and game theory can be used as an analytical tool to understand the outcome (Berger and Offe 1982; Grafstein 1988; compare Bianco and Bates 1990; Tsebelis 1990).

Walter Korpi has argued that the high degree of unionization in Sweden should not be attributed to that country's having developed some form of corporatist political system, which essentially forces wage-earners to join unions, but rather arises from workers' self-interest in collective action (Korpi 1983:7–25). But why then do workers in capitalist countries have such different interests in furthering their own interests by collective action? Obviously, this problem cannot be solved without discussing what causes this variation in the formation of workers' preferences as to whether or not to join unions. This is where institutionalist analysis comes in because, contrary to rational choice and game theory, institutions to a large extent explain preference formation, the ordering of preferences, and the number as well as the resources of the player (March and Olsen 1984:739; Douglas 1987). I contend that the explanation of the variation in degree of unionization to a great extent lies in the variation of the operational logic of the national public unemployment schemes.

COMPARING PUBLIC UNEMPLOYMENT SCHEMES

All major industrialized Western countries introduced some form of public or publicly supported unemployment-insurance system before World War II. These schemes took two different institutional forms: (1) as a compulsory system administered by government agencies and, (2) as a voluntary but publicly supported scheme administered by unions or union-dominated funds. The latter system is also called the Ghent system, after the Belgian town in which it was established in 1901.

In order to understand the difference in operational logic between these systems, it is necessary to examine briefly the *mode of administration* of insurance against such a thing as unemployment. One of the major problems in designing an unemployment scheme is how to identify that part of the nonworking population that should be entitled to support. This cannot be done in a simple way using precise rules defined in laws such as those regarding pensions or child allowances. First of all, people not belonging to the labor force must be excluded. It is always difficult to decide if a person really is a part of the supply to the labor market. Second, workers are not just unemployed in general, they are *as individuals* unable to find work at a certain place and time, within a certain trade, and at a certain level of payment. It is thus often the case that an unemployed worker can find a job if he or she is willing to move, to take a job outside his or her trade or below his or her qualifications, or to accept a job at a lower level of payment. Therefore, the paramount question in the implementation of an unemployment-insurance scheme is to decide what kind of job an unemployed worker cannot refuse without losing the insurance benefit. In the literature about unemployment insurance, this is known as the problem of defining "the suitable job" (Lester 1965; Erici and Roth 1981). In contrast to the case with capital, there is no such thing as labor power in general, as each and every unit of labor power is physically attached to an individual human being with unique characteristics (Rothstein 1990).

This means that what constitutes a suitable job must be decided for each and every individual seeking support from the insurance scheme. This can be done only by granting a considerable measure of discretion to the "street-level bureaucrats" that are necessary to manage the scheme (see Lipsky 1980). As can easily be imagined, these questions are very delicate, and who has the power to decide them is a matter of paramount importance for both unions and workers. The unemployed worker does not wish to be forced to take a job that he or she, for some reason, finds unsuitable. This need not of course be due to idleness. Indeed both the society's and the individual's interest may require that the unemployed worker resist accepting any job immediately available, if for instance it would cause serious damage to his or her skills or impose large social costs (if moving is necessary, for example). To wait for a suitable job instead of taking any available job is thus in many cases perfectly rational from both an individual and a social standpoint. On the other hand, if suitable jobs are available, unemployed workers are expected to leave the dole queue and accept them.

From a union perspective, the critical task is to ensure that workers are not forced to accept jobs at wages below the union-set level, because unions then lose control of the supply of labor power (Unga 1976). When unions started setting up their own unemployment funds in the nineteenth century, benefits were primarily seen as a way to prevent unemployed workers from underbidding the union wage rates; relieving distress came second (Harris 1972:297; Edebalk 1975).

Given our concern with institutional power, the paramount question is: Who shall be given the power to decide the question of suitable jobs in general, as well as in individual cases? It is obviously not enough for the union movement to influence the enactment of the general rules governing the scheme, because the critical issues are necessarily decided in the course of applying rules to each specific case (see Lipsky 1980).

In the case of the Ghent system, the unemployment insurance is administered by the unions or by union-run unemployment funds; and it is thus union officials who possess institutional power in the implementation of the unemployment scheme. Usually this insurance is tied to union membership – that is, all union members must also be members of the insurance system – but it is possible, de jure, to be a member of the insurance scheme without being a member of a union. In a compulsory system, it is typically government officials who have the aforementioned institutional power, and union membership has nothing to do with entitlement to unemployment insurance.

Others have forcefully argued that in order to enhance the working class's political strength, public policies should provide universal entitlements and avoid individual means tests and voluntary insurance schemes based on principles of "self-help" (Esping-Andersen and Korpi 1984; Esping-Andersen 1985:33). The Ghent system in unemployment insurance, however, is clearly based on these principles. We should therefore expect countries with a Ghent system to have a low degree of unionization. But as shown in Table 2.1, the facts are exactly the opposite.

As can be seen from Table 2.1, the five countries with the highest degree of unionization all have the same public unemployment-insurance scheme, the Ghent system, while all the other countries have some type of compulsory system. Hence it seems reasonable to conclude that institutional power in the administration of government labor-market institutions is important in determining union density, or working-class strength. This is because with a Ghent system: (1) unions can make it difficult for nonunion members to obtain the insurance; (2) unions control, or greatly influence, the determination of what constitutes a suitable job; and (3) unions can, by controlling the scheme, increase their control over the supply of labor power. Table 2.1 also lists an index of left-party participation in government and number of potential union members, because these two variables have, as stated earlier, been shown to be strongly correlated with union density (Wallerstein 1989). In order to compare the relative strength of these three variables, a multivariate regression analysis is presented in Table 2.2.

Table 2.2 shows that all three variables have an independent explanatory effect of about the same standardized size. Together they explain 82% of the variation in union density. Controlling for the variables measuring left-party participation

Table 2.1. *Union density, potential union membership, left-party participation in government and the public unemployment insurance system*

Country	Union density (%)	Potential membership (thousands)	Left government	Ghent system
Sweden	86	3,931	111.84	Yes
Denmark	83	2,225	90.24	Yes
Finland	80	2,034	59.33	Yes
Iceland	74	81	17.25	Yes
Belgium	74	3,348	43.25	Yes[a]
Ireland	68	886	0.00	No
Norway	58	1,657	83.08	No
Austria	57	2,469	48.67	No
Australia	51	5,436	33.75	No
United Kingdom	43	25.757	43.67	No
Canada	38	10,516	0.00	No
Italy	36	15,819	0.00	No
Switzerland	34	2,460	11.87	No
Germany (West)	31	23,003	35.33	No
Netherlands	29	4,509	31.50	No
Japan	28	39,903	1.92	No
USA	18	92,899	0.00	No
France	15	18,846	8.67	No

[a]Belgium has a mixed system of compulsory insurance but union participation in the administration (Flora 1987:776).
Sources: Union density – definition in Kjellberg 1983, figures from Kjellberg 1988 (figures for 1985 or 1986) except Australia, Iceland, and Ireland that are taken from Wallerstein 1989 (figures for 1979, 1975, and 1978, respectively). System of public unemployment insurance – Flora 1987 and Kjellberg 1983 except Australia (Castles 1985:ch 3) and Iceland (Nordiska Rådets Utredningar 1984:10:220). Potential membership – figures from Wallerstein 1989. The measure is the sum of the number of wage and salary earners and the unemployed. Index of left government – Wilensky 1981 (quoted in Wallerstein 1989). The index includes all Communist, Socialist, Social Democratic, and Labor parties except the Italian Socialist and Social Democratic parties in the period from 1919 to 1979. Sample – all industrialized countries where unions have been free to organize since 1945, except Luxembourg, New Zealand, excluded because it has compulsory union membership (Davidson 1989:ch. 6), and Israel, excluded because its main union is also one of the country's largest employers.

in government and size of the labor force, the Ghent system makes a difference of about 20% in union density.[2] Taking the "visual" result from Table 2.1 into consideration, we can say that it is possible to have a fairly strong union movement without a Ghent system, but that in order to have really strong unions, such a system seems necessary. It must be recalled, however, that this statistical analysis does not help us understand how the causal link operates. It might well be true that already very strong labor movements have introduced Ghent systems, rather

Table 2.2. *Cross-national differences in union density as a function of unemployment-insurance scheme* (GHENT), *left-party government* (LEFT), *and* (*natural log of*) *potential union membership* (SIZE)

Independent variable	Unstandardized coefficient	Standardized coefficient	Standard error
Constant	86.77	0.00	17.50
LEFT	0.23	0.34	0.09
SIZE	−5.80	−0.41	1.90
GHENT	20.29	0.38	8.60
	Number of cases: 18		
	r^2 .82		

Note: Data from Table 2.1. GHENT was set at 1 and non-GHENT set at 0 with the exception of Belgium, which was set at 0.5 because the country has a mixed system. Results are significant at the .5 level.

Using the natural log of SIZE means that the percentage increase, rather than the absolute increase, is what matters for union density.

than vice versa. In order to get a handle on this problem, we must go from static comparison to diacronic comparative analysis.

HISTORICAL COMPARISON

The first question here is whether a correlation existed between union strength and system of unemployment insurance at the time the schemes were established. If it did, our hypothesis about the importance of institutional power in government labor-market administration must be reconsidered. Historical data about union density is not easily available, and when available, it is of doubtful reliability. For some of the eighteen countries in the statistical analysis, figures of a reasonable reliability are available, but not for all years. As the 1930s have been said to be the crucial decade in this case (Skocpol 1988), it is fortunate that accurate figures are available for these years. Fortunately, data about when different unemployment schemes were introduced are both available and reliable.

The data in Table 2.3 show that there is no significant correlation between union strength and type of unemployment scheme in the 1930s. The four countries with the highest level of unionization had either compulsory insurance or no public insurance at all. The mean of union density in the countries with a compulsory scheme was slightly higher than for those with a Ghent scheme (33% compared to 25%). Hence it seems fair to conclude that in general it has *not* been already especially strong labor movements that have introduced union-controlled public unemployment-insurance schemes. Moreover, the effect of the Ghent system on union density seems to be considerably delayed. In any case, the question

Table 2.3. *Union density, 1930, by type of public unemployment scheme and year of introduction*

Country	Union density (%)	Unemployment-insurance scheme	Year of introduction
Germany	48	Compulsory	1927
Australia	44	Compulsory	1922[a]
Sweden	41	—	—
Austria	38	Compulsory	1920
Denmark	37	Ghent	1907
Netherlands	30	Ghent	1916
Belgium	28	Ghent	1901
Great Britain	26	Compulsory	1911
Norway	23	Ghent	1906
United States	11	Compulsory[b]	1935
France	9	Ghent	1905

[a] Queensland.   [b] Ten states.
Sources: Union density (Kjellberg 1983:36f); unemployment scheme and year of introduction (Pettersen 1982:199).

is then who introduced what kind of scheme? Did the different labor movements have the political strength and the strategic skill necessary to institutionalize the Ghent system? Note that the political force behind the establishment of any form of social insurance is notoriously difficult to isolate. For instance, a Conservative Party in government might unwillingly introduce a social policy in order to deny the opposing Labor Party a political weapon. It seems rather unlikely, though, that a labor party in government would need in this way to bow to the pressure of an opposing Conservative or Liberal Party. Hence, who holds government responsibility should be of interest here.

In view of the results mentioned previously about the positive impact of a Ghent system on the organizational strength of the working class, the results in Table 2.4 are surprising. Voluntary systems seem above all to have been favored by Liberal governments, while Labor governments have, with one exception, introduced compulsory schemes. How can this seemingly paradoxical result be understood? One possible explanation is that individual responsibility and self-help organization have strong roots in liberal ideology, while the notion of social insurance as a right of citizenship has strong support in socialist ideology. Perhaps then ideology has sometimes taken primacy over strategic calculation (cf. Lewin 1988).

Although there is no space in this essay for a detailed description of why these countries institutionalized the system they did, some important details can be mentioned. In France a Ghent system was introduced as early as in 1905, but

Table 2.4. *Party in government and introduction of different public unemployment insurance schemes*

Type of scheme	Party in government		
	Labor	Liberal	Conservative
Compulsory	3 (AU, NE, NO)	2 (IT, UK)	3 (BE, FR, GE)
Voluntary	1 (SW)	4 (DE, FR, NE, SZ)	2 (BE, FI)

Source: Alber 1984:170.

union leaders' reluctance to collaborate with the state left the insurance system practically a dead letter. This was probably due to the strong syndicalist, and thus antistate, influence in the French labor movement. The same thing happened in Norway where a Ghent system was introduced in 1906, although the Norwegian labor movement was left-socialist and communist oriented rather than syndicalist (Pettersen 1982; Alber 1984:153f). In Norway some union-run funds that had been established went bankrupt, and the whole system was discredited during the 1920s and early 1930s because the unions could not perform the necessary economic supervision, which is to say cut benefits and raise payments. In 1938 a Labor government introduced a compulsory system in collaboration with the Liberal Party and the Conservative(!) Party. It seems there was no discussion about the effects this would have on unionization (Pettersen 1982). In the Netherlands in 1949 as in Norway, a Labor government replaced a voluntary system with a compulsory one (Alber 1984).

In Britain, on the other hand, the union movement condemned the introduction of a compulsory scheme unless it was managed by organized labor, and argued that the insurance should be restricted to union members. However, this was denied them when the Liberal government introduced the world's first compulsory system in 1911 (Harris 1972:317f). Under questioning by the president of the Board of Trade, the Parliamentary Committee of the British Trades Unions Congress (TUC) argued that if the insurance was not restricted to union members, "You will have men to support who never have been and never will be self-supporting. They are at present parasites on their more industrious fellows and will be the first to avail themselves of the funds the Bill provides" (quoted in Harris 1972:317f).

In Denmark the union movement argued strongly for a Ghent system, which was introduced by a Liberal government in 1907. The Liberal government seems simply to have miscalculated in believing that unemployment funds would be established by liberal Friendly Societies and not by the socialist unions. Although critical of aspects of the insurance scheme, the Danish unions were quick to establish funds or enroll existing union funds in the scheme, and hence a Ghent system was established. Afterward, the Danish labor movement fought hard to preserve the system, in contrast to their more radical Norwegian fellows (Andersen et al. 1981). Thus, as confirmed by Alber, the initial union response to differences in the structure of unemployment insurance schemes varied considerably (Alber 1984:154, compare Harris 1972:299f). Some labor movements were unable to introduce a Ghent system even though they wanted to, while other labor movements saw no strategic advantage in a Ghent system.

As shown in Table 2.4, there is, nonetheless, one country in which a Labor government did manage to introduce a Ghent system: Sweden in 1934. If there is such a thing as strategic behavior in the process of designing political institutions, then Sweden deserves a closer look.

THE SWEDISH CASE

Unionization came late but rapidly to Sweden. For the reasons stated, that is, to reduce the temptation of unemployed workers to undermine union solidarity, many unions established their own unemployment funds during the late nineteenth and early twentieth centuries (Heclo 1974:68). One of the labor movement's first demands upon the government was for the establishment of a public unemployment-insurance system. Compared to many similar countries, especially Denmark and Norway, the Swedish labor movement succeeded rather late in its efforts to introduce a public unemployment-insurance scheme (1934; see Table 2.3). There were two major reasons for this delay. One is that, beginning in 1918, Sweden developed a unique unemployment policy, the main substance of which was to organize relief works rather than to distribute unemployment benefits. The unemployed were typically sent away to distant relief-work camps where conditions were very harsh, to put it mildly. Cash benefits were also provided, but not on a basis of entitlement to insurance; they were granted only after a series of rigorous individual means tests. Those who refused to take jobs at the relief-work camps and who could not be supported by their unions had no choice but to endure the humiliation of asking for help at the poor-relief agencies.

The problem with this system was that the wages paid at the relief works were far below the union rate. This meant that some employers, mainly the local municipalities, could buy labor power outside the unions' control. It was generally believed that the only cure for unemployment was to lower the wage level, and the relief-works system explicitly promoted this by providing labor at a lower price than the unions would (Heclo 1974; Unga 1976). This wage-deflationary policy naturally led to intense industrial disputes. The bourgeois parties, who had a majority in Parliament throughout the period between the wars, supported this deflationary policy; moreover, they decided that all workers belonging to trades in which unions were involved in industrial disputes should be cut off from any help, relief works, or cash benefits. The Unemployment Commission could even in some cases force unemployed workers to act as strikebreakers on penalty of losing any form of assistance. This unemployment policy came thus to be a paramount threat to union control over the supply of labor. Two Social Democratic minority governments actually chose to resign (in 1923 and 1926), when they could not get a parliamentary majority in favor of changing the system. It may be said that this policy, and its administration, were the most hotly contested issues between the labor movement and the bourgeois parties during the 1920s. The bourgeois parties, together with the employers' federation, saw in the operation of this unemployment policy a major weapon with which to weaken the labor movement, while for the labor movement the policy and its administration were seen as the very incarnation of the bourgeois class character of the capitalist state (Rothstein 1985a).

The demand for an unemployment-insurance scheme to replace the established system was thus the main issue for the Swedish labor movement during the 1920s, but because of the established relief-work policy and the controversies it provoked, the matter resulted in a deadlock. No less than four government commissions produced reports and detailed plans for the introduction of such a policy before 1934, but because of intense resistance from the Conservative and Agrarian parties, they never materialized into legislation (Heclo 1974:99–105; Edebalk 1975). Apart from arguing for the necessity of lowering the wage level, these two parties claimed that such a system would only further the organizational strength of the unions and thus the Social Democratic Party. But the bourgeois front was split, as one of the two Liberal parties (the Prohibitionist) was generally in favor of introducing public unemployment insurance.

The two major variants of unemployment insurance discussed previously were of course also considered in the Swedish debate. The Liberals, who had been in government from 1926 to 1928 and from 1930 to 1932, found themselves in a difficult position. On the one hand they hesitated to introduce a compulsory scheme because they considered the costs too high and the administration too complicated. A Ghent system had neither of these drawbacks, but the Liberals realized such a system would strengthen the labor movement and thus be detrimental to their own political interests. (After the unions' defeat in the general strike of 1909, unions with unemployment funds managed to keep their members to a much higher degree than those without. Hence the impact of the Ghent system on union strength had at that time been "proven" in Sweden; see Edebalk 1975.) Another argument against the Ghent system was that the union-run unemployment funds would be merged with the unions' strike funds (Unga 1976:112).

From early on, the Social Democratic Party favored the introduction of a Ghent system. But when the combined effects of the relief-work system and rising unemployment hit the unions in the late 1920s, they started to press the Social Democrats to strike a deal with the Liberals in order to introduce an insurance scheme whether compulsory or attached to the unions. However, the Liberals, although in government from 1930 to 1932, never managed to introduce a bill proposing a compulsory scheme. One reason was that unemployment insurance was considered suitable only for "normal" times of unemployment, which the early 1930s certainly were not. The other reason was that the lessons learned from the British and German compulsory schemes during the economic crisis was not particularly encouraging (Heclo 1974:97).

After their electoral victory in 1932 the Social Democrats formed a minority government. In order to introduce unemployment insurance, therefore, they needed support from at least one of the bourgeois parties. The only prospect was the Liberals, but they were more inclined to a compulsory than a Ghent system. However, after failing in 1933, the Social Democrats managed, by striking a deal with a section of the Liberals, to introduce a Ghent system in 1934. In order to reach this compromise they had to sacrifice an important part of their original proposal concerning the rules and regulations of the scheme. First, the union unemployment funds had to be licensed and supervised by the National Board of Social Affairs. Second, workers outside the unions also were given the right to become members of the funds. Third, the level of benefits was set rather low, and the rules governing entitlement to support (e.g., gauged by the number of days in work and contributions from individual members) were very restrictive. Finally, the employers were not obliged to contribute to financing the insurance (Heclo 1974:102–5; Edelbalk 1975). Notwithstanding these concessions, the compromise meant that the implementation of the scheme was to be managed by union-run funds, which is to say union officials were given the power of deciding the important question of a suitable job. Moreover, in practice, although not in law, workers would not be expected to take jobs at workplaces affected by industrial conflict, nor accept wages below the union rate. In sum, the Social Democrats compromised greatly about the content of the scheme (i.e., the actual policy) in order to be able to institutionalize an insurance scheme that would greatly enhance their future organizational strength. The question that has to be answered is whether this strategy was intentional – that is, whether this was a case of deliberate and (which seems to be something rare) successful institutional design in political history (Miller 1988; Tsebelis 1990).

The answer is yes, for we can, in this case, identify the specific political agent behind the strategy: the Social Democratic Minister of Social Affairs Gustav Möller. When speaking in Parliament in 1933 about accepting the demands of the Liberals, he declared that they were very difficult for him to accept, but that he nevertheless would do so because

I do not want, if I can prevent it, . . . the Swedish Parliament to let this possibility slip away, which we perhaps have, to take away from the agenda the struggle about the very principle about, whether Sweden should have publicly supported unemployment insurance or not. (Parliamentary Records, Second Chamber 1933–50;96, my translation)

He admitted the scheme to be introduced was not very impressive and would not be especially efficient in helping the unemployed masses. But, he argued, if the principle was settled, then the substance could be improved later on (Parliamentary Records, First Chamber [PRFC] 1933–47:47f). It should be mentioned that Möller said this in 1933, when the bill in fact was rejected by Parliament because some Liberals got cold feet. When it was actually accepted a year later, Möller had to make even greater concessions to the Liberals (Edebalk 1975). Interestingly enough, the Communists, for their part, strongly opposed the bill as they preferred a compulsory state-administered system. In the debate in Parliament in 1934, Möller openly argued that one of the advantages of a voluntary system compared to a compulsory one was that it would support only those workers who "show such an interest in the insurance system . . . that they take the initiative to create or to join an unemployment insurance fund" (PRFC 1934–37:12, my translation).

As early as 1926, in a widely distributed political pamphlet, Möller had emphasized the importance a Ghent system would have for the union movement and argued such a system was preferable to a compulsory scheme.He did not deny such a system would be rather "union-friendly," but according to Möller nothing was wrong, in principle, in the state supporting only those workers who had taken an interest in their own and their families' well-being. Workers who had not shown such an interest – those choosing to be "free-riders" instead of joining the union movement – should, according to Möller, be sent away to the relief-work camps, if helped at all (Möller 1926). The central moment seems to have been a meeting with the executive committee of the trade union conference in 1930, where Möller persuaded the union leaders that the labor movement, although beset by difficulties arising from high unemployment, should press for a Ghent system because it "would force workers into the unions" (quoted in Unga 1976:118, my translation).

The problem for the Social Democrats at that time (1930) was the risk that the Liberal government would propose a bill to Parliament introducing a compulsory scheme; hence proposing a voluntary system would made the party "look ridiculous" (Unga 1974:118). Thus, mainly for tactical reasons (hoping that the Liberal government would not take action), the Social Democrats demanded in Parliament that an insurance system be introduced no matter what type (Edebalk 1975). But after the Social Democrats formed the government in 1932 and Möller became minister of social affairs, there was no question about which system he preferred (Unga 1976). It should be mentioned that this was neither the first nor the last time Gustav Möller combined strategic political skill with a remarkable sense of the importance of designing the administrative institutions of the welfare state (Rothstein 1985b). In this case, in order to further his (that is, the labor movement's) long-term interest, policy substance was traded for institutional design.

Although this is not the place for a "life and letters," some details about Möller should be given. One important fact is that Gustav Möller was not only minister of social affairs, he was also party secretary from 1916 to 1940. In the

Swedish Social Democratic Party, this position is second in the hierarchy, and it
carries special responsibility for the party organization. One can easily imagine
that this position gave Möller a special sensitivity to the problem of free-riding.
In contrast to most other European Social Democratic parties, which, when in
government during this period, often made people of minor importance responsible for social affairs, Möller's position shows the importance the Swedish party
at that time placed on social policy (Therborn 1989). Second, Möller had been
in the forefront in the fight against the Unemployment Commission and the threat
its policies posed to the union's organizational strength.

The scheme established in 1934 was to be almost a complete failure as a means
of helping the unemployed masses during the 1930s. But Möller did not consider
the insurance system to be a method for curing unemployment during crises. For
this, he relied on a massive program of job creation that was implemented during
1934–9 (Heclo 1974:104; Rothstein 1986). One of the reasons the insurance did
not work well was that very few unions actually applied to register their funds,
or establish new funds, under the scheme. This issue often aroused intense debate within the unions during the second half of the 1930s. One example is the
powerful metalworkers' union, where the majority of the board argued for accepting the conditions and putting the union fund under the scheme (because
doing so would be economically favorable). However, at the union's conferences
in 1936 and 1939, it was decided to put the question to a vote. In both cases the
members voted against the proposal. The most powerful argument, made mostly
by communists and left-socialists, was based on a lingering suspicion of having
anything to do with government labor-market authorities (Erici and Roth 1981).

Möller's prediction in 1934, that the substantive rules in the insurance system
could be changed in the future, was vindicated in 1941 when a unanimous Parliament changed the rules in favor of the unions. From that date the scheme
started to grow; that is, unions started to apply to register their funds under the
scheme or create new funds. Since then, the rules have been successively changed
in favor of the union funds and the unemployed. To take economic contributions
as an example: From an original 50–50 basis, the scheme has been changed to
one in which, since the 1970s, the government pays almost all the costs of the
system (Erici and Roth 1981). Although since the mid-1960s the institutional
principles have been attacked by the bourgeois parties and the employers' federation, who argue that the connection between union membership and the insurance should be cut, no such institutional changes have been made (Lindkvist
1989). While it is legally possible for any wage-earner to be a member only of
the insurance fund, unions make this very difficult in practice (and also more
expensive). Those wage-earners who have succeeded in being members of the
funds but not the unions amounted in 1986 to about 0.6 percent of the total
number insured (Statens Offentliga Utredningar 1987:56).

One of the reasons the bourgeois parties, although in government from 1976
to 1982, did not succeed in changing the system, is that not only the blue-collar

unions, but also the comparatively strong white-collar unions in Sweden have forcefully defended union power in the administration of the scheme, and so, for electoral reasons, it was difficult for the bourgeois parties to resist strong demands from these unions (Hallgren 1986:131–58). Hence an institution such as a Ghent system can be considered to some extent self-reinforcing, because it tends to strengthen the very forces that have a positive interest in preserving the institution. Thus, strange as it may seem, Sweden is today a country where the bourgeois parties, and the employers' organization, press for the introduction of a compulsory unemployment-insurance scheme, even at the price of raising public expenditure, while the labor movement successfully fights to keep it a voluntary scheme (see Hallgren 1986).

SUMMARY AND CONCLUSIONS

The theoretical aim of this chapter has been to show that institutional analysis can serve as a bridge between structural and agent-oriented analysis in political science. Since the seminal work of Mancur Olson, rational choice and game theorists have tried to find out how people solve the prisoner's dilemma. Writing from a game-theoretical perspective, Jonathan Bendor and Dilip Mookherjee have been forced to admit that such an approach can explain neither why patterns of collective action persist nor why they arise. They state that "the emergence of cooperation is a hard problem – one that may require other methods of analysis" (Bendor and Mookherjee 1987:146). As should be obvious, I agree. Moreover, game theorists have usually pointed at the important role of iteration (repeated play) in explaining collective action. William Bianco and Robert Bates, also writing from a game-theoretical perspective, have recently shown the limited impact of iteration, and instead pointed at the important role that "leaders" play in initiating collective action among rational, self-interested individuals. What leaders need, according to them, is an appropriate strategy and reputation among followers. As might be expected, I agree, but I want to add that in order to find the actual leader and to identify his or her "incentives and capabilities" used in creating the institution that makes collective action possible (solves the prisoner's dilemma), game theory seems to be of limited value (Bianco and Bates 1990:133). The value of this approach only emerges when we have a more substantial theory from which to draw hypotheses about why some players, resources, and institutions are more important than others.

When it comes to institutional analysis, I have tried to show four things. The first is that in order to understand the importance of political institutions, institutional theory is not enough. The reason is simply that one needs a theory about *what kind* of institutions are important for *what issues*. Without generalizing, I have shown in the case of explaining working-class organizational strength that Marxism and institutional theory go together. The former has been used to identify the important agents and institutions, and the latter to explain how and why they make a difference. Second, as the statistical analysis shows, the institutionalization of government labor-market policy is important in explaining variation in working-class organizational strength among the Western industrialized countries. Third, organized class power stems not only from socioeconomic factors, but also from the power that social classes at times are able to invest in political institutions. There is thus definitely a dialectical relationship between government institutions and class formation.

Moreover, I have tried to move beyond the question of the mere importance of institutions. Even if institutions give an advantage to some social forces, there remains the question of intentionality. It has two dimensions: The first is whether the *creation* of a political institution should be considered an intentional act, or if instead it results from social evolution. If the creation is intentional, then the question arises of the outcome of the institution's operation – that is, whether the outcome is what the creative agent expected or not. My knowledge of political history tells me the latter result is the most common one. For a Swedish example, one can point to the Social Democratic Party's efforts in 1907 to keep a "winner take all" majority electoral system, which if successful would have created a Tory-like party in Sweden (instead of three different and oft divided bourgeois parties), making the long reign of the Social Democrats very improbable (see Pontusson 1988). It was the party's sheer luck to be forced to accede to the Conservative Party's demand for a proportional electoral system in 1906–7 (Lewin 1988:69–79).

Nevertheless, two things have been shown in this case. The first is that many labor movements seem simply to have made the wrong choice in deciding what system of unemployment insurance to strive for. "Designing social structures" (Miller 1988), or creating the right kind of "positive loops" (Skocpol 1988), or being a rational goal maximizer when creating institutions (Tsebelis 1990) seems thus not so simple. Unions, especially, seem to have been unaware of what type of unemployment-insurance institution would be advantageous to them. This was also true in the Swedish case in which, when under pressure, the unions seemed willing to trade long-term institutional power for short-term interests. Moreover, when the Ghent system was introduced, they hesitated to join and thereby strengthen the system. Before 1941 the Swedish Ghent system was so weak that it could easily have been changed into a compulsory scheme.

In the Swedish case it has been shown both that the establishment of the Ghent system was deliberate and that it has had the outcome expected by its creator(s). Political institutions are certainly sources for the determination of political behavior, but *homo politicus* cannot be considered a total structural cum institutional dope. In some, albeit probably rare, historical cases, people actually create the very institutional circumstances under which their own as well as others' future behavior will take place. It is thus possible not only to bind oneself to the mast in order to avoid being tempted by the sirens' song, but also at times to use the ropes to structure the future choices of others as well (Elster 1979).

NOTES

1 In a letter in March 1875 to August Bebel, the leader of the German Social Democrats, Friedrich Engels criticized the Gotha Party program for not paying due attention to the fact that the trade union is "the real class organization of the proletariat" (quoted in Bottomore 1985:482).
2 The unstandardized coefficient for SIZE (-5.8) shows that a doubling of the potential union membership would reduce union density by $\ln(2)(5.8) = (.69) < (5.8) \approx 4.0$ percentage points. The unstandardized coefficient for LEFT (0.23) indicates that three years of Social Democratic majority government ($= 9$ points in Wilensky's index) would increase union density by approximately 2 percentage points (cf. Wallerstein 1989:492).

REFERENCES

Alber, Jens. 1984. "Government Responses to the Challenge of Unemployment: The Development of Unemployment Insurance in Western Europe." In Peter Flora and Arnold J. Heidenheimer, eds. *The Development of Welfare States in Europe and America*. New Brunswick, N.J.: Transaction Books.

Åmark, Klas. 1986. *Facklig makt och fackligt medlemskap*. Lund: Arkiv.

Amenta, Edwin, and Theda Skocpol, 1986. "States and Social Policies." *Annual Review of Sociology* 12:131–57.

Andersen, John, Per Jensen, Jorgen E. Larsen, and Carsten Schultz. 1981. "Klassekamp og reformisme." Unpublished paper, Department of Sociology, University of Copenhagen.

Bendor, Jonathan, and Dilip Mookherjee. 1987. "Institutional Structure and the Logic of Ongoing Collective Action." *American Journal of Political Science* 81:129–54.

Berger, Johannes, and Claus Offe. 1982. "Functionalism vs Rational Choice." *Theory and Society* 11:521–6.

Bianco, William T., and Robert H. Bates. 1990. "Cooperation by Design: Leadership, Structure and Collective Dilemmas." *American Political Science Review* 84:133–47.

Bottomore, Tom, ed. 1985. *A Dictionary of Marxist Thought*. London: Macmillan.

Callinicos, Alex. 1989. *Making History. Agency, Structure and Change in Social Theory*. Oxford: Polity Press.

Castles, Francis. 1985. *The Working Class and Welfare*. Wellington: Allen and Unwin.

Cerny, Philip G. 1990. *The Changing Architecture of Modern Politics*. London: Sage.

Cohen, Gerald. 1978. *Karl Marx's Theory of History. A Defence*. Oxford: Oxford University Press.

Davidson, Alexander. 1989. *Two Models of Welfare*. Stockholm: Almqvist and Wiksell International.

Douglas, Mary. 1987. *How Institutions Think*. London: Routledge and Kegan Paul.

Edebalk, Per-Gunnar. 1975. *Arbetslöshetsförsäkringsdebatten*. Lund: Department of Economic History.

Elster, Jon. 1979. *Ulysses and the Sirens*. Cambridge: Cambridge University Press.
    1985. *Making Sense of Marx*. Cambridge: Cambridge University Press.
    1989. *The Cement of Society*. Cambridge: Cambridge University Press.

Erici, Bernt, and Nils Roth. 1981. *Arbetslöshetsförsäkringen i Sverige 1935–1980*. Stockholm: Arbetslöshetskassornas samorganisation.

Esping-Andersen, Gösta. 1985. *Politics against Markets*. Princeton, N.J.: Princeton University Press.

Esping-Andersen, Gösta, and Walter Korpi. 1984. "Social Policy as Class Politics in Post-War Capitalism: Scandinavia, Austria and Germany." In John H. Goldthorpe, ed. *Order and Conflict in Contemporary Capitalism.* Oxford: Oxford University Press.

    1985. "From Poor Relief towards Institutional Welfare States: The Development of Scandinavian Social Policy." In Robert E. Eriksson, ed. *The Scandinavian Model: Welfare States and Welfare Research.* New York: M. E. Sharpe.

Flora, Peter, ed. 1987. *Growth to Limits. The Western European Welfare States Since World War II. Vol 4.* Berlin: de Gruyter.

Giddens, Anthony. 1979. *Central Problems in Social Theory.* London: Macmillan.

Goldfield, Michael. 1987. *The Decline of Organized Labor in the United States.* Chicago: University of Chicago Press.

Grafstein, Robert E. 1988. "The Problem of Institutional Constraint." *Journal of Politics* 50:577–9.

Hallgren, Sive. 1986. *Från allmosa till rättighet.* Stockholm: Tidens förlag.

Harris, John. 1972. *Unemployment and Politics.* Oxford: Clarendon Press

Heclo, Hugh. 1974. *Modern Social Policies in Britain and Sweden.* New Haven, Conn: Yale University Press.

Kjellberg, Anders. 1983. *Facklig organisering i tolv länder.* Lund: Arkiv.

    1988. "Sverige har fackligt världsrekord." *LO-tidningen* 9:10–11.

Knight, Jack. 1988. "Strategic Conflict and Institutional Change." Paper presented at the annual meeting of the American Political Science Association, Washington, D.C.

Korpi, Walter. 1983. *The Democratic Class Struggle.* London: Routledge and Kegan Paul.

    1985. "Power Resource Approach vs. Action and Conflict. On Causal and Intentional Explanation of Power." *Sociological Theory* 3: 31–45.

Lester, Richard. 1965. "Unemployment Insurance." In *International Encyclopedia of the Social Sciences.* London: Macmillan.

Levi, Margaret. 1990. "A Logic of Institutional Changes." In Karen Schweers Cook and Margaret Levi, eds. *The Limits of Rationality,* Chicago: University of Chicago Press.

Lewin, Leif. 1988. *Ideology and Strategy. A Century of Swedish Politics.* Cambridge: Cambridge University Press.

Lindkvist, Ann. 1989. "Fackföreningsrörelsen och arbetslöshetsförsäkringen." Working Paper, Department of Government, University of Uppsala.

Lipsky, Michael. 1980. *Street-level Bureaucracy. Dilemmas of the Individual in Public Services.* New York: Russell Sage Foundation

March, James H., and Johan P. Olsen. 1984. "The New Institutionalism. Organizational Factors in Political Life." *American Political Science Review* 78:734–49.

Miller, Trudi. 1988. "Designing Social Structures." Paper presented at the annual meeting of the American Political Science Association, Washington, D.C.

Möller, Gustav. 1926. *Arbetslöshetsförsäkringen jämte andra sociala försäkringar.* Stockholm: Tiden.

    1938. "The Swedish Unemployment Policy." *The Annals of the American Academy of Political and Social Sciences* 197.

Mouzelis, Nicos. 1984. "On the Crises of Marxist Theory." *British Journal of Sociology* 25:112–21.

    1988. "Marxism or Post-Marxism." *New Left Review* 167:107–23.

Noble, Charles F. 1988. "State or Class? Notes on Two Recent Views of the Welfare State." Paper presented at the annual meeting of the American Political Science Association, Washington, D.C.

Nordiska Rådets Utredningar (Reports from the Nordic Council).
Offe, Claus, and Helmuth Wiesenthal. 1980. "Two Logics of Collective Action." In Maurice Zeitlin, ed. *Political Power and Social Theory.* Greenwich, Conn: JAI Press.
Olofsson, Gunnar. 1979. *Mellan klass och stat.* Lund: Arkiv.
Olson, Mancur. 1965. *The Logic of Collective Action: Public Goods and the Theory of Groups.* Cambridge, Mass.: Harvard University Press.
Parliamentary Records, First Chamber.
Parliamentary Records, Second Chamber.
Peretz, David. 1979. *The Governments and Politics of Israel.* Boulder, Colo. Westview Press.
Pettersen, Per A. 1982. *Linjer i norsk sosialpolitikk.* Oslo: Universitetsforlaget.
Pontusson, Jonas. 1988. "Swedish Social Democracy and British Labour. Essays on the Nature and Conditions of Social Democratic Hegemony." Western Societies Program Occasional Paper no 19. New York Center of International Studies, Cornell University, Ithaca, N.Y.
Przeworski, Adam. 1985. *Capitalism and Social Democracy.* Cambridge: Cambridge University Press.
Rothstein, Bo. 1985a. "The Success of the Swedish Labour Market Policy: The Organizational Connection to Policy." *European Journal of Political Research* 13: 153–65.
1985b. "Managing the Welfare State: Lessons from Gustav Möller." *Scandinavian Political Studies* 13:151–70.
1986. *Den socialdemokratiska staten. Reformer och förvaltning inom svensk arbetsmarknads- och skolpolitik.* Lund: Arkiv.
1990. "State Capacity and Social Justice: The Labor Market Case." Paper presented at the meeting of the American Political Science Association, Aug. 28–Sept. 2, 1990, San Francisco.
Schmidt, Folke. 1977. *Law and Industrial Relations in Sweden.* Stockholm: Almqvist and Wiksell International.
Shalev, Michael. 1983a. "Class Politics and the Western Welfare State." In S. E. Spiro and E. Yuchtman-Yaar, eds. *Evaluating the Welfare State.* New York: Academic Press.
1983b. "The Social Democratic Model and Beyond. Two Generations of Comparative Research on the Welfare State." *Comparative Social Research* 6:315–52.
Shepsle, Kenneth A. 1989. "Studying Institutions – Some Lessons from the Rational Choice Approach." *Journal of Theoretical Politics* 1:131–47.
Skocpol, Theda. 1988. "Comparing National Systems of Social Provision: A Polity Centered Approach." Paper presented at the International Political Science Association meeting, Washington, D.C.
Statens Offentliga Utredningar (Government Public Commission).
Steinmo, Sven. 1989. "Political Institutions and Tax Policy in the United States, Sweden and Britain." *World Politics* 41:500–35.
Streeck, Wolfgang. 1981. *Gewerkschaftliche Organisationsprobleme in der sozialstaatlichen Demokratie.* Königstein: Athenäum.
Therborn, Göran. 1989. "Arbetarrörelsen och välfärdsstaten." *Arkiv för studier i arbetarrörelsens historia.* 41–2: 3–51.
Tsebelis, George. 1990. *Nested Games. Rational Choice in Comparative Politics.* Berkeley: University of California Press
Unga, Nils. 1976. *Socialdemokratin och arbetslöshetsfrågan 1912–34.* Lund: Arkiv.
von Beyme, Klaus. 1980. *Challenge to Power. Trade Unions and Industrial Relations in Capitalist Countries.* London: Sage.

Wallerstein, Michael. 1989. "Union Growth In Advanced Industrial Democracies." *American Political Science Review* 83:481–501.

Weir, Margaret, and Theda Skocpol. 1985. "State Structures and the Possibilities for 'Keynesian' Responses to the Great Depression in Sweden, Britain, and the United States." In Peter B. Evans, Dietrich Rueschemeyer, and Theda Skocpol, eds. *Bringing the State Back In*. Cambridge: Cambridge University Press.

Wilensky, Harold L. 1981. "Leftism, Catholicism and Democratic Corporatism: The Role of Political Parties in Recent Welfare State Development." In Peter Flora and Arnold J. Heidenheimer, eds., *The Development of Welfare States in Europe and America*. New Brunswick, N.J.: Transactions Books.

Wright, Eric O. 1985. *Classes*. London: Verso.

3

The rules of the game: The logic of health policy-making in France, Switzerland, and Sweden

ELLEN M. IMMERGUT

Explaining change is a central problem for institutional analysis. If institutions are purported to have a kind of staying power, then how can the same institutions explain both stability and change? If institutions limit the scope of action that appears possible to different actors, why can they sometimes escape these constraints? This essay uses the case of national health insurance politics to show how institutions can explain both policy stability and policy change. The key to the analysis is a break with "correlational" thinking. Rather than analyzing policy-making in terms of correlations between policy inputs (such as demands from various social groups or past policy legacies) and policy outputs (such as specific pieces of legislation) the strength of institutional analysis is to show why policy inputs and policy outputs may be linked together in different ways in different political systems.

THE PROBLEM

National health insurance constitutes an excellent case for institutional comparison. Nearly every West European government has considered proposals for national health insurance, that is, compulsory public programs that insure citizens for medical treatment. Although the same health programs have been proposed, however, the policy results differ. Political conflicts over national health insurance have resulted in large differences in the role of government in health care provision. The causes of these different results are not self-evident. Not only have policy-makers deliberated quite similar proposals, but similarly situated interest groups seem to have interpreted their interests in similar ways. Doctors, in particular, have traditionally viewed national health insurance programs as a threat to their professional independence. For while these public programs ex-

This essay includes excerpts from "Institutions, Veto Points, and Policy Results: A Comparative Analysis of Health Care," *Journal of Public Policy* 10, no. 4 (1990):391–416. For helpful comments, I would like to thank Jens Alber, Douglas Ashford, Peter Hall, Desmond King, Renate Mayntz, Fritz Scharpf, George Tsebelis, Sven Steinmo, and Kathleen Thelen.

pand the market for medical care by using collective resources to pay for medical services, they also generate financial incentives for governments to regulate the medical profession.

Once governments begin to pay for medical services, they inevitably take steps to control the price of these services and hence to control the incomes and activities of doctors. National health insurance programs thus engender an inherent conflict of interest between governments and doctors as the respective buyers and sellers of medical services; these programs menace the economic autonomy of doctors. Nevertheless, despite the reputation of the medical profession as an insurmountable political veto group, some European governments have overcome professional opposition to introduce both national health insurance programs and substantial restrictions on the economic activities of physicians. In other nations, by contrast, medical protests have blocked government efforts to introduce national health insurance as well as controls on doctors' fees. Given that medical associations throughout Western Europe possess a legal monopoly of medical practice and are regarded as highly influential politically, how then can one explain the significant variation in West European health policy? Why have some governments been able to "socialize" medicine?

This essay compares the politics of national health insurance in France, Switzerland, and Sweden. Politicians in all three nations proposed national health insurance as well as controls on doctors' fees. From similar starting points, however, the health systems of France, Switzerland, and Sweden developed in divergent directions as a result of the specific legislative proposals enacted into law in each country. In Switzerland, national health insurance was rejected. Consequently, the role of government in the health care market is limited to providing subsidies to private insurance. In France, by contrast, the government succeeded in introducing national health insurance, a compulsory public insurance program that pays for medical treatment by private doctors, as well as limited controls on doctors' fees. The Swedish government has gone the furthest, first establishing national health insurance and then converting this program to a de facto national health service that provides medical treatment directly to citizens through publicly employed doctors working in public hospitals. The policy results of this series of political conflicts are three health systems that represent the two extremes and the center of government intervention in health: The Swedish can be considered the most socialized health system in Europe, the Swiss the most privatized, and the French a conflict-ridden compromise between the two. Consequently the economic autonomy of doctors has been most restricted in Sweden and least in Switzerland.

The balance of this essay argues that these divergent policy outcomes cannot be explained by differences in the ideas of policy-makers, differences in political partisanship, or differences in the preferences and organization of various interest groups. Instead, it argues that these outcomes are better explained by analyzing the political institutions in each country. These institutions establish different rules of the game for politicians and interest groups seeking to enact or to block policies. De jure rules of institutional design provide procedural advantages and impediments for translating political power into concrete policies. De facto rules arising from electoral results and party systems change the ways in which these formal institutions work in practice. Together these institutional rules establish distinct logics of decision-making that set the parameters both for executive action and interest group influence.

ALTERNATIVE EXPLANATIONS

One leading explanation for health policy is the theory of "professional dominance." By achieving a monopoly of medical practice, doctors are thought to be able to set the limits to health policy and to determine their conditions of practice under government health programs. Doctors are the sole experts qualified to judge the effects of these public programs on health. Further, these programs depend on the cooperation of doctors, for government health programs are meaningless unless doctors will agree to treat the patients covered by these programs. As the ultimate political weapon, doctors should (in theory) be able to block any health policy proposals to which they are opposed by calling for a medical strike.[1]

Medical dominance does not, however, explain empirical differences in the ability of the French, Swiss, and Swedish medical professions to influence legislative decisions. The first reason, as the following case studies will establish, is that doctors' opinions regarding national health insurance and restrictions on doctors' fees were nearly identical: Swiss, French, and Swedish doctors all objected to these reform proposals. More precisely, elite private practitioners in each country considered the expansion of government in the health insurance area a threat to their economic autonomy. These doctors viewed economic freedom as the precondition for professional freedom. They wished to preserve the status of physicians as independent practitioners and to avoid complete financial dependence on governmental authorities. The ability of these physicians to impose their views on policy-makers, however, differed radically.

Second, the resources available to these doctors do not account for their different degrees of success in blocking proposals for socialized medicine. Although the process of professionalization in Sweden, France, and Switzerland took different paths, by the outset of the twentieth century each of these medical professions had achieved a legal monopoly of medical practice.[2] Indeed the numbers of physicians were more stringently controlled in Sweden and France than in Switzerland. Consequently, in terms of market scarcity, the Swedish medical profession was the most advantageously placed of the three, with 89 doctors for every 100,000 inhabitants in 1959, as compared to 107 in France and 141 in Switzerland (see Table 3.1).[3] Nevertheless, although the Swedish doctors were in shortest supply, it was not the Swedish doctors that were most influential, it was the Swiss.

Table 3.1. *Market scarcity, organizational resources,*
parliamentary representation of doctors

Year	Doctors per 100,000 population		
	Sweden	France	Switzerland
1958	89.2	106.7	140.6
1975	171.5	146.3	185.8
	Membership in medical association (%)		
1930	76	63	—
1970	92.2	60–5	97
	Doctors in Parliament (%)		
1970	1	12.2	3

Sources: 1. Number of doctors. James Hogarth, *The Payment*
of the Physician. Some European Comparisons (New York:
Macmillan, Pergamon Press, 1963), pp. 60, 139, 281; R. J.
Maxwell, *Health and Wealth. An International Study of Health*
Care Spending. (Lexington, Mass.: Lexington Books, D. C.
Heath and Company for Sandoz Institute for Health and Socio-
Economic Studies, 1981), pp. 148–9, 130–1, 151–2.
    2. Memberships. *Läkartidningen* (Journal of the Swedish
Medical Association), April 19, 1930, p. 516; Swedish Medi-
cal Association membership figures; Jean Meynaud, *Les Groupes*
de Pression en France. Cahiers de la Fondation Nationale des
Sciences Politiques No. 95. (Paris: Librairie Armand Colin,
1958), p. 66; Jean-Claude Stephan, *Economie et Pouvoir Méd-*
ical (Paris: Economica, 1978), pp. 38–9; Gerhard Kocher,
Verbandseinfluss auf die Gesetzgebung. Aerzteverbindung,
Krankenkassenverbände und die Teilrevision 1964 des Kran-
ken- und Unfallversicherungsgesetzes, 2d ed. (Bern: Francke
Verlag, 1972), p. 25.
    3. Parliamentarians. Swedish figures for 1960, Lars Sköld
and Arne Halvarson, "Riksdagens Sociala Sammansättning
under Hundra År," in *Samhälle och Riksdag. Del I.* (Stockholm: Almqvist and Wicksell, 1966), pp. 444, 465; Henry H.
Kerr, *Parlement et Société en Suisse* (St. Saphorin: Editions
Georgi, 1981), p. 280.

In organizational terms, on the other hand, the French medical profession
should have been the weakest. The most generous estimates place 40% to 60%
of the profession as members of medical unions, as opposed to well over 90% in
Sweden and Switzerland. Moreover, whereas Swedish and Swiss doctors were
organized into single medical associations, French doctors were represented by
competing organizations beset by political differences.[4] Again, however, it was

not the French doctors that were the least successful in the political sphere, it was the Swedish. Finally, as far as strikes were concerned, the cases will show that the political victories of physicians' associations were never linked to strikes. Politically influential physicians' associations did not need to resort to strikes. In sum, medical monopoly, market scarcity, strikes, and organizational strength do not account for differences in the ability of national medical professions to defend their economic autonomy against government intervention. Instead, strategic opportunities arising from the design of political institutions explain the extent to which doctors could veto proposed health policies.[5]

A second possible explanation might focus on political demands for national health insurance programs, particularly from unions and leftist political parties. There are differences in both the degree of unionization and the votes received by socialist parties in these countries. But they do not conform either to the policy outcomes or to the political process in these countries. As Table 3.2 shows, Swedish workers and employees were more highly unionized than the French or Swiss. Swiss workers, in turn, were more highly unionized than the French. Yet, for reasons related to the organization of Swiss political institutions, Swiss unions were less effective than French unions in demanding health insurance reform. Thus, while levels of unionization can potentially explain why the Swedish government might be under more pressure to provide extensive public programs in health, they cannot explain the difference between the French and Swiss results. Moreover, the factor of unionization does not enter the political contests over national health insurance in a manner compatible with the "working-class power" thesis. All three governments appeared eager to enact national health insurance programs, indicating that in all three nations electoral pressures were sufficient to place the same health policies on the political agenda. The difference between the cases hinged not on the initial pressures for health policy but rather on how these pressures were brought to bear on politicians during the legislative process itself.

Political partisanship, on the other hand, is more convincing as an explanation. The combined vote for Socialist and Communist parties does fit the policy outcomes. However, evidence from the actual political debates discredits this hypothesis. While parliamentary votes and political allegiances structured the political decision-making process, a simple model of partisanship does not capture the texture and substance of these conflicts. National health insurance politics did not boil down to a confrontation between parties of the Left versus those of the Center and Right. Swedish Social Democrats did not triumph over the bourgeois parties by outvoting them. All of the Swedish parties agreed on national health insurance and the earliest steps in this direction had been taken by the liberals. French Communists and Socialists did not band together against Gaullists and the Catholic Left; French health insurance initiatives were imposed by de Gaulle through executive fiat. Swiss Social Democrats were not overcome by the Radical Democrats and Catholic Conservatives; rather, a coalition for

Table 3.2. *Working-class strength (unionization and left voting)*

	Union membership as percentage of labor force			Total union/employee association density (%)	Left voting Socialists (%)/ Communists (%)	
	1939–40	1950	1960	1960	1944	1959
Sweden	36	51	60	73	46.5/10.3	47.8/4.5
France	17	22	11	19.8	23.8/26.1	15.7/19.2
Switzerland	19	29	28	30.3	28.6/—	26.4/2.7

Sources: 1. Union membership. John D. Stephens, *The Transition from Capitalism to Socialism* (London: Macmillan, 1979), p. 115; Jelle Visser, "Dimensions of Union Growth in Postwar Western Europe," European University Institute Working Paper No. 89 (Badia Fiesolana, San Domenico (FI): European University Institute, 1984), pp. 29, 65, 77.

2. Left vote. Peter Flora et al., *State, Economy, and Society in Western Europe, 1815–1975. A Data Handbook in Two Volumes. Vol. 1. The Growth of Mass Democracies and Welfare States* (Frankfurt: Campus Verlag, 1983), pp. 115, 143, 147. Swedish figures from 1944 and 1960; French from 1945 and 1958; Swiss from 1943 and 1959.

national health insurance composed of all three parties was defeated in a popular referendum. Thus political parties across the board were interested in national health insurance programs, and some of the most important initiatives came in fact from nonsocialist parties. Institutional dynamics specific to these three political systems determined to what extent executive governments were able to introduce proposed reforms. These institutional mechanisms – and not the number of votes going to the Left – set the limits to what was politically feasible in each country.

A third approach to the politics of enacting social programs has focused on the state. Both actors within the state, such as bureaucrats, and the institutions of government themselves are said to shape policy conflicts to such an extent that policies are no longer recognizable as products of the demands of various social groups. Such an outlook has variously stressed the role of civil servants, state administrative capacities, policy legacies, state structures, and the more classical issues of state, such as the national interest and political legitimacy. If applied in a static manner, however, such an approach cannot explain legislative changes. The health policies of France, Switzerland, and Sweden shared common starting points but diverged when new laws were introduced. Policy legacies or path dependency cannot account for such watersheds. Neither can state capacities explain health policy outcomes. Switzerland has a federal form of government, yet federalism was not the obstacle to national health insurance. France has a centralized state, but regulation of the medical profession proved politically impossible for many years. Furthermore, unless state structures change each time that new policies are proposed, it is unclear why administrative structures or state capacities sometimes limit the scope of policy-making and sometimes do not.

The institutional analysis elaborated here emphasizes the importance of executive power for policy-making. The motivations for pursuing national health insurance legislation were indeed linked to questions of political rule. But in order to understand the factors that facilitated or impeded executive governments in enacting their legislative programs, one must consider the ways in which political institutions mediated specific political contests. There is no direct link between a given set of political institutions and a particular policy result. Institutions do not allow one to predict policy outcomes. But by establishing the rules of the game, they do enable one to predict the ways in which these policy conflicts will be played out.

THE RULES OF THE GAME

In order to explain differences in the ability of interest groups to obtain favorable policy outcomes and in the ability of executive governments to enact their legislative programs, this essay analyzes the institutional dynamics of political decision-making. I use a formal perspective on institutions, stressing constitutional rules and electoral results, to show why political decision-making follows characteristic patterns in different polities. Political decisions are not single decisions made at one point in time. Rather, they are composed of sequences of decisions made by different actors at different institutional locations. Simply put, enacting a law requires successive affirmative votes at all decision points. By tracing the formal structure of these decision points as well as examining the party allegiances of the decision-makers at these points, one can understand the logic of the decision-making process.

Political decisions require agreement at several points along a chain of decisions made by representatives in different political arenas. The fate of legislative proposals, such as those for national health insurance, depends upon the number and location of opportunities for veto along this chain. If the politicians that occupy the executive are to enact a new program, they must be able to muster assenting votes at all of the decision points along this chain. Conversely the ability of interest groups to influence such legislative outcomes depends upon their ability to threaten the passage of the law and, hence, to convince those representatives holding critical votes to block the legislation. The probability of veto is not random, however. Vetoes can be predicted from the partisan composition of these different arenas and from the rules for transferring decision-making from one arena to the next. Constitutional provisions create veto opportunities by setting forth procedural rules that establish a division of power amongst elected representatives. Formal rules, such as the separation of executive and legislative powers or the division of legislatures into two chambers determine the number of decision points required for legislative enactment, and therefore the number and location of potential vetoes. Second, veto opportunities are affected by electoral results and features of the party system that affect the distribution of partisan representatives into the different political arenas; political power depends on votes, but votes as they are distributed within distinctly organized political systems. Thus the essence of a political system is the way in which political institutions partition votes into different jurisdictions in combination with the partisan distribution of these votes. These straightforward political and institutional factors produce complex logics of decision-making that provide different opportunities and constraints on both political leaders and interest groups.

The rational choice literature provides some important insights for understanding these decision-making logics. According to these theories, majority rule is insufficient for reaching political accords. With diverse dimensions of political preference, majority votes for a given policy proposal can always be countered by alternative majorities. Institutional mechanisms put a stop to this so-called cycling of preferences by restricting unlimited choice, and therefore allow binding decisions to be made. In other words, the normal political condition is not consensus; the normal condition is a diversity of preferences. Institutional rules resolve conflicts by limiting the points of decision where alternative proposals can be considered. This is how they forge consensus. American studies of institutions have analyzed some examples of the ways in which institutional mechanisms lead to stable outcomes by restricting choice. Executive vetoes allow the executive to block legislative proposals and therefore to maintain the status quo. Or, historically, the division of legislatures into two chambers, with different property qualifications or constituency sizes, established an upper house whose members could be counted on to exert a moderating influence by vetoing proposals from the lower house. Congressional committees, whose members are self-selected to share some preferences in common, are able to propose changes and get them through the legislature, because they can veto alternative proposals from the full house. Such institutional mechanisms ensure stability in policy outcomes and institutional arrangements because they allow a core of political representatives to veto legislative proposals.[6]

In turning to European cases, however, some revisions must be made in the starting assumptions of institutional analysis. While American studies have often assumed that the executive brakes change while legislators or voters promote changes, in the European cases examined here, the political executive was prepared to promote policy changes while vetoes were made in subsequent arenas. A second difference is the importance of political parties and party discipline in reducing choice by binding representatives to a particular party line. Third, some veto points were created by the concentration of politicians with particular interests in a given political arena such as a parliamentary committee or an upper house. But equally important to these cases were veto points that arose in places where majorities were not limited, and where one can observe exactly the cycling of preferences predicted by rational choice theory. Both the classical veto points and the latter points of uncertainty were critical for interest-group influence in these cases. Rather than focusing on one particular institutional mechanism, this study examines political systems at work during the policy process and shows how distinctive mechanisms were relevant to the outcomes in each case. We can understand the political systems and the specific mechanisms that arise within them by spelling out the effects of constitutional rules and electoral results.

Figure 3.1 illustrates the impact of constitutional rules and electoral results on political decision-making. The ability of an executive government to introduce a policy depends on its capacity for unilateral action – that is, on the probability that the executive decision will be confirmed at subsequent points of decision. If the executive is constitutionally independent from the Parliament – that is, if its decisions do not require parliamentary approval – the executive may take direct action without concern for the Parliament. In this case the executive decision is the final decision; the Parliament does not have veto power.

But if the constitution requires parliamentary approval, the decision-making process moves to the Parliament. Here, however, partisanship and party discipline make a difference. If the executive government enjoys a stable parliamentary majority and party discipline is in force, the probability that an executive decision would be overturned by the Parliament is extremely low. Under these circumstances, one cannot expect the majority of members of Parliament (MPs who belong to the same political party as the executive) to deviate from the executive decision. Thus, although the Parliament is formally required to ratify the executive decision, the effects of partisanship will lead the Parliament to rubber-stamp the legislation; the executive arena will remain the effective point of decision.

If, however, the executive is not supported by a stable parliamentary majority, or if party discipline does not require members of Parliament to vote with their fellow party members in the executive, the probability that parliamentary representatives would override executive decisions is much greater. In such a situation, one would expect significant policy changes and even vetoes from parliamentary representatives; the Parliament would emerge as a veto point.

Similar factors govern the relationship between the parliamentary arena and the electoral arena. In most political systems, parliamentary decisions are the last step in enactment of laws. However, where the possibility for popular referenda on legislative decisions exists, this formal constitutional rule allows the electorate to override parliamentary decisions. In such a case, the electoral arena becomes an effective veto point. Or, when electoral shifts or approaching elections make members of Parliament especially sensitive to voter reactions, the electoral arena may become a de facto point of decision in a particular political system.

In sum, constitutional rules and electoral results produce different constraints on the ability of executive governments to introduce new policies. These institutional and political hurdles direct decision-making along different paths in different polities. Opportunities for veto determine whether the effective point of

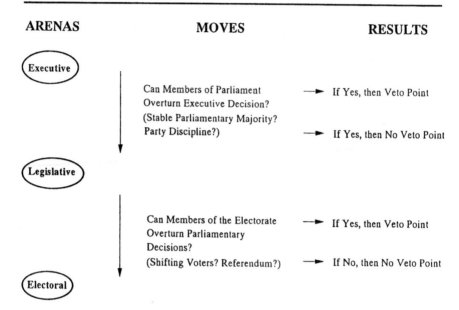

Figure 3.1. Political arenas and veto points

decision will be the executive arena, the parliamentary arena, or the electoral arena. The specific mechanisms for veto determine precisely which politicians or voters have the power to ratify or to block policy proposals. As described, the veto points are not physical entities, but points of strategic uncertainty that arise from the logic of the decision process itself. Even a small change in constitutional rules or electoral results may change the location of the veto points and their strategic importance. In this way, formal constitutional rules and electoral results establish a framework in which policy-making takes place. This is the context for interest group influence.

Interest-group "power" is not a property possessed by interest groups by virtue of some characteristic like the number of members they enroll, the money they collect, or even the contacts they have with politicians. Although efforts have been made to understand interest-group influence in terms of the social or economic position of these groups as well as their organizational resources, factors exclusive to these groups are insufficient for explaining influence. Political influence comprises the relationship of these groups to the political system, and hence, it cannot be understood without an analysis of the receptivity of political institutions to political pressures. The response of politicians to interest groups, it will be argued here, does not depend upon the social origins or the personal weaknesses of these representatives. Instead, specific institutional mechanisms structure the decision process in a given polity, and by so doing, provide interest groups with different opportunities for influencing political decisions. Depending upon the logic of the decision process, different political strategies are available to interest groups, and different groups are privileged by the political institutions in each country.

The following sections of this essay show how such standard political factors affected health policy-making in France, Switzerland, and Sweden. Irrespective of differences in partisanship, all three executive governments were prepared to enact national health insurance and to restrict the economic independence of the medical profession. National health insurance legislation was prepared in the executive bureaucracy after consultation with representatives of interest groups and political parties. The critical difference between the cases turned on the ability of the political executive to ratify these proposals in subsequent arenas.

In Sweden the political executive could count on decisions being routinely confirmed by the parliament. This pattern of executive dominance was made possible by institutions established to conserve the power of the monarchy and the Conservative Party during the transition to democracy. Proportional representation and an indirectly elected first chamber helped the Social Democrats achieve stable parliamentary majorities. Because the executive government rested on secure parliamentary majorities, executive decisions were automatically ratified by parliamentary votes. This combination of institutional design and electoral victories effectively constrained decision-making to the executive arena. But in this context, Swedish doctors were politically disadvantaged. In the executive arena, their views were outweighed by those of the main producer groups – employers and trade unions – and, in contrast to French and Swiss doctors, they did not have recourse to an alternative veto point to override the executive-level consensus.

In France the Parliament of the Fourth Republic offered unexpected opportunities for interest group influence. Unstable parliamentary coalitions and lack of party discipline impeded executive governments from enacting legislation. Executive proposals were not supported by parliamentary votes; instead, each proposal was countered by alternative parliamentary majorities. Consequently the Parliament became a bottleneck in the French political process and hence the de facto point of decision. This unique decision structure was the context for French interest-group influence. French doctors profited from their parliamentary contacts to demand legislative concessions, and as a group that generally wished to block legislation rather than to see it enacted, these doctors were inadvertently advantaged by the difficulty of French parliamentarians in reaching any binding decision at all. The same features of the political system benefited and disadvantaged other groups. Interest groups important to the members of the governing coalitions, such as small businessmen and Catholics, wrested legislative benefits, while those with party affiliations outside the governing coalitions, such as the Communist union, had little influence. Only when the executive resorted to constitutional change in order to circumvent the parliamentary veto point could French health legislation be enacted.

In Switzerland the constitutional right of voters to challenge legislation through referenda pulled decision-making into the electoral arena. In this arena the instability of majority rule proved a deterrent to proposals for policy change; referendum votes were more often negative than positive. Consequently the referendum was viewed as a threat to legislation. This created a strategic opportunity for the interest groups, like Swiss doctors, who found that they could use the referendum threat to gain concessions from policy-makers. Swiss doctors never resorted to medical strikes; they simply threatened to block legislation by calling for referenda. Other interest groups as well, like chiropractors, relied on the referendum threat to obtain policy concessions. Unions, by contrast, were disadvantaged by this mechanism. To groups that wished to promote legislation, the referendum mechanism could provide only Pyrrhic victories.

In each case institutional rules established a distinct logic of decision-making that set the parameters both for executive power and interest-group influence. Consequently the institutions determined where the balance point between different interest group demands and the programmatic goals of the executive was to be found. In contrast to some of the other analyses in this volume, such as those by Hall, King, and Weir, this essay does not argue that institutions screen out or encourage certain policy ideas. Nor does it argue that institutions change the subjective perceptions of political actors about their interests. This is not to say that institutions could never exert such effects. Rather, selecting a case where both the policy ideas and the views of politicians and interest groups happened to be similar allows these factors to be held constant.

This study singles out the impact of political institutions on the ability of each of these actors to prevail in policy conflicts. By providing different opportunities for vetoing legislation, the institutions change the relative weights of these actors as well as the most opportune strategy available to these actors for promoting similarly defined interests (as in the essays by Dunlavy, Hattam, and Rothstein). In Sweden the executive could enact legislation without fearing vetoes from the parliamentary or electoral arenas; the lack of a block of opposing votes restricted decision-making to the executive arena. In France unstable parliamentary majorities shifted decision-making to the parliamentary arena. In Switzerland decision-making was moved to the electoral arena. The rules of the game established distinct political logics that account for three distinct patterns of political behavior and policy results.

THREE CASES

Direct parliamentary rule

During the French Fourth Republic, French doctors as well as several other interest groups were able to gain concessions from the legislature. The French Parliament constituted a veto point for several reasons. The Constitution of the

Fourth Republic, like that of the Third Republic, was based on the principle of direct parliamentary rule. The executive government was dependent on the Parliament because it was invested by parliamentary coalitions and it could not take action without parliamentary approval. In practice the weakness of the system stemmed not from these constitutional provisions but from the fact that the French electoral system and party practices did not produce stable parliamentary majorities. Had this been the case, the executive government would have had a clear mandate for policy decisions. Instead, the fragmented party system and the lack of internal party discipline made it difficult to form and to maintain decisive parliamentary majorities. Furthermore, the disjuncture between parliamentary majorities and electoral alliances (related to the two rounds of voting, which kept the smaller parties alive and hampered majorities), meant that a single election result could provide the basis for a wide variety of parliamentary coalitions, further increasing the scope for parliamentary manoeuvering.

Thus, while the ideal view of a parliamentary system is that elections establish a distribution of parliamentary seats, and that this distribution is then used to invest an executive, in France these different political arenas – the electoral arena, the parliamentary arena, and the executive arena – were disarticulated.[7] There were virtually no restrictions on the alliances that could be formed or the policy proposals that could be considered. The parties were free to change their positions, and often did so as the unstable electoral situation encouraged opportunistic ploys to attract new voters. Consequently any political party or interest group dissatisfied with an executive decision could hope to achieve a different outcome in the parliamentary arena. Furthermore, given the instability of the governing coalitions, renewed discussion in the parliamentary arena not only might produce a change in policy, but it might cause the government to fall. This instability made the executive government vulnerable to members of political parties – particularly those that controlled swing votes in building or breaking a governing coalition – or to interest groups that could claim connections to these MPs. Under conditions of unstable governing coalitions and weak party discipline, where at any moment majorities could unravel or new allegiances could form, the political game became one of disrupting the coalition.

This potential to disrupt the governing coalition was the key to interest-group power in the French Fourth Republic. Interest groups aimed their appeals at individual members of parliament, particularly during the handling of policy issues in the parliamentary committees and during local election campaigns, when individual candidates were pressured to declare their allegiance to specific local interest groups.[8] Success depended upon reaching individuals central to the coalitions rather than upon building centralized interest organizations with large memberships. This strategic context changed the probability that a particular interest group could veto proposed legislation. Consequently interest groups important to members of Parliament critical to the governing coalitions had no reason to be disposed toward cooperation. The medical profession, for example, was highly overrepresented in the Parliament, and with doctors spread through several of the parties needed to build governing coalitions, the profession enjoyed the privileges that accrue to swing voters. In the Fourth Republic, physicians and pharmacists together held 5.8% of the seats. More important, they constituted 10.5% of the Radicals, 6.9% of the Catholic left party (the MRP), and 6.5% of the Socialists (the SFIO; refer to Table 3.1).[9] Personalized bargaining, without the protection of party discipline, only enhanced this power. Several other interest blocs, such as farmers, small employers, and special interest groups, such as wine producers, wielded parliamentary clout out of proportion to the number of voters represented by their memberships. With the power to block parliamentary action, and with the parties always seeking to capture new voters, these groups were in a position not only to make demands, but also to escalate these demands at will.

At several unusual constitutional junctures, however, this parliamentary stalemate was broken by direct action on the part of the executive government. Specific constitutional protections of the Liberation period and the Fifth Republic prevented the overturning of executive decisions by parliamentary representatives. When members of Parliament could no longer override the executive, the instability of the parliamentary majority no longer mattered; the veto point was no longer relevant. Consequently the locus of decision-making shifted from the Parliament to the executive, and one witnessed a corresponding change in the dynamics of policy-making. The groups who had been under little pressure to compromise when they could threaten to withdraw parliamentary support from the executive government were suddenly excluded from executive decisions.

French national health insurance was introduced in precisely such an extraordinary period. The executive could issue legislation directly by ordinance, the Parliament was merely consultative, and it was composed, in any case, overwhelmingly of representatives of the resistance coalition. Based on the economic and social program drawn up by the *Conseil National de la Résistance* in the spring of 1944, the Social Security Ordinances were promulgated directly by the executive on October 4 and 9, 1945. Although employers and preexisting health insurance carriers (the old mutual societies and private insurance companies) protested, the executive government utilized the route of direct legislation to introduce a universal social insurance system that covered all salaried employees for health, old age, and work accidents. The plan was to establish a single type of insurance fund, called the *caisse unique,* that would, eventually, cover all French citizens for all risks. The ordinances extended social insurance coverage to the majority of the working population and greatly improved insurance benefits. In an obvious electoral manoeuvre, the executive seized the opportunity to introduce the legislation only days before the first parliamentary elections and the referendum to ratify the Constitution were to be held.[10]

Direct executive privilege was short-lived, however. Almost from the start, the need to make concessions to constituencies of the Liberation coalition weakened the administration's scheme. Particularly with the return to parliamentary democracy, party competition increased, which opened up opportunities for an onslaught of particularistic claims. The medical profession criticized the national health insurance program and blocked regulation of doctors' fees by governmental authorities, insisting instead that local negotiations between health insurance funds and medical associations be used to establish doctors' fees. The Catholic Trade Union and the Catholic left party (MRP) forced the government to remove family allowances from the general social security scheme, and to introduce free elections for the seats on the governing boards of the social security funds. (Free elections would increase the number of Catholic representatives, at the expense of the Communist CGT.) White-collar employees and the self-employed protested their inclusion in the same insurance scheme as workers, thereby putting an end to the movement for universal coverage under a single scheme.[11] The lack of a firm parliamentary coalition provided the opportunity for this interest-group log-rolling.

These concessions to special interests created problems that plagued the French health insurance system for the next twenty years. The use of negotiations to regulate doctors' fees did not work; the plethora of special schemes weakened the social security administration; and competition between various unions turned the social security elections into arenas of political competition that hampered unified leadership of the health insurance administration.

Although doctors' fees were to be regulated through negotiations between local medical associations and local sickness insurance funds, the medical associations simply refused to negotiate. Rural doctors were in principle prepared to negotiate; their patients could not afford the high fees charged by urban specialists in any case. But the urban elite pressured medical association leaders not to negotiate. Consequently patients did not receive full reimbursement for the costs of medical treatment. In response the social insurance funds attempted to push for legislation. But elite physicians were well-placed to veto parliamentary initiatives. Visits by the organization of insurance funds (the FNOSS) to the main parliamentary groups resulted in many bills, but no party dared to oppose the medical profession by actually depositing the bill in the Assembly.[12] With unstable governing coalitions, a solid bloc of deputies, spread through several parties that were regularly included in the government, was in a pivotal position.

The Fourth Republic was equally blocked in the area of hospital reform. Plans for more efficient hospital administration had been submitted to the National Assembly in 1954 and 1957. Hospitals should be freed from local political control by municipal councils and mayors; instead professional administrators and prefects should play a stronger role. In the name of efficiency, the reports argued that doctors should no longer divide their time between a number of activities including private clinics and public hospitals, but should work in full-time hospital positions.[13] As in the case of doctors' fees, however, parliamentary stalemate had precluded any action.

With the emergence of the Fifth Republic, however, the rules of the game were radically changed. Under the 1958 Constitution, the executive government was effectively freed from the Parliament. Direct election of the executive, greater possibilities for direct executive legislation by decree without parliamentary approval, and a strict separation between the ministries and the Assembly established an independent executive government, one that would no longer be undermined by the lack of stable parliamentary majorities. In the case of health policy, the most important provisions were those that allowed the executive to impose legislation without parliamentary ratification. This transformed the logic of French policy-making.

Within two years of taking office, the de Gaulle government introduced reforms that completely reorganized the hospital system and imposed a new system of fee controls on the medical profession. All of these reforms were enacted by decree or ordinance, with no parliamentary discussion whatsoever. The first of these, the Réforme Debré, established full-time, salaried hospital practice. As a transitional measure, senior doctors would be able to receive a limited amount of private patients within the public hospitals, but this private practice was to be phased out completely.[14] Doctors' fees would be directly regulated by the government. In order to pressure local medical associations to negotiate official fee schedules, individual doctors would be able to sign contracts with the funds. The patients of these doctors would be reimbursed at more favorable rates than doctors that did not sign contracts. These individual contracts had been demanded by the health insurance funds since 1928, but had always been blocked by the French Medical Association. Now French Medical Association control over the fee negotiations was undercut by allowing individual doctors to decide whether or not to sign; the government had added an element of market competition in order to buttress its new institutional framework. In addition the ministers of labor, health, and finance would set maximum fees that would apply in the event that no fee schedules were negotiated.

The French Medical Association protested the government's "politics of fait accompli," and charged that as a result of the decrees, "medical fees will become an affair of the State, and, at the same time, the profession will cease, in our point of view to be a liberal profession, because it will lose, definitively, its economic independence."[15] French doctors fought these measures in the courts, the Parliament and the market, but without success. The Constitutional Council upheld the Debré reform in January 1960. In the legislature an absolute majority in the Senate (155 senators belonging to the Independents, the Gauche Démocratique, the Peasants, or that were unaffiliated, as well as three former ministers of health) and an absolute majority in the National Assembly (241 deputies, including about one-half of the Gaullist UNR deputies) presented propositions for new laws to regulate relations between the medical profession and the social insurance funds.[16] Nevertheless, now independent from the Parliament, the executive held firm and refused to reconsider the decrees.

Escape to the market arena proved equally unsuccessful. Pressured by the Medical Union of the Seine, the French Medical Association launched an administrative strike to block the reform. But this time, in contrast to earlier efforts, the government had succeeded in dividing the profession. The individual contracts allowed the many doctors who would benefit from the system to bypass the medical association leadership. Within a few months the strike was broken. The rift between doctors who were for and against the fee schedules continued to deepen, however. When the French Medical Association signed an agreement with the social security funds in July 1960, the economic liberal faction split off, forming the Fédération des Médecins de France.

The medical profession was not the only group affected by the decrees of May 12, 1960. For in conjunction with the measures to control fees – a clear improvement in social security benefits – the government reorganized the administrative structure of health insurance and social security. The power of the regional social security directors, directly responsible to the minister of labor, were greatly strengthened at the expense of the elected administrative boards. Like the solution to doctors' fees, the administrative reform was not a new idea; it had been debated since the introduction of the social security system and was the preference of both members of the Ministry of Labor and employers. Previous political circumstances had not permitted administrative reform, however. Now it was imposed from above. The social security funds and the unions – the CGT, the CFTC, and the CGT-FO – supported the controls on fees as an increase in benefits, but adamantly opposed the administrative component of the reform, calling it the *étatisation* of the funds. At the same time, small employers opposed the reform because they would lose some of the privileges of their separate health and social security scheme. The only interest group that supported the reform was the employers' association, which was dominated by large industrialists. The industrialists supported both the regulation of doctors' fees and the administrative changes as rationalizing measures that would contain costs.[17]

In the French case the parliamentary veto point enabled a select set of interest groups to exert legislative pressure through their ability to threaten the parliamentary majority. Once the executive government was able to circumvent the parliament, however, reforms were passed despite the protests of these traditional veto groups.

Direct democracy

Swiss political institutions were designed differently from French institutions and had different effects on policy-making. A series of institutional mechanisms restricted the powers of the national government. The jurisdiction of the federal as opposed to the cantonal governments was limited to areas specifically set forth in the constitution; a constitutional amendment was required to enlarge the scope of the federal government. The political executive was composed of a seven-member council, the Bundesrat, which divided power among representatives elected by the parliament in proportion to the political parties. The legislative branch was divided into two chambers, one elected by proportional representation, and one elected by the cantons, which would be expected to dampen the effects of proportional representation because the more conservative rural cantons would be overrepresented in the second chamber. Finally all legislation was subject to direct electoral veto through the referendum.

Although all of these provisions slowed policy-making, it was in practice the referendum that constituted the critical veto point. Proponents of national health insurance successfully launched a popular initiative to revise the constitution to allow the federal government to legislate national health insurance in 1890. At several points, both before and after the Second World War, agreement was reached among the parties represented in the executive Bundesrat, and national health insurance legislation was enacted into law by both chambers of the parliament. Nevertheless, national health insurance was subsequently vetoed through referendum challenges.

The referendum had a dual impact on Swiss policy-making. The referendum effectively moved decision-making from the executive and parliamentary arenas into the electoral arena. In referendum votes Swiss voters did not follow partisan loyalties. In fact, statistically, referendum votes were more often negative than positive.[18] These votes followed the predictions of theories of collective action: Voters who were affected by the potential costs of legislation turned out at higher rates than voters affected by potential benefits. Furthermore, recent studies of Swiss referenda show voter participation, which averages 40 percent, to be correlated to socioeconomic status, with higher rates of participation for individuals with higher incomes and higher levels of educational attainment.[19] Precisely these voters, however, were least likely to benefit from national health insurance or other forms of social protection.

The unintended consequences of the referendum go beyond specific instances of defeat, however. Swiss policy-makers were loath to see legislation subject to a referendum challenge after a lengthy process of executive and parliamentary deliberation. Not only was the outcome uncertain, but the chances of failure were greater than those of success. In order to avoid such defeats, they attempted to ensure that legislation was "referendum-proof." Ironically, this placed a great deal of power in the hands of interest groups.[20] Interest groups had sufficient memberships to collect the signatures necessary to launch referenda and the organizational resources to mount referendum campaigns. Although these groups could not control the *outcome* of referendum votes, they *could* control whether or not a referendum was called; interest groups were thus the gatekeepers to the referendum. Furthermore, whereas the general public did not have a clear channel for expressing its views on legislation, interest groups presented policy-makers with very specific demands to which they could respond. Hence the most efficacious means for policy-makers to prevent a possible veto of legislation was to address interest-group concerns early on in the legislative preparations: "The most successful referendums are those which do not take place. The circles that might have fought the law do not do so because it contains what they want. This is the explanation for the compromise character of a large part of federal legislation; parliament does not make laws in a sovereign way but always under the threat of a referendum."[21]

The ability of interest groups to force issues out of executive and parliamentary arenas and into the electoral arena provided groups willing to block the legislation entirely if their demands were not met with a great deal of leverage over health care policy-making. Even at the executive and parliamentary stages, politicians were forced to consider carefully the views of interest groups. Because even rather narrow interest groups could rely on the referendum weapon, access to policy-making was opened up to a variety of smaller groups. Expert commissions, rather than counting ten to twenty members as in the Swedish case, often consisted of more than fifty representatives. Furthermore, as any one group could veto, decision-making had to be unanimous, lest the losing minority would decide to topple the reform at the electoral stage. As in the French case, the possibility of vetoing legislation reduced the incentives for these groups to compromise. Thus policy decisions were shifted to the electoral arena; many extremely small and minority groups were able to exert a large political influence; and unanimity was imposed as the decision rule.

Swiss doctors were able to wrest many concessions from this legislative process. As in other nations, there were two general areas of concern to the profession: (1) the role of the state in the health insurance market, and (2) the freedom of the profession to determine its own fees. Swiss health insurance was organized around a system of federal subsidies to voluntary mutual funds. The insured bought their own policies directly from the mutuals. The mutuals were required to be nonprofit in order to receive the subsidies, but in practice, many private insurance companies simply opened nonprofit divisions that qualified as nonprofit carriers. Doctors' fees were to be regulated through agreements negotiated between local sickness funds and cantonal medical societies. But, as in France, agreements were not always reached, and when reached, they were not always followed.

After the Second World War, the Federal Office of Social Insurance (under the direction of the Bundesrat, collectively governed by three Radical Democrats, two Catholic Conservatives, one Social Democrat, and one member of the Citizens', Farmers', and Artisans' Party) developed reform plans to expand the role of government by converting the system of federal subsidies to a compulsory national health insurance plan and to control doctors' fees. While preparing a more general compulsory insurance law, the executive submitted a proposal for compulsory health insurance for low-income earners and a program of x-rays to combat tuberculosis.

Both chambers of the Parliament approved the TB law – the cantonally elected

Ständerat approved it unanimously and the proportionally elected Nationalrat gave approval by all but three votes. But interest groups moved the policy process to the electoral arena, where the law was defeated by a national referendum. Though it was launched by French Swiss liberals, the Swiss Medical Association played an active role in this referendum campaign, as did the Swiss Employers' Association, the Swiss Farmers' Association, and the Swiss Small Business Association. On the other side, supporting the law were all of the unions, all of the employee associations, the church organizations, and the association of sickness funds.

Given the evident fact that the groups that supported this law had much larger memberships than those that opposed the law, how can one explain this defeat? The sickness funds, themselves, wondered why this was the case and complained that they needed to educate their membership.[22] However, while policy-makers, the sickness funds, and union organizations might have understood the collective benefits of national health insurance, and the role of the TB law as the first step in establishing national health insurance, the TB law had little appeal to the individual voters that participated in the referendum. The law called for compulsory insurance for low-income earners. Anyone with a high income had no particular interest in this compulsion unless for some reason they were concerned about the uninsured. For those with low incomes, persons that in any case tended not to vote, the law provided only the compulsion to insure themselves, not government financial aid. Moreover, the initial impetus for the law was a popular plebiscite calling for maternity insurance. But the Federal Office of Social Insurance had decided to begin its efforts with health insurance.

Thus, when the issue of national health insurance was moved from the executive and parliamentary arenas – where there was widespread agreement on the law – to the electoral arena, a different set of criteria became relevant. While political elites were concerned with the percentage of the population covered by health insurance, preventive medicine, and their ability to control the overall costs of the system through collective financing and regulating doctors' fees, individual voters viewed the relative costs and benefits of the legislation in individual terms. Further, as key actors in the decision to launch a referendum, interest groups were able to demand concessions from both the executive bureaucracy and the parliament.

This process was seen clearly in the aftermath of defeat of the 1949 TB referendum. On the basis of the defeat, the Swiss Medical Association, and the Employers', Farmers', and Small Business associations petitioned the government to withdraw its plans for health insurance reform. In 1954 the Department of Social Insurance prepared a plan for compulsory maternity insurance, increased federal subsidies for health insurance, and introduced controls on doctors' fees. The Department withdrew its proposal, however, when preliminary consultations with interest groups indicated that their positions were "too divided" for the government to pursue reform.[23] In a political system where any interest group, no matter how small, could launch a referendum, and given the uncertain outcome of the referendum, it did not make sense to continue deliberations without the unanimous support of these groups.

As a total reform of the health insurance system had been shown to be politically unfeasible, the Federal Office of Social Insurance announced in 1961 that it intended to pursue a partial reform, which, "must be designed in such a way so as to assure its prospects of acceptance without a referendum battle."[24] To this end, the reform would not include national compulsory health or maternity insurance, or limits on doctors' fees. The reform would be limited to a large increase in the federal subsidies to private health insurance. The executive, in other words, was attempting to protect itself from the electoral arena, the veto point. As interest groups could not be denied access, as in the French case, the process was to be closed off by keeping certain issues off of the agenda.

Nevertheless, the medical association managed to reinsert the issue of doctors' fees into the debate, and its ability to do so was clearly linked to the referendum threat. The medical association was not satisfied that the government had agreed to drop its plans for controls on doctors' fees, which the association called "the first step toward socialized medicine."[25] The association now wished to obtain a ruling that it was legal for physicians to charge patients different fees according to their incomes, a system of sliding fees known as class divisions. In addition the medical association demanded that payment from sickness funds to doctors (direct third-party payment) be replaced by direct payments from patients, who would in turn be reimbursed by the funds. The association built up a war chest estimated at 1 million Swiss francs by increasing its membership fees and hired a public relations firm. This strategy emulated the successful American Medical Association's campaign against national health insurance between 1948 and 1952, which was funded by a special assessment of $25 from each of its 140,000 members, and during which $4.6 million was spent.[26] The Swiss Medical Association was not the only group to remind the Parliament of its power to veto legislation, however. Swiss chiropractors, who were not recognized by the association, collected nearly 400,000 signatures for a petition demanding that treatments by chiropractors be covered on the same basis as treatments by licensed physicians. This created a dilemma: The medical profession was adamantly opposed to the inclusion of the chiropractors, but with such a large number of signatures, the chiropractors could clearly veto the reform.

The parliamentary treatment of the reform was a long and drawn out process that lasted nearly two years. Although both houses of Parliament agreed to increase the federal subsidies, the issue of doctors' fees created problems. The behavior of the medical association was severely criticized, with one supporter of the physicians stating that the leadership had been "overrun by a more-or-less radicalized mass."[27] Nevertheless, the final results clearly benefited the groups that could launch a referendum and penalized those that could not. The medical profession was granted freedom to set fees according to income and reimbursement payment. Over the protests of the Swiss Medical Association, chiropractors were incorporated into the system on the same basis as licensed physicians. The victory of the chiropractors demonstrates that the referendum threat is more essential than professional status. The sickness funds were dissatisfied, however. But at a delegates' meeting of the organization of sickness funds (Konkordat) it was decided not to pursue a referendum challenge. As Konkordat president Hänggi explained, no party or union would be willing to fight the reform, and the chiropractors, delighted at the outcome, would constitute fierce competition in a referendum battle.

Better a little bit of progress with this revision than none at all. . . . For one must be clear about one thing: in a referendum battle, "medical rights" [fees according to patients' incomes] would not play a major role; instead, the talk would be of the improvements in benefits and Federal subsidies, that is, about the material improvements for the insured. The basic conflicts over medical rights, which are of interest to few, would remain obscure to most people; certainly, they would hardly unleash the groundswell of opposition that would be necessary to topple this law.[28]

After more than three years of debate, then, a reform process that was intended to be simple and uncontroversial had become protracted and ridden with conflict. Referendum politics blocked the introduction of national health insurance and hampered subsequent efforts to regulate medical fees. With these early steps effectively precluded, discussion of restrictions on private practice became a nonissue. National maternity insurance, a subject of debate since the constitutional initiative of 1945, had somehow gotten lost in the shuffle. The ever present possibility to force decisions into the electoral arena discouraged compromises and allowed even very narrow interests, for example the chiropractors, to play a central role in the reform process. In the Swiss political system, the concept of power was defined by the referendum and the rules of the game were set by an interpretation of how the referendum works, just as in the French case, the logic of the system revolved around controlling the unpredictable Parliament.

Majority parliamentarism

In contrast to the French and Swiss political systems, Swedish political institutions provided for a chain of decision with no veto points. The executive government was able to make and enforce policy decisions with little probability of veto at later points in the chain. This was the result of a coincidence of features of institutional design with unexpected electoral victories. Political bargains worked out in the transition from monarchical rule in 1866 and in the subsequent extensions of the franchise in 1909 and 1918 had established a system with some of the same institutional checks as in France and Switzerland. The Parliament was to balance the power of the executive, while the indirectly elected first chamber of the bicameral parliament was to restrain the effects of proportional representation. However, whereas in France conflicts between the political executive and the Parliament resulted in stalemate, in Sweden institutions were developed to mediate these jurisdictional conflicts. The use of Royal Commissions, consultative bodies of interest-group and political representatives appointed by the executive to draft legislative proposals, as well as the associated *remiss* process, during which interest groups were requested to submit written comments, expanded as the monarch sought to avoid the Parliament and parliamentary representatives preferred that policy negotiations take place outside of the royal bureaucracy.[29]

In 1932 the unexpected Social Democratic electoral victory and alliance with the Farmers' Party effected a sea change in the Swedish system that Olle Nyman has called a shift from minority parliamentarism to majority parliamentarism. The very institutions that were designed to block popular change abruptly switched to the favor of the Social Democrats. The Royal Commissions, introduced to allow the monarchical bureaucracy to avoid parliamentary opposition, now helped to promote Social Democratic legislation. The Upper House of the Parliament, long a veto point used by Conservatives, suddenly ensured continued Social Democratic rule despite electoral fluctuations.[30]

After this electoral realignment, the system worked as though the veto points had disappeared. Once a decision had been taken in the executive arena, the Parliament was unlikely to change it, as the executive government rested on stable parliamentary majorities. Similarly, with proportional representation and fairly stable electoral results, parliamentary decisions were generally not challenged by reactions from the electorate. In contrast to Switzerland, interest groups or voters could not veto legislation with referenda; this decision was strictly parliamentary, which in the case of stable parliamentary majorities meant that the party that controlled the executive could control the use of the referendum. In contrast to France, the electorate did not contain pockets of "surge" voters that tempted politicians to defect from the parliamentary coalitions.[31] Only on the very rare occasion of an electoral realignment – or the threat of one – did the electoral arena become significant for specific policy proposals. Consequently policy-making was concentrated in the executive, with interest-group representatives under pressure to compromise as the probability was high that executive proposals would pass unscathed through parliamentary deliberations. The political logic of this system entailed building a majority coalition in the executive arena.

Within this political system, the Swedish medical profession was placed at a disadvantage. In executive proceedings, its views were always weighed against the views of the trade union confederation, the white collar union, and the employers' association. The profession had better contacts in the Parliament, but the Conservative members of Parliament that were ready to veto the executive proposals were outnumbered. The profession also had success in obtaining newspaper coverage for its viewpoints, but only in the rare instances when there was an electoral threat was this effective.

As in France and Switzerland, the government in Sweden took steps in the postwar period to expand health insurance and to control doctors' fees. National health insurance was introduced in 1946, when the Social Democrats held a majority in both chambers of parliament. Not every interest group was completely in favor of national health insurance. But in contrast to the French and Swiss cases, doctors, employers, and white-collar workers did not have recourse to a veto point. Unable to threaten parliamentary or referendum vetoes, each group expressed misgivings but agreed to cooperate. The Swedish Employers' Federation pointed to the virtues of voluntary insurance and questioned the financial wisdom of immediately introducing national health insurance, but essentially agreed to the reform. The white-collar union noted that most of its members would not benefit from the reform, but, in the name of solidarity, it lent its support. The Swedish Medical Association stated that it preferred voluntary to compulsory insurance, and urged the government to concentrate on more pressing public health needs. It would, however, go along, particularly as the proposal provided for a reimbursement mechanism for payment and for a free choice of doctor. In this context, the medical profession or other interest groups were not in a veto position. The government had the parliamentary votes necessary to enact the law, and there was no alternate channel of *political* influence, like the French Parliament or the Swiss referendum, where the doctors could make their own point of view prevail over a majority consensus.

Two years later the situation had changed. The opposition parties were gearing up for the 1948 electoral campaign and hoped that the 1947 balance-of-payments crisis would erode Social Democratic electoral support. The release of a government report calling for the creation of a National Health Service, by placing all hospital and office doctors on a government salary and eliminating all forms of private medical practice, provided a focus for a conservative backlash. The nonsocialist press depicted this proposal, which was known as the Höjer reform, as a doctrinaire call for the immediate socialization of medicine and the downgrading of doctors from free professionals to state civil servants. The Conservative newspaper, *Svenska Dagbladet,* editorialized, "Mr. Höjer's goal emerges with frightening clarity: the profession's total socialization and the economic levelling of physicians."[32] Doctors, employers and the three nonsocialist parties – the Farmers, the Liberals, and the Conservatives – actively campaigned against the reform. No other legislative proposal received as much nor as critical press coverage in 1948 as the Höjer reform.[33] But the pattern was the same for economic and tax policy, as well: The nonsocialist parties relied on the press to carry out an electoral campaign that has been singled out as being unusually aggressive and ideological in tone.[34]

The potential breakdown of future prospects for Farmer–Labor coalition governments as well as electoral losses placed the Social Democratic Party in a vulnerable position. Although the Social Democratic MPs held sufficient seats to enact any reform, potential electoral losses presented opponents of Social

Democratic policies with a veto opportunity. These electoral pressures created a strategic opening for the medical profession. Unlike its grudging acceptance of national health insurance, now the profession declared itself absolutely opposed to the Höjer reform. In face of these electoral pressures, the Social Democratic government backed down completely, not only with regard to the Höjer reform, but also with respect to a controversial proposal for a new inheritance tax, as well as other elements of its economic program.

As soon as this moment had passed, however, the Social Democratic government went ahead with a number of health policies, often without consulting the medical association. The overall direction of these policies was to reduce the market power of doctors, by increasing their numbers and reducing the scope of private practice. Over the opposition of the association, the number of doctors was increased by a factor of 7 between 1947 and 1972. Private beds were removed from public hospitals in 1959, and, at the same time, all hospitals were required to provide public outpatient care. These clinics competed with private office practitioners and with the private office hours of hospital doctors and were therefore viewed as a threat to private practice. Finally, in 1969, private medical consultations were banned from public hospitals, outpatient hospital care was made virtually free of charge by setting patient fees at a flat rate of 7 crowns (kronor), and hospital doctors were placed on full-time salaries.

At no time was the profession able to avail itself of a similar strategic opening as that of 1948. In 1969 Conservative MPs supported the profession and voted against the law to eliminate private practice from hospitals and to reduce patient fees to 7 crowns. Nevertheless, with an absolute majority, the Social Democrats had no trouble in passing the reform and did so with the full support of the Center and Liberal parties. Conservatives complained that the parliamentary vote was "a mere formality . . . the real decision has taken place over the heads of the MPs."[35]

The Swedish state was able to take steps to control the medical market because its actions could not be vetoed in alternative arenas. This was not simply a matter of Social Democratic electoral victories. Similar expansions of public health insurance, controls on doctors' fees, and salaried payment had been supported by French Gaullists, and by nearly unanimous votes from the full spectrum of Swiss political parties. The Swedish executive was able to go further than these other governments because the initial policy changes were not blocked; rather, they led to further interventions.

Nor were these policy changes a result of peculiar preferences on the part of the medical profession or a result of any inherent economic or organizational weaknesses. Swedish private practitioners complained that the Seven Crowns reform entailed "the total socialization of Swedish health care overnight, through changed employment conditions for hospital doctors and the economic freezing-out of private practitioners."[36] Like French and Swiss doctors, the Swedish private practitioners viewed market autonomy as the key to professional freedom.

Indeed, Swedish doctors attacked the medical association leadership for not protesting more forcefully against the Seven Crowns reform. The association might have been able to organize a strike or some other economic action against the reform. In the past, economic protests had been quite successful. Thus Swedish medical opinions did not differ radically from those in other countries, nor did the medical association seem incapable of collective action.[37]

The striking difference between the Swedish medical profession and the others lay in its strategic political position. While strikes had indeed been effective in the past, for example in increasing doctors' fees, these victories were short-lived. After each successful strike, the government took a *political* step to constrain the private market, such as removing private beds from public hospitals or eliminating the fee system entirely, as under the Seven Crowns reform. Despite membership protests, the leadership of the Swedish Medical Association argued that it was "stuck" in a situation where it was difficult to bargain with resolution and strength.[38] Not only did the Social Democratic government hold the parliamentary votes that would ensure passage of the legislation, but like the de Gaulle government, it buttressed its reform by changing market incentives to both doctors and patients. In France the individual contract had assured the widespread acceptance of the negotiated fee schedules by making it much cheaper for patients to go to the doctors that agreed to lower their fees, thereby breaking the French doctors' strike. In Sweden the Seven Crowns reform made private office practice less attractive to patients, because hospital outpatient care was now virtually free, whereas in private offices patients were required to pay the full fee and were later reimbursed for a portion of the fee. This would make it difficult for doctors wishing to protest the Seven Crowns reform to flee to the private sector.

Thus the idea that doctors can block any reform by going on strike appears to be a myth. In economic conflicts the government can use political means to change the terms of the conflict. And we might note that the medical association that received the greatest concessions from the government, the Swiss doctors, never went on strike and seems to have profited both from the electoral reactions to health insurance referenda and the fears of policy-makers that it might launch a referendum. In Sweden the Social Democratic government was able to convert its electoral gains into concrete policy decisions because political bargains worked out within Royal Commissions were enforced by stable parliamentary majorities, which closed off veto opportunities for dissident groups. Only when electoral realignments provided a strategic opportunity for veto did interest groups defect from this game of cooperative bargaining.

CONCLUSIONS

In studying these episodes of reform, one reaches the conclusion that the medical profession has had less impact on health policy than is generally believed to be the case. To the extent that it has an impact, this has been caused by opportunities presented by different political systems, and not by differences in medical organizations or differences in medical licensing and market monopoly. Veto opportunities allow political decisions to be overturned at different stages in the policy process. This has provided interest groups with different routes of political influence in the three systems. In Sweden decisions were made in the executive arena, through a consensual process that depended on majority rule. In France decisions during the Fourth Republic were made in the Parliament, where groups with ties to swing voters were sufficient to veto decisions. When the constitution of the Fifth Republic allowed the executive to circumvent the Parliament, this veto power was eliminated. In Switzerland the ability to veto decisions by calling for referenda allowed opposed interest groups to threaten credibly to veto health insurance legislation. Thus it is not the preferences of the profession that have shaped the health systems, but the preferences of a wide variety of groups and strata of the electorate as they are channeled through political processes that are differentially sensitive to these pressures.

Constitutional rules and electoral results set distinct limits on the ability of executive governments to introduce reforms. These barriers, in turn, served as useful tools for interest groups that wished to block legislation or that were willing to threaten to stop the process unless their demands were met. Consequently the peculiarities of these institutional mechanisms changed the array of relevant political actors and the implicit decision rules in each case (see Figure 3.2). The Swiss referendum allowed even very small groups to veto legislation unilaterally; this allowed such groups to resist pressures for interest aggregation, and unanimity was imposed as the decision rule. In France opportunities for parliamentary concessions privileged those groups central to the coalitions: Catholic unions, doctors, small businessmen. By contrast, direct executive rule privileged unions at the Liberation, industrialists in the Fifth Republic. In Sweden executive decision-making privileged the large producer organizations, who alone needed to agree for a majority decision to be made and to be enforced. This system of open but narrow channels of access to the state encouraged aggregation of interests and the massive organization-building known as Organization Sweden.

In each case, distinctive patterns of policy-making emerged as politicians and interest groups strove to use the institutional mechanisms in each system. By making some courses of action more difficult and facilitating others, the institutions redefined the political alternatives and changed the array of relevant actors. The institutions, in other words, established a strategic context for the actions of these political actors that changed the outcome of specific policy conflicts. This view of institutions breaks with a tradition in institutional analysis. Some of the most compelling arguments about institutions have viewed institutions as an independent variable. For example, electoral laws predict levels of voter turnout; corporatist institutions predict levels of inflation, economic growth, and citizen unruliness.[39]

	Arena	Actors	Decision
Sweden	Executive	LO, SAF, TCO	Majority Rule
France IV Republic	Parliament (unstable coalitions)	CFTC, CGC, CGMPE, CNPF, CSMF	Hierarchy/ Privilege (degree to which group is critical to regime)
V Republic (Liberation)	Executive (rule by decree)	CNPF (unions at Liberation)	
Switzerland	Electorate (Referendum)	SÄV, SAV, SGV, SBV, chiropractors (if willing to veto, potentially sickness funds, unions, and employee associations)	Unanimity

Figure 3.2. Arenas, actors, and decision rules. *Sweden:* LO, Landsorganisationen i Sverige (Swedish Trade Union Confederation); SAF, Sveriges Arbetsgivarförening (Swedish Employer Association); TCO, Tjänstemännens Centralorganisation (Swedish White-Collar Employees [and Managers] Central Organization). *France:* CFTC, Confédération Française des Travailleurs Chrétiens (French Confederation of Christian Workers); CGC, Confédération Générale des Cadres (French Union of White-Collar Employees [and Managers]); CGPME, Confédération Générale des Petites et Moyennes Entreprises ([French] General Confederation of Small and Medium Enterprises); CNPF, Conseil National du Patronat Français (National Council of French Employers); CSMF, Confédération des Syndicats Médicaux Française (Confederation of French Medical Unions). *Switzerland:* SAV, Schweizerischer Arbeitgeberverein, also called Zentralverband Schweizerischer Arbeitgeber-Organisationen (the Swiss Employers' Association); SÄV, Schweizerischer Ärzteverein (Swiss Medical Association), or Verbindung der Schweizer Ärzte; SBV, Schweizerischer Bauernverein (Swiss Farmers' Association); SGV, Schweizerischer Gewerbeverein (Swiss Artisans' Association).

This essay, by contrast, relies on a two-step causal model. It makes a clear distinction between political actors and their strategies versus the institutional frameworks within which this action takes place. The actors formulate their goals, ideas, and desires independently from the institutions. The institutions become relevant only in strategic calculations about the best way to advance a given interest within a particular system. Over time, there may of course be some spillover – if a particular goal is unachievable, it may after a while be dropped. But at a given point in time, the model presented here does not depend on actors socialized by institutions to restrict their goals or interests.

The origins of the institutions, as well, are chronologically independent from the actors and their strategies. That is, institutions are most certainly created by social actors engaged in a struggle for political power. However, the actors that participated in the battles over institutional design are not necessarily, and in fact only rarely, identical to those that participate in later policy conflicts. Thus the view that institutions are somehow congealed social structure is not especially helpful. To understand the impact of institutions on contemporary policy conflicts, one must analyze the incentives, opportunities, and constraints that institutions provide to the current participants.

Within these institutions, more than one course of action was possible; the unfolding of events depended as much on historical accident and the inventiveness of these actors as on the institutional constraints. Moreover, these actors often made mistakes. The institutions tell us what courses of action are likely to bring success or failure, but they do not predict the final choices made by these actors. Thus the social logic of history is not to be replaced by a new efficiency of history based on political institutions.

Political institutions can be thought of as the outermost frame for political conflicts. The institutions help to define the terms of these conflicts by shaping the practical meaning of political power and providing the basis for developing the rules of thumb of political strategy. The institutions explain many aspects of the life within them – the types of interest organizations that will be successful, the pressures to consolidate interests, the usefulness of membership mobilization, and the degree to which cooperation versus defection is likely to be a fruitful strategy. But the interests, strategies, and resources of political actors cannot explain the institutions, so I prefer to start thinking about politics with the institutions. But no view of politics can rely exclusively on either institutions, on the one hand, or interests and actors, on the other; both components are necessary to our understandings of the past and to our role as the subjects of the future.

NOTES

1 For reviews of theories of professional power see Andrew Abbott, *The System of the Professions. An Essay on the Division of Expert Labor* (Chicago: The University of Chicago Press, 1988); Jeffrey Berlant, *Profession and Monopoly: A Study of Medicine in the United States and Great Britain* (Berkeley: University of California Press, 1975); Giorgio Freddi and James Warner Björkman, eds., *Controlling Medical Professionals: The Comparative Politics of Health Governance* (Newbury Park, Calif.: Sage Publications, 1989); Eliot Freidson, *Profession of Medicine: A Study of the Sociology of Applied Knowledge* (New York: Dodd, Mead, 1970); Donald Light and Sol Levine,

"The Changing Character of the Medical Profession: A Theoretical Overview," *The Milbank Quarterly* 66, Suppl. 2 (1988):10–32; Theodore R. Marmor and David Thomas, "Doctors, Politics and Pay Disputes: 'Pressure Group Politics' Revisited," *British Journal of Political Science* 2 (1972):421–42; Magali Sarfatti Larson, *The Rise of Professionalism. A Sociological Analysis* (Berkeley: University of California Press, 1977); Paul Starr, *The Social Transformation of American Medicine* (New York: Basic Books, 1982); Deborah A. Stone, *The Limits of Professional Power* (Chicago: Chicago University Press, 1980).

2 Legal monopoly of medical practice, supervised by government bureaucracies, and including penalties for unlicensed practice was established in Sweden in 1663, and in France in 1892. Coordination of cantonal licensing requirements was established in Switzerland in 1867, but not all cantons participated, no bureaucracy controlled the numbers of physicians and no sanctions were in place for unlicensed practitioners. Several cantons used the institutions of direct democracy to introduce legislation allowing unlicensed practice. Consequently medical monopoly was not firmly established until the 1920s, when two cantons revoked legislation permitting unlicensed practice, and when the Swiss Medical Association became a more effective licensing body. Entry barriers to practice remained lowest in Switzerland, as evidenced both by weaker laws and by the resulting high numbers of doctors. On Switzerland and France, Matthew Ramsey, "The Politics of Professional Monopoly in Nineteenth-Century Medicine: The French Model and Its Rivals," in Gerald L. Geison, ed., *Professions and the French State* (Philadelphia: University of Pennsylvania Press, 1984), pp. 225–305; on France, Monika Steffen, "The Medical Profession and the State in France," *Journal of Public Policy*, 7, no. 2 (1987):189–208; on Sweden, Peter Garpenby, *The State and the Medical Profession. A Cross-National Comparison of the Health Policy Arena in the United Kingdom and Sweden 1945–1985* (Linköping: Linköping Studies in Arts and Sciences, 1989). For more discussion of these issues, as well as the case studies, see my book, *Health Politics: Interests and Institutions in Western Europe* (Cambridge: Cambridge University Press, 1992).

3 The figures were originally cited as inhabitants per doctor, that is, 1,120 in Sweden, 940 in France, and 710 in Switzerland, in James Hogarth, *The Payment of the Physician. Some European Comparisons* (New York: Macmillan, Pergamon Press, 1963), pp. 60, 139, 281.

4 William A. Glaser, *Paying the Doctor: Systems of Remuneration and Their Effects* (Baltimore: Johns Hopkins Press, 1970); Gerhard Kocher, *Verbandseinfluss auf die Gesetzgebung. Aerzteverbindung, Krankenkassenverbände und die Teilrevision 1964 des Kranken- und Unfallversicherungsgesetzes*, 2d ed. (Bern: Francke Verlag, 1972); *Läkartidningen* (Journal of the Swedish Medical Association) 1978: 1986–2000; Roland Mane, "Où va le syndicalisme médical?" *Droit Social* 25, (1962):516–29; Jean Savatier, "Une Profession libérale face au mouvement contemporain de socialisation," *Droit Social*, 25 (1962):477–9. Jean-Claude Stephan, *Economie et Pouvoir Médical* (Paris: Economica, 1978), pp. 38–9.

5 This is the argument made by Harry Eckstein in *Pressure Group Politics: The Case of the British Medical Association* (London: Allen and Unwin, 1960). See also Arnold J. Heidenheimer, "Conflict and Compromise between Professional and Bureaucratic Health Interests. 1947–1972," in Arnold J. Heidenheimer and Nils Elvander, eds., *The Shaping of the Swedish Health System* (London: Croom Helm, 1980), pp. 119–42; J. Rogers Hollingsworth, *A Political Economy of Medicine: Great Britain and the United States* (Baltimore: Johns Hopkins University Press, 1986); Rudolf Klein, "Ideology, Class and the National Health Service," *Journal of Health Politics, Policy and Law* 4 (1979):484; Stone, *Limits of Professional Power*.

6 Kenneth A. Shepsle, "Institutional Equilibrium and Equilibrium Institutions," in Herbert Weisberg, ed., *Political Science: the Science of Politics* (New York: Agathon, 1986), pp. 51–81; T. H. Hammond and G. J. Miller, "The Core of the Constitution," *American Political Science Review* 81, (1987):1155–73; Kenneth A. Shepsle and Barry R. Weingast, "The Institutional Foundations of Committee Power," *American Political Science Review* 81 (1987):85–104. On decision rules, see Fritz W. Scharpf, "Decision Rules, Decision Styles, and Policy Choices," *Journal of Theoretical Politics* 1 (1989):149–76. On political logics, Douglas E. Ashford, "The British and French Social Security Systems: Welfare State by Intent and by Default," in Douglas E. Ashford and E. W. Kelley, eds., *Nationalizing Social Security* (Greenwich, Conn.: JAI Press, 1986), pp. 96–122.

7 Duncan MacRae, *Parliament, Parties and Society in France, 1946–1958* (New York: St. Martin's Press, 1967); Maurice Duverger, *Institutions politiques et droit constitutionnel.* Vol. 2. *Le système politique français* (Paris: Presses Universitaires de France, 1976); Henry Ehrmann, *Politics in France,* 3d ed. (Boston: Little, Brown, 1976), pp. 298–9.

8 Ehrmann, *Politics in France,* pp. 194, 196–7.

9 Pierre Birnbaum, *Les Sommets de l'Etat* (Paris: Editions du Seuil, 1977), pp. 50, 71.

10 Pierre Laroque, "La Sécurité Sociale de 1944 à 1951," *Revue Française des Affaires Sociales* 25, no. 2 (April–June 1971):11–25.

11 Henry C. Galant, *Histoire Politique de la Sécurité Sociale Française, 1945–1952.* Cahiers de la Fondation Nationale des Sciences Politiques No. 76 (Paris: Librairie Armand Colin, 1955).

12 Henri Hatzfeld, *Le Grand Tournant de la Médecine Libérale* (Paris: Les Editions Ouvrières, 1963), pp. 78–103; *Revue de la Sécurité Sociale* (Journal of the health and social security funds), March 1957, pp. 9–12; interview, Clément Michel, ex-director of the FNOSS, June 7, 1984.

13 Jean Imbert, "La réforme hospitalière," *Droit Social* 21, no. 9–10 (Sept.–Oct. 1958):496–505.

14 Haroun Jamous, *Sociologie de la Décision: la réforme des études médicales et des structures hospitalières* (Paris: Editions du Centre Nationale de la Recherche Scientifique, 1969).

15 Archives Nationales. Direction de la Sécurité Sociale. Ministère des Affaires Sociales et de la Santé. "Travaux préparatoire à la réforme de la Sécurité Sociale de 1960," SAN 7515, Feb. 24, 1960.

16 *Le Monde,* May 19, 1960, May 21, 1960; Jacques Doublet, "La Sécurité Sociale et son évolution [octobre 1951–juin 1961]," *Revue Française des Affaires Sociales* 25, no. 2 (April–June 1971):41.

17 Archives, SAN 7517 on position of CGT; cf. *Droit Social,* no. 3 (March 1960):179, and no. 4 (April 1960):242 for other union opinions. Doublet, *Sécurité Sociale,* pp. 41–2 for details on the special service.

18 J. F. Aubert, "Switzerland," in D. Butler and A. Ranney, eds., *"Referendums." A Comparative Study of Practice and Theory* (Washington, D.C.: American Enterprise Institute for Public Policy Research, 1978), pp. 46, 48–9.

19 Schweizerische Gesellschaft für Praktische Sozialforschung (GFS) "Analyse der eidgenössichen Abstimmung vom 6. Dezember 1987," GFS Publications 12, no. 34 (March 1988).

20 Aubert, "Switzerland"; Christopher Hughes, *The Parliament of Switzerland* (London: Cassell, 1962); Alfred Maurer, "Switzerland," in Peter A. Köhler and Hans F. Zacher, eds., *The Evolution of Social Insurance. 1881–1981. Studies of Germany, France, Great Britain, Austria and Switzerland* (London: Frances Pinter; New York:

St. Martin's Press, 1982), pp. 384–453; Leonhard Neidhart, *Plebiszit und pluralitäre Demokratie. Eine Analyse der Funktion der Schweizerischen Gesetzreferendums* (Bern: Francke Verlag, 1970).

21 Aubert, "Switzerland," pp. 48–9.

22 *Konkordat der schweizerischen Krankenkassen, Tätigkeitsbericht* (Concordat of Sickness Funds, annual report), 1958–1960 (Solothurn: Konkordat, 1960), p. 47.

23 "Botschaft des Bundesrates an die Bundesversammlung zum Entwurf eines Bundesgesetzes betreffend die Änderung des Ersten Titels des Bundesgesetzes über die Kranken- und Unfallversicherung (vom 5. Juni 1961)," *Bundesblatt* (Swiss Federal Government Proceedings) 113, no. 25, I (1961):1418.

24 Department of Social Insurance cited in Neidhart, *Plebiszit und pluralitäre Demokratie*, p. 337.

25 Cited in *Amtliches Stenographisches Bulletin der schweizerischen Bundesversammlung. Ständerat* (Parliamentary debates of States' Council). *Stenbull SR* (1962): 119.

26 Kocher, *Verbandseinfluss auf die Gesetzgebung*, p. 147.

27 Obrecht, *Stenbull SR*, 1963, p. 104.

28 Hänggi, March 24, 1964, cited in Kocher, *Verbandseinfluss auf die Gesetzgebung*, p. 131.

29 Gunnar Hesslén, "Det Svenska Kommittéväsendet intill år 1905. Dess uppkomst, ställning och betydelse," unpublished Ph.D. dissertation, filosofiska fakultetet i Uppsala humanistiska sektion, Uppsala. 1927, pp. 357, 360, 377; Steven Kelman, *Regulating America, Regulating Sweden: A Comparative Study of Occupational Safety and Health Policy* (Cambridge, Mass.: MIT Press, 1981), pp. 131–2; Hugh Heclo and Henrik Madsen, *Policy and Politics in Sweden: Principled Pragmatism* (Philadelphia: Temple University Press, 1987).

30 Olle Nyman, *Svensk Parlamentarism 1932–1936. Från Minoritetsparlamentarism till majoritetskoalition*, Skrifter Utgivna av Statsvetenskapliga Föreningen i Uppsala genom Axel Brusewitz No. 27 (Uppsala: Almqvist and Wicksell, 1947); on role of First Chamber, Douglas V. Verney, *Parliamentary Reform in Sweden, 1866–1921* (Oxford: Clarendon Press, 1957), p. 217.

31 MacRae, *Parliament, Parties and Society in France*.

32 *Svenska Dagbladet*. Swedish Conservative newspaper *(SvD)*, March 10, 1948, pp. 3–4.

33 Anita Jarild Ög, "Diskussion kring Medicinalstyrelsens betänkande, 'Den öppna läkarvården i riket,' " unpublished paper from the pro-seminar in Political Science, Uppsala University, 1962, p. 10.

34 Nils Elvander, *Svensk Skattepolitik 1945–1970. En Studie i partiers och organisationers funktioner* (Stockholm: Rabén och Sjögren, 1972).

35 *Riksdagens Protokoll FK* (Parliamentary debates of the First Chamber), *39* (1969), p. 72.

36 Gunnar Biörck, *SvD*, Nov. 17, 1969, p. 4.

37 For a fuller discussion and alternative interpretations on this point see Mack Carder, and Bendix Klingeberg, "Towards a Salaried Medical Profession: How Swedish was the Seven Crowns Reform?" in Arnold J. Heidenheimer and Nils Elvander, eds., *The Shaping of the Swedish Health System* (London: Croom Helm, 1980), pp. 143–72; Arnold J. Heidenheimer, "Conflict and Compromise between Professional and Bureaucratic Health Interests. 1947–1972," in Heidenheimer and Elvander, pp. 119–42.

38 *Läkartidningen*, November 5, 1969, pp. 4625–8, November 19, 1969, p. 4826, Dec. 1969, p. 4964; cf. Carder and Klingeberg, "Towards a Salaried Medical Profession."

39 I am thankful to Fritz Scharpf for this point, including these examples. For his discussion of the issues of strategy and institutional constraints, see Fritz W. Scharpf, *Crisis and Choice in European Social Democracy,* trans. Ruth Crowley and Fred Thompson (Ithaca, N.Y.: Cornell University Press, 1991), pp. 7–14.

4

The movement from Keynesianism to monetarism: Institutional analysis and British economic policy in the 1970s

PETER A. HALL

The 1970s witnessed a revolution in British economic policy. When the decade began, Britain was the paradigmatic case of what has often been termed the Keynesian era.[1] By the 1980s Britain was leading again but in a different direction. Under Prime Minister Margaret Thatcher, monetarist modes of economic policy-making replaced their Keynesian antecedents. How are we to explain this change in direction? That is the empirical question to which this chapter is addressed.

For those who are interested in the role of institutions in political life, the evolution of British economic policy during the 1970s also poses an important set of theoretical challenges. First, it invites us to explore the relationship between institutions and political change. Institutions are usually associated with continuity: They are by nature inertial and linked to regularities in human behavior. As a result political analysts have been able to demonstrate how national institutions impose a measure of continuity on policy over time.[2] However, macroeconomic policy-making in Britain is a case of change, even radical change, in policy. We can use it to examine what role, if any, institutions play in the process whereby policies change. The question is whether institutional factors contribute to the explanation of change as well as continuity.

The shift from Keynesian to monetarist modes of policy-making also provides an appropriate case for the kind of analysis we associate with historical institutionalism. As most of the essays in this volume indicate, those who approach the world from the standpoint of historical institutionalism accord prominence to the role of institutions in political life, but they are not concerned with institutions alone. Rather, their analyses explore the role of several variables – often encapsulated as institutions, interests, and ideas – in the determination of political

For comments on drafts of this chapter, I am grateful to the participants in the Boulder conference and especially Douglas Ashford, Peter Katzenstein, Peter Lange, Frank Longstreth, Theda Skocpol, Sven Steinmo, and Kathy Thelen as well as Judith Goldstein, Geoffrey Garrett, and Rosemary Taylor. For research support, I would like to thank the German Marshall Fund.

outcomes.[3] The extended process whereby Britain moved from Keynesian to monetarist policies involved underlying changes in the world economy, a clash between social and political interests, and a contest between competing interpretations of the economy. Therefore, by examining it we can situate the impact of institutions within a broader matrix of competing interests and ideas as well.

Within this matrix, institutions interact with interests and ideas in a variety of ways. By providing routines linked to processes of socialization and incentives for certain kinds of behavior, they contribute to the very terms in which the interests of critical political actors are constructed. By making organized activity and the expression of political views more or less viable for certain groups, they affect the power with which the interests of key social groups are pressed. In many instances the routines that have been institutionalized into the policy process filter new information, affecting the force with which new ideas can be expressed. In some cases institutions act as vehicles for individual or collective intentions. In other cases they alter behavior in such a way as to produce wholly unintended consequences of considerable moment for a nation. As we shall see, the institutions associated with economic policy-making in Britain did not fully determine any of the outcomes of interest to us here, but they structured the flow of ideas and the clash of interests in ways that had a significant impact on these outcomes.

THE COURSE OF BRITISH POLICY

In broad terms the evolution of British policy in the two decades following 1970 is clear. It is well represented by the differences between the economic policies that the Thatcher government pursued during the early 1980s and those to which preceding governments had adhered with little interruption since the Second World War.[4] Under Thatcher inflation replaced unemployment as the central target of macroeconomic policy. Her government rejected reliance on an active fiscal policy in favor of efforts to secure balanced budgets. Monetary policy, once seen as subsidiary, became the principal instrument of macroeconomic management and was oriented, initially at least, to the rate of growth of the money supply. The Thatcher government discontinued the incomes policies that had been a long-standing feature of British policy and, after thirty-five years of rising public expenditure and taxation, it sought lower levels of both.[5]

In large measure these changes represented a revolution in ideas that is best captured in terms of the concept of *policy paradigms*. In technically complex fields of policy, such as that of macroeconomic policy-making, decision-makers are often guided by an overarching set of ideas that specify how the problems facing them are to be perceived, which goals might be attained through policy and what sorts of techniques can be used to reach those goals. Ideas about each of these matters interlock to form a relatively coherent whole that might be described as a policy paradigm. Like a gestalt, it structures the very way in which policy-makers see the world and their role within it.[6]

The economic doctrines associated with Keynesianism and monetarism are ideal examples of this sort of policy paradigm. Each is based on a fundamentally different model of the economy. After all, the economy is simply a set of human relationships and material flows that cannot be perceived by the naked eye. It must be interpreted or modeled to be understood, and from divergent models flow different prescriptions for policy. Thus the discrepancies to be found between the policy recommendations of Keynesians and monetarists were not simply incidental. They derived from very different conceptions of how the economy worked.

Keynesians tended to regard the private economy as unstable and in need of government intervention; monetarists saw the private economy as basically stable and government intervention as likely to do more harm than good. Keynesians saw unemployment as a problem of insufficient aggregate demand, while monetarists believed that a "natural" rate of unemployment was fixed by structural conditions in the labor market that would be relatively impervious to reflationary policy. Keynesians regarded inflation as a problem arising from excess demand or undue wage pressures that might be addressed by an incomes policy; monetarists argued that inflation was invariably a monetary phenomenon containable only by controlling the money supply.[7]

In the 1970s and 1980s, then, Britain witnessed a shift in the basic policy paradigm guiding economic management. Thatcher's policies were not simply ad hoc adjustments to pieces of policy; they were rooted in a coherent vision associated with monetarist economics. Today mainstream economics has synthesized portions of both the monetarist and Keynesian paradigms. In the 1970s, however, two competing doctrines contended for control over British policy, and the monetarist paradigm emerged victorious.

If we are going to trace the impact of institutions on this revolution, however, we must do more than note that it took place. For our purposes the precise trajectory of British policy is also important and can best be understood as a series of stages. In particular, although the basic paradigm guiding policy changed only in 1979 with the election of the first Thatcher government, several steps in a monetarist direction were taken by the preceding Labour government during 1976 to 1979.

The economic policies of the 1970–4 Conservative government under Edward Heath might well be seen as the starting point of the British journey toward monetarism. They represent the high-water mark of Keynesian policy-making. Although Heath was elected on a platform that promised reductions in public spending, lower levels of government involvement in the economy, and movement toward greater market competition, his government responded to rising levels of unemployment and inflation during 1971–2 in classic Keynesian manner with substantial increases in public spending, a relaxed monetary policy, a statutory incomes policy, and massive industrial subsidies.[8] In short, Heath's initial effort to break with the Keynesian formula ended in an abrupt about-turn back toward it.

The opening years of a new Labour government elected in 1974 under Harold Wilson mark a second stage in the evolution of British policy. The Labour government arrived in office just in time to greet rising levels of inflation and economic stagnation associated with the oil price shock of 1973–4. It responded by pumping money into the economy to counteract the effects of recession in the hope that the trade unions would adhere to a voluntary incomes policy.[9] In short, the initial response of the British authorities to the economic shocks of the mid-1970s was highly Keynesian.

In 1976, however, British economic policy turned in a monetarist direction. As early as October 1976, the new Labour prime minister, James Callaghan, broke with postwar tradition to tell his party conference that a fiscal stimulus could no longer be used to counteract rising levels of unemployment. Within a year, monetary targets had assumed considerable importance in economic policy-making and the government had embarked on the deepest cuts in public expenditure ever accomplished in postwar Britain. In short, British policy changed to a significant degree even before Thatcher took office. However, as some commentators put it, the policy-makers of 1976–78 were at best "unbelieving monetarists."[10] They pushed policy in a monetarist direction unenthusiastically and without fully renouncing the Keynesian principles on which the postwar consensus had been based.

The full renunciation came in 1979 when a Conservative government under Margaret Thatcher was elected and began to put a full-blown monetarist program into operation. This is the last stage of the policy evolution examined here, although, as the 1980s progressed, monetarist policies themselves underwent another process of change.

In some respects these changes in British policy paralleled those adopted elsewhere in the world. By the end of the 1980s many governments had become hesitant about Keynesian reflation and more interested in controlling the monetary aggregates, reducing taxation and expenditure, and expanding the role of market mechanisms in the allocation of resources. However, several features of the British case were distinctive and especially worthy of explanation. Not only did the shift from Keynesian to monetarist modes of policy-making follow a particular trajectory in Britain, it also came relatively early and in an unusually abrupt and radical fashion. Other nations tended to follow the British lead hesitantly and in a more piecemeal way. In most cases their governments altered some dimensions of policy but left others intact. Few embraced the monetarist program with the fire or coherence of the Thatcher government.[11]

INSTITUTIONS, IDEAS, AND INTERESTS

The dynamic whereby Britain moved from Keynesian to monetarist policies was a complex one in which institutions, interests, and ideas all played significant roles. Before turning to the impact of institutions, which is the principal concern of this essay, a brief look at the other components of the process is in order.

Economic developments

Two economic developments, experienced by most nations but especially intensely by Britain, had a significant causal impact on the movement toward monetarism. The first was the substantial acceleration of inflation that the world witnessed in the 1970s. British inflation rose dramatically to peak at 25 percent annually in the spring of 1975. The second was the general stagnation of economic production accompanied by rising rates of unemployment that Britain experienced in common with most of the industrialized world after the oil and commodity price increases of 1973–4. The origins of these developments are a matter of controversy but, whatever the causes, the results were clear. British economic performance deteriorated sharply during the 1970s.[12]

In significant measure, the move toward monetarism was a response to the persistently poor performance of the economy during the 1970s and the apparent inability of Keynesian policies to rectify the situation. As is often the case, disillusionment with the results of past policy set in motion a search for alternatives.

However, economic developments alone do not explain why Britain settled on monetarism as an alternative, nor do they explain the more particular trajectory of British policy. There was no one-to-one correlation between economic change and policy response. Britain's initial response to rising levels of inflation and unemployment was decidedly Keynesian. Policy turned in a monetarist direction only after a substantial time lag. Moreover, cross-national evidence suggests that monetarism, of the sort pursued in Britain, was not the only possible response to the economic difficulties of the 1970s. Many other nations reacted to similar problems with quite different policies. Therefore an adequate explanation for the course of British policy must contain some additional variables.

Contending social interests

Like most kinds of policy, a macroeconomic strategy tends to favor the material interests of some social groups to the disadvantage of others. Although both have some generalized merit, Keynesian and monetarist policies are not exceptions to this rule. Perceiving this, the organizational representatives of the working class generally argued for Keynesian policies during the 1970s, while the spokesmen for capital leaned more strongly toward monetarism. Among the segments of British capital, those in the financial community tended to favor monetarist policies more than did many industrialists. Within the labor movement, public sector employees tended to resist the monetarist program more forcefully than did workers in the private sector.

To neglect the conflicts of material interest at stake in the promulgation of a policy is invariably a mistake, even when these are not an apparent component of the policy process. Even when hidden or highly mediated, the struggle for power and resources is invariably a critical part of the framework in which politics is conducted.[13] As we shall see, the distribution of power among broad social groups with divergent interests became a factor in the movement from Keynesianism to monetarism at several points. In particular, the initial steps toward monetarism were precipitated by a shift in the relative power of organized labor and finance capital over policy-making during the 1970s; and the penultimate step toward full-blown monetarism was made possible by a bitter electoral contest for the support of key social groups, in which the Conservatives drew significant segments of the working class away from the social coalition behind Labour.[14] In recent years it has become clear that the movement from Keynesianism to monetarism in Britain ultimately involved a broader series of conflicts among segments of the working class and capital from which clear winners and losers emerged.[15]

However, here as elsewhere, those conflicts were mediated in a significant way by political and economic institutions that channeled contention in certain directions, privileged some actors at the expense of others, and profoundly affected the balance of power at any one time. If monetarism could well be said to represent the victory of some groups over others in British society, the process whereby monetarist policies replaced Keynesian ones cannot be seen exclusively in these terms. The institutions of the British policy process shaped both the terms in which the contending groups would see their interests and the relative power with which the latter would be pursued.

The flow of ideas

The shift from Keynesian to monetarist modes of policy-making is ultimately a story about the movement of ideas, as the concept of competing policy paradigms underscores. The availability and appeal of monetarist ideas was central to the direction of change in British macroeconomic policy. As the problems of inflation and unemployment proved persistent in the face of Keynesian prescriptions, policy-makers naturally began a search for alternative solutions; and, among the proffered alternatives, monetarist doctrine displayed special merits. In particular, it spoke directly to the problem of inflation, which was coming to preoccupy the British, at a point when Keynesian solutions seemed increasingly unwieldy and more focused on issues of unemployment.

However, the evolution in British policy was not primarily the result of changing views among economists. Because the Keynesian and monetarist policy paradigms turned on highly divergent views of the economy, it was very difficult to secure definitive evidence for the superiority of one over the other in the terms of economic science. As a result, in the 1970s and early 1980s when British policy turned toward monetarism, the vast majority of British economists, both inside and outside the civil service, remained resolutely Keynesian.[16] In this case the movement of policy preceded, rather than followed, the weight of professional opinion. Under Thatcher the Conservatives took up the monetarist case as much for political, as economic, reasons and then imposed monetarist policies on a rather reluctant set of economic officials.

As in so many other cases, the influence of the new ideas in this case depended heavily on the circumstances of the day, some economic but others highly political and all conditioned by the institutional framework within which policy was made and power over policy acquired. The mere existence of monetarist ideas did not ensure that they would be accepted by policy-makers. The problem is to explain why those ideas, rather than others, were taken up by key actors and why those actors, rather than others, were able to secure influence over policy.[17]

Institutional factors

The central concern of this essay is the role that the institutional context of policy-making played in the evolution of British policy. How should we conceptualize the institutional setting in which British economic policy has been made? The concept of institutions is used here to refer to the formal rules, compliance procedures, and customary practices that structure the relationships between individuals in the polity and economy. Institutions may be more or less formal but invariably serve to regularize the behavior of the individuals who operate within them.[18]

With regard to the direction of British economic policy and the distribution of power in the political economy, it may be useful to think in terms of three levels of institutions, each with a particular impact on these outcomes.

1. At an overarching level, the basic organizational structures we associate with a democratic polity and a capitalist economy can be said to contribute to the general balance of power between labor and capital and to militate in favor of some lines of policy over others. Notable at this level are the constitutional provisions for regular elections and economic institutions that leave the ownership of the means of production in private hands. The impact of this overarching structural framework on economic policy has been explored by a variety of scholars.[19] It tends to impose very broad constraints on the direction of policy.

2. At one level down, a number of features intrinsic to the basic organization of the state and society in each nation might also be said to affect the distribution of power among social groups and the kinds of policies that can be formulated or implemented most readily. At this level we see more variation across nations; and an important body of literature associates these institutional differences with divergent patterns of economic policy. Institutional features relevant at this level might include the structure of the trade union movement (including its degree of density, concentration, and centralization), the organization of capital (including

its managerial forms, the nature of employer organization, the relationship among segments of capital, and the way in which they are inserted into the international economy), the nature of the political system and the structure of the state (including the nature of the party system, the administrative division of responsibility within the state, and its receptivity to external advice).[20]

3. Although not always as sharply delimited as the preceding factors, the standard operating procedures, regulations, and routines of public agencies and organizations should also be seen as institutional factors of some importance for policy outcomes. Some of these may be relatively formal, others more informal but no less potent. As a group, institutional factors of this sort are more mutable than those at the preceding levels: A regulation is changed more readily than a regime. However, routines and regulations of this sort are far from transitory. They can privilege some kinds of initiatives or the interests of some social groups over others with great consequences for the distribution of power and the direction of policy.[21]

THE PROGRESS OF POLICY

Policy under the Heath government, 1970–4

Although it is unconventional to open an account of the turn toward monetarism with the policies of the 1970–4 Heath government, the latter provide a basepoint that can tell us a great deal about the importance of the changes that were to follow. Here is a case of the dog that didn't bark. Many of Heath's objectives were similar to those that Thatcher would pursue ten years later. His electoral platform emphasized the importance of lowering taxes, reducing public spending, reviving market competition, and limiting state intervention in the economy. Confronted with rising levels of unemployment and inflation, however, Heath backed away from each of these objectives toward a traditional Keynesian reflation.[22] The contrast with the first Thatcher government is striking. In the face of an even deeper recession, Thatcher refused to alter the course of a highly deflationary monetarist program.

How can we account for the different behavior of the two governments? Some say that Thatcher was simply more determined. She was a self-confessed "conviction" politician, but Heath was also justly known as a highly stubborn political leader. It is significant that Thatcher's term in office followed the years of Heath government: Her behavior was clearly influenced by the negative lessons conventionally drawn from Heath's about-turn. Of potentially even greater importance, however, was the state of the monetarist paradigm when Thatcher came to office. By 1979 it was a fully elaborated alternative to the reigning Keynesian paradigm with a significant base of institutional support in the City, among economists at several universities, and in the media. Thatcher was able to resist massive pressure from inside and outside the government to reverse the course of policy in 1980–81 in large measure because she could draw on the monetarist paradigm to explain what others saw as unanticipated events and to rationalize her resistance to demands for change.

By contrast, when faced with similar pressure to alter his initial policy positions, Heath had no conceptual framework with equivalent coherence or institutional support on which to base his resistance to demands for a reversal of course. Monetarist ideas enjoyed some currency among American and British economists in the early 1970s, but they had no substantial base of institutional support within the British policy-making system. Although many elements of the Heath program resembled those later pursued by Thatcher, the former were simply a loose collection of aspirations formulated in a relatively ad hoc fashion, lacking the coherent backing provided by a full-fledged policy paradigm. As a result, when Heath encountered unexpected economic developments that seemed to dictate a change in policy, he had nothing to fall back on for guidance other than the one policy paradigm already institutionalized in the policy process, namely the Keynesian paradigm. In the face of rising unemployment and inflation, it dictated reflation and an incomes policy, which the government accordingly pursued.

It is notable how deeply the Keynesian paradigm had been institutionalized in the British policy process by the early 1970s. The structure of British government lent itself to the institutionalization of a particular policy paradigm. In contrast to the American polity, where many different agencies have a voice in a policy process that is highly permeable to multiple sources of outside advice, the British system vested a few senior civil servants in the Treasury with a virtual monopoly over authoritative economic advice. A small, hierarchical organization dominated by career civil servants, the Treasury alone enjoyed access to the latest economic data and to the government's macroeconomic model on whose forecasts policy was based. By 1970 both the equation systems in the Treasury's econometric models and its standard operating procedures for formulating a budget judgment institutionalized a Keynesian view of the economy.[23] Outside the government, there were virtually no informed sources of alternative advice. The only other institution generating economic forecasts was the National Institute for Economic and Social Research and it, too, was resolutely Keynesian. Given how deeply entrenched the Keynesian paradigm was within the institutions of the British policy process, it is not surprising that the Heath government retreated toward traditional formulas shortly after taking office.

Policy in the opening years of Labour government, 1974–5

In 1974 an economic crisis, precipitated by massive oil price increases, and the election of a Labour government under Harold Wilson initiated a second stage in the evolution of British economic policy during the 1970s. How would a new government respond to a new economic crisis?

Once again the degree to which the Keynesian paradigm was institutionalized within the Treasury was central to the response. Although the oil price increases had significant wealth effects on the British economy and rising rates of inflation were altering the savings ratio and fiscal multiplier in such a way as to render the economy resistant to traditional reflation, Treasury officials had difficulty appreciating these developments. The forecasts that their econometric models generated were based on parameters derived from regressions on past data that could not reflect these more recent changes in underlying economic relationships. The seats on the train of econometric equations always face backward. Partly as a result, many Treasury officials were inclined to treat the stagnation of 1974 much as if it were a normal recession for which reflation was prescribed.[24]

Equally important at this point, however, were several institutional features of the British polity. Prominent among them was the electoral constraint. Labour had been elected with a minority government in February 1974 and another election was anticipated shortly. Therefore the government faced strong incentives to reflate by expanding spending programs tied to further electoral support. In addition, because the trade unions enjoyed a position of extraordinary institutional power within the Labour Party itself, Labour governments had difficulty imposing unwanted austerity measures on them. Those difficulties were intensified by growing union opposition to the incomes policies of the 1960s. Accordingly the 1974 Labour government had pinned its hopes for wage restraint on a nebulous Social Contract with the unions, by which the latter were supposed to practice voluntary wage restraint in exchange for favorable economic, social, and industrial relations policies. The government pursued expansive spending policies in the hope of securing union cooperation but was left defenseless when many trade unions naturally sought substantial wage increases in the face of rapidly rising inflation. A rapidly rising public sector wage bill expanded public spending even further.

As a result, public expenditure increased by 6.1 percent in volume terms during 1974–5 alone; and within two years the government had spent half again as much as its initial public spending plans projected for its entire term of office. The public sector deficit for 1974–5 exceeded all expectation, rising to almost 10 percent of gross domestic product (GDP). If we can reasonably think of each government as having a given economic increment that reflects the amount of reflation and debt-financed public spending that it can afford during its term of governance, the 1974–9 Labour government inadvertently spent the entire increment during its first year in office. This episode of profligacy set the stage for the radical changes in policy that were to come.

POLICY CHANGE IN 1976–7

In 1976 and 1977 British economic policy turned in a somewhat monetarist direction. These years mark a critical transition stage in the movement toward monetarism. On the one hand, the deep spending cuts and restrictive monetary policies of these years reflected more than the normal deflationary stance that Keynesians might be expected to adopt in such circumstances, and they were accompanied by a new concern for the rate of growth of the monetary aggregates. The policy-makers of this era admitted that they were inspired in part by disillusionment with the capacity of Keynesian techniques to cope with the problems of contemporary economic management. On the other hand, these policies did not yet represent full acceptance of the monetarist paradigm. They were ad hoc measures taken in response to the collapse of the Keynesian paradigm. Those who implemented them remained essentially Keynesian in their outlook and aspirations. Full embrace of the monetarist paradigm came only after the election of a new Conservative government in 1979.

How, then, are we to explain the about-turn that economic policy took in 1976–7? Some would attribute it to the demands of the International Monetary Fund from which Britain sought a conditional loan in the autumn of 1976; and the IMF certainly played a role in these developments.[25] However, the shift in policy began well before the IMF negotiations of autumn 1976 and continued after the government had again secured room for maneuverability in 1977–8. Even within the Labour cabinet, there was a good deal of feeling that the overspending of 1974–5 and ensuing balance-of-payment problems demanded a new round of expenditure cuts.[26]

Moreover, the austerity measures of 1976–7 soon went beyond the consensus of cautious Keynesians. A substantial number of the economic policies adopted in this period were virtually forced on the government by the financial markets. In this respect the radical change in policy that took place between 1974–5 and 1976–7 reflects a most interesting shift in the distribution of power among social forces. The expansionary policies of 1974–5 were largely a response to the power of organized labor. Consequently many commentators regard the 1970s as a decade when the trade unions gained overwhelming power in the British polity. But this is not the whole story. The power of the trade unions peaked in 1974–5. After they agreed to enforce a rigid incomes policy in the spring of 1975, the unions began to lose both their leverage over the government and their influence over the rank and file. From 1976 to 1977 it was the power of finance capital, working through the financial markets, that rose dramatically. If the early 1970s brought increases in the power of the trade unions, the second half of the decade saw an important shift of power over policy toward the financial markets.

In part the growing power of the financial markets was a direct consequence of past policy. As the expansive policies of the early 1970s propelled the public sector deficit upward, the government had to borrow more heavily from the financial markets; and its growing dependence on debt rendered the government increasingly sensitive to the views about economic policy expressed in those markets.[27] In addition, however, a series of changes in the institutional practices of the markets for government debt (the gilt markets) that happened to occur in these years substantially reinforced the power of the markets vis-à-vis the government. Here was a classic case of unintended consequences.

The relevant changes began in 1971 when the Heath government introduced a series of reforms, associated with the White Paper on Competition and Credit Control (CCC), designed to allow greater competition in the banking sector by eliminating quantitative controls on credit. Once the quantitative controls that had been the fulcrum for monetary policy since 1958 were removed, the government was to exercise influence over the monetary aggregates and overall levels of credit in the economy primarily by varying interest rates, notably the bank rate (minimum lending rate) fixed by the Bank of England. The full story of CCC cannot be told here.[28] Suffice it to say that the primary object of the reform was credit control and the management of competitive conditions in the banking system and not the gilt markets. However, the reform had significant, if imperfectly understood, side effects on the gilt market.

Before CCC the Bank of England managed the gilt market according to a "cashiers' " approach to market management. In a nutshell its premise was that the best way to ensure demand for government bonds was to minimize the risks associated with holding them by minimizing changes in interest rates and therefore in bond prices.[29] Since monetary control under the new CCC system was now to be achieved primarily by allowing fluctuations in interest rates, however, a system for marketing gilt based on limiting changes in interest rates proved to be incompatible with it. Accordingly the authorities developed a new approach that might be termed the "economists' " approach to gilt management.[30] If the premise behind the so-called cashiers' approach was that gilt could be made attractive by minimizing the losses investors could suffer, the premise behind the economists' approach was that gilt could be made attractive by offering investors the possibility of large profits. In order to sell gilt, the authorities would force interest rates up just enough so it would seem to the market that rates could go no higher. Believing interest rates would next fall, investors would then buy gilt because, as interest rates fell, bond prices would rise and they would be holding a rapidly appreciating commodity. The theory was that gilt might not be as secure an investment as it had been under the old regime but it would retain marketability based on the high return it could bring. British officials did not initially realize that CCC would require a new system for marketing gilt, but by 1974 they had been forced to implement the new system.

Once in place, however, the new system precipitated many changes in the behavior of purchasers and brokers in the gilt market. First, it vastly increased the cohesiveness of the market, namely the extent to which purchasers of gilt acted together. Previously purchases of gilt had been relatively even over time but, in order to avoid losses under the new system, investors had to act at precisely that point when interest rates seemed to peak. The herd instinct, always present in such markets, was deeply reinforced. As a result, the authorities might sell gilt only in dribbles for several months; and then, after moving the bank rate up a notch, suddenly sell millions of pounds' worth of bonds in a day.

Second, these new practices in the gilt market made it much more important for brokers and purchasers to predict changes in interest rates with some accu-

racy. A number of bankruptcies among brokerage houses in the early years of
the new system rammed this point home. As a result the brokerage houses began
to hire young economists in increasing numbers to monitor government policy
with a view to predicting interest rate changes and gilt prices. Brokers developed
much greater interest in the government's overall economic policy; and they
began to speculate publically about that policy in a rapidly growing number of
circulars published for the benefit of their clients. By 1976 dozens of these publications were circulating in the City, including Philips and Drew's *Economic
Forecasts*, Greenwell's *Monetary Bulletin*, Capel's *Discussion Papers*, Messel's
Monthly Monitor, Rowe and Pitman's *Market Report*, Vickers da Costa's *The
British Economy*, and many others. The views promulgated in these circulars
were widely followed by investors and given coverage in the quality press. The
Chancellor of the Exchequer himself began to complain about the influence now
wielded by these "teenage City scribblers."

The new market practices and the circulars to which they gave rise were responsible both for accelerating the speed with which the markets responded to a
change in government policy and for rendering that response increasingly mon-
olithic. As the cohesiveness of the market increased, so did its leverage vis-à-vis
the government. Just as investors generally bought gilt in one grand rush, so they
held off together when conditions seemed unpropitious. The more they held back,
the more desperate the government became to sell gilt and the more likely it
became that the authorities would have to offer better terms, either by increasing
interest rates or by ruling out such increases through reductions in the public
sector borrowing requirement (PSBR). In short, there was a growing element of
self-fulfilling prophecy to the new dynamic in the gilt market. The cohesiveness
of the market made it increasingly easier for purchasers of gilt to extract policy
concessions from the government.[31]

A third consequence of these developments was the appearance of growing
concern inside the City for the rate of growth of the money supply. Since their
principal task was to predict the direction of interest rates and bond prices, most
of the young economists flowing into the City were naturally interested in the
monetary aggregates. These economists gradually discovered that the amount of
gilt the government had to sell depended on the relationship between the rate of
growth of the money supply (M3), the level of bank lending to the private sector,
and the size of the PSBR – all of which could be predicted reasonably accurately.
Once the government adopted a target for M3, as it did from 1976, its need to
sell gilt could be predicted with remarkable facility.[32] Once such predictions
became possible, the market could wait with little risk for the government to
raise interest rates or cut public spending and the PSBR, knowing that the authorities had little choice if they were to meet their targets. In effect, with unparalleled cohesiveness and a remarkable arsenal of information, the market could
virtually hold the Government to ransom.[33]

What is most interesting is that these developments did not involve any conspiracy on the part of the financial community vis-à-vis the government. The City has never been notoriously sympathetic to Labour governments, but the periodic unwillingness to purchase gilt that forced concessions on the government in this period was not produced by an organized movement. It was simply the summary result of a series of decisions made by individual investors trying to follow market cues so as to maximize their own profits. If the relevant incentives for unified action had not been present in the institutionalized practices of the market, those individuals would willingly have broken ranks in their own interest.[34]

A similar dynamic developed in the foreign exchange markets in the 1970s. Although it cannot be described in detail here, this market also put increased pressure on the government in the 1970s. Massive growth in the Euromoney markets during the decade generated huge sums of capital that could be moved relatively quickly from one currency to another, and the foreign exchange market began to respond to many of the same signals as the British bond markets. As a result, speculative pressure in the two markets began to reinforce one another, and the government often found itself simultaneously unable to market gilt or fend off a run against sterling unless it initiated further increases in interest rates and/or reductions in public expenditure.

The newfound power of the financial markets was not lost on either side. The permanent secretary of the Treasury observed of this period: "If markets take the view that policies pursued by a particular country are likely to damage assets held in that country or in that country's currency, they are likely to behave in ways which can actually enforce a policy change. Market behavior has become a significant input into decision-making."[35] One broker waxed almost philosophical: "The gilt-edged market is in some sense a contemporary extension of the checks and balances that Bagehot spoke of. It is a check on Labour Governments, on socialism, and on their tendency to increase public expenditure too much. This is especially true now that we have monetary targets."[36]

As a consequence, increases in interest rates and reductions in public spending were forced on the government at numerous points in the 1976–8 period. One reflection of the new climate was a dramatic increase in the number of major financial statements issued by the chancellor each year. Another was the renewed attention the government gave to monetary policy, reflected for instance in its decision to let the exchange rate appreciate in the fall of 1977 despite adverse effects on exports rather than allow inflows of foreign exchange to expand the money supply.[37] Behind the unbelieving monetarism of 1976–7 lay a set of institutional changes that had intensified pressure from the financial markets.

The shift to wholehearted monetarism under Thatcher

If the 1976–8 years mark a period of transition, the full move to monetarist modes of policy-making came only with the election of a new Conservative government under Margaret Thatcher in May 1979. Once in office, that government began to shift the orientation of economic policy quite dramatically. It lifted exchange controls, set a fixed target for sterling M3 and raised the minimum lending rate by 3 points to 17 percent to enforce its targets. Its first budget took a new approach to macroeconomic management based on a medium-term financial strategy that set explicit targets for the rate of growth of the money supply several years ahead. Reducing the rate of inflation became the foremost priority of government policy and reducing the public sector deficit its principal means to that end. Although monetary policy was relaxed slightly at the end of 1980, the 1981 budget was deflationary yet again, despite the sharpest increase in unemployment that Britain had experienced since 1930. With these measures, Thatcher embarked on a course that broke radically with the character of British economic management since the war.[38]

In order to explain this final step toward monetarist modes of policy-making, we must answer two questions. Why did Thatcher and the Conservative Party embrace a monetarist approach to economic policy? Why were they elected to office in 1979? Once again the answers lie in a complex interaction of interests and ideas in which institutional factors played a critical mediating role.

The explanation should begin with the collapse of the preceding paradigm and what is often referred to as the Keynesian consensus. A change in the situation of the economy initiated the process. Inflation and unemployment began to rise simultaneously in Britain during the 1970s, calling the trade-off that most Keynesians postulated between these two variables into question and generating effects that Keynesian models had difficulty anticipating or explaining. One result was a series of mistaken forecasts. These were naturally followed by some serious failures of policy to produce the results that had been intended. Such policy failures set in motion a set of institutional developments of some moment.

In the first instance, the monopoly of authority that the Treasury had enjoyed over matters of economic policy began to erode and a range of new institutions associated with what might be termed an outside *marketplace in economic ideas* developed in Britain. As economic problems intensified and the capacity of the Keynesians in the Treasury to deal with them satisfactorily seemed to decline, a number of outside institutions were established to provide alternative analyses of the economy and economic policy. Prominent among these were the research departments of brokerage houses, which expanded in response to changes in the financial markets noted above and whose circulars constituted an influential *samizadt* on economic matters. Independent institutes were also formed and gained new prominence, such as the Centre for Economic Forecasting at the London Business School, the Cambridge Economic Policy Group, and the Centre for Policy Studies established by the Conservative Party. When some disgruntled members of Parliament forced the Treasury to release the details of its model for forecasting the British economy in 1976, these institutes gained an important additional resource.

The 1970s saw an unparalleled expansion in the amount of coverage given to sophisticated economic matters in the British press, much of it monetarist in tone. From 1975 to 1979 thousands of articles with a monetarist slant appeared in *The Times, The Financial Times, The Economist, The Daily Telegraph,* and elsewhere in the press. The government faced an avalanche of opinion, all the more significant because few British economists held monetarist views during these years. Why, then, did so many journalists take them up? Many began to popularize monetarist ideas because they were searching for a standpoint from which to mount informed criticism of the government's policies. As one influential journalist put it: "This was a period of intense humiliation for a lot of thinking people within Whitehall and the City. . . . A number of us made a conscious decision to pin these people bloody-well down."[39] Others took up monetarist analyses simply because the latter became the "angle" of the day. As one explained, "We saw monetarism as the major alternative to the Keynesian orthodoxy that ruled in Britain and we were interested in it from that angle."[40]

As an institution, the media are a critical transmission belt between the state and society that is sometimes neglected by those who focus on the traditional channels of interest intermediation. However, because the media fasten onto particular issues in search of an angle, they act more as a magnifying glass than as a mirror for popular opinion. The ferocity with which economic journalists took up monetarist issues during the 1970s was central to their popularization in Britain.

The nature of the British party system also played an important role in the progress of monetarist ideas. In the British system, where two parties are usually the only viable candidates for office and the victor generally governs alone, the party that is out of office is always casting about for a coherent standpoint from which to mount an effective attack on the government's performance, especially in issue areas of great concern to the electorate.[41] Thus, many Conservatives began to show interest in monetarism as a coherent standpoint from which to attack the Labour government's lackluster economic policies. They faced strong institutional incentives to pick up and press the alternative economic doctrine.

Moreover, monetarist ideas had a special appeal for those on the right wing of the Conservative Party, who gained influence after the 1974 electoral failure of the moderates under Heath. In monetarism they found a highly coherent rationale for many of the policy initiatives they had long favored. Monetarist doctrine provided cogent economic reasons for cutting public spending and taxation, reducing the public sector deficit, rejecting incomes policies, shrinking the public sector, and limiting the legal power of the trade unions.[42] Accordingly Sir Keith Joseph and Margaret Thatcher deliberately schooled themselves in monetarist doctrine and founded the Centre for Policy Studies to promulgate such ideas more widely within the party.

The Conservative electoral victory of 1979 was the result of many circumstances. However, the evidence suggests that two factors made a crucial difference to the outcome.[43] One was the popularity of the Conservatives' policy positions, including a number pertaining to the economy that were closely tied to a monetarist outlook. The other was an electoral backlash against the difficulties the preceding Labour government had experienced with the implementation of an incomes policy, intensified by popular resentment against the wildcat strikes that broke out in the public sector during the 1979 "winter of discontent."

Given Britain's poor economic performance, Labour faced an uphill electoral battle. But the electorate reacted with special force against the tortuous efforts to secure voluntary wage restraint that were the hallmark of the 1974–9 years. In this respect the organization of labor was relevant to the rise of monetarism in Britain. The fragmented nature of the British trade unions had made it especially difficult for the government to implement a successful incomes policy. Each round of crisis bargaining carried a political cost. The authority of the government itself seemed to have been undermined by its constant efforts to placate the unions; and the popularity of the unions themselves dropped precipitously between 1974 and 1979.

In the face of this crisis, monetarism seemed to contain a formula for restoring governmental authority. The monetarists claimed that the government could control inflation – and the unions – simply by adhering to a rigid target for monetary growth. They believed that monetary targets would force the trade unions to accept moderate wage increases or risk unemployment. One of the subtexts, in effect, of the 1979 Conservative campaign was an attack on the trade unions. Some of the most popular planks in Thatcher's platform were promises to ban secondary picketing and stop social security payments to the families of strikers. With these and further promises to sell off council houses and lower income taxes, Thatcher put together an electoral coalition that drew many middle-class voters and important segments of the working class away from the Labour Party.[44]

CONCLUSION

As even this brief summary suggests, the movement from Keynesian to monetarist modes of economic policy-making in Britain was a complex process with many ingredients. In it, economic developments, conflicts of interest among social groups, and new ideas all played a role. However, the process as a whole was structured by the institutional framework that characterizes the British polity and policy process.

What do institutions do? Let us summarize the impact that each level in the institutional framework of British policy-making had on the course of policy. In overarching terms, British policy-making takes place within a framework marked by the combination of capitalist relations of production and democratic electoral institutions. On the one hand, this framework did not dictate a monetarist solution to the economic difficulties of the 1970s, as the divergent paths taken by many other nations with a similar political-economic framework indicate. On the other hand, it tended to impose broad constraints on policy-makers that militated strongly against radical schemes involving substantial alterations to the existing relations of production. The power of businessmen to oppose such schemes is unusually great where they control means of production and investment so vital to economic prosperity and where the electoral constraint soon translates any downturn in business confidence and prosperity into a loss of votes.

Even more germane to the actual course of policy was the organization of the state and society in Britain. Prominent among their features was the organization of the British trade union movement. Powerful enough to create strong inflationary pressures, it was also organizationally fragmented enough to render neocorporatist solutions to the problems of unemployment and inflation, of the sort associated with incomes policies, especially difficult to attain. As we have seen, the difficulties the 1974–9 Labour government experienced persuading a fragmented trade union movement to adhere to a wage norm paved the way for its 1979 electoral defeat and for the popularity of monetarist ideas in many quarters. In this case we can see how the institutions devised to represent the interests of a social group, such as the working class, themselves affect the definition and expression of those interests. A less fragmented union movement might have been inclined to pursue neocorporatist solutions longer than the British unions did and it might have been able to implement them more effectively.[45]

Several features of the British political system also seem to have affected the course of policy. On the one hand, a party system characterized by intense two-party competition, compared to the continental pattern of coalition governments, gave the Conservatives strong incentives to seek a clear alternative to Labour policies, of the sort that they found in monetarism. On the other hand, once in office, the Conservatives had the capacity to institute radical changes in economic policy in part because the British system of "responsible" government vests great power in a cabinet and its prime minister. It is difficult to imagine a German, French or American administration carrying through such a substantial break with the past as the British achieved; and, indeed, their efforts to do so were all dissipated more quickly than those of the British.[46]

This analysis suggests that, while we are used to thinking of institutions as factors of inertia tending to produce regularities in politics, some kinds of institutional configurations may be systematically biased in favor of change. The combination of responsible cabinet government and a two-party political system that we find in Britain may be precisely such a configuration.[47] A two-party system gives the party that is out of office strong incentives to propose innovative lines of policy so as to develop a distinct profile in the eyes of the electorate and a basis from which to mount an effective critique of the incumbent party. A system of responsible cabinet government concentrates power effectively enough to permit a new government to implement distinctive innovations in policy.[48]

The unusually concentrated character of the British media also played an important role in this episode. Four newspapers dominated the national market for a quality press in Britain during the 1970s, and three gave an extraordinary amount of coverage to monetarist ideas and issues at a time when they were still largely unaccepted by British economists. Such coverage intensified the pressure for monetarist policies that the government faced in 1976–9 and paved the way for those seeking to persuade the Conservative Party of the advantages of a monetarist program.[49] In this case a particular configuration of institutions provided the proponents of a new set of ideas with an influential platform from which to launch them.

At the very least this case reminds us that the electoral systems and popular media associated with democratic polities can be important institutional sites for the initiation of political change. While many of the institutional features of the state itself tend toward inertia, democratic political systems contain avenues for innovation. Monetarist policies were virtually imposed on a reluctant set of officials by politicians responding to the media and the matrix of incentives in the electoral arena.

Finally the standard operating procedures adopted by British officials constitute a third level of institutions with a substantial impact on the trajectory of policy. The routines and decision-making procedures of the Treasury acted as filters for response to outside economic developments. Both the Heath and Wilson governments initially reacted to rising levels of unemployment and inflation in a quintessentially Keynesian manner in some measure because a Keynesian approach to economic management had been routinized into the standard procedures of the Treasury. They were built into the econometric model that became increasingly central to policy-making in the early 1970s. It was the failure of this model, built on estimates of past economic relationships, to anticipate the changing relationships in the economy during the 1970s that led to many mistaken forecasts and growing disillusionment with Keynesianism itself.

The inertial impact of these routines was further reinforced by the structure of the British Treasury itself. Operating in considerable secrecy, it was staffed by career civil servants and vested with great authority over macroeconomic policy-making. Partly for this reason, monetarist doctrines gained influence faster in the Bank of England, where senior officials were close to the financial community, and among politicians who were ultimately to press them upon officials.

Similarly, we have seen how a change in the operating procedures of the financial markets altered the incentive structure facing investors there in such a way as to intensify pressure on the government for monetarist policies in the 1976–9 period. Here is a classic case in which institutional reform had significant unintended consequences and one that demonstrates how the power of particular social interests is shaped by the institutional framework in which they find themselves. The institutional reforms associated with Competition and Credit Control greatly enhanced the power of the financiers operating in the gilt markets vis-à-vis the British government during the second half of the 1970s. Although a wider struggle for power and resources among social groups often lies behind the surface of policy-making, that struggle is mediated by political and economic institutions that channel it in certain directions and privilege some groups at the expense of others. Those institutions transmute as well as transmit the preferences of such groups and they can have a crucial, if often unintended, impact on the outcome.

In sum, institutions alone did not produce the changes made to British economic policy during the 1970s. The latter were the outcome of a complex process driven, in large measure, by the problems generated by new economic developments, the pressure of competing social interests expressed in both the financial and electoral markets, and by the apparent viability of old and new economic ideas for the purposes at hand. However, the institutional setting in which British policy was made contributed a good deal to the precise trajectory that policy was to follow. The institutionalized routines of the policy process structured the interpretation that policy-makers put upon the new economic developments. The configuration of the labor and financial markets intensified pressure for some lines of policy over others, and the institutional character of the media and electoral arena added public and political appeal to some economic ideas more than others.

Institutions emerge from this analysis as critical mediating variables, constructed by conscious endeavor but usually more consequential than their creators intended. They are not a substitute for interests and ideas as the ultimate motors of political action, but they have a powerful effect on which interests and ideas will prevail. Institutions are a force not only in instances of political inertia but in cases of political change as well. As such, they deserve the attention that has been devoted to them.

NOTES

1 For basic reviews of British policy during the Keynesian era, see F. T. Blackaby, ed., *British Economic Policy 1960–74* (Cambridge: Cambridge University Press, 1979); Andrew Shonfield, *Modern Capitalism* (New York: Oxford University Press, 1969); and J. C. R. Dow, *The Management of the British Economy 1945–1960* (Cambridge: Cambridge University Press, 1964).

2 Examples of neoinstitutionalist studies examining stable patterns of policy include Peter A. Hall, *Governing the Economy: The Politics of State Intervention in Britain and France* (New York: Oxford University Press, 1986), ch. 9; Geoffrey Garrett and Peter Lange, "Performance in a Hostile World: Economic Growth in Capitalist Democracies, 1974–82," *World Politics* 38, no. 4 (July 1986); Fritz Scharpf, "Economic and Institutional Constraints of Full-Employment Strategies: Sweden, Austria, and West Germany, 1973–82" in John Goldthorpe, ed., *Order and Conflict in Contemporary Capitalism* (New York: Oxford University Press, 1984), pp. 257–90; Sven Steinmo, "Political Institutions and Tax Policy in the United States, Sweden and Britain," *World Politics* 61, no. 4 (July 1989):500–35; and John Zysman, *Governments, Markets and Growth* (Ithaca, N.Y.: Cornell University Press, 1983).

3 For a more general statement reflecting this view, see James March and Johan Olsen,

"The New Institutionalism: Organizational Factors in Political Life," *American Political Science Review* 78, no. 3 (Sept 1984):734–49. It is also well represented in the essay by Margaret Weir in Chapter 7 of this book and her "Ideas and Politics: The Acceptance of Keynesianism in Britain and the United States," in Peter A. Hall, ed., *The Political Power of Economic Ideas: Keynesianism across Nations* (Princeton, N.J.: Princeton University Press, 1989), pp. 53–86.

4 Although there were three Thatcher governments, 1979–83, 1983–7, and 1987–91, for the sake of simplicity I will refer to all of them as the Thatcher government.

5 For surveys of the economic policies of the Thatcher government, see Peter Riddell, *The Thatcher Decade* (Oxford: Basil Blackwell, 1990); Geoffrey Maynard, *The Economy under Mrs. Thatcher* (Oxford: Basil Blackwell, 1988); and Martin Holmes, *The First Thatcher Government* (Brighton: Wheatsheaf, 1985).

6 See Peter A. Hall, "Policy Paradigms, Social Learning and the State," *Comparative Politics* (forthcoming).

7 See Peter A. Hall, *The Political Dimensions of Economic Management* (Ann Arbor, Mich.: University Microfilms, 1982), ch. 1; K. Cuthbertson, *Macroeconomic Policy* (London: Macmillan, 1979); K. A. Chrystal, *Controversies in British Macroeconomics* (Oxford: Philip Allan, 1979).

8 On the Heath policies, see Hall, *Political Dimensions of Economic Management*, ch. 2; Martin Holmes, *Political Pressure and Economic Policy* (London: Butterworths, 1982); and Jock Bruce-Gardyne, *Whatever Happened to the Quiet Revolution?* (London: Charles Knight, 1974).

9 See David Coates, *Labour in Power?* (London: Longman, 1980); and Hall, *Political Dimensions of Economic Management*, ch. 3.

10 See William Keegan and Rupert Pennant-Rae, *Who Runs the Economy?* (London: Temple Smith, 1979); Samuel Brittan, *The Economic Consequences of Democracy* (London: Temple Smith, 1977).

11 For accounts of the trajectory of economic policy in this period in several other industrialized nations, see Peter A. Hall, "State and Market," in Peter A. Hall, Jack Hayward, and Howard Machin, eds., *Developments in French Politics* (London: Macmillan, 1990); Paul Roberts, *The Supply-Side Revolution* (Cambridge, Mass.: Harvard University Press, 1984).

12 For a general review of economic performance in this period, see Andrea Boltho, ed., *The European Economy* (Oxford: Oxford University Press, 1982), esp. chs. 1, 2.

13 For an influential statement of such a position, see Peter A. Gourevitch, *Politics in Hard Times* (Ithaca, N.Y.: Cornell University Press, 1986).

14 This is a point well made by Geoffrey Garrett, "The Politics of Structural Change: The Construction of Social Democracy in 1930s Sweden and Neoliberalism in 1980s Britain," Cornell University Western Societies Program, Occasional Papers, forthcoming.

15 For analyses that emphasize this point, see Joel Krieger, *Reagan, Thatcher and the Politics of Decline* (Cambridge: Polity Press, 1986); Stuart Hall and Martin Jacques, eds., *The Politics of Thatcherism* (London: Lawrence and Wishart, 1983); and Bob Jessop et al., *Thatcherism: A Tale of Two Nations* (Cambridge: Polity Press, 1989).

16 By the 1990s, of course, many aspects of monetarist doctrine had been integrated into the conventional wisdom of neoclassical economics, but this was not the case in the period under scrutiny here. For further discussion of the incommensurability of the policy paradigns at that point see Hall, *Political Dimensions of Economic Management*, ch. 1.

17 For further elaboration on this approach to explaining the impact of new economic ideas, see Hall, ed., *Political Power of Economic Ideas*, esp. the introduction and conclusion.

18 For an elegant analogous formulation, see G. John Ikenberry, "Conclusion: An Institutional Approach to American Foreign Economic Policy," *International Organization* 42, 1 (Winter 1988).

19 For further elaboration see Adam Przeworski and Michael Wallerstein, "The Structure of Class Conflict in Democratic Capitalist Societies," *American Political Science Review* 76 (1982):215–38; Adam Przeworski, *Capitalism and Social Democracy* (Cambridge: Cambridge University Press, 1985); Charles Lindblom, *Politics and Markets* (New York: Basic Books, 1977); Fred Block, "The Ruling Class Does Not Rule: Notes on the Marxist Theory of the State," *Socialist Review* 33 (May–June, 1977):6–28; Claus Offe, *Disorganized Capitalism* (Cambridge, Mass.: MIT Press, 1985); Claus Offe, *Contradictions of the Welfare State* (Cambridge, Mass.: MIT Press, 1984); and Hall, *Governing the Economy*, ch. 10.

20 For a limited sample of relevant arguments, see: Hall, *Governing the Economy*, ch. 9; Peter Evans, Dietrich Rueschemeyer, and Theda Skocpol, eds., *Bringing the State Back In* (Cambridge: Cambridge University Press, 1985); John Goldthorpe, ed., *Order and Conflict in Contemporary Capitalism* (New York: Oxford University Press, 1986); Bernard Elbaum and William Lazonick, eds., *The Decline of the British Economy* (Oxford: Oxford University Press, 1986); Suzanne Berger, ed., *Organizing Interests in Western Europe* (Cambridge: Cambridge University Press, 1982); Robert Boyer and Jacques Mistral, *Accumulation, Inflation, Crises* (Paris: Presses Universitaires de France, 1983).

21 Cf. Hugh Heclo and Aaron Wildavsky, *The Private Government of Public Money* (London: Macmillan, 1979). Much of the literature in organization theory is pertinent here. For overviews see Paul C. Nystrom and William H. Starbuck, *Handbook of Organizational Design* (New York: Oxford University Press, 1981); Graham Allison, *The Essence of Decision* (Boston: Little, Brown, 1971); Stewart Clegg and David Dunkerley, *Organization, Class and Control* (London: Routledge and Kegan Paul, 1980); Herbert Simon, *Administrative Behavior* (New York: Free Press, 1976).

22 See Michael Stewart, *Politics and Economic Policy in the UK since 1964* (London: Pergamon, 1978), ch. 5.

23 Cf. Paul Ormerod, *Economic Modelling* (London: Heinemann, 1979).

24 Cf. Barbara Castle, *The Castle Diaries, 1974–76* (London: Weidenfeld and Nicolson, 1980); Harold Wilson, *The Final Term* (London: Weidenfeld and Nicolson, 1980); Ninth Report from the Expenditure Committee, *Public Expenditure, Inflation and the Balance of Payments*. H. C. 328 (London: HMSO, 1974).

25 Cf. H. Fay and S. Young, *The Day the Pound Died* (London: The Sunday Times, 1977).

26 See Castle, *Castle Diaries, 1974–76*, p. 546 et passim. Extensive documentation for the account given here of British economic policy can be found in Hall, *Political Dimensions of Economic Management*.

27 Public sector borrowing as a percentage of gross domestic product rose from 3.2% in 1962–7 to 6.8 % in 1972–7. In the five years to 1980, the government had to sell £41,825 million worth of public sector debt; and, by 1980, it had some £57 billion worth of bonds outstanding, equivalent to 42% of GDP compared with a U.S. debt of 16% of GDP at that time. In 1977 government bonds absorbed 90% of the U.K. capital market as opposed to only 30 % of the U.S. domestic capital market. See Adam Ridley, "Public Expenditure in the United Kingdom: The Biggest Crisis of Them All," in Ruble and Veler, eds., *Wachsende Staatshaushalte* (Bonn: Ahntell, 1978), Table 10; *The Times* (London), Nov. 26, 1979, p. 17; *The Bank of England Quarterly Bulletin* (June 1979), pp. 138 ff.

28 For more detailed accounts of Competition and Credit Control, see Michael Moran, *The Politics of Banking* (London: Macmillan, 1988); Hall, *Political Dimensions of*

Economic Management, ch. 3; K. K. Zawadzki, *Competition and Credit Control* (Oxford: Basil Blackwell, 1981).

29 From the investors' point of view, this meant that gilt was a safe, if low-return investment, on which one just might make a good profit should interest rates fall.

30 This and the cashiers' theory are explained in David Gowland, *Monetary Policy and Credit Control* (London: Croom Helm, 1978), pp. 28 et passim.

31 The major limit to this leverage was imposed by the fact that large institutional investors generally put their inflows of funds into overnight paper while they waited for the gilt market to move and, after a period, the resulting imbalance in their asset portfolios began to incline them more strongly toward reentry into the gilt market.

32 Cf. G. T. Pepper, "The Uses of Monetarism for Practical Working Economists," *Journal of the Institute of Actuaries* 96, no. 1 (1970):403.

33 What these City circulars were doing was defining – and, in the process, creating – the "confidence" that the financial community had in various government policies. They were perfectly explicit. To take only one example, the report that stockbrokers Rowe and Pitman prepared immediately after the 1979 budget declared that: "If . . . the financial markets consider that the consequences of the fiscal policies announced in the Budget will be a Borrowing Requirement in excess of £8.5 billion, confidence will be impaired and interest rates will have to move upwards again in order to keep monetary growth under control." *Market Report* (March 1979):p. 3.

34 Although I do not pursue it here, this sort of dynamic also lends itself to a game-theoretic interpretation. These developments were initiated by a change in the strategy of the Government that altered the payoff matrix for investors in bonds, who altered their behavior accordingly and then devised means for improving their access to the relevant information. New institutions devised for this purpose, in turn, made coordination of market behavior more feasible and enhanced the leverage that operators in the market had vis-à-vis the government.

35 Sir Douglas Wass, "The Changing Problems of Demand Management." Lecture to the Johnian Society, Cambridge University, Feb. 15, 1978, p. 99.

36 Interview, London (July 10, 1980).

37 For details, see Hall, *The Political Dimensions of Economic Management,* ch. 7.

38 Although there is not space to follow the trajectory of policy under the Thatcher government here, it should be noted that monetarist policy itself underwent some significant changes during the 1980s. In particular, monetary control proved much more difficult than Thatcher had anticipated and by the middle of the decade the money supply had become only one of several targets at which monetary policy was aimed. Nonetheless, the nature of policy over the 1980s remained sharply different and the ideas that guided it remained quite different from those that had prevailed in preceding decades. For more extensive discussion of Thatcher's policies, see Riddell, *The Thatcher Decade* and Peter Smith, *The Rise and Fall of Monetarism* (Harmondsworth: Penguin, 1988).

39 Interview, London, Aug. 11, 1980.

40 Samuel Brittan, private communication.

41 Cf. A. M. Gamble and S. A. Walkland, *The British Party System and Economic Policy 1945–83* (Oxford: Oxford University Press, 1984).

42 See Andrew Gamble, "The Free Economy in the Strong State" in Ralph Miliband and John Saville, eds., *The Socialists' Register 1979* (London: Merlin, 1979), pp. 1–25; and Robert Behrens, *The Conservative Party from Heath to Thatcher* (Farnsborough: Saxon House, 1980).

43 See Ivor Crewe, "Why the Conservatives Won" in Howard Penniman, ed., *Britain at the Polls, 1979* (Washington, D.C.: American Enterprise Institute, 1981), pp. 263–306.

44 Geoffrey Garrett, "Endogenous Electoral Change: The Political Consequences of Thatcherism," paper presented to the Conference of Europeanists, Washington, D.C., April 1990.

45 On this point, there is a large literature; see especially John Goldthorpe, ed., *Order and Conflict in Contemporary Capitalism* (Cambridge: Cambridge University Press, 1984) and Peter Lange, Geoffrey Garrett, and Michael Alvarez, "Government Partisanship, Labor Organization and Macroeconomic Performance, 1967–1984," *American Political Science Review* (forthcoming).

46 In Germany the government is usually constrained not only by its coalition partners but by a powerful Bundesrat and independent central bank. Thus, the famous *wende* of the new Kohl government proved to be quite moderate. In the United States, Congress, the Federal Reserve Bank, and an independent judiciary limit the capacity of a new administration to pursue a coherent economic strategy. Thus the Reagan administration rapidly retreated from its promises to control the budget deficit and soon encountered opposition to its tax reforms. In France the government can be constrained both by the power of the presidency and the legislature, if the opposition is well represented there. Thus the program of the 1986–9 Chirac government, while inspired by Thatcher's ideas, never attained the same results. See Peter Katzenstein, *Politics and Policy-making in West Germany* (Philadelphia: Temple University Press, 1987); Andrei Markovits, ed., *The Political Economy of Germany* (New York: Praeger, 1982); David Stockman, *The Triumph of Politics* (New York: Norton, 1985); Howard Machin and Vincent Wright, eds., *Economic Policy and Policy-Making in Mitterrand's France* (London: Pinter, 1985).

47 For an analogous but slightly different argument, see John Keeler, *The Limits of Democratic Reform* (Oxford: Polity Press, forthcoming), ch. 3.

48 The caveat that must be entered here, of course, is that the dynamics of two-party electoral competition can lead the parties to converge on a similar set of platforms in order to secure as many votes from the center of the political spectrum as possible. Cf. Anthony Downs, *An Economic Theory of Democracy* (New York: Harper & Row, 1957). It may well be that deep dissatisfaction among the electorate is the necessary trigger for a dynamic of innovation, as opposed to one of convergence, to operate.

49 See Wayne Parsons, *The Power of the Financial Press* (London: Edward Elgar, 1989); and Peter A. Hall, *Political Dimensions of Economic Management*, ch. 6.

5

Political structure, state policy, and industrial change: Early railroad policy in the United States and Prussia

COLLEEN A. DUNLAVY

The historical relationship between politics and industrial change remains a fascinating and complex subject, fraught with theoretical and practical implications alike. In what ways has politics shaped patterns of industrialization since the late eighteenth century? To what extent has the process of industrial change, in turn, altered domestic configurations of power? Scholars have wrestled with these deceptively simple questions for decades. For generations of students, the classic inquiries of scholars such as Karl Polanyi (1957) and Alexander Gerschenkron (1962), rooted in the experiences of the 1930s, set the initial contours of debate; most recently economists, historians, and political scientists have opened exciting new lines of inquiry by refurbishing and extending the economic institutionalism that also flourished in the 1930s.[1] Binding the old and the new is a shared passion to understand the subtle, historical interaction of polity and economy.

The contributions of this new economic institutionalism to the historical study of politics and industrial change are many and substantial. Concerned principally to explain economic performance, the new economic institutionalists clearly acknowledge the importance of politics, not only in the familiar sense (as overt struggles for advantage) but also as embodied in institutions that reduce uncertainty and facilitate exchange, both economic and political.[2] At its best, moreover, historical analysis in this vein explores the workings of institutions at sev-

For advice and counsel I am indebted to Suzanne Berger, Alfred D. Chandler, Jr., Joshua Cohen, Rainer Fremdling, Victoria Hattam, Diane Lindstrom, and Merritt Roe Smith. I have also benefited from comments at the Boulder conference (particularly those of Peter Katzenstein), from the friendly prodding of the volume's editors, and from readings by Frank Dobbin, Richard R. John, Steven Lewis, and Cecil O. Smith. This essay is a revised version of Dunlavy 1991 and part of a larger study (to be published by Princeton University Press) that has received generous support from the Council for European Studies, German Academic Exchange Service, Lincoln Educational Foundation, Fulbright Commission, Social Science Research Council, International Research and Exchanges Board, National Museum of American History (Smithsonian Institution), American Council of Learned Societies (with funding from the National Endowment for the Humanities), and University of Wisconsin-Madison Graduate School. Responsibility for the results is mine (as are all translations).

eral levels of aggregation, paying explicit attention not only to the individual firm and to relations among firms but also to the state as the institution that specifies and enforces property rights (North 1981; North and Weingast 1989).

Yet, on closer inspection, the literature seems oddly incomplete. The problem is not the direction of the causal arrow. If the net is widely cast, practically every scholar who explores the impact of politics on industrial change has a counterpart who reverses the causal arrow, focusing principally on the way that industrial change affects politics, while others seek to assess reciprocal effects. Instead, the imbalance arises in the units of analysis commonly deployed in the political and economic spheres. This becomes apparent if one draws a broad distinction between studies, on the one hand, of the elements of polity or economy and, on the other, of the overall structure of the two spheres. Studies of the multitude of discrete elements that compose an economy or a polity appear in abundance in both spheres; they focus on capitalists, politicians, or state officials; on workers or voters; on firms or political parties; on markets or elections; on trade associations or bureaucracies; on property rights or civil rights; on economic ideology or political ideology. But studies that proceed on a macrostructural level – concerned not with the discrete components per se but with the *relationships* among them and with the structures that they create – have tended to restrict their horizons to the economy. Scholars working in this mode focus on industrial structure, labor-market structure, economic structure, and so on, which is not surprising, given that industrialization itself is normally viewed as a process of structural change. But they rarely apply the same perspective to the polity. In its view of politics, the literature remains wedded to a volitional perspective that sees individuals or groups, rather than political structure, as the relevant causal forces.[3] The impact of the structure of political institutions in a strictly nonvolitional sense lies on the frontiers of the field, largely unexplored.

It is here, at its frontiers, that the new economic institutionalism intersects with the new *historical* institutionalism on display in this volume. Like its counterpart in economics, this line of inquiry sees institutions and individuals as intimately intertwined: Individuals pursue their goals, formulate policy, even create or alter institutions, all in the familiar, volitional sense; but, as they do so, their own strategic choices are shaped by the institutional context in which they operate (March and Olsen 1984; Smith 1988). In applying this insight to the political realm, however, the new historical institutionalists take it a step further, using it to explore the consequences not only of particular institutions but also of the structure of political institutions on a national scale. In this volume, for example, Ellen Immergut (see Chapter 3) and Victoria Hattam (see Chapter 6) both place national political structures at the centerpoint of their respective studies of national health insurance politics and working-class formation. Peter Hall's work on economic policy (1986 and Chapter 4), moreover, demonstrates the impressive power of an analysis that is sensitive to the institutional organization of capital, labor, and the state – in effect, viewing both economy and polity in structural terms. In its attention to national political structures, the new historical institutionalism offers new tools for understanding the relationship between politics and industrial change.

In that spirit this essay offers a comparative study of the content and process of early railroad policy-making in the United States and Prussia, a piece of a larger study of the impact of the two political structures on the contours of the nascent industry. A full treatment would, of course, also explore the impact of the two political structures on the interface between polity and economy (i.e., on the process of organizing railroad interests) and on the economy itself (i.e., on the development of railroad technology),[4] but a case study that focuses, as this one does, on the relationship between national political structures and the political component of industrial change (industrial policy) suffices to illustrate the approach. Section I explains why these two cases make an illuminating comparison. Section II outlines American and Prussian railroad policies in the 1830s and 1840s, arguing that the American state governments actually tended to favor less liberal policies through the mid-1840s than the Prussian central state did. Section III explains this rather unexpected difference in terms of the two political structures and the distinctive patterns of policy-making that they engendered in a capitalist context. Section IV carries the story forward to the 1850s, the decade when the industrial changes that railroad development set in motion, in turn, initiated a process of institutional change that ultimately lessened the force of intervention in the United States while enhancing it in Prussia.

A study of this kind aids in understanding historical patterns of state intervention, but systematic comparison offers more than that: Unlike a single-country study in which the background conditions tend to be taken for granted, this comparison highlights the structural dimensions of economic policy-making in a changing industrial context. In a nutshell, the contrasting stories of American and Prussian intervention in the 1830s and 1840s underscore the way that the nature of the political structure shaped the state's ability to promote capitalist enterprise – enhancing it in the United States and diminishing it in Prussia – and how this, in turn, determined the extent to which the state was able to sustain regulatory initiatives. The reversals of the 1850s then bring the causal arrow full circle, so to speak, showing how this sprawling, capital-intensive technology – the harbinger of a new, industrial capitalism – recast the economic context, altering the significance of the two political structures and, therefore, the tenor of railroad policy as well.

I. COMPARATIVE RATIONALE

Why compare the United States and Prussia? Not long ago, the choice would have struck many observers as fundamentally ill-conceived, for conventional views of their respective patterns of industrialization stood in marked contrast. Whether the subject was Prussian industrialization or the German industrialization for which it is often taken as a surrogate, scholars typically described the process as late, rapid, and proceeding "from the top down," led by institutions such as the state, banks, and cartels. Studies of the American process, on the other hand, tended to treat it as an example of early industrialization, a "bottom-up" process driven by price changes, perhaps, or by American ingenuity, initiative, or values, but not by public or private institutions.[5]

But closer scrutiny quickly softens the contrast. For much of the nineteenth century, Prussia (and, later, the German empire) does in fact make an ideal case for comparison with the United States, or at least as close as one is likely to come in historical research. As Jürgen Kocka (1980:16–23) points out, the literature on the two countries discloses remarkable, if rather broad, similarities in their patterns of industrialization.[6] The earmarks of early industrialism were clearly visible in both countries by the 1830s,[7] and in both the process took a predominantly capitalist form.[8] By the end of the nineteenth century, moreover, the United States and the German Empire, with its Prussian core, had become the leading challengers to British industrial power. By then, striking parallels had also become evident in the organizational nature of American and German industrialism; where the United States saw the emergence of giant trusts at the turn of the century, Germany of course had its giant cartels.[9] Both countries, in short, might usefully be viewed as moderately "backward" industrializers.[10]

The characterization is apt for another reason as well. *Vormärz* Prussia[11] and the antebellum United States were once thought to map out opposite ends of a "strong-state, weak-state" spectrum, but several decades of research have rendered these images increasingly untenable as well. On the American side, revisions began in the 1940s when a group of scholars set out to reevaluate the state governments' role in antebellum American industrialization.[12] These studies of state legislation and political rhetoric – the first to take federalism seriously, one might say – collectively laid to rest the myth of laissez-faire during the antebellum period. Since then, scholars of the antebellum political economy have examined the American state from another angle, shifting attention to the role of the state and federal courts in economic growth.[13] Others, meanwhile, have taken a closer look at the federal government's role before the Civil War and discerned interventionist tendencies in the federal legislature and executive as well.[14] The cumulative effect is clear: It has become impossible to speak of "laissez-faire" in the antebellum American context. On the Prussian side, too, historians have begun to rethink the state's role in industrialization as mounting evidence has undermined the conventional image. Initially, few historians questioned the extent of the state's involvement in economic activity during the first half of the nineteenth century; instead, they debated its consequences – beneficial or not, intended or not. On balance, the first round of revisions found *Vormärz* Prussian policies to have been rather contradictory in nature, some encouraging industrialization but others either hampering economic change or proving irrelevant.[15] Historian Clive Trebilcock (1981:74–8) has gone a step further, however, debunking what he labels "myths of the directed economy" in nineteenth-century Germany. By 1840, he argues, even the Prussian state had shifted away from the "regimented" forms of state involvement that had characterized the eighteenth century, turning instead to a collection of indirect policies that aimed to encourage industrialization mainly by offering advice and guidance. As he rightly notes (1981:78), "these methods are not easily reconciled with traditional expectations as to the behaviour of 'authoritarian' German states." Revisions from both sides, in short, have blurred traditional images of the two states: The antebellum United States had more of a state than previously thought, while Prussia had less. In this sense, too, "moderately backward" seems an appropriate characterization.

Yet the fact remains that their political structures exhibited sharp differences in the first half of the nineteenth century. The key difference lay in the degree to which governmental powers were separated, both vertically among levels and horizontally among branches of government. In the United States, federalism spelled out a vertical separation of power that gave the American state governments not only a strong voice in the formulation of public policy but also the power to alter the constitutional structure itself.[16] In addition, they possessed the power to determine their own internal structure and to control the activities of lower levels of government. Thus during the antebellum period political power was concentrated mainly at the middle level of the American political structure, rather than above or below that point.[17] In *Vormärz* Prussia, in contrast, the uppermost level of government effectively determined both public policy and the structure of the state itself, despite a considerable degree of de facto decentralization.[18] Provincial assemblies had been established in 1823 as a partial concession to demands for political liberalization, but, except for strictly provincial matters, they shaped public policy mainly in an advisory capacity and certainly had no formal power to alter the political structure itself. Real power lay at the top of the structure in the hands of the king, whose personal authority was limited mainly by the power of the bureaucracies. Where legislative matters were concerned, two bodies – the Council of State (Staatsrat) and the Council of Ministers (Staatsministerium) – served the king directly but, even though they frequently exerted considerable influence, their powers too proved merely advisory when push came to shove. On an informal basis, a ring of personal advisors around the king could and often did prove more powerful than either the Council of State or the Council of Ministers. Together these institutions, formal and informal, constituted the Prussian central state. The only real challenge to its power came from the lowest levels of government, the district assemblies and magistrates, which were firmly under the control of the local nobility.[19] To the extent that the interests of central state officials coincided with those of the landed nobility at the local level, as they often did, the two together formed an interlocking power structure. Differences in the vertical separation of powers thus defined two distinct structures, one federal and the other largely unitary.

At each level of government, moreover, the two structures differed in another crucial respect: the degree to which power was separated among branches of government. In the United States a relatively well-developed horizontal separation of powers served to limit executive power both at the national and at the state level. This naturally gave greater prominence to legislative bodies and carried with it a fairly high degree of formal popular representation at both the state-government and the national level.[20] In practice, therefore, Congress and the state legislatures tended to dominate the policy-making process at their respective levels of government, their power tempered mainly by the courts and in a few cases by strong executives at the state level.[21] In *Vormärz* Prussia governmental powers were less distinctly separated. To a certain extent, the executive (Verwaltung) and judiciary had been disengaged as part of the Stein-Hardenburg reforms, but the executive and legislative functions in Prussia remained formally combined. Since representative bodies played only an advisory role, the bureaucracies at the national and district level dominated the policy-making process.[22]

Viewed both vertically and horizontally, then, the American and Prussian political structures looked quite different. The distinguishing mark of the Prussian unitary-bureaucratic state before 1848 was its twofold concentration of power at the national level in the executive branch. In the United States, federalism and (horizontal) separation of powers combined to produce a highly fragmented political structure, one marked by a twofold dispersion of power that gave the state legislatures a prominent place in policy-making. Economic policy in this period, consequently, emanated from different quarters in the two political structures: Where the state legislatures decided, for example, whether to incorporate companies or to grant rights of eminent domain in the United States, the central bureaucracies did so in Prussia. Hence, if there is anything to be learned about the impact of different political structures on the process of economic policy-making – and, therefore, on the process of industrial change – comparing events in these two countries should at least provide a few clues.[23]

Early railroad development provides a fertile terrain for comparison because of its pivotal role in the industrialization of the two "moderately backward" nations. Here, too, we find remarkable similarities in the timing, pace, and nature of development, yet intriguing differences in state policies. In both countries, railroad plans first surfaced in the 1820s and the basic networks had been laid down by the 1850s.[24] Prussia never matched the United States in railroad mileage, of course – no country did – but it led the German states by 1850 and they in turn led the Continental countries.[25] Despite discrepancies in the scale of construction, however, railroad demand for raw materials and industrial products provided a strong impetus to industrial change in both countries, as did the national markets that they opened.[26] At the same time, because most railroads were privately owned and operated in both countries (through the 1870s), their unprecedented demand for capital set in motion broad changes in American as well as Prussian capital markets. The railroads were the first to make extensive use of the joint-stock form of corporate organization, the first to offer large volumes of industrial securities to the public, and thus the first to attract broad segments of the public to the stock market. In short, they constituted the first "big business" in both countries.[27] As such, they introduced policy-makers in both countries to the distinctive problems of industrial capitalism. Yet, for all of the similarities, railroad policies initially moved in quite different directions in the two countries, as the next section seeks to demonstrate.

II. EARLY RAILROAD POLICIES

Since the argument here turns on "liberalism," an exceedingly troublesome term, it may help to begin with definitions. Without being too precise about it, one may simply define it by gesturing toward the schools of thought commonly associated with John Locke and Adam Smith.[28] In the classical sense, *political liberalism* prevails to a greater extent in a political structure that places limits on autocratic or oligarchic power and allows formal representation for a relatively broad segment of the population. Since the American political structure's vertical and horizontal separation of powers was designed to do just that, it seems reasonable to characterize the antebellum American structure as politically liberal. And it should be equally obvious that the Prussian *Vormärz* structure, with its twofold concentration of power, qualifies as politically illiberal, at least in relative terms.[29]

Economic liberalism can also be defined, in the abstract at least, in a straightforward manner. The central concern here is not the structure of political institutions but rather the nature of the economic policies that those institutions produced. What is at issue, accordingly, is not the degree of individual autonomy in political affairs afforded by the structure of political institutions, but rather the degree of individual autonomy in economic matters admitted by the general pattern of economic policy – here, railroad policy. To assess state policies in a relative sense, it will do, as a first approximation, simply to say that economic liberalism prevails more where the state does less, providing a suitable context for market operations but otherwise abstaining from action; conversely, it obtains less where the state does more. Put differently, the more that state economic policies shift the balance of decision-making power in favor of the state, the more "interventionist" and therefore less liberal they are.[30]

In practice, of course, railroad policy from the start was an extraordinarily complex affair. In the United States, this was doubly true since federalism produced, to borrow Harry Scheiber's term (1975:97), a "mosaic" of state policies. Fortunately, the messy problem of federalism recedes when one views events from the perspective of "the American state" writ large and, accordingly, assesses the state governments' policies as if they had issued from a unitary state. In that sense, variations among state-government policies matter no more or less than discrepancies in the Prussian state's treatment of the various provinces.

Even without the complications of federalism, however, relations between the railroads and the state comprehended a diverse array of topics. To simplify the task, therefore, this section focuses on two aspects of state–railroad relations during the 1830s and 1840s that have traditionally been taken as the hallmarks of positive and negative intervention: direct and indirect state participation in railroad development, and efforts to protect existing sources of state revenues from railroad competition.

Put simply, direct and indirect state participation in railroad development proceeded on a much grander scale in the United States during the 1830s and 1840s than it did in Prussia. In both countries enthusiasm for railroad projects intensified in the late 1820s and early 1830s, but Prussia, unlike the United States, had no state-owned railroads in operation through the 1840s; as we will see, private enterprise built all of the Prussian railroads that opened before the Revolution of 1848. In the United States, in contrast, relations between the state and the railroads initially took on a more "statist" complexion, as some familiar facts attest. A number of state governments entered the field of state enterprise boldly in the 1830s, building and operating railroads themselves. These included Pennsylvania, Georgia, Michigan, Indiana, and Illinois. Economic depression and fiscal troubles forced some overextended state governments to sell off their railroads during the 1840s, but even then not all state governments divested. Pennsylvania retained ownership of the Philadelphia and Columbia Railroad, part of its Main Line of public works, until 1857, while Georgia's Western and Atlantic Railroad remained state property throughout the nineteenth century. Virginia and Tennessee, meanwhile, moved against the trend, both assuming the role of railroad entrepreneurs in the 1850s.[31]

The pattern of state investment in private railroads followed similar contours, for the American state governments – and, with their approval, the municipalities – proved far more generous in providing financial aid for private railroads than the Prussian state initially did. In individual cases investment in private railroads by the American state governments and municipalities matched or exceeded the contributions of private capital, producing a wealth of privately managed "mixed enterprises" in the transportation sector. By 1839 Maryland's investment in the Baltimore and Susquehanna Railroad, for example, represented 63% of its total capital, while the city of Baltimore had contributed more than 28%; hence, private capital accounted for less than 9%. Beginning in the 1830s, the state of Virginia extended to railroads its policy of subscribing 40% of the shares of worthy internal-improvements projects as soon as the public had taken 60%; by the late 1840s, it was, in practice, buying 60% of their shares itself. The state of Massachusetts provided 70% of the capital that had been invested in the Western Railroad by its completion in 1841. By the late 1850s the state of Maryland, together with the cities of Baltimore and Wheeling (Virginia), had contributed nearly half of the Baltimore and Ohio Railroad's share capital and more than half of its loan capital. And so on.[32]

In aggregate terms the investment of state and local governments in American railroads – state and private – reached impressive levels during the antebellum period. During the 1830s the state governments alone contributed roughly 40% of all railroad capital.[33] Thereafter the pace of investment slowed, largely because of depressed economic conditions in the late 1830s and attendant fiscal crises that produced what Carter B. Goodrich (1950:148–51) terms a popular "revulsion" against state enterprise. But even though the economic downturn dealt a blow to the tradition of state enterprise – in some cases written into new state constitutions – it did not obliterate the tradition altogether. As Goodrich notes (1950:148), "the shift in policy was by no means final." Except in the old Northwest states, aid soon flowed again and, where it did taper off, municipalities tended to take up the slack.[34] Altogether, state and local investment still accounted for an estimated 25% to 30% of the roughly $1 billion invested in railroads before the Civil War. To a Prussian railroad promoter, the Berlin banker Joseph Mendelssohn, the state governments' contributions seemed self-evident; American railroads had been built by the state governments, he declared in 1844, unlike German railroads, which had been and would be built "through thick and thin" by private capital with little state assistance.[35]

The Prussian state, in fact, invested very little capital in its private railroads during the first phase of Prussian railroad development, from the 1820s to 1842. Only on two occasions during those years did the state step in when railroad promoters encountered financial difficulties, and then its total assistance amounted to a mere $1.4 million (2 million Taler) or less than 7% of the $21 million in railroad stocks and bonds that had been chartered by then. Beyond that the railroads received no systematic infusion of capital from the state before 1842; Prussian railroad construction, as W. O. Henderson (1975:48) notes, was simply "left to private enterprise."[36]

In the early 1840s, however, just as the "revulsion" against American state enterprise set in, flagging railroad investment in Prussia forced state officials to reevaluate their policy stance. By then they had begun to take a more positive view of the new transportation technology, encouraged both by the new (and younger) king, Frederick William IV, and by improvements in the technology itself, and were under pressure for action from the provincial assemblies. Finally, the state began to provide more systematic aid. After seeking the approval of delegates from the provincial assemblies, King Frederick William IV authorized an aid package for railroads deemed of national importance. This included a continuing expenditure of up to $1.4 million (2 million Taler) annually, to be used to guarantee interest on the shares of those railroads; $350,000 (500,000 Taler) for railroad surveys; and a railroad fund, capitalized initially at $4.2 million (6 million Taler). The railroad fund was to be used to purchase shares in the railroads to which the state had given interest guarantees. In practice during the 1840s the state usually bought one-seventh of a railroad's stock and guaranteed 3.5% interest on the remaining, publicly held shares.[37]

But even though the program appeared ambitious on paper, state investment remained comparatively meager. By the end of 1846, when a total of some $88 million (126 million Taler) in railroad capital had been chartered, the railroad fund had paid in about $2.4 million (3,380,000 Taler) on nominal stock purchases totaling $3.7 million (5,350,000 Taler), while its obligations for interest guarantees totaled about three-quarters of a million dollars (1.1 million Taler).[38] Even with this new increment, the Prussian state's direct financial impact on early railroad development proved far from impressive. As Rainer Fremdling shows, the share of total chartered capital on which it had guaranteed interest slipped from a peak of 39% in 1843, just after the new policy took effect, to 19% in 1848. Meanwhile, its nominal stock holdings, relative to the total chartered capital, had peaked at 7% in 1844 and declined to 4% in 1848.[39] In aggregate terms, then, state enterprise – both direct and indirect – featured more prominently in American than in Prussian railroad development until the late 1840s. Prussia's parsimonious railroad policy, as Richard Tilly (1966:485) notes, "contrasts sharply with the substantial program of 'internal improvements' carried out in the United States after 1815."

Through much of the antebellum period, moreover, some American state governments also proved better able to protect existing investments from railroad competition. Both New York and Pennsylvania, for example, resorted to transit taxes on railroad freight traffic in an effort to protect state investment in canals.[40] Initially New York state laws actually prohibited freight transportation on railroads that paralleled the Erie Canal. By the mid-1840s the legislature allowed railroads that paralleled state canals to carry freight in the winter when the canal was closed, but only if they paid tolls into the state canal fund. By the late 1840s they could carry freight year around, but now they had to pay canal tolls year around. Not until 1851 were all such restrictions finally removed.[41] Even then, it might be noted, agitation to reimpose the tolls persisted. As Governor Myron H. Clark put it in a special message to the legislature in 1855,

There is no interest of the State of greater importance, or which has a more extended influence upon its growth and prosperity than its works of internal improvement. They are enduring and valuable monuments of the wisdom and foresight of those who projected them and have, to an incalculable degree, developed the resources, increased the wealth, and contributed to the general prosperity of the commonwealth. It is the duty of the legislature, therefore, to guard jealously their interests and to secure to them that degree of protection which their importance and the vested right of the State alike demand.[42]

As late as 1859 or 1860 "canal conventions" around the state continued to agitate for reimposition of the tolls; only after the Civil War did the movement dissipate.[43]

Pennsylvania adopted a similar strategy in defense of its Main Line system of canals. In the late 1830s, Governor Joseph Ritner (1901:384–6) vetoed two "general improvement" bills because of the aid that they would have given to projects that ran parallel to the state works. It was a "ruinous policy," he declared; if the legislature insisted on pursuing such a course, it might as well just abandon the state works. In 1846 the legislature did indeed charter the Pennsylvania Railroad, which ran parallel to the state works; but, to protect the state works, it required the railroad to pay a transit tax of 5 mills per ton-mile on freight carried more than 20 miles between March and December. This tax, reduced to 3 mills in 1848 but made effective throughout the year, was not eliminated until 1861.[44]

Prussian officials, too, initially worried about the effects of railroad competition on state revenues. Their concerns, however, focused on state revenues from passenger coach travel. Prussian postal authorities had a virtual monopoly of passenger traffic on post roads and, although postal service was not officially intended to produce profits, postal revenues, in practice, supplemented the general state budget. Accordingly, when the first railroad plans surfaced, Postmaster General von Nagler and the Prussian ministers quickly recognized the threat to state revenues that railroads posed.[45]

But the Postmaster General's efforts to impose a tax on the railroads foundered fairly quickly on resistance from the private companies. Nagler initially demanded "compensation" from the railroads for the anticipated loss of revenues and even extracted several agreements to that effect from individual lines. But the railroads continued to object strenuously, precipitating extensive ministerial deliberations in 1837. These eventually produced a provision in the 1838 railroad law that required the railroads to pay an annual tax geared to their net profit, in effect a tax resembling those imposed on railroads that paralleled American state canals. But, finally, under the weight of renewed protests from the railroads, the king intervened and rescinded that provision of the law before it could take effect. Collection of a railroad tax did not actually begin until a new law was passed in 1853.[46]

In these two policy areas, then, the American state legislatures proved more willing or, at least, better able to intervene than Prussian officials were. Evidence from other policy areas, such as the military's influence and railroad rate regulation, points to the same conclusion: "economic liberalism" better characterized Prussian railroad policies than it did American policies.[47] Broadly speaking, the two political economies, viewed through the lens of early railroad development, looked like mirror images of each other: Prussia, with its illiberal political structure, adopted more liberal railroad policies; while the United States, with a more liberal political structure, adopted less liberal railroad policies.

III. EXPLAINING DIVERGENCE

What accounts for these rather striking patterns of political structure and economic intervention? Why would a comparatively representative government prove to be more interventionist in its policy-making? And why would a relatively authoritarian state largely abstain from direct intervention? Several alternative solutions to this puzzle deserve evaluation: the force of tradition, embodied in ideas about the state's proper role in the transportation sector; the configuration of socioeconomic interests; and the structure of political institutions.[48] This section considers each in turn.

Did most Americans simply believe that railroads, like all other public thoroughfares, should be subject to a large measure of government promotion and regulation, while Prussians tended to look askance at both forms of intervention? For the United States this explanation works reasonably well (despite conventional understanding), but it does not work for Prussia. In both countries, in fact, tradition mandated a leading role for the government both in promoting and in regulating transportation improvements.

Consider first the question of promoting transportation projects. In the United States, events at the state and national levels left little doubt about the extent of continuing popular support for an established tradition. During the antebellum period, the state and lower levels of governments, reflecting the "canal mania" that reigned until the coming of the railroad, contributed nearly three-quarters of all canal investment; four-fifths of the governments' share, it should be noted, went into publically owned works (Goodrich, 1968:366–7). The railroad era, as we have seen, carried forward this tradition of state and local activism, albeit in somewhat diminished form. Even at the national level, moreover, proposals to give the federal government a leading role in the construction of roads and canals surfaced repeatedly, from Albert Gallatin's comprehensive plan of 1808 onward. In the aftermath of the War of 1812, President James Madison set the stage for antebellum debate when he impressed upon Congress "the great importance of establishing throughout our country the roads and canals which can best be executed under national authority." In the 1830s at least one official, General Edmund P. Gaines, took Madison seriously, lobbying long and hard on behalf of an ambitious plan to have the military build more than 4,000 miles of railroads at an estimated cost of $64 million (Campbell, 1940:369–73). To be sure, *federal* aid to internal improvements constituted one of the most contentious political issues in the antebellum era, and the more modest congressional initiatives that did reach the stage of legislation frequently ran afoul of presidential vetoes on constitutional grounds. But that does not diminish the fact that Congress repeatedly passed legislation that would have given the federal government a stronger role.[49] And the policies actually adopted in state legislatures and city councils across the country bespoke a firm tradition of government support for transportation improvements.

In Prussia, too, the railroad era came at the end of – but in this case departed from – a long tradition of government support for transportation improvements. Prussian peasants were required to build and maintain local roads, much as American citizens did in lieu of paying highway taxes. But responsibility for canal construction fell to the state, a tradition that extended back as far as the fourteenth century, and highway construction had also begun to absorb considerable state resources by the late eighteenth century. Even though state officials had made important moves in the early nineteenth century to liberalize the Prussian economy, it would be too much to say that such ideas were applied to transportation as well. Indeed, throughout the decades when private capital was building the railroads, the state continued to provide highways itself. And as the railroad era got under way, it should be noted, a large segment of public opinion seems to have favored state construction or, at least, a more energetic role for the state. The "economic liberals," particularly those from the western provinces, generally supported the idea of state construction, and in 1841 the provincial assemblies petitioned the crown to use an anticipated state revenue surplus to promote railroad construction. Moreover, when Friedrich Wilhelm IV convened delegates from the provincial assemblies in 1842 to consider (among other things) whether and how the state might encourage private railroad construction, the delegates took it upon themselves to discuss state construction as well. Of those who favored railroad construction in any form (89 of the 97 delegates), 47 preferred state construction and 42 opposed it.[50] In short, traditional conceptions of the state's proper role in railroad construction may explain why the American state governments did so much to promote railroad construction, but they do not account for the Prussian state's hesitancy on that score.

Much the same can be said of regulation. In both countries the railroads were initially viewed merely as a new kind of highway and therefore one to be regulated in the time-honored fashion. From the start the American state governments carried over to the railroads their traditional prerogatives to regulate transportation companies. Railroad rates, for example, were initially governed by individual charter provisions and later by general legislation. As George H. Miller (1974:30–1) explains, "legislative regulation of rates was a normal practice of the early railroad era. . . . The power to alter railroad tolls, barring the existence of a legislative contract to the contrary, was taken for granted."[51] In Prussia, too, the national railroad law, adopted in 1838, made clear the state's intent to regulate railroads in the traditional fashion, for it reserved to the state broad powers to oversee the activity of the private corporations. As Josef Enkling concludes, Prussian railroads *would* have amounted to "mixed enterprises" (*gemischtwirtschaftliche Unternehmungen*) from the outset, "*if* [the law's provisions] had been strictly followed in practice." But as a rule most of them were simply not enforced before 1848.[52] The American tradition of promoting *and* regulating transportation enterprises proved its resilience during the early decades of railroad development, but the parallel Prussian tradition did not. Despite similar conceptions of the state's role vis-à-vis transportation projects, railroad policies ran in different directions in the two countries.

Another explanation – at least for the salience of promotion in the United States and its comparative absence in Prussia – may lie in the configuration of interests favoring and opposing such projects. That is, one might think that railroad construction faced more opposition in Prussia than in the United States, a difference then reflected in the strength of each state's promotional efforts. But this line of argument, a standard in treatments of Prussian railroad history, does not hold up either. The pattern of interests, in fact, looked much the same in the two countries. In both, commercial and political (including military) considerations brought railroad development a significant degree of support in the abstract. Even in Prussia, as noted, 90 percent of the delegates from the provincial assemblies, where the nobility maintained a strong presence, declared themselves favorably disposed toward railroad construction in 1842 ("Die Verhandlungen . . ." 1881). But, when it came to specific projects, enthusiasm often fractured under the weight of pragmatic opposition. For, in both countries, the inherent disjunction between the long-term, generalized benefits of internal improvements and the short-term, disruptive effects that particular projects exercised on the local economy inevitably generated conflict. This kind of pragmatic concern underlay even the Prussian Junkers' reputed opposition to railroad construction. As Dietrich Eichholtz (1962:42) writes of their role in *Vormärz* railroad history, "one surely cannot speak of a principled opposition of the Junkers to railroad construction." Why not? Because they had turned increasingly to production for the market in the decades before 1848. When they did actively oppose railroad construction, they did so (like Southern planters and western Massachusetts farmers) largely because they feared that it would change trade patterns to their disadvantage. In both countries the railroad question generated conflicts of interest, and interests tended to break down along similar lines.[53]

If neither ideas nor interests provide a complete explanation for patterns of early railroad policy, then the key to the puzzle lies elsewhere. A closer look at the constraints that each political structure imposed on the policy-making process suggests that it lies in the distinctive dynamics that each political structure generated in a capitalist context.

In Prussia state officials shed their initial skepticism and, in the late 1830s, came to accept the view that railroad construction should be encouraged. But the task required a great deal of capital, far more than the monarchy had at its disposal. In theory the Prussian state could have financed construction through taxation or borrowing, as the American state governments did, but not in practice. Following a protracted recovery from the Napoleonic wars, the state budget had only just been put in sufficient shape by the early 1840s to allow a long-awaited reduction of taxes. Hence, the ministries were hardly in a political position to press for new taxes of the magnitude required to finance state railroad construction. Nor could they afford to raise the capital by borrowing, for this carried an even higher political price. According to the terms of the so-called National Debt Law of 1820, the state could not take out loans of more than $12.6 million (18 million Taler) without the approval of a parliament. This was a concession – a "credible commitment," as North and Weingast (1989) would put it – apparently extracted by the monarchy's creditors after the Napoleonic Wars. State officials had found ways to live with (and occasionally circumvent) it, until the coming of the railroads with their unprecedented capital needs and high visibility. Then the issue stood clearly posed. In order to finance construction itself, the crown would have to convene a parliament: marshaling the financial means to pursue a policy defined here as economically less liberal would require political liberalization.[54] In the eyes of the *Vormärz* crown, the price was simply too high. To be sure, convening delegates from the provincial assemblies in 1842 signaled a small concession by the king to liberal demands, but in reality little changed. The Prussian state retained its illiberal characteristics and railroad construction proceeded under the aegis of private enterprise.

Having made that choice, state officials then found it necessary to cede to the railroads' demands for a measure of freedom from government supervision, if the much-desired railroads were to be built at all. The railroad men, with cries of "alarmed capital," quickly turned the government's difficult position to advantage and used it to good effect in fending off regulation.[55] Time and again they warned that state efforts to regulate the industry would scare off investors.[56] David Hansemann, an "economic liberal" who headed the Rhenish Railroad and favored state construction himself, was particularly vocal on the subject. "It cannot be emphasized enough," he wrote (1841:110–11) in a critique of the 1838 national railroad law, "if the state wants to satisfy the great desire for railroads through private industry, then it must also give prospective capital all possible guarantees of lucrative and secure investment; this is the best means of attracting and retaining capital." At the heart of the matter, as he saw it (1841:24–7), lay a compromise: If the state wanted private capital to build the railroads, then "the least that the state must do is to prescribe good statutory regulations for the railroad system that will infuse not only native but also foreign capitalists with lasting trust and in that way attract capital to the larger railroad projects as well."[57] In short, private capital would build the railroads but, in doing so, it would extract a price for its services.

In a sense, then, the railroad era carried forward for a time the distinctive compromise between state and bourgeoisie that had prevailed in Prussia since 1815. As Wolfgang Klee (1982:100) writes, "Economic progress had to take place, had to show entrepreneurs (especially in the Rheinland) that the desired economic conditions, which made other western countries seem like a liberal economic paradise to the capitalists, could also be achieved without a parliament or a constitution." Obviously, one way to promote economic growth was for the state to build the railroads itself – the route taken, for example, by Belgium – but the Prussian monarchy did not have the financial resources to do so and it could not obtain them without liberalizing its polity.[58] Hence, in order to promote economic growth and yet resist political liberalization, state officials were forced by the logic of the situation to accord the railroads a substantial measure of freedom from state intervention.

In the United States, too, the pattern of railroad policies in the 1830s and 1840s reflected constraints imposed by the political structure itself. Because greater formal representation and more distinct separation of powers gave prominence to the state legislatures, a different dynamic drove policy-making in the United States, for the state legislatures proved, above all, more receptive to competing political demands. Hence, while American railroad promoters usually could marshal the political strength to obtain railroad charters, their opponents, empowered by the franchise, often proved capable of imposing constraints on them. "Charter log-rolling" not only produced an abundance of railroads, as some historians have noted[59]; when opposition to particular projects reached sufficient proportions, log-rolling also generated regulatory measures.

The political origins of the transit tax imposed on the Pennsylvania Railroad illustrate the way that legislative policy-making itself encouraged interventionist economic policies. In 1846 the Baltimore and Ohio Railroad applied to the Pennsylvania legislature for a charter to extend its road from Cumberland, Maryland, to Pittsburgh; at the same time, however, Philadelphia interests backed the proposed Pennsylvania Railroad, which would run parallel to the state canal between Harrisburg and Pittsburgh. With the western and southwestern counties of Pennsylvania solidly behind the Baltimore and Ohio Railroad, and the eastern region lobbying for the Pennsylvania Railroad, the rival projects unleashed conflict of tremendous proportions. At one point, twenty-two western counties even threatened to secede from Pennsylvania if the Baltimore and Ohio Railroad did not receive a charter.[60]

The Pennsylvania legislature ultimately resolved the conflict with a three-part compromise. First, it provisionally granted both charters, thus accommodating both east and west. Then, to the satisfaction of Philadelphia interests, it made the Baltimore and Ohio's charter contingent on the Pennsylvania Railroad's progress in raising capital and getting construction under way; if it failed to do so in a specified period of time, the Baltimore and Ohio's charter would take effect. Finally, the legislature inserted the provision in the Pennsylvania Railroad's charter that required it to pay a transit tax on freight. This was, in effect, the price of consent from the southwestern counties. They not only stood to gain little from construction of the Pennsylvania Railroad but also feared higher taxes if traffic declined on the state canals. The railroad transit tax served, in effect, as a partial consolation prize.[61]

In short, because the liberal structure of the American state empowered conflicting interests at the level of the state governments, the Pennsylvania Railroad received its charter but also labored under a transit tax. Noting how the Prussian state, once it had committed itself to private construction, stepped in to protect the railroads from competing interests, German historian Thomas Nipperdey (1983:192) concludes that "[i]n a fully democratic order the railroad would scarcely have been built." But the American experience in the antebellum state legislatures suggests differently. Not only would more railroads have been built in Prussia; more of them would have paid canal tolls, transit taxes, and the like.

When federalism is given proper weight, the early years of railroad development suggest that economic liberalism prevailed to a lesser extent in the United States than in Prussia, precisely because of the different constraints imposed by the two political structures on policy-making in a capitalist context. Because both economies were largely capitalist, private interests, through their control over the allocation of resources, set limits on the exercise of state power; as a consequence, the Prussian central state and the American state legislatures, each in their own way, engaged in a process of negotiation with private interests as the first railroads were built. But the Prussian state with its illiberal structure proved more constrained – and private interests, more empowered – by its dependence on private capital to build the railroads; accordingly, state officials found themselves hamstrung in their efforts to regulate the railroads. In the United States, in contrast, the state legislatures operated in a more liberal structure, the logic of which permitted and encouraged greater intervention. This serves as a clear warning not to assume that economic and political liberalism necessarily come as a package. In Prussia the twin goals of promoting economic growth and preserving an illiberal political structure mandated the adoption of liberal economic policies; in the United States the more representative policy-making process encouraged less liberal economic policies.

IV. THE TRANSFORMATIVE 1850S

Both patterns proved short-lived, however. Railroad development served as the opening wedge in a process of industrial change that transformed both nations into leading industrial powers by the end of the century. In initiating that transformation, the railroads introduced the twin phenomena that defined the new industrial order: capital intensity and increasing geographic scale. On the railroads, capital intensity manifested itself in two ways: in the unprecedented amounts of capital that single enterprises commanded; and in high fixed costs, which radically changed competitive behavior. The railroads also brought a vast extension of the geographic scale of enterprise, for they were the first business enterprises whose transactions and property holdings alike extended over great distances. This first encounter with industrial capitalism had different consequences in the two countries, however, because of differences in political structure. In Prussia the unprecedented amounts of capital that railroad construction demanded – *pace* Gerschenkron – forced a modicum of political liberalization. In the United States the combination of high fixed costs and geographic sprawl undermined the states' traditional regulatory authority. These institutional changes, in turn, altered the interventionist thrust of railroad policy in the two countries. As the process of industrial change laid bare the structural constraints on the American state legislatures' power, the interventionist thrust of American railroad policy became increasingly attenuated. In newly liberalized Prussia, meanwhile, railroad policy took an "American turn" as state officials began promoting *and* regulating the railroads with greater energy.

Hints of this transformation were already visible in the early 1840s, when, as noted earlier, American and Prussia railroad policy began to move in opposite directions. The American state governments began to divest themselves of state railroads – the second stage of what Carter Goodrich (1968) calls a "state in, state out" pattern of economic policy; during the same years, the Prussian state began somewhat tentatively to move "in." These trends not only continued in the 1850s, but gained momentum and took on added dimensions.

The transformation in Prussia, begun with the change of state policy in 1842, moved ahead a few years later, when the question of railroad construction again forced the crown further down the path toward liberalization. In 1847 the king called a joint meeting of the provincial assemblies (the United Diet) to seek approval of a set of financial measures that included a state loan of some thirty to forty million Taler. Roughly twice what the 1820 debt law allowed the crown to borrow without parliamentary approval, the loan was intended to finance state construction of the great Eastern Railroad, which would run from Berlin to Königsberg in the far northeastern reaches of Prussia. But the delegates held their ground, insisting that the provisions of the National Debt Law be abided by, and so did the king, who refused to allow the United Diet full parliamentary powers. Revolution came the following year.[62] In that sense the unprecedented levels of capital required for railroad construction – in the Prussian political context – helped to precipitate a transformation of the Prussian political structure.

By no means did a fully liberal regime emerge. The new political structure only took final form after a conservative reaction corrected the "excesses" of the revolution. With the crown in the lead, a coalition composed of *Landtag* conservatives, the bureaucracies, the nobility, the Protestant orthodoxy, and the officer corps of the standing army undid many of the revolutionary reforms between 1848 and 1854, retaining their outward constitutional forms but strengthening the power of the aristocracy, the bureaucracy, and the monarchy within them. At the national level, the attack centered on parliament. Not only was the Council of State revived but, more important, the Upper House was transformed into a House of Lords (Herrenhaus) in 1854. This was done in such a way that eligibility for three-quarters of the seats, formerly reserved for the largest tax-payers, was now restricted to an elite among the nobility – those possessing "old" and "established" estates – while the remaining 90 percent of the nobility, including the bourgeois nobles (*bürgerliche Rittergutsbesitzer*), were excluded. Those changes had, in turn, been made possible by replacing universal suffrage with a three-class system based on wealth. Governmental powers, moreover, remained intertwined, for the executive continued to influence the other branches of government through its ministers, who sat not only in the legislature but also on the final court of appeal (Ober-Tribunal). Even the king retained substantial power, since the ministers served at his, rather than Parliament's, pleasure. But bureaucratic control did attenuate somewhat, for the two houses of the Prussian Assembly now influenced policy – including railroad policy – through their powers of approval over state expenditures. Thus the revolution and its aftermath produced a constitutional monarchy in which central-state officials, while still powerful, nonetheless shared policy-making powers with Parliament.[63]

Once a degree of political liberalization had been achieved, the constraints that the old illiberal structure had imposed on economic policy lost their force. The necessity of obtaining parliamentary approval for state loans, as Klee (1982:118) observes, had previously made state railroads too "expensive" from a political standpoint. But now both a parliament and a constitution existed; now the state had greater latitude to raise the capital that it needed to "cultivate" state railroads. In the early 1850s, August von der Heydt of the Elberfeld banking family, head of the new Ministry for Commerce, Industry, and Public Works now responsible for railroad policy, stopped chartering private railroads for a time and launched a program of state railroad construction. By a variety of means, Minister von der Heydt, who became known as the "state railroad minister" for his enthusiasm to nationalize Prussian railroads, also took over the administration of some of the private lines.[64] Thus the revolution brought, as Tilly (1966:495) notes, "a turning point in Prussian fiscal history." Now that it had parliamentary support, the state dramatically increased borrowing and spending to further railroad development.

In the meantime the political dynamic first manifested in 1842, which coupled regulation with promotion, became more pronounced after the revolution, for Minister von der Heydt also brought the remaining private railroads under control in ways that the state had not done before 1848. In 1853, as noted earlier, he reasserted the state's authority to tax the railroads, securing passage of a tax on their net profits.[65] The central thrust of his efforts, however, aimed to reconstitute state control of rates and schedules. This he accomplished by adopting a technique explicitly tying promotion to regulation, one that had initially been tried out soon after the shift in state policy in 1842: He forced the private companies – when they wanted to increase their capital, for example, or to receive an interest guarantee – to accept charter amendments that gave the state control of rates and schedules.[66] In a related effort, von der Heydt also instituted night-train service on the major railroads in order to facilitate mail delivery, an extensive and ultimately successful campaign known at the time as the "night train affair" (*Nachtzugangelegenheit*).[67] In another well-known initiative, finally, von der Heydt drove down freight rates for the transportation of coal from Upper Silesia to Berlin.[68] In sum, as the Prussian state undertook an ambitious program to promote railroad development, it also reclaimed its regulatory powers in a variety of ways as the 1850s progressed.

Thus, in Prussia, the railroads' unprecedented capital intensity – in this case, their sheer demand for capital – precipitated a revolution; the revolution changed the political structure, which in turn altered the policy-making process; with a measure of political liberalization came less liberal economic policies. Before 1848 the constrained circumstances had offered little leeway for state action, whether promotional or regulatory. After 1848 the state could borrow virtually at will. The ''alarmed capital'' argument that the railroads had used to fend off regulation, moreover, lost its force as the major private lines went into operation and as state investment increased. Both trends enhanced the ministries' leverage. In the 1850s, consequently, Prussian railroad policy came to resemble the less liberal policy that the American structure had produced earlier.

In the United States, meanwhile, the state governments during the 1850s began to find themselves in a position that strangely resembled the Prussian state's predicament before 1848. Having partially divested themselves of railroads, they had lost some of the regulatory leverage that came with promotion. Now the railroads' capital intensity (manifested in high fixed costs) and their geographic sprawl precipitated a virtual revolution. The state legislatures' traditional methods of regulating transportation rates proved ill-equipped to deal with the peculiar competition that high fixed costs induced; as a consequence, rate regulation – in a federal-legislative structure – became thoroughly politicized. Then, when the railroads began to cross state lines, the legislatures' problems escalated. In the ensuing political struggle, American railroads took up the ''alarmed capital'' argument, developed a second version of it peculiarly suited to a federal structure, and used both to evade regulation with increasing ease in the 1850s. The state legislatures found their power undermined both by the federal political structure and by horizontal separation of powers. Understanding how the railroads precipitated this transformation requires a closer look at the state legislatures' traditional methods of regulation.

Initially the American state legislatures, as George H. Miller (1971) argues in a brilliant study, sought to regulate railroad rates in the same way that they had traditionally regulated transportation prices – by setting maximum tolls for use of the highway or, at least, by reserving the right to lower them.[69] This reflected two characteristics of traditional forms of transportation such as turnpikes or canals: The road- or waterway itself was owned by one party who set tolls for its use under noncompetitive conditions, while competition prevailed among the various parties (e.g., boatmen or stage companies) who provided transportation for passengers and freight. The legislatures thus regulated tolls for the use of the road or waterway but relied on competition among carriers to keep carrying charges at reasonable levels. At first, this approach seemed appropriate for railroads as well, since most of the early railroads did not face significant competition from other roads; like turnpike or canal companies, they enjoyed a monopoly in providing the roadway for use by the public. Even when it became clear in the late 1830s that safety and managerial efficiency would not allow multiple carriers on the railroads,[70] traditional methods still seemed workable, for now the railroads enjoyed a monopoly in providing both services. The legislatures, therefore, could simply regulate both by setting maximum rates. Tradition, as Miller emphasizes, provided firm support for the legislatures' right to regulate transportation prices under monopoly conditions.[71]

But, from the start, the railroads also presented an unprecedented regulatory problem of another kind: discriminatory rates. To an unprecedented degree, rate discrimination characterized the railroads because they were the first enterprises to operate under such high fixed costs. Fixed costs, in contrast to variable costs, did not change significantly with an increase or decrease in the volume of traffic carried or the distance travelled. Fixed costs on the railroads included such items as administrative expenses, depreciation on buildings and equipment, insurance, taxes, interest, and routine maintenance; variable costs generally consisted of wages and the other expenses of loading, unloading, and running trains as well as certain maintenance expenses that varied with the intensity of train operation.[72] High fixed costs, the hallmark of mass production later in the century, radically changed competitive behavior by introducing the practice of increasing production and cutting prices in hard times,[73] a phenomenon first apparent on the railroads.

From the beginning, railroad managers understood the practical significance of high fixed costs. "This elementary fact of economic life," George H. Miller (1971:17) notes, "was responsible for most of the early assumptions behind rate-making policies." As he explains:

Since the total cost of operation did not increase in proportion to the amount of traffic, a large volume of business was thought to be desirable, permitting overhead expenses to be distributed over a maximum number of units. This in turn seemed to justify low inducement rates. It was also evident that costs did not increase in proportion to the distance traveled because switching and terminal expenses were the same for short as for long hauls. It seemed practical therefore to seek long-haul traffic at lower rates per mile than were asked for short hauls.

Asymmetries in the flow of traffic back and forth provided additional incentives for discrimination.[74] "Almost from the outset," notes Miller (1971:17), such considerations "produced wide departures from a rate structure based simply on distance."

As quickly became apparent, traditional modes of regulation had little to say about the railroads' discriminatory rate structures. In writing charters, legislators traditionally focused exclusively on the problem of *high* rates, but both low inducement rates and long haul–short haul differentials meant that selected shippers paid rates that were *lower* than customary rates. Hence, maximum rates fixed in statute law did not address this peculiar new problem. Yet, common sense said that distance-based discrimination, in particular, was unjust, for transportation charges had always been proportional to the distance traveled. Thus a person who shipped goods, say, 100 miles should have to pay twice as much as someone who shipped goods only half the distance. (This was the basic premise of the pro-rata movements of the 1850s.) "It was clear from the outset," Miller (1971:23) observes,

that many, if not all, of these acts of discrimination were violations of the basic legal principle associated with common carriers: public transportation companies were obligated to treat all their customers fairly and without favor. When they did not do so the courts were supposed to offer remedies. For protection against unequal treatment, therefore, the people first turned to the courts, expecting to find their rights firmly established in the common law.

But they did not. The common law proved equally inadequate, for it, too, traditionally defined the problem in terms of high rates; unjust discrimination occurred only when the rate charged was "higher than the customary or prevailing rate" (1971:28). The courts had no precedent to follow where low rates were concerned. "As long as the higher rate was reasonable in itself," Miller (1971:32) explains, "there was no relief. . . . The common law provided no protection against the practice of rate cutting." In the late 1840s and early 1850s, therefore, constituents suffering discrimination took the issue back to the state legislatures.

About the same time, new developments in the railroad business completed the legislatures' introduction to the distinctive regulatory problems of the new industrial order and, in doing so, exposed the structural constraints on their power. As the eastern trunklines reached completion between 1849 and 1854, the volume of through traffic increased and competition intensified. This, in turn, magnified complaints from small and short-haul shippers as well from those shippers and communities that were not situated at points of trunkline competition and, therefore, paid higher rates. When competition among the trunklines became the norm, moreover, the premises on which legislative and judicial regulation traditionally rested seemed increasingly irrelevant, for competition now prevailed among the various trunklines as "highways" rather than as "carriers." The opening of the long-distance trunklines also raised that most intractable of questions: the competence of the state legislatures to regulate what was rapidly becoming the first interstate business. Thus, when the issue of rate regulation returned to the legislatures in the 1850s, the long-standing consensus undergirding their right to regulate rates disintegrated under the weight of industrial change. As Miller (1971:32) observes, "railroad reform became a political issue."

In those altered circumstances, the fractures designed into the American political structure in earlier days took on new significance. In the ensuing political battles, which raged from the 1850s through the 1880s, both federalism and separation of powers became weapons that the railroads sought to use to advantage. For, as Harry N. Scheiber (1975:115–16) argues, the American political structure offered several "routes of escape for business interests that were 'caught' in a particular state's policy of discrimination or stringent regulation." Federalism itself offered two separate avenues of escape from the state legislatures. Business could take a "lateral" route, in theory at least, moving from a "hostile" to a "benign" state. And, indeed, American railroad partisans, like Prussian railroad men, quickly used the "alarmed capital" argument precisely for this purpose. Two variants of the argument emerged in the 1850s, both of which exploited the structural constraints of federalism. One closely resembled the argument on which Prussian railroad men had relied: Regulation would scare off investors and inhibit further railroad development; the other, uniquely useful in a federal structure once interstate traffic developed, warned that regulation would imperil the capital in existing roads because through traffic would avoid the state that regulated its railroads. The first major controversy, which erupted in Rhode Island in 1850 when local shippers complained that rates on the New York, Providence, and Boston route discriminated against local traffic, brought both arguments into play. In the mid-1850s, critics of pending legislation to equalize rates charged that it would "alarm capital and crush enterprise"; rate regulation, they warned, would "effectually put a stop to any new railroads in our midst."[75] By the late 1850s, as another depression set in and competition with railroads in neighboring states intensified, the second version of the argument came into play. Now legislators began to worry that regulation would divert traffic away from its own lines; as John K. Towles (1909:318–19) explains, "the competition of other lines forced the Rhode Islanders to give a free hand to their own roads."

As railroad development progressed, the two versions of the "alarmed capital" argument varied in importance. Where the railroad network was thinner, the "Prussian" variant – stressing the threat to new investment – tended to carry greater weight. In those areas, the communities that had rail transport but suffered from rate discrimination tended to support regulation. The railroads, however, drew political support from the "have-not" communities, which feared that they would never obtain rail service if regulation scared off new investment.[76] Then, as the density of the railroad network increased, the "American" variant – warning that regulation would divert through traffic to other states – accordingly became more pronounced.[77] Such considerations lay behind the 1850 decision to abolish the canal tolls on railroads that paralleled the Erie Canal. Throughout the remainder of the decade, New York State railroads, allied with merchants in New York City, fought off canal tolls and equalized rates by arguing that higher rates for through traffic would divert commerce to other coastal cities and send New York City into decline.[78] Similar arguments were heard in Pennsylvania. Because of the tonnage tax that continued in force on the Pennsylvania Railroad, Governor James Pollock warned in 1858, "the produce of the west is forced upon the competing railroads of other States and to other markets than our own." The Pennsylvania Railroad and its supporters eventually used the same argument a few years later to remove the tonnage tax that its traffic had borne since 1846.[79] Once interstate traffic became a reality, federalism simultaneously undermined the regulatory thrust inherent in the legislative policy-making process and enhanced the leverage to be gained from the American version of the alarmed capital argument.

By the 1870s, moreover, the railroads as well as their opponents had both learned to exploit federalism in a second way, this time by moving "upward" to seek national, in place of state, legislation.[80] For the railroads' opponents, this seemed the only way to regulate an industry that had become national in scope; for the railroads, it became a means of defense against hostile state legislatures. And once the railroads crossed state lines, it should be noted, national legislation also better suited their needs. As early as 1854 one railroad official in New England implied as much. Even though he and his colleagues agreed that legislation governing such matters as common carrier liability, train speeds, and employee work rules would help the industry, state-level legislation, he argued, "would be . . . inexpedient, because of the difficulty of obtaining any united and uniform laws in the various States through which some railroads run."[81] National legislation had its attractions for both parties.[82]

Once the railroad question had become thoroughly politicized, separation of powers also became a valuable weapon as railroad partisans sought to fend off regulation. In this sense, too, business interests could move laterally – not by threatening to divert traffic to adjacent states but rather by avoiding hostile legislatures in favor of the state courts. New England railroad men opted for this strategy as early as 1850. Even though they would have preferred help from the state legislatures, they feared the consequences of seeking it. If the railroads took their problems to the legislatures, a Boston and Lowell official warned, "they would do the Railroads more harm than good." Thomas Hopkinson of the Boston and Worcester Railroad concurred; he "greatly feared that the burdens would be rather increased than diminished." A few years later, he again advised caution, deeming it "a bad policy to be bringing to bear directly on railroad corporations so much of the kind attention of legislators."[83] Another official, meanwhile, was convinced "that Railroads would have a better chance in New Hampshire Courts, than in the New Hampshire Legislature."[84] If the state courts also proved hostile, moreover, businessmen could again exploit the opportunities of federalism, moving "upward" by taking their complaints from the state to the federal courts. As through traffic became more important, the railroads resorted to this alternative with increasing frequency on diversity-of-citizenship grounds. Best known are the Granger cases, where the railroads sought quite explicitly, as Miller (1971:172) puts it, "to find sanctuary in the federal courts."[85]

In the new industrial order, in short, the federal-legislative structure of the American state exacerbated the already substantial difficulties of regulating capitalist enterprise. The expansion of railroads across state lines from the 1850s onward cast the problem in sharp relief: In the altered economic circumstances, the American political structure came to resemble a matrix (cf. Elazar 1987:37) that offered state-chartered railroads alternative "escape routes," as Scheiber so aptly puts it. As they sought to cope with industrial capitalism, the state governments' regulatory efforts ultimately foundered, in part because their jurisdiction in a federal structure was simply not adequate to the task and also because they operated in a structure that divided powers among the various branches of government.[86] Conflict over railroad regulation shifted decisively to the national level in 1886 when the Supreme Court declared unconstitutional the states' efforts to regulate interstate rates (*Wabash v. Illinois*). This made it clear that regulation would have to come from Congress. After a decade of stalemate, Congress quickly passed the Interstate Commerce Act (1887), creating the nation's first independent regulatory commission (Fiorina 1986; Gilligan, Marshall, and Weingast 1990). Neither the interests at stake nor the solution adopted were new; the novelty lay in the way that they were negotiated at the national level. However reluctantly, state officials on the Supreme Court and then in Congress had bowed to the new industrial realities. Prussian officials, in contrast, headed a unitary state that commanded the necessary jurisdiction from the outset; once the issue of railroad capital touched off the revolution of 1848 and the structure of the state had been transformed, they put it to good use.[87]

V. CONCLUSION

The key to the striking patterns of political structure and economic policy that prevailed in both countries thus lies in the nature of the two political structures themselves. The distinctive ways that the two political structures shaped the policy-making process pushed railroad policies in distinctive, if diametrically opposed, directions in the early years. In the end the conventional images of the American and Prussian states as the prototypical weak and strong states turn out to contain more than a kernel of truth – but only after the railroads' capital intensity had, in effect, transformed both political structures. Earlier, the two states, viewed through the lens of early railroad policy, do not conform to conventional images. The Prussian state's much vaunted strength proved largely illusory when it confronted the new, capital-intensive technology, while the American state governments began the railroad era empowered by a firm tradition of state promotion *and* regulation, one now largely obscured by the difficulties that beset them in the 1850s. When federalism is taken seriously and functional equivalents – the Prussian central state and the American state governments – are set side by side, the American state receives higher marks for interventionism during the early years and thus appears the stronger of the two. Behind the veil of federalism lay a moderately statist pattern of industrialization, driven by the exigencies of legislative policy-making and interstate competition.

Eventually, however, the railroads' capital intensity and geographic reach precipitated a transformation of both states, altering the formal structure of the Prussian state while shifting the seat of regulatory power within the American structure. In Prussia the problem of raising the extraordinary sums of capital that railroad construction demanded pushed the issue of political liberalization to the point of revolution. Only after the Prussian political structure had undergone a degree of liberalization was the state able to exercise the authority that it had possessed in theory from the outset. In light of the interventionist tendencies that the American state legislatures exhibited in the 1830s and 1840s, this outcome does not seem at all paradoxical. Over the long term, however, the Prussian state, partially liberalized but unencumbered by federalism and separation of powers, proved better equipped to regulate the first "big business." In the United States, in contrast, the peculiarities of railroad rate-making quickly challenged the state legislatures' traditional regulatory authority; and then, when the legislatures confronted interstate railroads in the 1850s, their power waned. Unlike the Prussian state, the American state governments, lacking jurisdiction beyond their boundaries and absent interstate policy coordination,[88] did not have the capacity to sustain their policies, for the railroads used the political structure itself to fend off the state legislatures. Only after several decades of political struggle, and a civil war that facilitated a permanent expansion of federal power, was the American state's authority to regulate industrial capitalism partially reconstituted at the national level (Bensen 1990; Skowronek 1982), although the conflict that the railroads unleashed persists to this day.

The vagaries of American and Prussian railroad policy highlight two general points about political structure and the making of industrial policy in a capitalist society. First, they caution one against the temptation to think that the impact of a given set of institutions on economic policy can be "read" directly from the institutional structure itself. Perhaps the most that can be said is that the dynamics of legislative policy-making encourage intervention. Generalizing any further requires due attention to the finer details of political structure and economic context. This comparative study of railroad policy, like the chapters by Hattam and Hall in this book, suggests that the significance of different political institutions ultimately depends on the particular circumstances in which they operate. The American state legislatures initially proved reasonably adept at promoting and regulating private enterprise; but after the rise of large-scale, capital-intensive enterprise, their position in a federal-legislative structure gutted their efficacy. Likewise, the Prussian central state appeared all-powerful until the advent of capital-intensive enterprise revealed the extent of its dependence on private economic interests.

Second, the two cases provide additional insight into Immergut's notion of "veto points." The history of American railroad policy testifies to the critical importance of the fractures that Immergut notes – gaps that occur when power is divided among the discrete elements that compose a set of political institutions and that offer opportunities to apply political pressure. In some measure, no doubt, federalism and separation of powers had empowered business interests and hampered legislative control from the beginning; but the "veto points" in the American political structure that became visible in the new industrial context engendered by the railroads' capital intensity and geographic sprawl doomed the state legislatures' efforts to regulate private enterprise. The Prussian story reinforces the lessons to be learned on the American side, for there it was precisely the absence of such openings that facilitated regulation in the 1850s.[89]

Before 1848, however, the Prussian experience reveals a different kind of fracture. This one arose from the peculiar division of power that prevailed in Prussian political economy before 1848, one in which political power resided in the crown but economic power was largely in private hands. In a sense it constituted an analogous fracture in a larger frame of reference, a disjunction between the spheres of political and economic power. As a consequence the crown had to depend on private capital to achieve its most important political goal, economic growth via railroad development. Prussian railroads – as American railroads would in the 1850s – exploited this dependence to fend off regulation. By liberalizing the political structure (when finally forced to do so), and thus closing the gap between polity and economy, Prussian state officials, in effect, diminished the state's vulnerability.

All along the American state had been less vulnerable in this respect, because legislative policy-making permitted and encouraged both state promotion and regulation. Instead, the state legislatures ultimately stumbled on federalism and separation of power – in short, on the American political structure itself – as the economic context changed. Historical experience in other policy areas, moreover, suggests that the pattern of railroad policy-making did not long remain unique.[90] If the relative weakness of American railroad policy since the 1850s constitutes one piece of the larger puzzle of "American exceptionalism," then the key to this larger puzzle also seems to lie in the subtle, pervasive, and enduring impact of the exceptional American political structure.

NOTES

1 North 1981; Williamson 1985; Bates 1990; North and Weingast 1990.
2 See Chandler 1977; North 1981; Williamson 1985; Bates 1990. Cf. Bates 1988. For the sake of convenience, I have stretched the term "new economic institutionalism" to include "positive political economy" (Alt and Shepsle 1990), since the latter represents the fruits of the former when applied to the political sphere. Both apply the "logic of choice" (Coase 1988:3) to their respective domains.
3 Cf. Smith 1988:96–7; Gordon 1989:84; Bates 1990. North (1981), it should be noted, departs from his colleagues in seeing not only calculated self-interest and efficiency seeking but also ideology as a factor that motivates individual or group behavior.
4 See details, see Dunlavy 1988 and 1990.
5 For examples, see Henderson 1958 and 1975 on Germany; and North 1966 and Cochran 1981 on the United States. Douglass North gives much greater weight to institutions in his later works.
6 See also Bowman 1986 and Chandler 1990.

7 For Germany, see Hoffmann 1963:96; Tilly 1966:484–97; Hardach 1972:65–70; Henderson 1975:23; Mottek 1987:77. For the United States, see North 1961:69–70, and 1963:45; Bruchey 1968:76–91, and 1988:26, 59; and Cochran 1981:78–100.

8 Both countries had a fairly well-developed public sector of the economy as the railroad era opened. In Prussia, the state, particularly through the Overseas Trading Corporation (Seehandlung) and the Mining Office (Oberbergsamt), owned a number of manufacturing and mining enterprises. In the United States, state enterprise came primarily in the form of state government participation in banking and transportation. Yet in neither country did the public sector carry so much weight that the economy could not be called capitalist. For Prussia the classic work is Henderson 1958; cf. Henderson 1975. For the United States, see Callender 1902; Taylor [1951]/1968:352–83; and Goodrich 1960. The extent to which agriculture in the Prussian East and American South took a capitalist form is a matter of considerable controversy; for an introduction, see Bleiber 1983, esp. pp. 102–6; Harnisch 1983:116–44; and Bowman 1986:36–67.

9 Horn 1979:124–5; Kocka 1980:18–19.

10 Cf. Gerschenkron 1966.

11 *Vormärz* refers to the period from the Congress of Vienna in 1815 to the revolution in March of 1848.

12 The pioneering state-level studies were Heath 1954; Primm 1954; Hartz 1968; and Handlin and Handlin 1969. These studies, which were sponsored by the Social Science Research Council, had their origins in the New Deal era; for details on the project, see Handlin and Handlin 1969:viii–x and appendix G. Related works include Goodrich 1960; Harry N. Scheiber 1969. For reviews of the literature over the years, see Lively 1955; Broude 1959; Goodrich 1970; Pisani 1987; and Scheiber's numerous insightful essays. For a recent study that bring new questions to this line of inquiry, see Gunn 1988.

13 Here scholars have followed the lead of Hurst 1956. For overviews of the literature, see Scheiber 1981 and Pisani 1987. For an innovative structural perspective on the courts, see Hattam 1990.

14 Smith 1985; O'Connell 1985; Hoskin and Macve 1988; Bourgin 1989. Although published recently, Bourgin's book, like the SSRC studies, was a product of the New Deal experience; for details see its foreword.

15 See Hardach 1972:73–7; Sperber 1985:280–4. For an overview of the Prussian state's activities, see Ritter 1961.

16 Friedrich 1968:5–6; cf. Elazar 1968 and 1987.

17 Scheiber 1975. The internal political structure of the state governments depended on the arrangements specified in their constitutions, subject only to the (national) Constitution's stricture (art. IV, sec. 4.) that they have "a Republican Form of Government." The Constitution did not elaborate on the subject, and it has generally been accepted that the form of the state governments that existed when the Constitution was adopted implicitly defined "republican." U.S. Congress, Senate 1938:548–9.

18 This description draws on Koselleck 1976:65–8, and 1980:219–36; Bleiber 1983:99–100; Ruf 1983:173–7. Cf. Heffter 1950 and Obenaus 1984. King Friedrich Wilhelm III reigned from 1797 until his death in 1840; he was succeeded by Friedrich Wilhelm IV, who died in 1861. Although weaker than in the United States, a degree of decentralization actually characterized Prussia throughout the nineteenth century, reflecting the country's persistently heterogeneous economic and social structure and evidenced in enduring domestic conflict "between ministerial centralism and provincial regionalism." Schütz 1983:28–31. Cf. Koselleck 1976:58, 63.

19 Central state officials appointed the magistrates (Landräte), but they did so from a list of candidates nominated by the district assemblies. Since the local nobility held the

preponderance of power in the latter, they could ensure that the magistrates came from their own ranks. In 1812 the district magistrate had been replaced by a district director, appointed directly by the state rather than by the district assembly; due to opposition from the nobility, however, the district-magistrate system was soon reinstated. Not until 1872 was the district magistrate made a civil servant (Ruf 1983:176).

20 By 1830 only five state governments still retained property qualifications on suffrage while another eight required voters to be taxpayers. In addition, most had moved to popular election of governors and presidential electors. A glaring exception to the shift toward manhood suffrage remained in place, of course, as long as slaves and (in some states) free blacks had no voting rights (Porter 1918:110, 148; Morris and Morris 1982:198).

21 On the structure of the state governments, see Morris and Morris 1982:132–3, 198. By the 1830s New York State under the Albany Regency had developed one of the strongest executives, its power most apparent in the areas of banking, education, and internal improvements. "For some time there has appeared in the administration of the State of New York," Michael Chevalier noted with approbation in 1835, "a character of grandeur, unity, and centralisation, that has procured it the title of the *Empire-State*" (Chevalier 1969:370–7, quotation from p. 371, original italics).

22 See note 18. The provincial assemblies (Provinziallandtage) were each headed by a marshal who was personally appointed by the king. In these bodies, noble (*ritterliche*) landowners held half of the votes, urban landowners a third, and peasant landowners a sixth, the nobility (*Standesherren*) voting as individuals and the others holding votes as a group.

23 Cf. Sewell 1967; Skocpol and Somers 1980.

24 Kocka 1987. The following works provide the best overview of Prussian railroad development: Klee 1982; Fremdling 1985. For the United States, see Meyer et al. 1917; Fishlow 1965; Taylor [1951]/1968:74–103.

25 In 1850, when the United States boasted more than 14,000 kilometers of track, Britain had 9,800; the German Confederation, 7,100 (including 3,000 km in Prussia); France, 2,900; and Belgium 900 km. In per capita terms, the United States had 6 km of track for every 10,000 inhabitants while Prussia had 1.8 km. Taylor 1960:526–7; U.S. Bureau of the Census 1960:Ser. A2, p. 211; Mitchell 1978:315–16; Fischer et al. 1982; Fremdling 1985:48.

26 For the United States, see Fogel 1964; Fishlow 1965; O'Brien 1977; Fogel 1979. For Germany, see Fremdling 1977, 1983, and 1985.

27 For Prussia, see Bösselmann 1939:48–49, and Obermann 1972; for the United States, see Chandler 1954, 1965, and 1977; for comparative perspectives, see Kocka 1987 and Chandler 1990.

28 For historical and theoretical insight, see Deane 1978; Hall 1987. Cf. Grampp 1965. Like Hartz 1955, Grampp defines his subject so broadly ("in a liberal economy the state may do whatever the people want it to do and that it is able to do," I:ix) that the term gives little purchase on the matters of greatest interest – the differences of opinion about the state's proper role that have so agitated political debate for two centuries.

29 Cf. Smith 1968:278. Friedrich 1968:6 treats the question whether a federal or a unitary structure is "more appropriate" in a given situation as a matter of "practical politics," but, as Elazar 1968:354 notes, federalism "as a political device" is usually valued as "a means of safeguarding individual and local liberties" through the dispersion of power.

30 For an influential neoclassical formulation of economic liberalism, see Friedman 1962:22–36. Adam Smith himself envisioned a larger role for the state than is commonly recognized. The term "intervention," it should be noted, implies a notion of

intrinsically separate political and economic spheres that runs counter to the broader argument here. In the interests of accessibility, however, I have retained it.

31 For details, see Phillips 1906; Burgess and Kennedy 1949:96; Goodrich 1949:371–2, and 1950:145–50; Taylor [1951]/1968:90–1, 382–3; Parks 1972.

32 Gerstner 1843:222; Poor 1860:580; Goodrich 1949:360–5; Taylor [1951]/1968:92–4.

33 As early as 1838, the state governments alone had incurred debts totaling $42.9 million for railroad development (Taylor [1951]/1968:92, 374; and Adler 1970:10). It would be helpful to have data on total railroad investment to this date, but such do not seem to be available. Two years later, however, a foreign observer reported what was probably an upper limit of $105.9 million (Gerstner 1843:334–7). This suggests a minimum contribution from the state governments of 40 percent.

34 Goodrich 1950:148–51, quotation from p. 148.

35 Joseph Mendelssohn to [August] Leo in Paris, June 29, 1844, in Staatsbibliothek Preussischer Kulturbesitz (West Berlin), Musikabteilung, Mendelssohn Archiv, Bankhaus Mendelssohn & Co., Vol. IX, Section VI. I am indebted to Dr. Hans-Günter Klein for allowing me access to this collection before it had been catalogued.

36 For a detailed study of early policy, see Paul 1938:250–303. Through the Seehandlung the state purchased 1,000,000 Taler ($700,000) of stock in the Berlin-Anhalt Railroad and loaned the company an additional 500,000 Taler ($350,000). The Finance Ministry also invested 500,000 Taler in Berlin-Stettin railroad bonds, buying them at par when they were selling below par on the stock exchange and agreeing to forgo ½ percent interest for six years (Schreiber 1874:8–9; Henderson 1958:119–47). I have converted Taler to dollars at a rate of $0.70. See Gerstner 1839:vol. 1, p. ii, and 1843:viii; Kgl. Legations-Kasse, Berlin, Sept. 17, 1840, Zentrales Staatsarchiv Merseburg, Historische Abteilung II (hereafter, ZStA Merseburg), Rep. 2.4.1, Abt. II, No. 7694, Vol. I, p. 34r; [Ministry of Foreign Affairs] to Royal Prussian General Consul König in Alexandria [Egypt], Feb. 25, 1861, in ibid., p. 108r; Bowman 1980:795r.

37 For details, see Extract, Friedrich Wilhelm to Council of Ministers, Nov. 22, 1842, in ZStA Merseburg, Rep. 93E, No. 546, Vol. I, pp. 2r–3v; Cabinet Order, Friedrich Wilhelm to Minister von Bodelschwingh, Dec. 31, 1842, in ibid., pp. 23r–v; Friedrich Wilhelm to Minister von Bodelschwingh, April 28, 1843, in ibid., p. 31r; Reden 1844:303–4; Schreiber 1874:9–12; "Die Verhandlungen . . ." 1881; Enkling 1935:66–9; Henderson 1958:163–6; Klee 1982:105–8, 215.

38 Bösselmann 1939:202; report of the General State Treasury (General-Staats-Kasse) on the status of the Railroad Fund in 1846 in ZStA Merseburg, Rep. 93E, No. 546, Vol. I, pp. 122r–123r; "General-Dispositions-Plan für die Verwendung des Eisenbahn-Fonds in den Jahren 1847 bis einschliesslich 1856" in ibid., pp. 142r–143v.

39 Fremdling 1985:126. For details on the state's participation in individual railroad lines to 1869, see Rapmund 1869. Bösselmann 1939:201–2 provides useful summaries of railroad stocks and bonds issued up to 1850.

40 Maryland and New Jersey also imposed transit taxes on through passenger traffic, but they did so to generate state revenue in a politically inexpensive fashion. Until the 1870s, both states garnered a substantial portion of their revenue from such taxes, a strategy that increased in popularity during the Civil War. See Merk 1949:2–3. A Maryland legislative committee that advocated state construction of the Washington branch of the Baltimore and Ohio Railroad in 1830 argued that "it would . . . ensure a permanent and valuable revenue to the State . . . [so that] every system of revenue burthensome to the citizens of the state, unfair in its operation or injurious to the morals of the community, might at once be dispensed with and abolished." Maryland House of Delegates, Committee on Internal Improvement, *Report of the Committee*

on Internal Improvement, Delivered by Archibald Lee, Esq., Chairman, December session, 1830–1 (Annapolis, 1831), p. 5. The line was eventually built by the Baltimore and Ohio Railroad, but the legislature gave it considerable financial aid (as did local governments) and at the same time imposed the transit tax mentioned above. Once it had established the Baltimore and Ohio Railroad as a comfortable source of revenue, moreover, the legislature refused repeatedly to consider chartering competing lines to Washington. Merk 1949:4.

41 Meyer et al. 1917:316–17, 354–55; Van Metre n.d.:52–7; Taylor [1951]/1968:85.
42 New York State Assembly, Doc. No. 97, 78th session, 1855, quoted in Van Metre n.d.: 56–7.
43 New York [pseud.] 1860:3, 27–8; Towles 1909; Merk 1949:1, 7.
44 Pollock 1902:937; Van Metre n.d.:57–9; Meyer et al. 1917:395; Schotter 1927:7–8; Merk 1949:1–2 Hartz 1955:267–8. This and related legislation were reprinted in *By-Laws of the Board of Directors . . .* 1847. The state finally sold the Main Line to the railroad in 1857. According to that agreement, the railroad would thenceforth be exempt from state taxes, including the tonnage tax. But the state supreme court declared the provision unconstitutional, so the tax was reinstated until finally repealed in 1861.
45 Enkling 1935:9–10, 28, 52; Paul 1938:260, 269–71; Klee 1982:99.
46 Enkling 1935:45–8; 78–9; Henderson 1958:179; [Magdeburg-Leipzig Railroad] 1843:170r. Details on other aspects of the dispute between the railroads and the post office may be found in the sources cited in note 45.
47 Two years before the revolution, for example, the finance minister instructed the railroads to submit the annual reports required by the 1838 law. As §34 of the law made clear, these were necessary in order for the state to exercise its powers to regulate tolls. His action thus implied an effort to enforce that provision of the law for the first time. It had little immediate effect, however, except that it helped the railroads to surmount the barriers to collective action. The details are summarized in Dunlavy 1990 and treated in more detail along with other aspects of state policy in Dunlavy 1988:322–429.
48 Cf. Hall 1983; March and Olsen 1984; Skocpol 1985; Smith 1988; Steinmo 1989.
49 Taylor [1951]/1968:18–21, quotation from p. 19; Scheiber 1982:1–13; Bourgin 1989:127–75. Even though in 1817 Madison vetoed the Bonus Bill (which would have used monies derived from chartering the Bank of the United States to finance internal improvements), he did not object to the proposal itself but rather wanted a specific constitutional amendment so that it would not require a broad construction of the Constitution. See the works by Scheiber and Bourgin cited here. As Taylor [1951]/1968:20–1) points out, "Despite a great parade of constitutional scruple, successive chief executives and congresses actually approved grants to aid in building specific roads, canals, and railroads." Even Andrew Jackson's administration, known for its hostility to federal action, spent nearly twice as much each year on internal improvements as did that of John Quincy Adams, "the great champion of internal improvements." Annually the Adams administration spent $702,000 while Jackson's spent $1,323,000.
50 "Die Verhandlungen . . ." 1881:4, 7; Ritter 1961:140–1, 144–6; Taylor [1951]/1968:16; Henning 1973:80; Koselleck 1976:77; Klee 1982:100–1, 107.
51 Cf. Meyer et al. 1917:558; Taylor [1951]/1968:88–9, 379.
52 "Gesetz über die Eisenbahn-Unternehmungen, vom 3. November 1838," *Gesetz-Sammlung für die Königlichen Preussischen Staaten*, No. 35, reprinted in Klee 1982:appendix; Gleim 1888:804–6; Enkling 1935:75, italics added.
53 For a fuller treatment, see Dunlavy 1988:37–109.
54 For this general line of argument and additional details, see Reden 1844:4; Kech 1911:50; Enkling 1935:66; Henderson 1958:124, 163–5, and 1975:48–9; Tilly 1966;

Klee 1982:10–11. The origins of the 1820 agreement clearly call for additional research; as one historian has written recently, it became "quite central" to Prussian politics in the *Vormärz* period. Nipperdey 1983:278.

55 I have borrowed the term "alarmed capital" from Miller 1971, who draws it from the mid–nineteenth-century American context. See subsequent discussion.

56 Cf. Gleim 1888:291–6; Enkling 1935:43, 51–2.

57 See also Hanseman 1837; Klee 1982:101.

58 On this general dilemma during these years, see Chevalier 1969:275–6.

59 Hartz 1968:44–5; Scheiber 1975:89. "Charter log-rolling" involved banks as well as transportation projects and sometimes linked the two. The 1835 charter for Second Bank of the United States, for example, required it to subscribe to the stock of ten transportation companies (mainly railroads and canals) and to make "grants of financial assistance" to another eleven turnpikes and roads (Hartz 1968:46–7). As part of the "revulsion" against state enterprise, some of the new state constitutions explicitly forbade chartering more than one railroad at a time (Goodrich 1950:146).

60 Hungerford 1928:241–2; Hartz 1968:42–4; Stover 1987:66–7.

61 Hungerford 1928:242–4; Hartz 1968:43, 52–3, 267–8; Stover 1987:68. The Baltimore and Ohio's charter would have required it to pay transit taxes on both freight and passengers. See *By-Laws of the Board of Directors . . .* 1847:26.

62 The railroad loan was one of two financial measures that state officials presented to the United Diet; the other concerned agricultural credit. For details and background, see Henderson 1958:124, 163, 165–8; Tilly 1966:489; Klee 1982:110–13.

63 Heffter 1976:177–96; Hahn 1977:3–27; Dietrich 1983:204–5; Nipperdey 1983:679–83.

64 Henderson 1958:171–80; Klee 1982:119–25. By 1852 the first state line had opened in its entirety; by the 1870s roughly half of Prussian railroad mileage was state-owned. Bismarck was not able to convince the German Reichstag to nationalize the railroads, but he did succeed in persuading the Prussian Landtag to allow the state to buy up the major private railroads during the 1880s. See Klee 1982 for an overview. The German state railroads as such did not come into existence until the end of the Great War.

65 Henderson 1958:179–80, 185; Klee 1982:122, 124; Brophy 1991.

66 Enkling 1935:55–6. The 1843 case involved the Upper Silesian Railroad. See [Upper Silesian Railroad] 1867:60–7. For a later example, see [Magdeburg-Leipzig Railroad] 1850:88.5r.

67 Although the railroads contested his action in the courts, von der Heydt had won the battle by the mid-1850s. See Henderson 1958:180–2; Klee 1982:215–16; Roloff 1916:885. The Berlin-Hamburg Railroad, supported by the Mecklenburg and Hamburg governments, put up strong resistance. See note 89.

68 Henderson 1958:182–3; Klee 1982: 126, 129.

69 The following paragraphs rely on the excellent discussion in Miller 1971:1–41. Citations are given only for quotations from Miller or for additional sources. See also Levy 1967:135–9.

70 Cf. *Evidence . . .* 1838.

71 Cf. Levy 1967:135–6.

72 Cf. Chandler 1977:116–9; and Klein 1990.

73 See the excellent discussion in Lamoreaux 1985:46–86.

74 For an early argument in favor of long-haul, short-haul differentials, see [Boston & Worcester Railroad] 1840a:7–8. For a general discussion of rate making at the time, see [Boston and Worcester Railroad] 1840b.

75 *Manufacturers' and Farmers' Journal*, January 20, 1854, quoted in Towles 1909:316–17. Cf. Miller 1971:33–4.

76 Miller 1971:39; Scheiber 1975:99. Cf. [Atchison, Topeka and Santa Fe Railroad

Company] 1879. This tract discussed the threat to new construction ("if a stringent tariff law is enacted, *it will be impossible to obtain one dollar of foreign capital for* [new railroads]," p. 42, original italics) and emphasized the company's political support in areas that did not yet have railroads (p. 43) but, given its location in a comparatively thin part of the railroad network, it did not mention the potential diversion of traffic.

77 Cf. Miller 1971:34–40.

78 Miller 1971:34–5, 217. Cf. Merk 1948:1.

79 Pollock 1902:937; Miller 1971:36–7. The Pennsylvania Railroad did not escape rate regulation altogether in 1861; in another "compromise," the tonnage tax and "other disabilities" were eliminated in exchange for a prohibition against long-haul–short-haul differentials (Miller 1971:36).

80 Cf. Scheiber 1975:115–16.

81 *Journal . . .* 1855:17–18.

82 Gilligan, Marshall, and Weingast 1989.

83 *Journal . . .* 1855:17.

84 *Proceedings . . .* 1855:85–7.

85 See Scheiber 1975:76–8, 116; Miller 1971:172–93.

86 See Scheiber 1975 for a broader argument to this effect, although he emphasizes federalism.

87 The unanticipated absence of competition among carriers on the railroads also confounded Prussian officials, who followed traditional practice and regulated tolls but not carrying charges in the 1838 railroad law. In the context of a unitary state, however, the issue did not unleash political battles the way that it did in the American federal-legislative system. Ultimately, the Prussian solution to the problem of rates was nationalization; see Gleim 1881:827–9.

88 As successive administrations have sought to curtail federal regulation since the late 1970s, a number of state governments, stepping "into the breach," have sensibly taken the necessary step of coordinating their actions. See Stephen Labaton, "States March into the Breach," *New York Times* (national edition), December 18, 1989, sec. 3, p. 1.

89 The Berlin-Hamburg Railroad's efforts to resist Minister von der Heydt's 1852 order to run night trains (to facilitate mail delivery) are illuminating in this respect. It put up a strong fight, because it had the backing of the other governments whose territory it crossed. The company instituted night-train service only when state officials arrived to take physical possession of its offices. Even then, the company continued to fight the order in courts for several years, winning in the municipal court (Stadt-Gericht) but losing in the higher levels of the judicial system (Kammer-Gericht and Ober-Tribunal). The president of the Ober-Tribunal, the highest court of appeal, was the minister of justice. See Klee 1982:215–16, and the many documents in the Staatsarchiv Hamburg, especially Bestand Senat, Cl. VII, Lit. K^a, No. 11, Vol. 13, Berlin-Hamburg Railroad, Fasc. 114a–114d. On the resistance of other railroads, see Brophy 1991.

90 Scheiber 1975; Elliott, Ackerman, and Millian 1985; Robertson 1989; Hattam 1990.

REFERENCES

Adler, Dorothy R. 1970. *British Investment in American Railways, 1834–1898.* Muriel E. Hidy, ed. Charlottesville: University Press of Virginia for the Eleutherian Mills–Hagley Foundation.

Alt, James E., and Kenneth A. Shepsle, eds. 1990. *Perspectives on Positive Political Economy.* Cambridge: Cambridge University Press.

[Atchison, Topeka, and Santa Fe Railroad]. 1879. *Memorial of the Atchison, Topeka and Santa Fe Railroad Company, to the Senate and House of Representatives of the State of Kansas.* Topeka: George W. Martin.

Bates, Robert H. 1989. "Contra Contractarianism: Some Reflections on the New Institutionalism." *Politics and Society* 16:387–401.

    1990. "Macropolitical Economy in the Field of Development." In James E. Alt and Kenneth A. Shepsle, eds. *Perspectives on Positive Political Economy.* Cambridge: Cambridge University Press.

Bensel, Richard Franklin. 1991. *Yankee Leviathan: The Origins of Central State Authority in America, 1859–1877.* Cambridge: Cambridge University Press.

Bleiber, Helmut. 1983. "Staat und bürgerliche Umwälzung in Deutschland: Zum Charakter besonders des preussischen Staates in der ersten Hälfte des 19. Jahrhunderts." In Gustav Seeber and Karl Heinz Noack, eds. *Preussen in der deutschen Geschichte nach 1789.* Berlin: Akademie-Verlag.

Bösselmann, Kurt. 1939. *Die Entwicklung des deutschen Aktienwesens im 19. Jahrhundert: Ein Beitrag zur Frage der Finanzierung gemeinwirtschaftlicher Unternehmungen und zu den Reformen des Aktienrechts.* Berlin: Walter de Gruyter.

[Boston and Worcester Railroad]. 1840a. *Report of the Directors of the Boston & Worcester Rail Road, to the Stockholders, at Their Ninth Annual Meeting, June 1, 1840.* Boston.

    1840b. *Report of a Committee of Directors of the Boston and Worcester Rail-Road Corporation. On the proposition of the Directors of the Western Rail-Road, to reduce the rates of fare and freight on the two Rail-roads.* Boston.

Bourgin, Frank. 1989. *The Great Challenge: The Myth of Laissez-Faire in the Early Republic.* Foreword by Arthur Schlesinger, Jr. New York: George Braziller.

Bowman, Shearer Davis. 1980. "Antebellum Planters and Vormärz Junkers in Comparative Perspective." *American Historical Review* 85:779–808.

    1986. Planters and Junkers: A Comparative Study of Two Nineteenth-Century Elites and Their Regional Societies. Ph.D. dissertation, University of California, Berkeley.

Brophy, James M. 1991. Capitulation or Negotiated Settlement? Entrepreneurs and the Prussian State, 1848–1866. Ph.D. dissertation, Indiana University, Bloomington.

Broude, Henry W. 1959. "The Role of the State in American Economic Development, 1820–1890." In Hugh G. J. Aitken, ed. *The State and Economic Growth,* pp. 4–25. New York: Social Science Research Council.

Bruchey, Stuart. 1968. *The Roots of American Economic Growth, 1607–1861: An Essay in Social Causation.* New York: Harper & Row, Harper Torchbooks.

    1988. *The Wealth of the Nation: An Economic History of the United States.* New York: Harper & Row.

Burgess, George H., and Miles C. Kennedy. 1949. *Centennial History of the Pennsylvania Railroad Company, 1846–1946.* Philadelphia: The Pennsylvania Railroad Company.

By-Laws of the Board of Directors . . . Together with the Charter of the Pennsylvania Railroad Company, Its Supplement, and Other Laws. . . . 1847. Philadelphia: United States Book and Job Publishing Office.

Callender, Guy S. 1902. "The Early Transportation and Banking Enterprises of the States in Relation to the Growth of Corporations." *Quarterly Journal of Economics* 17:111–162.

Campbell, E. G. 1940. "Railroads in National Defense, 1829–1848." *Mississippi Valley Historical Review* 27:361–78.

Carr, William. 1979. *A History of Germany, 1815–1945.* 2d ed. New York: St. Martin's Press.

Chandler, Alfred D., Jr. 1954. "Patterns of Railroad Finance, 1830–50." *Business History Review* 28:248–63.

——— 1965. *The Railroads: The Nation's First Big Business, Sources and Readings.* New York: Harcourt, Brace and World.

——— 1977. *The Visible Hand: The Managerial Revolution in American Business.* Cambridge, Mass.: Harvard University Press, Belknap Press.

——— 1990. *Scale and Scope: The Dynamics of Industrial Capitalism.* Cambridge, Mass.: Harvard University Press, Belknap Press.

Chevalier, Michael. [1839] 1969. *Society, Manners and Politics in the United States.* Boston. Reprinted, New York: Burt Franklin.

Coase, R. H. 1988. *The Firm, the Market, and the Law.* Chicago: University of Chicago Press.

Cochran, Thomas C. 1981. *Frontiers of Change: Early Industrialism in America.* Oxford: Oxford University Press.

Deane, Phyllis. 1978. *The Evolution of Economic Ideas.* Cambridge: Cambridge University Press.

Dietrich, Richard. 1983. "Preussen zwischen Absolutismus und Verfassungsstaat." In Manfred Schlenke, ed. *Preussen-Ploetz: Eine historische Bilanz in Daten und Deutungen.* Würzburg: Verlag Ploetz Freiburg.

"Die Verhandlungen der Vereinigten ständischen Ausschüsse über die Eisenbahnfrage in Preussen im Jahre 1842." 1881. *Archiv für Eisenbahnwesen* 4:1–21.

Dunlavy, Colleen A. 1988. Politics and Industrialization: Early Railroads in the United States and Prussia. Ph.D. dissertation, Massachusetts Institute of Technology, Cambridge, Mass.

——— 1990. "Organizing Railroad Interests: The Creation of National Railroad Associations in the United States and Prussia." *Business and Economic History,* 2d ser. 19:133–42.

——— 1991. "Mirror Images: Political Structure and Early Railroad Policy in the United States and Prussia." *Studies in American Political Development* 5:1–35.

Eichholtz, Dietrich. 1962. *Junker und Bourgeoisie vor 1848 in der preussischen Eisehbahngeschichte.* Deutsche Akademie der Wissenschaften zu Berlin, Schriften des Instituts für Geschichte, Series 1, Vol. 11. Berlin: Akademie-Verlag.

Elazar, Daniel J. 1968. "Federalism." *International Encyclopedia of the Social Sciences* 5:355–7.

——— 1987. *Exploring Federalism.* Tuscaloosa: University of Alabama Press.

Elliott, E. Donald, Bruce A. Ackerman, and John C. Millian. 1985. "Toward a Theory of Statutory Evolution: The Federalization of Environmental Law." *Journal of Law, Economics, and Organization* 1:313–40.

Enkling, Josef. 1935. *Die Stellung des Staates zu den Privateisenbahnen in der Anfangszeit des preussischen Eisenbahnwesens (1830–1848).* Kettwig: F. Flothmann.

Evidence Showing the Manner in Which Locomotive Engines Are Used upon Rail-Roads and the Danger and Inexpediency of Permitting Rival Companies Using Them on the Same Road. 1838. Boston.

Fiorina, Morris P. 1986. "Legislator Uncertainty, Legislative Control, and the Delegation of Legislative Power." *Journal of Law, Economics, and Organization* 2:33–51.

Fischer, Wolfram, Jochen Krengel, and Jutta Wietog. 1982. *Sozial-geschichtliches Arbeitsbuch. Band I: Materialien zur Statistik des Deutschen Bundes 1815–1870.* Munich: C. H. Beck.

Fishlow, Albert. 1965. *American Railroads and the Transformation of the Ante-Bellum Economy.* Cambridge, Mass.: Harvard University Press.

Fogel, Robert W. 1964. *Railroads and American Economic Growth: Essays in Econometric History.* Baltimore: Johns Hopkins University Press.

1979. "Notes on the Social Saving Controversy." *Journal of Economic History* 39:1–54.

Fremdling, Rainer. 1977. "Railroads and German Economic Growth: A Leading Sector Analysis with a Comparison to the United States and Great Britain." *Journal of Economic History* 37:586–7.

1983. "Germany." In Patrick O'Brien, ed. *Railways and the Economic Development of Western Europe, 1830–1914.* New York: St. Martin's Press.

1985. *Eisenbahnen und deutsches Wirtschaftswachstum, 1840–1879: Ein Beitrag zur Entwicklungstheorie und zur Theorie der Infrastruktur.* 2d ed., enl. Untersuchungen zur Wirtschafts-, Sozial- und Technikgeschichte, Vol. 2. Dortmund: Gesellschaft für Westfälische Wirtschaftsgeschichte e.V.

Friedman, Milton. 1962. *Capitalism and Freedom.* Chicago: University of Chicago Press.

Friedrich, Carl J. 1968. *Trends of Federalism in Theory and Practice.* New York: Frederick A. Praeger.

Gerschenkron, Alexander. 1966. *Economic Backwardness in Historical Perspective: A Book of Essays.* Cambridge, Mass.: Harvard University Press, Belknap Press.

Gerstner, Franz Anton Ritter von. 1839. *Berichte aus den Vereinigten Staaten von Nordamerica, über Eisenbahnen, Dampfschifffahrten, Banken und andere öffentliche Unternehmungen.* Leipzig: C. P. Melzer. Excerpts in English translation, edited by Frederick C. Gamst, are published in *Railroad History,* No. 163 (Autumn 1990):28–73.

1843. *Die innern Communicationen der Vereinigten Staaten von Nordamerica.* 2 vols. Vienna: L. Förster.

Gilligan, Thomas W., William J. Marshall, and Barry R. Weingast. 1989. "Regulation and the Theory of Legislative Choice: The Interstate Commerce Act of 1887." *Journal of Law and Economics* 32:35–61.

1990. "The Economic Incidence of the Interstate Commerce Act of 1887: A Theoretical and Empirical Analysis of the Short-Haul Pricing Constraint." *RAND Journal of Economics* 21:189–210.

Gleim. 1888. "Zum dritten November 1888." *Archiv für Eisenbahnwesen* 11:804–6.

Goodrich, Carter B. 1949. "The Virginia System of Mixed Enterprise: A Study of State Planning of Internal Improvements." *Political Science Quarterly* 64:371–7.

1950. "The Revulsion against Internal Improvements." *Journal of Economic History* 10:145–50.

1960. *Government Promotion of American Canals and Railroads, 1800–1890.* New York: Columbia University Press.

1968. "State In, State Out – A Pattern of Development Policy." *Journal of Economic Issues* 2:366–7.

1970. "Internal Improvements Reconsidered." *Journal of Economic History* 30:289–311.

Gordon, Robert W. 1989. "Critical Legal Histories." In Allan C. Hutchinson, ed. *Critical Legal Studies.* Totowa, N.J.: Rowman and Littlefield.

Grampp, William D. 1965. *Economic Liberalism.* 2 vols. New York: Random House.

Gunn, L. Ray. 1988. *The Decline of Authority: Public Economic Policy and Political Development in New York State, 1800–1860.* Ithaca, N.Y.: Cornell University Press.

Hahn, Erich. 1977. "Ministerial Responsibility and Impeachment in Prussia, 1848–63." *Central European History* 10:3–27.

Hall, John A. 1987. *Liberalism: Politics, Ideology and the Market*. Chapel Hill: University of North Carolina Press.

Hall, Peter A. 1983. "Patterns of Economic Policy: An Organizational Approach." In S. Born, D. Held, and J. Krieger, eds. *The State in Capitalist Europe*. London: Allen and Unwin.

Hamerow, Theodore S. 1958. *Restoration, Revolution, Reaction: Economics and Politics in Germany, 1815–1871*. Princeton, N.J.: Princeton University Press.

Handlin, Oscar, and Mary Flug Handlin. 1969. *Commonwealth: A Study of the Role of Government in the American Economy: Massachusetts, 1774–1861*. Rev. ed. Cambridge, Mass.: Harvard University Press, Belknap Press.

Hanseman, David. 1837. *Die Eisenbahnen und deren Aktionäre in ihrem Verhältniss zum Staat*. Leipzig: Renger'sche Verlagsbuchhandlung.

———. 1841. *Kritik des Preussischen Eisenbahn-Gesetzes vom 3. November 1838*. Aachen: J. A. Mayer.

Hardach, Karl W. 1972. "Some Remarks on German Economic Historiography and Its Understanding of the Industrial Revolution in Germany." *Journal of European Economic History* 1:73–7.

Harnisch, Hartmut. 1983. "Zum Stand der Diskussion um die Probleme des 'preussischen Weges' kapitalistischer Agrarentwicklung in der deutschen Geschichte." In Gustav Seeber and Karl Heinz Noack, eds. *Preussen in der deutschen Geschichte nach 1789*. Berlin: Akademie-Verlag.

Hartz, Louis. 1955. *The Liberal Tradition in America: An Interpretation of American Political Thought since the Revolution*. New York: Harcourt, Brace and Company.

———. 1968. *Economic Policy and Democratic Thought: Pennsylvania, 1776–1860*. Cambridge, Mass.: Harvard University Press, 1948. Reprinted, Chicago: Quadrangle Books, Quadrangle Paperbacks.

Hattam, Victoria. 1990. "Economic Visions and Political Strategies: American Labor and the State, 1865–1896." *Studies in American Political Development* 4:82–129.

Heath, Milton Sydney. 1954. *Constructive Liberalism: The Role of the State in Economic Development in Georgia to 1860*. Cambridge, Mass.: Harvard University Press.

Heffter, Heinrich. 1950. *Die deutsche Selbstverwaltung im 19. Jahrhundert: Geschichte der Ideen und Institutionen*. Stuttgart: K. F. Koehler Verlag.

———. 1976. "Der nachmärzliche Liberalismus: die Reaktion der fünfziger Jahre." In Hans-Ulrich Wehler, ed. *Moderne deutsche Sozialgeschichte*. 5th ed. Cologne: Kiepenheuer and Witsch, pp. 177–96.

Henderson, W. O. 1958. *The State and the Industrial Revolution in Prussia, 1740–1870*. Liverpool: Liverpool University Press.

———. 1975. *The Rise of German Industrial Power, 1834–1914*. Berkeley: University of California Press.

Henning, Friedrich-Wilhelm. 1973. *Die Industrialisierung in Deutschland 1800 bis 1914*. Paderborn: Schöningh.

Hoffman, Walther G. 1963. "The Take-Off in Germany." In W. W. Rostow, ed. *The Economics of Take-off into Sustained Growth*. London: Macmillan.

Horn, Norbert. 1979. "Aktienrechtliche Unternehmensorganisation in der Hochindustrialisierung (1860–1920): Deutschland, England, Frankreich und die USA im Vergleich." In Norbert Horn and Jürgen Kocka, eds. *Law and the Formation of the Big Enterprises in the 19th and 20th Centuries*. Göttingen: Vandenhoeck and Ruprecht.

Hoskin, Keith W., and Richard H. Macve. 1988. "The Genesis of Accountability: The West Point Connections." *Accounting, Organizations and Society* 13:37–73.

Hungerford, Edward. 1928. *The Story of the Baltimore & Ohio Railroad, 1827–1927*. New York: G. P. Putnam's Sons.

Hurst, James Willard. 1956. *Law and the Conditions of Freedom in the 19th-Century United States*. Madison: University of Wisconsin Press.

Journal of the Proceedings of the General Railroad Association, at Their Meeting Holden in New York, November 23d, 1854. 1855. Newark, N.J.

Kech, Edwin. 1911. *Geschichte der deutschen Eisenbahnpolitik*. Leipzig: G. J. Göschen.

Klein, Maury. 1990. "Competition and Regulation: The Railroad Model." *Business History Review* 64:311–25.

Klee, Wolfgang. 1982. *Preussische Eisenbahngeschichte*. Stuttgart: Verlag W. Kohlhammer.

Kobschätzky, Hans. 1971. *Streckenatlas der deutschen Eisenbahnen, 1835–1892*. Düsseldorf: Alba Buchverlag.

Kocka, Jürgen. 1980. *White Collar Workers in America, 1890–1940: A Social-Political History in International Perspective*. Tr. Maura Kealey. Sage Studies in 20th Century History, vol. 10. Beverly Hills, Calif.: Sage Publications.

——— 1987. "Eisenbahnverwaltung in der industriellen Revolution: Deutsch-Amerikanische Vergleiche." In H. Kellenbenz and Hans Pohl, eds. *Historia socialis et oeconomica. Festschrift für Wolfgang Zorn zum 65. Geburtstag. Vierteljahrschrift für Sozial- und Wirtschaftsgeschichte*. Beiheft 84. Stuttgart: F. Steiner Verlag Wiesbaden.

Kolko, Gabriel. 1965. *Railroads and Regulation, 1877–1916*. Princeton, N.J.: Princeton University Press.

Koselleck, Reinhart. 1980. "Altständische Rechte, außerständische Gesellschaft und Beamtenherrschaft im Vormärz." In Dirk Blasius, ed. *Preussen in der deutschen Geschichte*. Königstein/Ts.: Verlagsgruppe Athenäum-Hain-Scriptor-Hanstein.

——— 1976. "Staat und Gesellschaft in Preussen 1815–1848." In Hans-Ulrich Wehler, ed. *Moderne deutsche Sozialgeschichte*. 5th ed. Cologne: Verlag Kiepenheuer and Witsch.

Lamoreaux, Naomi, R. 1985. *The Great Merger Movement in American Business, 1895–1904*. Cambridge: Cambridge University Press.

Levy, Leonard W. 1967. *The Law of the Commonwealth and Chief Justice Shaw: The Evolution of American Law, 1830–1860*. Cambridge, Mass.: Harvard University Press. Reprinted, New York: Harper & Row, Harper Torchbooks.

Lively, Robert A. 1955. "The American System: A Review Article." *Business History Review* 29:81–96.

[Magdeburg-Leipzig Railroad]. 1843. *Geschäfts-Bericht des Directorium der Magdeburg-Cöthen-Halle-Leipzig Eisenbahn-Gesellschaft für die Zeit vom 15ten Mai 1842 bis zum 7ten April 1843*. In Zentrales Staatsarchiv Merseburg, Rep. 77, Tit. 258ª, No. 2, Vol. 1, pp. 170–175r.

——— 1850. *Geschäfts-Bericht der Direction der Magdeburg-Cöthen-Halle-Leipzig Eisenbahn-Gesellschaft für das Jahr 1850*. In Staatarchiv Magdeburg, Rep. C20Ib, No. 2851, Vol. 3, pp. 88.2v–88.14v.

March, James G., and Johan P. Olsen. 1984. "The New Institutionalism: Organizational Factors in Political Life." *American Political Science Review* 78:734–49.

Merk, Frederick. 1949. "Eastern Antecedents of the Grangers." *Agricultural History* 23:1–8.

Meyer, Balthasar H., Caroline E. MacGill, and a staff of collaborators. 1917. *History of Transportation in the United States before 1860*. Washington, D.C.: Carnegie Institution.

Miller, George H. 1971. *Railroads and the Granger Laws*. Madison: University of Wisconsin Press.

Mitchell, B. R. 1978. *European Historical Statistics, 1750–1970*. Abridged ed. New York: Columbia University Press, Macmillan Press Ltd.

Morris, Richard B., and Jeffrey B. Morris, eds. 1982. *Encyclopedia of American History*. 6th ed. New York: Harper & Row.

Mottek, Hans Mottek. 1987. *Wirtschaftsgeschichte Deutschlands: Ein Grundriss*, Vol. II: *Von der Zeit der französischen Revolution bis zur Zeit der Bismarckschen Reichsgründung*. 3d ed. Berlin: VEB Deutscher Verlag der Wissenschaften.

New York (pseud.). 1860. *Legislative Restrictions on the Carrying Trade of the Railways of the State of New York: Viewed in Connection with Outside Competition*. New York.

Nipperdey, Thomas. 1983. *Deutsche Geschichte, 1800–1866: Bürgerwelt und starker Staat*. Munich: C. H. Beck.

North, Douglass [1949] 1961 *The Economic Growth of the United States, 1790–1860*. New York: W. W. Norton. (Original published by Prentice-Hall.)

——— 1963. "Industrialization in the United States (1815–1860)." In W. W. Rostow, ed. *The Economics of Take-off into Sustained Growth*. London: Macmillan.

——— 1981. *Structure and Change in Economic History*. New York: W. W. Norton.

——— 1990. "Institutions and a Transaction-Cost Theory of Exchange." In James E. Alt and Kenneth A. Shepsle, eds. *Perspectives on Positive Political Economy*. Cambridge: Cambridge University Press.

North, Douglass C., and Barry R. Weingast. 1989. "Constitutions and Commitment: The Evolution of Institutions Governing Public Choice in Seventeenth-Century England." *Journal of Economic History* 49:803–32.

Obenaus, Herbert. 1984. *Anfänge des Parlamentarismus in Preussen bis 1848*. Düsseldorf: Droste Verlag.

Obermann, Karl. 1972. "Zur Beschaffung des Eisenbahn-Kapitals in Deutschland in den Jahren 1835–1855." *Revue Internationale d'Histoire de la Banque* 5:315–52.

O'Brien, Patrick. 1977. *The New Economic History of Railways*. London: Croom Helm.

O'Connell, Charles F., Jr. 1985. "The Corps of Engineers and the Rise of Modern Management, 1827–1856." In Merritt Roe Smith, ed. *Military Enterprise and Technological Change: Perspectives on the American Experience*. Cambridge, Mass.: MIT Press.

Parks, Robert J. 1972. *Democracy's Railroads: Public Enterprise in Jacksonian Michigan*. Port Washington, N.Y.: Kennikat Press.

Paul, Helmut. 1938. "Die preussische Eisenbahnpolitik von 1835–1838: Ein Beitrag zur Geschichte der Restauration und Reaktion in Preussen." *Archiv für Eisenbahnwesen* 50:250–303.

Phillips, Ulrich B. 1906. "An American State-Owned Railroad: The Western and Atlantic." *Yale Review* 15:259–82.

Pisani, Donald J. 1987. "Promotion and Regulation: Constitutionalism and the American Economy." *Journal of American History* 74:740–68.

Polanyi, Karl. 1944. *The Great Transformation: The Political and Economic Origins of Our Time*. Reprinted, 1957, Boston: Beacon Press.

Pollock, James. 1902. "Annual Message to the Assembly, 1858." In George Edward Reed, ed. *Pennsylvania Archives*, 4th Ser., Vol. 7: *Papers of the Governors, 1845–1858*. Harrisburg: State of Pennsylvania.

Poor, Henry V. 1860. *History of the Railroads and Canals of the United States of America*. New York.

Porter, Kirk H. 1918. *A History of Suffrage*. Chicago: University of Chicago Press.

Primm, James Neal. 1954. *Economic Policy in the Development of a Western State: Missouri, 1820–1860*. Cambridge, Mass.: Harvard University Press.

Proceedings of the Convention of the Northern Lines of Railway, Held at Boston, in December, 1850, and January, 1851. 1851. Boston.

Rapmund, F. 1869. *Die finanzielle Betheiligung des Preussischen Staats bei den Preus-*

sischen Privateisenbahnen. Berlin: Verlag der königlichen Geheimen Ober-Hof-buchdruckerei.

Reden, Friedrich Wilhelm von. 1844. *Die Eisenbahnen Deutschlands.* Berlin: Ernst Siegfried Mittler.

Ritner, Joseph. 1901. "Annual Message to the Assembly, 1837." In George Edward Reed, ed. *Pennsylvania Archives.* 4th Ser, Vol. 6: *Papers of the Governors, 1832–1845.* Harrisburg: State of Pennsylvania, pp. 384–6.

Ritter, Ulrich P. 1961. *Die Rolle des Staates in den Frühstadien der Industrialisierung: Die preussische Industrieförderung in der ersten Hälfte des 19. Jahrhunderts.* Berlin: Duncker and Humblot.

Robertson, David Brian. 1989. "The Bias of American Federalism: The Limits of Welfare-State Development in the Progressive Era." *Journal of Policy History* 1:261–91.

Roloff. 1916. "Aus der Geschichte der Berlin-Stettiner Eisenbahngesellschaft." *Archiv für Eisenbahnwesen* 39:882–91.

Ruf, Peter. 1983. "Ansätze zur Erneuerung: Die preussischen Reformen 1807–1815." In Manfred Schlenke, ed. *Preussen-Ploetz: Eine historische Bilanz in Daten und Deutungen.* Würzburg: Verlag Ploetz Freiburg.

Scheiber, Harry N. 1960. *Ohio Canal Era: A Case Study of Government and the Economy, 1820–1861.* Athens: Ohio University Press.

1975. "Federalism and the American Economic Order, 1789–1910." *Law and Society Review* 10:57–118.

1980. "Public Economic Policy and the American Legal System: Historical Perspectives." *Wisconsin Law Review,* pp. 1159–89.

1981. "Regulation, Property Rights, and Definition of 'The Market': Law and the American Economy." *Journal of Economic History* 41:103–9.

1982. "The Transportation Revolution and American Law: Constitutionalism and Public Policy." In *Transportation and the Early Nation.* Indiana American Revolution Bicentennial Symposium. Indianapolis: Indiana Historical Society.

Schotter, Howard Ward. 1927. *The Growth and Development of the Pennsylvania Railroad Company: A Review of the Charter and Annual Reports of the Pennsylvania Railroad Company 1846 to 1926, Inclusive.* Philadelphia: Press of Allen, Lane and Scott.

Schreiber, K. 1874. *Die Preussischen Eisenbahnen und ihr Verhältniss zum Staat, 1834–1874.* Berlin: Ernst and Korn.

Schütz, Rüdiger. 1983. "Preussen und seine Provinzen." In Manfred Schlenke, ed. *Preussen-Ploetz: Eine historische Bilanz in Daten Deutungen.*Würzburg: Verlag Ploetz Freiburg.

Sewell, William H., Jr. 1967. "Marc Bloch and the Logic of Comparative History." *History and Theory* 6:208–18.

Skocpol, Theda. 1985. "Bringing the State Back In: Strategies of Analysis in Current Research." In Peter B. Evans, Dietrich Rueschemeyer, and Theda Skocpol, eds. *Bringing the State Back In.* Cambridge: Cambridge University Press.

Skocpol, Theda, and Margaret Somers. 1980. "The Uses of Comparative History in Macrosocial Inquiry." *Comparative Studies in Society and History* 22:174–97.

Skowronek, Stephen. 1982. *Building a New American State: The Expansion of National Administrative Capacities, 1877–1920.* Cambridge: Cambridge University Press.

Smith, David G. 1968. "Liberalism." *International Encyclopedia of the Social Sciences* 9:278.

Smith, Merritt Roe. 1985. "Army Ordnance and the 'American System' of Manufacturing, 1815–1861." In Merritt Roe Smith, ed. *Military Enterprise and Technologi-*

cal Change: Perspectives on the American Experience. Cambridge, Mass.: MIT Press.

Smith, Rogers M. 1988. "Political Jurisprudence, The New Institutionalism, and the Future of Public-Law." *American Political Science Review* 82:89–108.

Sperber, Jonathan. 1985. "State and Civil Society in Prussia: Thoughts on a New Edition of Reinhart Koselleck's *Preussen zwischen Reform und Revolution*." *Journal of Modern History* 57:280–4.

Steinmo, Sven. 1989. "Political Institutions and Tax Policy in the United States, Sweden, and Britain." *World Politics* 41:500–35.

Stover, John F. 1987. *History of the Baltimore and Ohio Railroad.* West Lafayette, Ind.: Purdue University Press.

Taylor, George Rogers. 1960. "Railroad Investment before the Civil War: Comment." In National Bureau of Economic Research, *Trends in the American Economy in the Nineteenth Century: Studies in Income and Wealth.* Princeton, N.J.: Princeton University Press.

[1951] 1968. *The Transportation Revolution, 1815–1860.* New York: Harper & Row, Harper Torchbooks.

Tilly, Richard. 1966. "The Political Economy of Public Finance and the Industrialization of Prussia, 1815–1866." *Journal of Economic History* 26:484–97.

Towles, John K. 1909. "Early Railroad Monopoly and Discrimination in Rhode Island, 1835–55." *Yale Review* 18:308–19.

Trebilcock, Clive. 1981. *The Industrialization of the Continental Powers, 1780–1914.* New York: Longman.

U.S. Bureau of the Census. 1960. *Historical Statistics of the United States, Colonial Times to 1957.* Washington, D.C.

U.S. Congress, Senate. 1938. *The Constitution of the United States of America (Annotated).* Senate Doc. No. 232, 74th Congress, 2d sess.

[Upper Silesian Railroad]. 1867. *Zur Feier des Fünfundzwanzigsten Jahrestages der Eröffnung des Betriebes auf der Oberschlesischen Eisenbahn, den 22. Mai 1867.* Breslau: Wilh. Gottl. Korn.

Van Metre, Thurman W. (n.d.). *Early Opposition to the Steam Railroad.* N.p.

Williamson, Oliver E. 1985. *The Economic Institutions of Capitalism.* New York: The Free Press.

6

Institutions and political change: Working-class formation in England and the United States, 1820–1896

VICTORIA C. HATTAM

THE PUZZLE

For the past century, English and American labor unions have adopted quite different strategies for advocating workers' interests and as a consequence have played very different roles in their respective political economies. In England the principal national labor organization, the Trades Union Congress (TUC), generally has looked to party and electoral politics as the cornerstone of its strategy; by forging strong ties with the Labour Party in the first two decades of the twentieth century, English unions have infused political debate with work-related issues and have advanced an extensive program of social reform. In contrast the American Federation of Labor (AFL) pursued a different strategy known as business unionism or voluntarism, in which workers' concerns were secured primarily through collective bargaining and industrial action on the shop floor.[1] At the high point of voluntarism, in the early decades of the twentieth century, the AFL largely eschewed political reform and adhered instead to a policy of nonpartisanship and political independence, even to the extent of opposing a wide range of government-sponsored social policies such as old age pensions, minimum wage and maximum hours laws, and compulsory health and unemployment insurance.[2]

To be sure, even in the golden era of AFL voluntarism American labor never withdrew from politics entirely. The AFL always maintained some contact with the Democratic Party, and continued to play a limited role in electoral politics. What has distinguished the American and English labor strategies was not engagement in politics per se, but rather the quite different terms on which each

I would especially like to thank Colleen Dunlavy, Ellen Immergut, Peter Lange, Richard Locke, Uday Metha, Jonas Pontusson, Theda Skocpol, Kathy Thelen, and the participants at the conference "The New Institutionalism: State, Society, and Economy in Advanced Industrial Societies," University of Colorado, Boulder, Colorado, Jan. 12–13, 1990, for comments on drafts of this essay. This chapter was first published in *Politics & Society,* 20, no. 2 (Spring 1992). It is reprinted with permission and minor revisions.

entered the political arena. After the turn of the century, the AFL both accepted and promoted a quite marked separation of work and politics in which the AFL participated in electoral politics but with little or no regard for work-based concerns. In England, on the other hand, divisions between work and politics have not been so sharply drawn as the Labour Party and its trade union allies explicitly have tried to infuse British politics with workplace concerns.[3]

The divergent labor movement development on the two sides of the Atlantic appears all the more perplexing when we recognize that for much of the nineteenth century the two labor movements followed a remarkably similar course. It was only in the last two decades of the nineteenth century that English and American labor strategies began to diverge. The puzzle, then, is to explain why movements that were at first so similar eventually turned to quite different spheres to further workers' interests. Or alternatively, why did the AFL break with the West European model and adopt instead the strategy of business unionism at the end of the century?

STATE STRUCTURE, IDEOLOGY, AND LABOR STRATEGY

The argument developed in this essay has two interrelated components: one institutional and one interpretative. The institutional argument claims that differences in state structure lead to differences in English and American labor strategy. Particular configurations of institutional power provided very different incentives and constraints for workers in the two countries and eventually channeled labor protest along different paths. While no government welcomed the increase in workers' power in the early nineteenth century, nations relied on quite distinct institutions to regulate workers' early attempts at organization. In Germany and France, for example, legislatures were responsible for regulating working-class organization through the socialist and Le Chapelier laws.[4] In the United States, however, courts were the principal institution for containing workers' collective action under the common law doctrine of criminal conspiracy.[5] The dominance of the courts over other branches of government, we will see, played a critical role in shaping labor strategy by providing few rewards for even successful political mobilization.

The English–American comparison is especially instructive because it provides a pair of most similar cases. Of all the advanced industrial societies, the English legal tradition and system of labor regulation most closely resembled that of the United States. To be sure, the courts were not the sole regulator of English labor, but shared responsibility with Parliament. Nevertheless, the same common law doctrine of criminal conspiracy along with the Combination Laws provided the two principal components of English labor policy.[6] In other Western democracies, the power of the courts was even more limited, thereby providing greater rewards for working-class mobilization than in either England or the

United States. If the more limited role of the English courts can be linked to the formation of a more politically active labor movement there, then the relationship between state structure and labor strategy should be clearer in other countries where the contrast with the United States is more pronounced.

The structural argument, however, only takes us part way in understanding the divergent patterns of labor movement development. After all, differences in the structure of the English and American states existed throughout the nineteenth century, but only came to play a decisive role in shaping labor strategy in the last quarter of the nineteenth century. The second leg of the argument adds an interpretative component that emphasizes the *changing significance* of state structures for working-class formation both over time and across organizations. Understanding how and why the role of the state changed over the course of the century takes us beyond structural considerations to the meaning and significance imparted to institutions by the working class. We will see that particular ideologies and cultural traditions were themselves constitutive of economic interests and institutional power. By attending more closely to the ideological and social context within which institutions are embedded we can develop a less static view of institutional power and thereby begin to unravel the changing role of the state in shaping labor movement development in England and the United States.

The essay proceeds in three parts. The first compares the English and American labor movements in the second half of the nineteenth century, between 1865 and 1896. Here different configurations of state power are shown to have played a decisive role in the AFL's turn to business unionism at the end of the nineteenth century. The second part returns to early state–labor relations in the 1820s and 1830s in order to show how ideology and culture mediated the nature and timing of state power. The final section looks beyond the English–American comparison to speculate on implications of the research for institutionalist accounts of politics more generally.

STATE STRUCTURE AND LABOR STRATEGY

Between 1865 and 1896, workers in both England and the United States organized collectively and began to demand state protection of the right to organize and strike. Before state protection could be secured, workers in both countries understood that the common law doctrine of criminal conspiracy had to be repealed. The conspiracy doctrine had long declared many forms of collective action to be a threat to public policy and individual liberty and had been used to regulate working-class organization from its inception. Beginning in the mid-1860s, workingmen's associations on both sides of the Atlantic embarked on an extensive campaign to repeal the conspiracy doctrine, or at least to exempt workers from prosecution under its reach.

The campaign to repeal the conspiracy doctrine was carried out in two stages in both countries. First, workers lobbied extensively for passage of anticonspiracy laws exempting labor from prosecution for criminal conspiracy. Once the legislation passed, the second stage ensued in which legislatures and the courts struggled over who was to interpret the new labor statutes. During the fist stage, English and American labor organizations adopted essentially the same strategies with very similar results. In England the Conference of Amalgamated Trades and later the Parliamentary Committee of the Trades Union Congress were the principal organizations lobbying for legislative reform. In the United States the campaign began at the state level, with the most extensive movements appearing in New York and Pennsylvania led by the New York Workingmen's Assembly and the Pennsylvania coal miners' unions. Beginning in 1881 state-level initiatives were joined at the national level by the Federation of Organized Trades and Labor Unions (FOTLU).[7]

Organizations in both countries employed quite sophisticated tactics in their political campaigns. Both labor movements displayed a detailed knowledge of their respective political institutions and carefully tailored their strategies to maximize passage of favorable legislation. English and American labor organizations followed legislative proceedings on a daily basis, sent deputations to relevant party officials, endorsed prospective candidates, educated the public, and even hired their own legal counsel to draft legislation to be introduced by friendly politicians.[8] Although by no means a radical political program, what is clear is that in the three decades following the Civil War, New York and Pennsylvania unions, like their English counterparts considered the state to be an important ally in their struggle with employers. Trade unions in both countries believed that workers' interests could be effectively protected through an extensive campaign for political reform.

Moreover, both the English and American anticonspiracy campaigns were equally successful, resulting in passage of eight anticonspiracy statutes between 1869 and 1891.[9] The particular form of state protection in both countries was almost identical: Neither country protected workers' right to organize unconditionally. Rather, all the anticonspiracy statutes limited protection to peaceful as opposed to coercive collective action. The English, New York, and Pennsylvania statutes all contained provisions against the use of force, threats, and intimidation that remained subject to criminal prosecution.[10] Despite these provisions, however, the English and American legislation delineated a legitimate sphere of workers' collective action and went a considerable distance in checking the courts' power to regulate industrial disputes in both nations.

Initially, then, the rewards for political mobilization seemed quite promising. In the 1870s and 1880s it looked as if both English and American workers could indeed protect their interests through political reform. Diligent organization and persistent pressure on their respective legislatures had paid off. Government policy toward labor had been effectively influenced through political channels, or so it seemed in the 1880s. Despite similar legislation, the level of state protection enjoyed by labor unions in England and the United States varied considerably. Passage of anticonspiracy laws by no means settled the question of government policy toward labor.

The courts and labor movement divergence

Implementation of the anticonspiracy statutes was not so straightforward, and followed a very different course in the two countries. The different patterns of implementation depended to a considerable extent on the balance of power between legislatures and the courts. Enforcing the right to organize and strike proved to be an especially elusive task for American labor, which had to contend with a more powerful and interventionist judiciary.

The history of the New York anticonspiracy laws captures in microcosm the underlying dynamics of the institutional struggle over labor regulation in the United States. The New York anticonspiracy laws of 1870, 1881, 1882, and 1887 did not put an end to conspiracy prosecutions altogether.[11] In fact, after each of the statutes had been passed, district attorneys continued to charge striking workers with criminal conspiracy. More important, state courts consistently ignored statutory provisions exempting workers from conspiracy and ruled in favor of the prosecution. Almost all of the postbellum conspiracy cases identified to date resulted in conviction, and many were accompanied by severe penalties and jail terms.[12] Whether or not American workers would be allowed to organize collectively in their negotiations with employers depended on the outcome of this three-cornered struggle between labor, the state legislature, and the state courts. The answer in the United States was resoundingly negative, as courts repeatedly overrode legislative initiatives in the last three decades of the nineteenth century.

The struggle between legislatures and the courts over which institution was to set the terms of industrial relations in the United States was negotiated repeatedly in the postbellum conspiracy trials. The issue at hand in each of the cases was whether or not the defendants' actions were protected from criminal prosecution under the newly enacted anticonspiracy statutes. The principal task for the prosecution attorneys in the postbellum conspiracy trials was to establish that strikers had "intimidated" their fellow workers, employers, or members of the public. The postbellum cases clearly demonstrate that the intimidation provisions contained in each of the anticonspiracy laws allowed for considerable judicial discretion when applying the statutes to actual disputes. No explicit force or violence need be used; the mere size of a picket line, the number of circulars distributed by union members, or an "attitude of menace" were held to intimidate, and as such provided sufficient grounds for conviction under the new statutes.[13]

The case of *People v. Wilzig* provides an excellent illustration of the persistence of conspiracy convictions despite passage of the anticonspiracy laws.[14] The case was formally one of extortion, but as Judge Barrett noted in his charge to the jury, the threat of conspiracy pervaded the case.[15] The dispute took place in the spring of 1886 with the boycotting of George Theiss's musical club on East Fourteenth Street in New York city. Early in March, Paul Wilzig and the other defendants came to Theiss's club and demanded that he dismiss his orchestra, bartenders, and waiters and hire instead union workers at union wages. Theiss protested that the musicians were already members of the Musical Union and that his brother-in-law was the head bartender and his son head waiter and that he did not want to dismiss them. The defendants refused to negotiate and gave Theiss twenty-four hours in which to comply with their demands. Theiss refused and a boycott was placed on his business.[16]

The boycott lasted fifteen days, during which "a body of men" picketed Theiss's club, distributed a circular condemning Theiss as "a foe to organized labor" and requesting customers to stay away from the club. At one point, the defendants "through their agents" entered the premises and plastered circulars on to the tables, in the bathrooms, and onto the frescoed walls. They also used "an infernal machine" to create such a stench in the place that the club had to be closed for several hours so as to ventilate the building. Finally the defendants were said to have set fire to scenery on the stage of the club. At times as many as five hundred bystanders gathered to watch the activity.

The dispute came to a head when the defendants threatened to establish a secondary boycott on Theiss's mineral water and beer suppliers. In order to head off the crisis, Theiss called a meeting of his employees, the defendants, and his suppliers. After eight hours of discussion, Theiss acceded to the defendants' demands and agreed to dismiss his current employees. Before the meeting ended, Beddles of the Central Labor Union demanded that Theiss pay the defendants $1,000 in order to cover the costs of the boycott. Again Theiss protested but eventually he gave in to this demand as well. The boycott was immediately called off and the dispute ended. Theiss was able to redress his grievance through the courts when the district attorney charged the defendants with extortion under the New York penal code.

The case was heard before Judge Barrett in the court of oyer and terminer.[17] In his charge to the jury, Judge Barrett summed up the current status of the conspiracy doctrine succinctly. First, Barrett acknowledged that the common law doctrine had been "greatly narrowed" by the recent anticonspiracy statutes. However, Barrett continued, the prevailing laws by no means licensed all forms of collective action due to the intimidation provisions included in the statutes. The task for the jury, then, was to determine whether the defendant's actions fell within these provisions. Barrett explicitly defined intimidation very broadly for the jury in the following terms:

Let us see what is meant by the word "intimidation." The defendant's counsel seem to have the idea that if a body of men, however large, operating in the manner suggested, only avoid acts of physical violence, they are within the law; and that the employer's business may be ruined with impunity, so long as no blow is struck, nor actual threat by word of mouth uttered. This is an error. The men who walk up and down in front of a man's shop may be guilty of intimidation, though they never raise a finger or utter a word. Their attitude may, nevertheless, be that of menace. They may intimidate by their numbers, their methods, their placards, their circulars and their devices.[18]

The conspiracy, for Judge Barrett, did not lie in workers' overt use of force or violence during the dispute. Rather their actions were intimidating because of the size of the protest, and the workers' attitude of menace, both extremely nebulous attributes for defining criminal action. All five defendants in the Wilzig case were convicted and received sentences ranging from one year and six months to three years and eight months of hard labor in a New York state prison.

Wilzig was by no means an exceptional case, as New York courts convicted striking workers for acting collectively in almost all the postbellum labor conspiracies.[19] Moreover, the same pattern of judicial obstruction can be seen in Pennsylvania as well, where a similar struggle to repeal the conspiracy doctrine was under way. There too, workers' demands were by and large successful: four anticonspiracy laws were passed, in 1869, 1872,1876, and 1891.[20] If anything, the Pennsylvania statutes were stronger and more comprehensive than the New York laws. The Pennsylvania legislation contained fewer limitations on workers' right to organize and strike, and tried to restrict judicial intervention in industrial disputes more explicitly than the New York statutes. Faced with a similar set of anticonspiracy laws, the Pennsylvania courts also were extremely reluctant to recognize workers' right to organize and strike under the new statutes.[21]

Perhaps the most notorious interpretation of an anticonspiracy statute was issued by a Pennsylvania county court in 1881.[22] The defendants, D. R. Jones, Hugh Anderson (both officers of the National Miners' Association) and approximately fourteen others were charged with conspiracy during a coal miners' strike at the Waverly Coal and Coke company in Westmoreland County, Pennsylvania. This dispute centered around the payment of lower wages by the Waverly Coal and Coke Company compared to other operators in the district. The Waverly miners, however, had signed a contract agreeing not to strike without giving the company sixty days' notice. If they broke this agreement, the miners had to forfeit 10 percent of the year's wages. On November 17 the Waverly miners met with two representatives of the National Miners' Association and agreed to go on strike to secure the "district price" if the Association would compensate them for their 10 percent forfeiture. The meeting was adjourned for a final decision the following evening. On their way to the town schoolhouse the following night, the defendants were arrested and charged with criminal conspiracy. Two counts were specified on the indictment. First, the defendants were charged with inducing workers to break their contract by suggesting that they ignore their sixty-day warning clause. Second, the defendants were charged with threatening to use a brass band to intimidate strikebreakers during the upcoming dispute.[23] The Westmoreland County court found the principal defendants guilty on both counts and stated that the presence of a brass band constituted "a hindrance within the meaning of the [anticonspiracy] act of 1876.''[24] The defendants were sentenced to pay the costs of prosecution, a fine of $100 each, and to be imprisoned for twenty-four hours in the county jail. The total cost of the fine amounted to $355.29, which the Miners' Association paid.[25]

By declaring the mere presence of a brass band to be an act of intimidation, the Pennsylvania court effectively rendered legislative protection of workers' collective action meaningless. The defense counsel appealed the lower court conviction to the Pennsylvania Supreme Court precisely on the grounds that the 1876 statute had legalized the miners' actions and that the county court conviction was in error. The defense requested that the Supreme Court provide an ''authoritative technical definition'' of the state's conspiracy laws because ''no law is as oppressive as an uncertain one.''[26] The decision to hear the appeal was discretionary, and the Pennsylvania Supreme Court determined not to take the case. Therefore no higher court ruling was given on the county court's extraordinary interpretation of the anticonspiracy statute.

Labor's response: Judicial obstruction and the turn to voluntarism

New York and Pennsylvania labor leaders were horrified by the postbellum conspiracy convictions and protested vigorously the class bias of the courts. As early as 1870, for example, the New York Workingmen's Assembly objected to the courts' ''unequal application of the law'' in which employers' combinations were not prosecuted under the conspiracy laws. ''Truly, it must be a crime to be a workingman, as it seems they only are amenable to the laws – they only are conspirators.''[27] The Wilzig decision was addressed explicitly by John Franey, chairman of the Assembly's Executive Committee, at the annual convention in September 1886.

This decision was rendered under the direct authority of no statute or legal enactment of any kind: it was made under cover of an artful misconstruction of a clause in the penal code regarding conspiracy. The word ''conspiracy'' has long been a facile legal weapon in the hands of capital, and the New York Judge and District Attorney only demonstrate their ability by finding a new definition for it in sending the Theiss boycotters to prison. It was a class decision in the interests of unscrupulous employers, and intended to intimidate and deter organized labor from even peaceably protecting its members.[28]

Similarly the president of the Assembly, Samuel Gompers, protested the postwar conspiracy convictions the following year.

Such trials, convictions and construction of the laws only tend to bring them [the judges] into discredit and contempt. It had been supposed that long ago the laws of conspiracy were in no way applicable to men in labor organizations having for their object the matter of regulating wages and hours of labor. If, as has now been decided, that the law of conspiracy still obtains in this question, the sooner it is repealed the better. Surely if monarchial England can afford to expunge obnoxious laws from her statutes, the Empire State of the Union can.[29]

By the mid-1880s, then, Franey, Gompers, and other New York and Pennsylvania labor leaders clearly considered the conspiracy convictions to be a travesty of justice and a considerable burden on American labor.[30] Their initial remedy for judicial obstruction was to return to the legislature for more effective protection. Neither New York nor Pennsylvania workers abandoned politics quickly. Instead, they redoubled their political efforts and tried to close the loopholes in the anticonspiracy laws through passage of more carefully drafted legislation. Thus the successive conspiracy statutes in New York and Pennsylvania between 1869 and 1891 were in many ways a testimony to organized labor's commitment to political change in the three decades following the Civil War.

By the turn of the century, however, the AFL had become disillusioned with the prospects of political reform. Their repeated campaigns to secure state protection of the right to organize were continually undermined by the courts. No matter how carefully the statutes were crafted, they seemed to have little or no capacity to curb the courts' power. Thus the postwar conspiracy convictions demonstrated repeatedly the difficulties of changing government policy toward labor through legislative channels. Moreover, it was not just the anticonspiracy laws that were blocked by the courts; the AFL's demands for improved hours, wages, and working conditions met with an equally ominous fate. Only where the anticonspiracy laws had been eroded through narrow interpretation, legislation establishing the eight-hour day, regular payment of wages, and prohibiting tenement manufacturing were declared unconstitutional.[31] Whether by judicial interpretation or the power of judicial review, the effect was the same; American labor frequently witnessed its hard won political victories being eroded by the courts in the postbellum decades. Not surprisingly, then, by the turn of the century many labor leaders began to articulate a deep-seated mistrust of politics and to advocate instead a change in strategy that would enable them to circumvent the unusual power of American judiciary.

The debate over the "political programme" at the AFL's Denver Convention captures nicely labor's increasing frustration with political reform. Delegates Beerman, Lloyd, Pomeroy, and Strasser opposed the ten-point platform precisely because the courts posed a major obstacle to effective political change. Although the delegates did not make explicit reference to the conspiracy laws, we can nevertheless see how the repeated pattern of political victory followed by judicial obstruction undermined their faith in the benefits of legislative change.[32] Delegate Pomeroy, for example, objected to plank 4, which called for "sanitary inspection of workshop, mine and home" in the following terms:

Under the kind of government with which we are infested at the present time everything of a legal nature that will permit the invasion of the people's homes is dangerous. This law could be used to destroy the sacredness that is supposed and did once surround the American home. I believe the home can be made sacred again, can be defended from the *violations of a judiciary that stretches laws at the dictation of their bosses, capital. . . .*

Leaving it [the plank] there, you leave a danger and a standing menace that has been already and will be used again against the rights of the citizens of this country.[33]

Delegates Beerman, Lloyd, and Strasser were less concerned with judicial interpretation and raised instead the specter of judicial review and the problems it created for political reform. Adolph Strasser summed up the frustration with legislative reform and began to articulate the basic features of voluntarist strategy during the debate over plank 3, calling for a "legal eight-hour workday." Rather than looking to the government as their savior, Strasser argued that workers would be better off if they directed their energy and resources to trade union organizing and protest on the shop floor.

There is one fact that cannot be overlooked. You cannot pass a general eight-hour day without changing the constitution of the United States and the constitution of every State in the Union. . . . I hold we cannot propose to wait with the eight hour movement until we secure it by law. The cigar makers passed a law, without the government, . . . and they have enforced the law without having policemen in every shop to see its enforcement. . . . I am opposed to wasting our time declaring for legislation being enacted for a time possibly after we are dead. I want to see something we can secure while we are alive.[34]

Perhaps the clearest account of the turn to voluntarism can be found in Samuel Gompers's autobiography in which he reflected on his "political work" in a chapter entitled "Learning Something of Legislation." Gompers had by no means always been a staunch advocate of business unionism. On the contrary, during the 1870s and 1880s, he campaigned actively to improve the workingmen's lot through political channels. Gompers's account of the New York cigarmakers' struggle to regulate tenement manufacturing in the City provides an uncanny parallel with the Workingmen's Assembly efforts to pass the anticonspiracy laws.[35]

Between 1878 and 1885 New York Cigarmakers Local 144 undertook an intensive campaign to abolish or at least improve the appalling conditions of tenement manufacturing. First, they lobbied for passage of an amendment to the federal revenue act that would have placed a prohibitive tax on cigars manufactured under tenement conditions. The amendment passed the House of Representatives in 1879 but did not make it out of the Senate. Second, the cigarmakers turned to the state level, where they tried to pressure the New York Assembly into prohibiting tenement manufacturing by using its police powers to regulate public health. An extensive lobby was maintained in Albany, with union representatives testifying regularly before the relevant committees, pledging representatives to support the bill, and endeavoring to elect their own representatives to the Assembly. After several abortive efforts a new state law prohibiting tenement manufacturing was passed in 1883.[36]

However, labor's hard-earned political victories for tenement reform, as with the anticonspiracy laws, seemed to have little or no real power. Soon after the tenement bill was passed, employers successfully challenged the constitutionality of the law in the New York courts on the grounds that the act violated the due process clause. As with the anticonspiracy statutes, New York unions were not so easily deterred and renewed their political work in order to enact a more effective statute that could withstand the scrutiny of the court. In May 1884 their efforts were again rewarded with a new, more carefully drafted law only to be overruled again by the New York Supreme Court and Circuit Court of Appeals.[37]

The Cigarmakers' unsuccessful struggle for tenement reform, according to Gompers, indeed taught him something about legislation, namely the ineffectiveness of securing effective change through political channels. "Securing the enactment of a law does not mean the solution of the problem as I learned in my legislative experience. The power of the courts to pass upon constitutionality of a law so complicates reform by legislation as to seriously restrict the effectiveness of that method."[38] When three decades of political work were continually undermined by the courts, New York and Pennsylvania workers began to look for other "methods" of protecting workers' interests within the confines of the divided American state.

The Cigarmakers' response to the failed tenement legislation might well have served as a blueprint for the shift in labor strategy more generally. Gompers described the change of tactics as follows:

After the Appeal Court declared against the principle of the law, we talked over the possibilities of further legislative action and decided to concentrate on organization work. Through our trade unions we harassed the manufacturers by strikes and agitation until they were convinced that we did not intend to stop until we gained our point and that it would be less costly for them to abandon the tenement manufacturing system and carry on the industry in factories under decent conditions. Thus we accomplished through economic power what we had failed to achieve through legislation.[39]

The AFL adopted a strategy of antistatist voluntarism, according to Gompers, precisely because of the frustration encountered in court for their political work. The power of the courts to set government policy convinced Gompers, Pomeroy, Strasser, and other members of the AFL that it was extremely difficult to secure enduring change through political channels.

To be sure, business unionism was not the only possible response to judicial obstruction. Indeed, at least two other reactions can be seen within the late nineteenth-century labor movement. On the one hand, the Socialist Party provided a very different way of negotiating the peculiarities of the American state. Instead of changing labor strategy as Gompers and the AFL suggested, Eugene Debs and the socialists called for a transformation of capitalist institutions. If the courts would not respond to workers' demands then workers must mobilize around a radical platform in order to create a more sympathetic regime. The task, from the socialists' perspective, was to change the state rather than refashion labor strategy.[40] William Hayward and the Industrial Workers of the World (the IWW, or Wobblies) represented a second alternative to business unionism. Their syndicalist program of direct action and shop-floor militance also contained a strong antistatist element. In many ways, business unionism and syndicalism were two sides of the same coin; both strategies enabled workers to avoid the frustrations of pursuing legislative reform within the divided American state by focusing their energies, albeit in very different ways, on the shop floor.[41]

The story told here does not explain why the socialist and syndicalist alternatives remained subordinate to the AFL's business unionism. All three strategies would have enabled workers to circumvent the power of the courts. What my research does explain, however, is why by 1900 the option of pursuing workers' interests through a labor party, or its equivalent, was no longer viable in the United States. The failure of New York and Pennsylvania campaigns to repeal the conspiracy doctrine laid bare the limitations of conventional party politics for influencing the state. Short of revolutionary transformation, there was little incentive for workers to mobilize politically as hard won political victories were continually obstructed by the courts. As long as the courts remained the primary institution for regulating labor, the antistatist strategy of business unionism seemed to many workers to provide a more promising means of securing workers' interests in the United States.

ENGLISH LABOR AND THE COURTS

Some might argue that the judicial interpretation of the New York and Pennsylvania anticonspiracy statutes reveals more about legislative politics than it does about the power of the courts. The New York and Pennsylvania statutes, so the argument might run, were simply symbolic victories that were never really intended to exempt workers from criminal prosecution. The statutes might have been passed with the intimidation provisions wittingly attached, legislators knowing full well that the judiciary could exploit these loopholes and continue to convict workers of criminal conspiracy. Fortunately, the limits of this argument can be gauged quickly by turning to the English case.

The English struggle for state recognition closely paralleled the New York and Pennsylvania movements. In the first phase, between 1867 and 1875, the Conference of Amalgamated Trades and the Parliamentary Committee of the Trades Union Congress lobbied Parliament for anticonspiracy legislation. The English campaign, like its New York and Pennsylvania counterparts, succeeded, resulting in two new anticonspiracy laws in 1871 and 1875.[42] The Trade Union Act of 1871 established two important checks on judicial power: Section Two granted unions immunity from prosecution under the common law doctrine of conspiracy and restraint of trade, while Section Four restored trade unions' right to register as Friendly Societies thereby protecting union funds from damage suits. Although the 1871 legislation went a considerable distance in protecting workers' industrial rights, Parliament, much like the New York and Pennsylvania legislatures, did not extend state protection unconditionally. Alongside the Trade Union Act of 1871, Parliament also passed the Criminal Law Amendment Act, which codified existing case law. The use of "violence, threats, intimidation, molestation or obstruction'' during industrial disputes remained illegal much as it had in the United States. A new campaign to repeal the Criminal Law Amendment Act was initiated by the Trades Union Congress and led to passage of the second anticonspiracy statute in 1875. The Conspiracy and Protection of Property Act went further than earlier legislation in protecting workers' right to organize by declaring all actions that were not themselves crimes when committed by an individual to be exempt from criminal prosecution if committed collectively. However, the 1875 statute continued to qualify state protection of workers' industrial rights under Section Seven, which declared the use of violence and intimidation to be criminal actions.

In 1875, then, the English and American labor strategy and legal status were very similar. Workers in both countries had set for themselves the task of securing state protection of the right to organize and strike. To change government policy toward labor, workers set about repealing the conspiracy doctrine through an extensive campaign of political reform. Moreover, the legislative victories in England and the United States were almost identical. Governments in both countries took clear steps to protect workers' right to organize, but also continued to identify specific actions beyond legislative protection. Implementation of the statutes, however, followed a very different course on the two sides of the Atlantic.

English employers were no more tolerant of working-class organization than their New York and Pennsylvania counterparts. When faced with a strike, they also were willing to testify as to the intimidating nature of their employees' behavior, thereby enabling workers to be convicted of criminal conspiracy under Section Seven of the 1875 Act.[43] Unlike their American counterparts, however, English courts did not continue to convict workers of conspiracy after 1875. Rather, English courts deferred to parliamentary authority and interpreted the provisions against the use of violence and intimidation more narrowly than either the New York or Pennsylvania courts.

Two of the leading English cases brought under the 1875 statute highlight the more limited role of the English courts. Two Queen's Bench cases, decided in 1891, *Curran v. Treleaven* and *Gibson v. Lawson,* like the postwar conspiracy cases in the United States, hinged on the question of how the courts should interpret the provisions against intimidation contained in Section Seven of the Conspiracy and Protection of Property Act.[44] In *Curran v. Treleaven,* the Court of Queen's Bench was faced with the question of whether or not ''injury to trade'' qualified as intimidation under the Conspiracy and Protection of Property Act.[45] Pete Curran, secretary of the National Union of Gas Workers and General Labourers of Great Britain, had been convicted by the court of petty sessions for ''wrongfully and without legal authority intimidating'' a Plymouth coal merchant named George Treleaven. The dispute centered on the use of nonunion labor to unload one of Treleaven's coal ships, the *Ocean Queen.* Union workers threatened to strike if Treleaven continued to hire nonunion workers. Union workers were charged with conspiracy on the grounds that they had intimidated Treleaven into fearing "injury to his business and consequently loss to himself." A strike to benefit workers, the prosecution argued, might have been legal, but a strike to injure the employer's business was an act of intimidation and as such was a criminal offense under Section Seven of the 1875 statute.[46]

The Court of Queen's Bench, however, disagreed with the prosecution's interpretation of the statute and adopted instead a more limited definition of intimidation. Unlike the American judiciary, English courts accepted a much wider range of industrial action as legitimate behavior, exempt from charges of criminal conspiracy. The Chief Justice delivered the opinion, denying that "injury to trade" was tantamount to intimidation, saying:

where the object [of a strike] is to benefit oneself, it can seldom, perhaps it can never, be effected without some consequent loss or injury to someone else. In trade, in commerce, even in a profession, what is one man's gain is another's loss, and where the object is not malicious, the mere fact that the effect is injurious does not make the agreement either illegal or actionable, and, therefore, is not indictable.[47]

The Queen's Bench reversed the lower court conviction and acquitted the workers, thereby affirming the earlier statutory protection of workers' industrial rights.

The more restrained approach of the English courts when interpreting the labor statutes can be seen especially clearly in a second case, which came before the Queen's Bench in the same term. In *Gibson v. Lawson*, the court again faced the issue if whether or not a particular strike action constituted a violation of Section Seven of the Conspiracy and Protection of Property Act. In delivering the opinion, Chief Justice Lord Coleridge explicitly deferred to parliamentary policy on the issue, and advocated a very limited role for judicial interpretation of statute law. For example, at one point in the opinion, Lord Coleridge noted that denying the appeal might appear to conflict with earlier convictions under the common law, especially the cases of *R. v. Druitt* and *R. v. Bunn*. The Chief Justice dismissed the apparent conflict, saying:

the cases of *Reg. v. Druitt* and *Reg. v. Bunn* in which Lord Bramwell and Lord Esher . . . are both said to have held the statutes on the subject have in no way interfered with or altered the common law, and that strikes and combinations expressly legalized by statute may yet be treated as indictable conspiracies at common law, and may be punished by imprisonment with hard labour. . . . We are well aware of the great authority of the judges by whom the above cases were decided, but we are unable to concur in these dicta, and, speaking with all deference, we think they are not law.[48]

Thus, the Queen's Bench rather dramatically repudiated past case law in order to comply with the recent parliamentary statutes. Moreover, Lord Coleridge explicitly acknowledged the supremacy of Parliament in his concluding remarks in the Lawson decision.

it seems to us that the law concerning combinations in reference to trade disputes is contained in 38 and 39 Vict. c 86, and in the statutes referred to in it, and that acts which are not indictable under that statute are not now, if, indeed, they ever were, indictable at common law.[49]

Gibson lost the appeal when the high court affirmed the lower court ruling and found the defendant not guilty of wrongful intimidation. The Queen's Bench, then, clearly reaffirmed Parliament's authority over labor policy. At least in the *Lawson* judgment, the court was willing to break with past case law in order to comply with new policies established in contemporary labor statutes.

In contrast to the New York and Pennsylvania workers, the English labor movement's struggle for state recognition was a more complete success. Not only did workers secure prolabor legislation through their intensive lobbying campaign, but these statutes actually protected workers from future conspiracy prosecutions. This more effective campaign for state protection, however, was not simply the product of more carefully drafted legislation, as both the American and English statutes contained similar intimidation provisions that could have been used by employers and the courts to secure subsequent prosecutions. Instead, the differences are more readily attributed to the effective division of political power between Parliament and the judiciary that was itself a legacy of past political struggles and social compromises negotiated at the end of the English Civil War. By deferring to the nineteenth-century labor statutes, the English courts were adhering to a long-standing tradition of Parliamentary supremacy, of which labor was now the unintended beneficiary.[50]

If the supremacy of Parliament indeed was the crucial factor in shaping labor strategy in England, then we must account for the resurgence of judicial hostility toward labor at the turn of the century. Did the revival of judicial hostility undermine past labor victories? Had the balance of power between the courts and Parliament changed? Why, after affirming the Conspiracy and Protection of Property Act so firmly in the 1890s, did the English courts hand down a series of antilabor decisions in the first decades of the twentieth century?

Taff Vale and civil liabilities

Even though the courts had deferred to Parliament when interpreting the Conspiracy and Protection of Property Act, the English struggle over state recognition of workers' industrial rights was by no means entirely resolved by the turn of the century. In the succeeding decades, unions were confronted with new attacks on their legal status, prompting further legislation to protect organized labor from renewed challenges in the courts. In fact, the most infamous antilabor cases were yet to come; *Quinn v. Leatham,* Taff Vale, and the Osborne judgment were handed down by the courts in the first two decades of the twentieth century, well after the legislative victories of 1871 and 1875.[51] These later cases, however, did not represent a change in judicial interpretation of the existing labor statutes, but rather reflected changes in other areas of common law doctrine that opened up entirely new legal issues that had not been covered by earlier legislation. All of these later convictions were brought as civil rather than criminal prosecutions and thus required additional parliamentary protection. The Conspiracy and Protection of Property Act had succeeded in protecting unions from *criminal* prosecution but had not been designed to, nor was it capable of, protecting workers from claims for *civil* liabilities.

The renewed attack on organized labor in the first two decades of the twentieth century was made possible both by developments in English corporation law during the 1890s and by the particular form of legislative protection provided by the English state. Prior to 1901, labor unions generally had been considered immune from prosecution for damages inflicted during industrial disputes due to their noncorporate status. Corporate officers had been protected from damage suits through the doctrine of limited liability which restricted damage claims to company property. Unions, fearing suits against the organization's funds, had chosen to remain unincorporated, thereby forgoing the "privilege" of limited liability but also protecting the union from civil liability claims.[52]

During the 1890s, however, English company law changed. In a series of nonlabor cases, the courts began to allow "representative actions" to be brought against unincorporated companies. This evolution of legal doctrine enabled the growing number of unincorporated companies to be held legally accountable by allowing individuals to be considered representatives of their organizations. In 1893 an enterprising attorney brought a representative action against a number of building trade unions in Hull. The Divisional Court, however, denied the action, and ruled that the defendants could be sued only as individuals and not as representatives of their unions. Although unsuccessful, the *Temperton v. Russell* case laid the legal groundwork for the historic Taff Vale decision of 1901.[53]

The Taff Vale railway company successfully sued the Amalgamated Society of Railway Servants precisely because the Law Lords overruled the Temperton decision and held that although not a corporate body, the union itself could be sued just as many *non*labor organizations had been in the previous decade. The court found for Taff Vale and ordered the union to pay damages of £23,000 and expenses, including legal costs of £42,000.[54] The decision was a major defeat for organized labor. The setback was short-lived, however; within five years Parliament passed the Trades Disputes Act, which established union immunity to civil liabilities as well as criminal conspiracies. Thus the new vulnerability was quickly foreclosed through further labor lobbying and renewed statutory protection of workers' industrial rights. Indeed, the campaign to repeal Taff Vale provided a major impetus to the newly established Labour Party, which led the campaign for legislative reform.[55] Again, as in 1875, the Trades Disputes Act was quite effective in protecting union funds from subsequent civil liability suits, thereby reaffirming the benefits of political action.

Changes in corporation law, however, were only partially responsible for the renewed prosecution of English unions. The particular form of legislative protection granted to English labor under the Conspiracy and Protection of Property

Act also contributed to the pattern of successive waves of statutory protection and judicial prosecution. Although clearly extending state protection to workers in the late nineteenth century, Parliament stopped short of enacting general rights for English workers. Instead, it used a more limited approach that protected workers' industrial rights against *specific* kinds of legal prosecution.[56] This form of state recognition has been characterized by Lord Wedderburn and others as a negative rather than positive definition of workers' rights, in that unions were provided with a series of "immunities" from particular legal doctrines rather than being granted a less qualified right to organize and strike.[57] Thus the legislative victories of 1871, 1875, and 1905 established distinct exemptions for labor from particular common law doctrines rather than enacting more wide-ranging industrial rights. Although the Conspiracy and Protection of Property and the Trades Dispute Acts were quite effective in shielding unions from criminal and civil liabilities, the negative definition of workers' rights left unions vulnerable to new or unanticipated legal actions. The emergence of representative actions in company law is a perfect example of the way in which the English statutes exposed unions to new prosecution strategies. With each legal innovation, labor had to return to Parliament in order to specify further the precise grounds of state protection.

Although both English and American labor regulation oscillated between periods of judicial hostility and statutory protection, the origins and impact of the pattern of state regulation was quite different in the two nations. In England, once statutory protections were enacted, the courts deferred to parliamentary authority and honored the immunities prescribed in successive labor legislation. The alternation between legislative protection and judicial prosecution did not stem from Parliament's inability to check the power of the English courts. Rather, Parliament was quite effective at limiting judicial interpretation, but only on the particular issues covered by the statute. In America, on the other hand, state legislatures had little or no success in redirecting judicial regulation of working-class organization and protest. Both the New York and Pennsylvania courts undermined the successive statutory protections and continued to convict workers of conspiracy on much the same grounds throughout the nineteenth century. Thus the successive waves of legislative protection and judicial prosecution in the United States reflected a different balance of power between the courts and legislature than existed in England in the same period.

AN INTERPRETATIVE TWIST: EARLY NINETEENTH-CENTURY PRODUCERS AND THE STATE

In many ways it is tempting to end the story of divergent labor movement development here and to attribute different labor strategies exclusively to differences in state structure. Although a state-centered analysis works well for the English–American comparison in the late nineteenth century, it is quite misleading to extrapolate from this historical period to other eras as well. In fact, when we extend the field of analysis to include the early nineteenth century we see that a very different set of state–labor relations prevailed.

Prior to 1860, American workers did not find themselves locked in a frustrating struggle with the courts. On the contrary, early workingmen's associations such as the New York and Philadelphia Working Men's parties (1827–31) and the New York Loco-foco or Equal Rights Party (1835–7) looked to the state as both the source and potential solution to their economic distress. Indeed, if we step back to the 1820s and 1830s we can see intriguing parallels between the Chartist and Working Men's parties in the United States. Moreover, New York and Pennsylvania workers were, if anything, more successful than their English counterparts at securing their political demands from the state. Laws establishing a system of compulsory education, general incorporation, and mechanics' liens, abolishing imprisonment for debt, and creating a more decentralized system of currency and credit were passed in several northeastern states before 1842. The Working Men's parties were by no means the only actors responsible for securing these reforms. But most scholars agree that skilled workers played an important role in placing these issues on the political agenda.[58]

Thus before the Civil War we see that the unusual power of the American courts over other branches of government did not hamper antebellum efforts at political reform. As yet, differences in state structure were of little consequence; working-class protest in England and the United States was not yet channeled along divergent paths. One last question remains, namely to explain why differences in state structure only became salient in the last quarter of the nineteenth century. Why, in short, did the role of the American state change so that American courts only came to block working-class political action after the Civil War?

The divergent patterns of state–labor relations after the Civil War cannot be explained by objective conditions alone. After all, state structure and policy remained relatively constant during the nineteenth century; moreover, workers were subject to conspiracy prosecutions both before and after the Civil War. Despite similar institutional arrangements and legal doctrine, conspiracy convictions did not become the focus of workingmen's ire before the Civil War. Instead of challenging the power of the courts, antebellum workers were engaged in a quite different program of political reform.[59] The more cooperative state–labor relations that prevailed in the first three decades of the nineteenth century can be understood, I believe, only by attending more carefully to changes in culture and ideology within which state institutions operated. We will see how long-standing eighteenth-century assumptions and the quite different cultural understandings they entailed continued to shape labor's perception of, and response to, the courts well into the nineteenth century.

Several scholars have begun to investigate the influence of republican ideology on workingmen's protest in the early decades of the nineteenth century.[60] Although not emphasized equally by all scholars, three assumptions seem to have been especially important. First, early nineteenth-century protesters continued to voice the republican belief in the constitutive power of politics. The economic distress and social conflict of the 1820s and 1830s, from this perspective, were the result of an inappropriate balance of political institutions and poor legislation rather than the product of some inevitable process of industrialization. The eighteenth-century belief in the formative power of politics is captured nicely by a chartist when he claimed: "Knaves will tell you that it is because you have no property, you are unrepresented. I tell you the contrary, it is because you are unrepresented that you have no property . . . your property is the result not the cause of your being unrepresented."[61] Similarly, the New York and Philadelphia Working Men's parties believed their economic plight to have been politically created and to be in need of political reform. "It is because every working man has *not* been a politician that bad legislation has taken place, that laws have been made granting *privileges* to a *few,* which privileges have enabled them to live without labor on the industry of the useful classes."[62] If only the appropriate configuration of political institutions and public policy could be established, then all productive citizens could share in the benefits of economic growth.

Second, in the early decades of the nineteenth-century workingmen continued to assert the importance of propertied independence as the basis of civic participation. Even though wage labor was increasing, skilled workers defended their claims to independence through the labor theory of value and claims of property rights in their trade. For example, Stephen Simpson of the Philadelphia Working Men's party analyzed the workingmen's plight as follows:

Capital is the superabundant aggregate stock of labour, in the hands of individuals, government, and nations. . . . All capital, therefore, is *produced* by the working men of a nation, although they seldom attain to or possess it, owing to a wrong principle, regulating the distribution of wealth, by which capital is almost always soley acquired by the idle speculator, the wary monopolist, or the sordid accumulator.[63]

The question was not simply one of economic interest and material gain, but rather of workingmen trying to assert their propertied independence and the associated right to participate in contemporary political debate. New York artisans joined the antebellum debate over financial reform by again laying claim to the labor theory of value and asserting property rights in their trade: "If you really think that we, the working men, have no *real interest* in the present contest, you are very much mistaken; for we think our labor is as good as your *real capital,* (the *produce* of labor,) and far better than your *false capital,* (the produce of exclusive and therefore unrepublican privileges;)."[64] Day laborers and the dependent poor might legitimately be excluded from politics, workingmen argued, but skilled artisans should be recognized as worthy members of the republic who were quite capable of remaining "independent at the polls."[65]

Finally, workingmen adhered to the long-standing eighteenth-century fear of dependence and corruption, which they believed led to tyranny and the abuse of political power. When faced with the reorganization of work and tremendous changes in production that we now refer to as industrialization, Chartists and workingmen across the Atlantic extended traditional republican fears from the political to the economic realm. The most urgent problem, the workingmen claimed, lay in the recent concentration of economic rather than political power. The National Bank and the "spurious currency" system were considered especially dangerous because they were creating unhealthy monopolies that were making the "rich richer, and the poor poorer," and the "many dependant on the few."[66]

Eighteenth-century ideology, however, did not remain at the level of rhetoric alone. Rather, these republican precepts were sustained by quite different social relations and political alliances as well. The primary social cleavage in the first three decades of the nineteenth century was not yet between labor and capital, or workers and employers, but centered instead on the division between the producing and nonproducing classes. Skilled artisans, small manufacturers, and yeoman farmers identified as producers and allied against bankers, lawyers, and speculators the quintessential members of the nonproducing classes. It is a mistake, from this perspective, to consider the Chartists and New York and Philadelphia Working Men's parties to be class-conscious "protosocialist" movements that mobilized workers as members of a distinct wage-earning class.[67] Instead, organizations such as the Birmingham Political Union and the Complete Suffrage Union in England and the Working Men's parties in New York and Philadelphia mobilized producers against the nonproducing classes. Skilled artisans and middle-class Radicals worked side by side within the same organization: No formal alliance was needed to sanctify their cooperation because both groups considered themselves producers and natural allies. Only gradually over the next fifty years would producers be distinguished into the working and middle classes.[68]

When producers mobilized politically in both England and the United States, they called for quite different demands from their counterparts after the Civil War. In essence the producers' platform called for economic and political power to be distributed more evenly throughout the nation and the conditions for civic participation ensured. The specific means of obtaining these goals varied on the two sides of the Atlantic as conditions producers faced differed in the two countries. In New York and Philadelphia, the Working Men's parties and Loco-focos advocated a series of antimonopoly reforms, especially targeted at the problems of finance and credit. First and foremost, New York and Philadelphia workingmen staunchly opposed the rechartering of the National Bank and demanded instead passage of more liberal banking laws that would give all productive citizens access to credit. As a result, producers believed that economic growth could proceed, but in a more decentralized way, thereby avoiding the dangers inherent in concentrations of economic and political power.[69]

In addition, New York and Philadelphia workingmen gave considerable attention to education reform and called repeatedly for creation of a system of state-funded schools. No industrious citizens, the producers argued, could hope to fulfill their duties of civic participation unless they had sufficient time and resources to inform themselves on the pressing issues of the day. Finally, New York and Philadelphia producers called for a number of smaller policy changes including abolition of imprisonment for debt, passage of a mechanics' lien law, and abolition of the militia system. Each of these demands, the producers believed, would help maintain the solvency and dignity of small producers in this period of rapid economic change.[70]

English producers, on the other hand, focused primarily on suffrage reform. Extending the vote, the Chartists claimed, was an essential prerequisite for alleviating the economic distress of skilled workers and small manufacturers who were presently being excluded from the benefits of economic growth. Chartist demands, however, were not limited to suffrage alone and often included attacks on the debilitating effects of speculators and middle men. Thomas Attwood's solution mirrored that of his New York and Pennsylvania counterparts: The system of finance and credit had to be changed in order to alleviate the current wave of economic distress.[71]

I do not want to imply that all was harmony and cooperation within the early nineteenth-century producers' organizations. Both the Chartist movement and Working Men's parties contained minority factions advocating more radical reforms. Fergus O'Connor and the "physical force" Chartists, for example, demanded universal manhood suffrage through a break with middle-class reformers and the use of violence if necessary. Similarly, Thomas Skidmore's proposal for the redistribution of property in the initial platform of the New York Working Men's party has been considered a decisive sign that working-class consciousness had emerged in New York City well before the Civil War.[72] Although O'Connor and Skidmore indeed called for a more complete break with the past than their rivals, it is a mistake to view them as the only authentic voices within the producers' ranks. By attending more closely to the eighteenth-century legacy, we can see a much wider range of producers' demands as equally legitimate, albeit different, responses to economic change. Financial reform, education policy, and general incorporation laws, for example, were not simply the concerns of middle-class reformers who infiltrated their organizations and deflected workingmen from their radical potential. Rather, each of these policy reforms was designed to create the conditions needed for producers to maintain their role as independent and respected citizens in their respective republics.

Moreover, it is important to note that neither O'Connor nor Skidmore were able to sway a majority of workingmen to their position and remained distinct minorities within both the Chartist and workingmen's movements. Throughout the 1820s through 1840s, the dominant factions within both the English and American protest movements remained firmly committed to the producers' program of republican reform and continued to attract both skilled artisans and middle-class allies into their ranks.[73]

Thus, when faced with declining wages and diminishing social status, producers were not transformed overnight into a new working class. Established social divisions and political alliances were not abandoned so lightly. Instead, the first wave of resistance to industrialization in the 1820s through 1840s was shaped by eighteenth-century ideology and social relations. Although early nineteenth-century protesters were by no means happy with their current situation, we should not assume that they wanted to break abruptly with the past. In fact, early nineteenth-century producers mobilized politically with the hope of returning their societies to their rightful paths. These early protesters, I have found, were more interested in reaffirming their position in the republic than they were in transforming nineteenth-century society along new class lines.

Adopting the producers' rather than wage-earners' concept of class enables us to understand the changing pattern of state–labor relations in the United States during the middle decades of the nineteenth century. The changing role of the state, in turn, was responsible for the divergent patterns of English and American labor movement development after the Civil War. In the early decades of the nineteenth century, when workingmen understood their economic plight in light of eighteenth-century assumptions, they looked to the state for very different reasons than their late nineteenth-century counterparts. Rather than demanding state protection of the right to organize and strike, antebellum protesters in both England and the United States mobilized collectively to secure the necessary conditions for their dual goals of decentralized economic growth and civic participation. Although not all the producers' demands were adopted immediately and many became the subject of heated political debate, it is important to note that the antebellum producers' demands were not eviscerated by the courts. Unlike workers' postwar demand for state protection of the right to organize, the central components of the producers' program for antimonopoly reform and civic participation could be accommodated quite easily within the existing legal order and did not require that the balance of power be renegotiated between legislatures and the courts.

Although I have shown how republican ideology entailed a quite different set of labor demands, which in turn enabled more cooperative state–labor relations to prevail before the Civil War, a critical reader might question my claim as to the importance of ideology, culture, and acts of interpretation as central to the shift in state–labor relations after the war. Why, the critic might argue, can we not explain the change in labor demands and the judicial obstruction that followed simply as products of industrialization? Workers' underlying interests changed, the argument might run, along with the reorganization of work and production that fueled industrialization. Shifts in ideology and culture after the Civil War, from this perspective, were largely derivative of changes in economic and social relations; acts of interpretation might appear to have shaped labor's relation to the state, but in fact they only masked the true source of causal change.

The limits of a materialist account of changes in state–labor relations after the

Civil War can be seen by shifting the field of analysis briefly from a comparison across countries and over time to a comparison across organizations in the same era. Contrasting the two principal labor organizations of the 1870s and 1880s, namely the Knights of Labor and the New York Workingmen's Assembly, enables us to hold economic and social conditions reasonably constant and as a consequence brings into sharper relief the influence of ideology and culture over labor's platform. As I have already presented a detailed account of this postwar comparison elsewhere, I will simply refer here to the central findings of my research.[74]

The producers' alliance did not break down quickly or in an orderly fashion, but rather disintegrated in a much more uneven pattern. In the three decades following the Civil War there was a proliferation of labor organizations in both England and the United States, each of which put forth its own interpretation and remedy for labor's current distress. Although most workers agreed that economic and social relations had changed in an undesirable fashion in the three decades immediately following the war, how workers understood these changes, the meaning they imparted to them, varied considerably across organizations.

When comparing the Knights of Labor and New York Workingmen's Assembly response to the postwar conspiracy trials I found that state–labor relations varied across organizations as well as over time. The Knights of Labor, unlike their trade union rivals, continued in the producers' tradition and did *not* make collective action and repealing the conspiracy laws a central component of their postwar program. Instead the Knights of Labor continued to advance an extensive program of antimonopoly reform and did not become embroiled in a protracted struggle with the courts.[75] The New York Workingmen's Assembly, on the other hand, adopted a quite different approach. The cornerstone of the Workingmen's Assembly program, we have seen, centered on obtaining state protection of the right to organize alongside a campaign to improve hours, wages, and working conditions for labor. The extended campaign to repeal the conspiracy laws led them headlong into an unsuccessful struggle with the courts, a struggle that was itself decisive in disillusioning New York and Pennsylvania workers with the prospects of political reform.

Differences in labor demands across postwar labor organizations cannot be accounted for readily by economic conditions and social relations alone because both the Knights of Labor and the New York Workingmen's Assembly were responding to the same conditions. Instead what we see is that different ideologies and interpretative frames played a considerable role in shaping workers' demands as workers struggled to make sense of the enormous changes that were taking place in the second half of the nineteenth century.

Once workers began to demand state protection of the right to organize both English and American workers set for themselves the task of changing legal doctrine or displacing the courts as the principal regulatory institution of industrial conflict. Labor's struggle for industrial rights, we have seen, followed very different paths in England and the United States largely as a consequence of the different configurations of state power in the two nations and ultimately led to very different patterns of labor movement development in the two nations.

CONCLUSION: STATE STRUCTURE AND LABOR STRATEGY IN HISTORICAL PERSPECTIVE

The history of judicial regulation of working-class organization in England and the United States points to three broad conclusions about historical and institutional arguments more generally. First, we can see clearly how different institutional arrangements provided very different incentives and constraints for workers and channeled protest along different paths. The political terrain on which workers organized indeed played a significant role in shaping working-class interests and strategy in England and the United States.

The contrasting behavior of the courts in the English and American political systems provided very different rewards for working-class political action and ultimately was responsible for the divergent development of the two labor movements at the end of the nineteenth century. In England, where the courts were less powerful and generally allowed Parliament to establish government policy toward labor, working-class political organization was systematically rewarded. The legislative victories of the English labor movement produced significant changes in government regulation of working-class organization. In contrast, equivalent legislative successes in New York and Pennsylvania provided very little leverage over government policy, which continued to be dominated by the judiciary with little or no regard for statute law. The inability of New York and Pennsylvania legislatures to check the power of the courts left American workers disillusioned with the prospects of even successful political mobilization. The divergent patterns of labor movement development after 1890, then, can be traced to the very different roles played by the courts during workers' struggle for state protection of industrial rights in the closing decades of the nineteenth century. After almost a century of parallel development, the English and American labor movements began to adopt quite different strategies, largely in response to the pattern of frustrations and rewards that flowed from the political systems within which they organized.

Second, the preceding research suggests that the nature of institutional power needs to be reconsidered. Although American courts played a decisive role in the turn to business unionism, the courts were by no means always so influential. In the first half of the nineteenth century, when producers pursued a very different program of reform, the unusual structure of the American state was of little significance. Producers did not find their programs thwarted by the courts and did not engage in an extensive program of legal reform. Instead, we have seen that the courts' role *changed* over the course of the nineteenth century. The distinctive structure of the American state shaped labor strategy only under specific conditions. Not until American labor decided it wanted what the courts had jurisdiction over, namely the right to collective action, did judicial regulation shape subsequent labor strategy. Ironically, the courts' power over American labor was dependent, to a considerable degree, on the substantive aspirations and goals of the very organizations they sought to regulate.

Questions of state structure and capacity alone cannot account for the changing significance of judicial regulation over the course of the nineteenth century. Instead, we need to adopt a more relational approach to institutional power in which we attend to both institutional structures as well as the larger social context within which they are embedded. By comparing state–labor relations across countries, eras, and organizations we have seen that judicial power varied enormously as different ideologies and cultures intersected with the same institutional structures in very different ways.

Finally, this study underscores the importance of attending to issues of interpretation in institutional analyses. How workers responded to industrialization, what they understood their interests to be during the nineteenth century, did not follow directly from the underlying economic and social relations. Instead, we have seen that there was considerable play in how workers interpreted the economic changes at hand. The influence of different interpretations was manifest in the distinct demands that different organizations advanced to protect workers' interests in the new economy. The particular visions, or interpretative frames, that dominated in any particular country, period, or organization had a considerable impact on workers' relation to the state and ultimately played a central role in shaping labor strategy. Ignoring questions of meaning and interpretation would, I believe, have prevented us from deciphering the origins of divergent patterns of labor movement development in England and the United States.

NOTES

1 For two excellent accounts of the American Federation of Labor's business unionism in the early twentieth century, see Michael Rogin, "Voluntarism: The Political Functions of an Anti-political Doctrine," *Industrial and Labor Relations Review* 15, no. 4 (July 1962):521–35; and Ruth L. Horowitz, *Political Ideologies of Organized Labor* (New Brunswick, N.J.: Transaction Books, 1978), ch. 1.

For English labor strategy at the turn of the century, see G. D. H. Cole, *British Working Class Politics, 1832–1914* (London: Routledge and Kegan Paul, 1965), esp. chs. 8, 11, 12, 14, 19; Sidney Webb and Beatrice Webb, *The History of Trade Unionism* (New York: August M. Kelley, 1965), esp. chs. 10 and 11; and Alan Fox, *History and Heritage: The Social Origins of the British Industrial Relations System* (London: Allen and Unwin, 1985). For an extensive list of legislation supported by the English Trades Union Congress at the end of the nineteenth century, see George Howell, *Labour Legislation, Labour Movements, and Labour Leaders* (London: T. Fisher Unwin, 1902), pp. 469–72.

2 See the following editorials by Samuel Gompers: "Economic Organization and the Eight-Hour Day," *American Federationist* 22, no. 1 (Jan. 1915); "Compulsory Arbitration's Latest Evangelist," *American Federationist* 21, no. 9 (Sept. 1914); "Trade

Union Health Insurance,'' *American Federationist* 23, no. 11 (Nov. 1916). More generally, see Horowitz, *Political Ideologies of Organized Labor*, ch. 1.

3 See Ira Katznelson, *City Trenches: Urban Politics and the Patterning of Class in the United States* (Chicago: University of Chicago Press, 1981). Although Katznelson identified the separation of work and politics nicely, he locates the origins of the separation early in the nineteenth century with the rise of capitalism. In contrast, I do not see ''city trenches'' taking hold until the last decade of the nineteenth century. Indeed I see the division between work and politics as a product of the AFL's unsuccessful struggle for legal reform in the post Civil War era. Earlier in the nineteenth century, workers were quite willing and able to advocate their workplace concerns through electoral and party politics. My alternative periodization of class and politics is elaborated in the remainder of this chapter.

4 For discussion of government regulation of working-class organization in France, see Julio Samuel Valenzuela, Labor Movement Formation and Politics: The Chilean and French Cases in Comparative Perspective, 1850–1950, unpublished Ph.D. dissertation, Columbia University, 1979; and Chris Howell, *Regulating Labor: The State and Industrial Relations Reform in Postwar France* (Princeton; N.J.: Princeton University Press, in press).

For discussion of government regulation of labor in Germany, see Mary Nolan, ''Economic Crisis, State Policy, and Working-Class Formation in Germany, 1870–1900,'' in Ira Katznelson and Aristide Zolberg, eds., *Working-Class Formation: Nineteenth-Century Patterns in Western Europe and the United States* (Princeton, N.J.: Princeton University Press, 1986). For a useful comparison of Britain, Germany, and the United States, see Gary Marks, *Unions and Politics: Britain, Germany, and the United States in the Nineteenth and Early Twentieth Centuries* (Princeton, N.J.: Princeton University Press, 1989).

5 For useful discussions of the conspiracy doctrine, see Hampton L. Carson, *The Law of Criminal Conspiracies and Agreements, As Found in the American Cases* (Philadelphia: Blackstone, 1887); Francis B. Sayre, ''Criminal Conspiracy'' 35 *Harvard Law Review* 393 (1922); Edwin Witte, ''Early American Labor Cases,'' 35 *Yale Law Journal* 825 (1926); and Alpheus T. Mason, *Organized Labor and the Law* (New York: Arno and the New York Times, 1969. Originally published in 1925).

Many accounts of American labor law limit the conspiracy doctrine to the period 1806 to 1842. The landmark case of *Commonwealth v. Hunt* 4 Metc. 111 (Ma. 1842) is said to have ended the use of conspiracy, and to have established the right to organize and strike for American workers. However, limiting conspiracy to the antebellum era is incorrect. There is considerable evidence of a revival of the doctrine in the 1860s through the 1890s. For example, see Hyman Kuritz, ''Criminal Conspiracy Cases in Post-bellum Pennsylvania,'' *Pennsylvania History* 18 (Oct. 1950):292–301; and Witte, ''Early American Labor Cases,'' pp. 828–32. For elaboration of the legal doctrine and cases in both the antebellum and postbellum eras, see Victoria Hattam, *Labor Visions and State Power: The Origins of Business Unionism in the United States, 1806–1896* (Princeton, N.J.: Princeton University Press, in press), ch. 2.

6 For discussion of English labor regulation, see M. Dorothy George, The ''Combination Laws,'' *Economic History Review* 6, no. 2 (April 1936):172–8; and John Victor Orth, Combination and Conspiracy: The Legal Status of English Trade Unions, 1799–1871, unpublished Ph.D. dissertation, Harvard University, 1971.

7 Excellent accounts of the English struggle for state recognition can be found in the following articles by H. W. McCready: ''British Labour's Lobby, 1867–75,'' *The Canadian Journal of Economics and Political Science* 22, no. 2 (May 1956):141–60; ''British Labour and the Royal Commission on Trade Unions, 1867–69,'' *University of Toronto Quarterly* 24, no. 4 (July 1955):390–409; ''The British Election of 1874:

Frederic Harrison and the Liberal Labour Dilemma,'' *Canadian Journal of Economics and Political Science* 20, no. 2 (May 1954):166–75; Cole, *Working Class Politics,* ch. 5, esp. p. 55; and Webb and Webb, *History of Trade Unionism,* ch. 5.

For the United States, see Victoria Hattam, "Economic Visions and Political Strategies: American Labor and the State, 1865–1896," *Studies in American Political Development* 4 (1990):82–129; and Kuritz, "Criminal Conspiracy Cases."

8 See *New York Workingmen's Assembly Proceedings 1870–1893* on microfilm at the Industrial and Labor Relations Library, Cornell University. Unless otherwise specified, hereafter cited as *Workingmen's Assembly Proceedings* followed by the year.; and McCready, "British Labour's Lobby," pp. 148–159; and Webb and Webb, *History of Trade Unionism,* pp. 280–91.

9 Four anticonspiracy laws were passed in New York and four in Pennsylvania. See *Laws of the State of New York,* Chapter 19, 1870; Penal Code Sections 168 and 170, 1881; Chapter 384, 1882; and Chapter 688, 1887; and Laws of Pennsylvania P.L. 1242, 1869; P.L. 1105, 1872; P.L. 33, 1876; and P.L. 230, 1891.

The three English statutes were the Trade Union Act, 35 Vict. c. 31, 1871; the Criminal Law Amendment Act, 35 Vict. c. 32, 1871; and the Conspiracy and Protection of Property Act, 38, 39 Vict. c. 86, 1875.

10 For example, see Section 168 of the New York Penal Code, 1881; and the Criminal Law Amendment Act, 35 Vict. c. 32, 1871.

11 See New York statutes identified in note 9.

12 Many American conspiracy cases, especially in the lower courts, went unreported. Thus some cases can be identified only through local newspapers and government reports. The following are the major postbellum conspiracy cases in New York and Pennsylvania identified to date: *Master Stevedores Association v. Walsh,* 2 Daly 1 (NY 1867); *People v. Van Nostrand,* (NY 1868) *Workingmen's Assembly Proceedings,* 1969:19; Cigar-maker's Union No. 66, Kingston, New York (1868), *Proceedings of the Second Session of the National Labor Union, in Convention Assembled, New York City, Sept. 21, 1868* (Philadelphia: W. B. Selheimer, 1868), p. 12. Hereafter cited as *NLU Proceedings, Second Session.* See also *Raybold and Frostevant v. Samuel R. Gaul of Bricklayers' Union No. 2, New York City, NLU Proceedings, Second Session,* 1868:12; *Iron Moulders' Union No. 22 v. Tuttle & Bailey, Brooklyn, Kings County, New York,* 1869, *Workingmen's Assembly Proceedings,* 1870:23; *Iron Moulders' Union No. 203, Harlem, New York v. United States Iron Works,* 1869, *Workingmen's Assembly Proceedings,* 1870:23; *Commonwealth v. Curren,* 3 Pitts. 143. (Pa. 1869); *Commonwealth v. Berry et al.,* 1 *Scranton Law Times* 217 (Pa. 1874); Xingo Parks and John Siney trials, Clearfield County, Pa. (1985), *1875), Pennsylvania Bureau of Industrial Statistics* 9:313–15; *Commonwealth ex re. E. Vallette et al. v. Sheriff,* 15 Phil. 393 (Pa. 1881); D. R. Jones trial, Westmoreland County, Pa. (1881), *Pennsylvania Bureau of Industrial Statistics* 9:378–83; Miles McPadden and Knights of Labor trials, Clearfield County (Pa.1882), *Pennsylvania Bureau of Industrial Statistics* 10 (1881–2):161–3; *Newman et al. v. the Commonwealth* 34 *Pittsburgh Law Journal* 313 (Pa. 1886); *People v. Wilzig,* 4 N.Y. Cr. 403 (1886); *People v. Kostka,* 4 N.Y. Cr. 429 (1886); Knights of Labor trials, Allegheny County (Pa. 1887), Kuritz, "Pennsylvania State Government and Labor Controls," 154; *People ex. Gill v. Smith,* 10 N.Y. St. Reptr. 730 1887; and *People ex rel. Gill v. Walsh,* 110 N.Y. 633 (1888); *People v. Radt et al.,* 71 N.Y.S. 846 (NY 1900); *People v. McFarlin et al.,* 43 Misc. Rep. 591, 89 N.Y.S. 527 (Pa. 1904); *People v. Makvirka,* 224 App. Div. 419, 231 N.Y.S. 279 NY 1928); and *People v. Commerford,* 233 App. Div. 2, 251 N.Y.S. 132 (NY 1931).

13 For example, see *People v. Wilzig; People v. Kostka;* and *Newman et al., v. The Commonwealth.*

14 See *People v. Wilzig.*

15 Ibid., 415.

16 The account of the dispute is taken from the prosecution arguments in the trial of Hans Holdorf, one of Wilzig's fellow defendants. Each of the defendants requested and was granted a separate trial. The Holdorf prosecution's account is reprinted in the Wilzig case report. See *People v. Wilzig,* 406–11.

17 In England special tribunals of oyer and terminer were established to hear some criminal cases. In the United States, some states followed the English tradition and used this same term to refer to their higher criminal courts.

18 *People v. Wilzig,* 414.

19 See the New York cases in note 12.

20 See Pennsylvania statutes identified in note 9.

21 See Pennsylvania cases in note 12. For useful discussion of some of the postwar Pennsylvania cases, see Kuritz, "Criminal Conspiracy Cases."

22 The Waverly coal miners' case was not reported in the Pennsylvania law reports. Nevertheless, accounts of the trial can be found in the *Pennsylvania Bureau of Industrial Statistics* 9 (1880–1881):378–82. See also Kuritz, "Criminal Conspiracy Cases," pp. 298–9; and Witte, "Early American Labor Cases," p. 831.

23 My account of the Waverly strike is based primarily on the *Pennsylvania Bureau of Industrial Statistics* 9:379–80. However, for reference to the specific counts on the indictment, see Kuritz, "Criminal Conspiracy Cases," p. 299.

24 See Kuritz, "Criminal Conspiracy Cases," p. 299.

25 See *Pennsylvania Bureau of Industrial Statistics* 9:380.

26 Ibid. and Witte, "Early American Labor Cases," pp. 830–1.

27 Quotations are taken from *Workingmen's Assembly Proceedings,* 1886, p. 3; and *Workingmen's Assembly Proceedings,* 1870, p. 23.

28 Quoted from *Workingmen's Assembly Proceedings,* 1886, p. 3.

29 Quoted from *Workingmen's Assembly Proceedings,* 1887, p. 6.

30 For additional complaints against the postwar conspiracy convictions by New York labor leaders, see the Nineteenth Annual Convention of the New York Workingmen's Assembly, where a resolution was passed condemning "the action of the Court of Appeals as partial to capital and inimical to labor, by deciding that the Tenement House Cigar Bill is unconstitutional." Quoted from *Proceedings of the Nineteenth Annual Convention of the Workingmen's Assembly of the State of New York: Held in the City of Albany, N.Y., January 20, 21, and 22, 1885* (New York: Brooklyn Times Print, 1885), p. 20. For additional complaints about the unequal application of the conspiracy law, see *Proceedings of the Twenty-third Annual Convention of the Workingmen's Assembly of the State of New York. Held in the City of Albany, N.Y., January 15–17, 1889* (West Troy, N.Y.: James Treaner, Book and Job Printer, 1889), p. 36; and *Proceedings of the Twenty-fourth Annual Convention, of the Workingmen's Assembly of the State of New York. Held in the City of Albany, N.Y., December 10th to 12th, 1889* (Binghamton, N.Y.: O. R. Bacon, 1890), p. 18. For comment on the dangerous separation of the judiciary from politics, see *Workingmen's Assembly Proceedings* 1886. Finally, the New York Bureau of Labor Statistics summed up labor's view of the postwar conspiracy trials in 1892 when the annual report claimed that the current effort to "revise" the conspiracy laws "backwards" has led to the current "feeling among our laboring class that the law is the poor man's enemy." Quoted from Hurwitz, *Theodore Roosevelt and Labor,* p. 53.

Labor leaders also denounced the postbellum Pennsylvania conspiracy convictions. For example, after the Siney and Parks trial in 1875 the *National Labor Tribune* declared "Again we repeat it, not a shot was fired, not a club raised, not a man hurt, not a house burned, not a dollar's worth of property destroyed and yet thirty men are tried and convicted; four of them sent to prison for a year and forever disgraced. Great heaven! Where was the riot; where the conspiracy? In the hearts of the legal mob that hounded these poor men to prison and no where else!'' Quoted from the *National Labor Tribune,* June 26, 1875, in Edward Killeen, ''John Siney: The Pioneer in American Industrial Unionism and Industrial Government,'' unpublished Ph.D. dissertation, University of Wisconsin, 1942, p. 297. For additional protests against the postbellum Pennsylvania conspiracy convictions, see also Kuritz, ''Pennsylvania State Government and Labor Controls,'' p. 58.

For remarkable corroboration of the New York case and for parallel developments in Colorado and Illinois, see Forbath, ''Shaping of the American Labor Movement,'' 102 *Harvard Law Review,* 1109 (1989).

31 For discussion of judicial review of labor legislation on hours, wages, and working conditions, see Fred Rogers Fairchild, *The Factory Legislation of the State of New York* (New York: Macmillan, 1905), chs. 1–7; Howard Lawrence Hurwitz, *Theodore Roosevelt and Labor in New York State, 1880–1900* (New York: Columbia University Press, 1943), chs. 2–3; Benjamin R. Twiss, *Lawyers and the Constitution: How Laissez Faire Came to the Supreme Court* (New York: Russell and Russell, 1962), chs. 4–6; and Forbath, ''Shaping of the American Labor Movement,'' part 11.

32 Delegates Strasser, Sullivan, and Beerman all suggested that since conspiracy was such a major concern it ought to be added to the program. However, this was opposed on the grounds that delegates had been instructed to vote on the platform as originally proposed and were not in a position to adjudicate completely new amendments. See *A Verbatum* [sic] *Report of the Discussion on the Political Programme at the Denver Convention of the American Federation of Labor, December 14, 15, 1894* (New York: The Freytag Press, 1895), pp. 15, 17, 62.

33 Quoted from *Verbatum* [sic] *Report of the Political Programme,* pp. 21–22, emphasis added.

34 Quoted from *Verbatum* [sic] *Report of the Political Programme,* pp. 19–20.

35 Generally see Samuel Gompers, *Seventy Years of Life and Labor* (New York: E. P. Dutton, 1925), vol. 2, ch. 11. For a more general discussion of Gompers' political activity, see Harold Livesay, *Samuel Gompers and Organized Labor in America* (Boston: Little, Brown, 1978), ch. 4.

36 My account of the Cigarmakers' campaign for tenement reform is compiled from Gompers, *Seventy Years,* pp. 186–98; Fairchild, *Factory Legislation,* ch. 2; and Bernard Mandel, *Samuel Gompers: A Biography* (Yellow Springs, Ohio: The Antioch Press, 1963), pp. 29–33. For an interesting discussion of these same events from Roosevelt's point of view, see Hurwitz, *Theodore Roosevelt and Labor,* pp. 79–89.

37 See Fairchild, *Factory Legislation,* ch. 2; and *In Re Jacobs,* 98 N.Y. 98 (1885).

38 Gompers, *Seventy Years,* p. 194.

39 Ibid., p. 197.

40 See Debs's testimony before the Senate investigation into the Pullman strike in *The Report on the Chicago Strike of June–July 1894 by the United States Strike Commission* (Washington, D.C.: Government Printing Office, 1895), pp. 129–80. See also Nick Salvatore, *Eugene V. Debs: Citizen and Socialist* (Urbana: University of Illinois Press, 1982), esp. ch. 5.

41 See Joseph Rayback, *A History of American Labor* (New York: Free Press, 1959), ch. 16.

42 See the Trade Union Act, 35 Vict. c. 31, 1871; and the Conspiracy and Protection of Property Act, 38, 39 Vict. c. 86, 1875.

43 For English cases involving the Conspiracy and Protection of Property Act, see the following: *Judge v. Bennett,* 1887, 52 J. P. 247; *R. v. McKeevit,* 1890, Liverpool Assizes, December 16 (unreported, discussed in Hedges and Winterbottom, *Legal*

History of Trade Unionism, 122; *Gibson v. Lawson,* 1891, 2 Q. B. 547; *Curran v. Treleaven,* 1891, 2 Q. b. 553; *Pete v. Apperley,* 1891, 35 S. J. 792; *R. v. McKenzie,* 1892, 2 Q. B. 519; *Lyons v. Wilkins,* 1899, 1 Ch. 255; *Walters v. Green,* 1899, 2 Ch. 696; *Charnock v. Court,* 1899, 2 Ch. 35; *Smith v. Moody,* Div. Ct., 1903, 1 K. B. 56; *Ward, Lock & Co. v. Printers' Assistants Society,* 1906, 22 TLR 327.

44 See *Curran v. Treleaven,* 1891, 2 Q. B. 553; and *Gibson v. Lawson,* 1891, 2 Q. B. 547.

45 *Curran v. Treleaven,* 536.

46 Ibid., 554–6.

47 Ibid., 563.

48 Ibid., 560.

49 Ibid., 560.

50 For discussion of the seventeenth-century social compromise, see Christopher Hill, *The Century of Revolution, 1603–1714* (New York: Norton, 1961); and Mauro Cappeletti, *Judicial Review in the Contemporary World* (New York: Bobbs-Merrill, 1971), esp. chs. 1, 2.

51 *Quinn v. Leathem,* 1901, A. C. 495; *Taff Vale Railway Co. v. Amalgamated Society of Railway Servants,* 1901, A. C. 426; and *Osborne v. Amalgamated Society of Railway Servants,* 1901, 1. Ch. 163; 1910, A. C. 87.

52 Webb and Webb, *History of Trade Unionism,* 595–6.

53 For discussion of representative actions, see R. Brown, "The Temperton v. Russell Case (1893): The Beginning of the Legal Offensive against the Unions," *Bulletin of Economic Research* 23, 1 (May 1971):55–6, 58–9, 66; and Webb and Webb, *History of Trade Unionism,* p. 601 and notes.

54 Webb and Webb, *History of Trade Unionism,* pp. 601–2.

55 The Trades Disputes Act, 6 Ed. VII c. 47 foreclosed the loophole. For discussion of the Act, see Hedges and Winterbottom, *Legal History of Trade Unionism,* pt. 11, chs. 4, 5. For discussion of Taff Vale and the Labour Party, see Henry Pelling, *A History of British Trade Unionism* (Suffolk: Penguin, 1963), ch. 7.

56 This argument draws largely on the work of Lord Wedderburn. For example, see Lord Wedderburn, "Industrial Relations and the Courts," *Industrial Law Journal* 9, 2 (June 1980):65–94.

57 See Wedderburn, "Industrial Relations and the Court"; Roy Lewis, "The Historical Development of Labor Law," *British Journal of Industrial Relations* 14, 1 (1976); and Brown, "The Temperton v. Russell Case."

58 Compulsory public education was established in New York, New Jersey, New Hampshire, Connecticut, and Massachusetts between 1834 and 1849. Imprisonment for debt was abolished in Connecticut, New Jersey, Pennsylvania, New Hampshire, Massachusetts, and Ohio before 1842. The ten-hour work day was established, at least in theory if not in practice, in 1835 for Philadelphia public employees, and in 1840 for all federal employees, and 1840 for all Pennsylvania workers. Two mechanics' lien laws were passed in New York in 1830 and 1841. Finally, President Jackson's veto of the National Bank in 1832, the New York Free Banking Act of 1838, and Van Buren's Independent Treasury Act of 1840 all were considered important victories for the producers' program of financial reform.

    For arguments linking these political victories to labor, see John R. Commons, *History of Labor in the United States* (New York; Macmillan, 1936), vol. 1, ch. 2, p. 220. and Rayback, *A History of American Labor.* chs. 6 and 7.

59 For a more extended discussion of workers' rather quiescent response to the conspiracy convictions before the Civil War, see Hattam, *Labor Visions and State Power,* ch. 3.

60 Gareth Stedman Jones, in particular, has pioneered work in this area. See the chapter,

"Rethinking Chartism," in his book *Languages of Class: Studies in English Working Class History, 1832–1982* (Cambridge: Cambridge University Press, 1983). See also John Smail, "New Languages for Labour and Capital: The Transformation of Discourse in the Early Years of the Industrial Revolution," *Social History* 12, no. 1 (Jan. 1987):49–71; and Fox, *History and Heritage*, esp. ch. 3.

For work along these lines on the United States, see Howard B. Rock, *Artisans of the New Republic: The Tradesmen of New York City in the Age of Jefferson* (New York: New York University Press, 1979); David Montgomery, "Labor and the Republic in Industrial America: 1860–1920," *Le Mouvement Social* 111 (1980):201–15; Bruce Laurie, *Working People of Philadelphia, 1800–1850* (Philadelphia: Temple University Press, 1980), ch. 4; Alan Dawley, *Class and Community: The Industrial Revolution in Lynn* (Cambridge, Mass.: Harvard University Press, 1976); Paul Faler, *Mechanics and Manufacturers in the Early Industrial Revolution: Lynn, Massachusetts, 1780–1850* (Albany: State University of New York Press, 1981); and Sean Wilentz, *Chants Democratic: New York City and the Rise of the American Working Class, 1788–1850* (New York: Oxford University Press, 1984), chs. 2, 4. However, these studies stop short of rethinking the concept of class sufficiently. Each of these studies modifies but ultimately adheres to the claim that a division between labor and capital was the central social cleavage by the mid-1830s. In contrast, I believe that the social divisions and class consciousness were more strongly influenced by eighteenth-century assumptions until the postbellum era.

For a general account of republican precepts, see J. G. A. Pocock, *Politics, Language and Time: Essays on Political Thought and History* (New York: Atheneum, 1973). In the American context, see Bernard Bailyn, *The Ideological Origins of the American Revolution* (Cambridge, Mass.: Harvard University Press, 1967).

61 Quoted in Stedman Jones, "Rethinking Chartism," p. 109.

62 Quoted from *The Man* 1, no 37 (April 3, 1834):146. Although he does not discuss workingmen's protest in terms of the eighteenth-century legacy, Pessen also notes the constitutive role given to politics in the workingmen's platforms. See Edward Pessen, *Most Uncommon Jacksonians: The Radical Leaders of the Early Labor Movement* (Albany: State University of New York Press, 1967), ch. 9.

63 Quoted from Stephen Simpson, *The Working Man's Manual: A New Theory of Political Economy on the Principle of Production the Source of Wealth* (Philadelphia; Thomas L Bonsal, 1831), p. 64. For excellent discussion of the labor theory of value in the secondary literature, see Bruce Laurie, *Working People of Philadelphia, 1800–1850* (Philadelphia; Temple University Press, 1980), pp. 76–8; and Wilentz, *Chants Democratic*, pp. 157–8.

64 Quoted from *The Man* 1, no. 57 (April 26, 1834):231.

65 Quoted from *The Man* 1, no. 29 (March 25, 1834):111.

66 Quotes are taken from *The Man* 1, no. 38 (April 4, 1834):149 and no. 59 (April 29, 1834):239. See also vol. 1, no. 21 (March 15, 1834):81.

67 Both the Webbs and Tholfsen describe early nineteenth-century movements as "proto-socialist." See Webb and Webb, *History of Trade Unionism*, p. 161; and Tholfsen, *Working Class Radicalism*, p. 86.

68 For further evidence of the producers' alliance, although presented in a somewhat different analytic cast, see Asa Briggs, "Thomas Attwood and the Economic Background of the Birmingham Political Union," *Cambridge Historical Journal* 9, no. 2 (1948):190–216; Trygve R. Tholfsen, "The Artisan and Culture of Early Victorian Birmingham," *University of Birmingham Historical Journal* 3 (1951–2):146–66.

69 For general discussion of the New York and Pennsylvania Working Men's parties and their programs, see Pessen, *Most Uncommon Jacksonians*, chs. 2, 7–12; Wilentz, *Chants Democratic*, ch. 5; and Laurie, *Working People of Philadelphia*, ch. 4. For

examples of opposition to the National Bank and discussion of finance and credit in the primary sources, see Simpson, *Working Man's Manual*, chs. 7–12, 16, 17; and *The Man* 1, no. 2 (Feb. 20, 1834):2; no. 8 (Feb. 28, 1834):1; and no. 27 (March 22, 1834):105.

70 Three different platforms were developed within the New York Working Men's Party. For Skidmore's platform, see the "Report of the Committee of Fifty"; for the John Commerford platform, see the "Proceedings of a Meeting of Mechanics and Other Working Men, held at Military Hall, Wooster Street, New York, on Tuesday evening, Dec. 29, 1829," and for the Robert Dale Owen position, see the minority report of the subcommittee on education, 1830. All three reports have been reprinted in John R. Commons et al., eds., *A Documentary History of American Industrial Society* (Cleveland: Arthur H. Clark, 1910), ch. 5, pp. 149–68.

71 For discussion of Attwood's views on finance and credit, see Briggs, "Thomas Attwood and the Economic Background of the Birmingham Political Union," pp. 204–11.

72 See Wilentz, *Chants Democratic*, ch. 5.

73 Fergus O'Connor and the "physical force" Chartists often receive special attention because of their more radical demand for universal manhood suffrage through a break with middle-class reformers and the use of violence if necessary. Similarly, Thomas Skidmore's proposal for the redistribution of property in the initial platform of the New York Working Men's Party is considered a decisive sign that working-class consciousness had emerged in New York well before the Civil War. Indeed factions within both the Chartists and Working Men's parties that did not support these more radical demands are often dismissed by scholars as the voice of middle-class reformers who had infiltrated the movements and were deflecting workers from their true course. For example, both William Cobbett, Richard Carlisle, and Thomas Attwood in England and Robert Dale Owen and Noah Cook in the United States are often portrayed by historians as diverting workers from economic issues and property relations toward questions of currency, cooperatives, and education reform. Only some segments of the protest movements are considered authentic and are thought to voice the real interests of the working class.

For discussion of Fergus O'Connor and the physical-force Chartists, see Trygve Tholfsen, "The Chartist Crisis in Birmingham," *International Review of Social History* 3 (1958):461–80; Clive Behagg, "An Alliance with the Middle Class: The Birmingham Political Union and Early Chartism," and Jennifer Bennett, "The London Democratic Association 1837–41: A Study in London Radicalism," both in James Epstein and Dorothy Thompson, eds., *The Chartist Experience: Studies in Working Class Radicalism and Culture, 1830–1860* (London: Macmillan, 1982).

For discussion of Skidmore and his views, see Wilentz, *Chants Democratic*, ch. 5. However, Wilentz overestimates Skidmore's power and dismisses other factions within the Working Men's Party as inauthentic. For a critique of Wilentz's interpretation, see Hattam, *Labor Visions and State Power*, ch. 3.

74 See Victoria Hattam, "Economic Visions and Political Strategies."

75 Where the New York Workingmen's Assembly demanded state protection of the right to organize, the Knights of Labor largely ignored the conspiracy laws and called instead for greater regulation of capital. Financial reform, regulation of interstate commerce, and antimonopoly policies were the mainstays of the Knights' political program. Unlike the Workingmen's Assembly platform, the Knights met with greater political success because the Granger laws, the Legal Tender acts, and the Interstate Commerce Commission were not continually eroded by the courts. To be sure, the Knights' demands were not completely exempt from judicial interpretation; yet the

Knights' judicial defeats were more readily reversed as courts gave way to renewed legislative initiatives at both the federal and state level.

The Knights' political demands met with less judicial obstruction than the Workingmen's demands largely because they did not present a major challenge to existing legal doctrine and practice. For example, rather than calling for repeal of the conspiracy laws, when the Knights actually addressed the question of conspiracy at the General Assembly in 1886, the "Special Committee on Conspiracy Laws" recommended that the conspiracy laws be "honestly and impartially applied" with equal vigor to "combinations of aggregated wealth" and "organized greed." Thus the Knights did not require that the courts relinquish their power, but rather called for extension of the conspiracy laws to employers' combinations as well. See Hattam, "Economic Visions and Political Strategies," pp. 119–24.

7

Ideas and the politics of bounded innovation

MARGARET WEIR

Social scientists have long been interested in the influence of ideas on government action. In Max Weber's classic formulation, innovative ideas could create
new "world images" and fundamentally reshape the terms of struggle among
interests.[1] A half century later, John Maynard Keynes, hoping to revolutionize
thinking about the government and the economy, made his famous observation
that "the power of vested interests is vastly exaggerated compared with the gradual encroachment of ideas."[2]

Such views are challenged by arguments that material interests, not ideas, are
the true motors of policy change. Those who emphasize the role of ideas are
often poorly equipped to respond to their critics because they have traditionally
devoted little attention to how ideas become influential, why some ideas win out
over others, or why ideas catch on at the time that they do.[3] In this chapter, I
argue that simply opposing ideas to material interests excludes many of the most
interesting questions about policy innovation. Instead, we need to understand
how ideas become influential by scrutinizing the fit between ideas and politics
and discerning how and why it changes over time. The way to do this is by
tracking the development and paths to influence that ideas and material interests
take within the institutional context of policy-making.

I pursue these questions by examining the development of employment policy
in the United States from the New Deal to the Reagan administration. Employment policy provides an excellent arena for exploring questions about when and
how politics and ideas combine to produce policy innovation and why some ideas
fail to influence policy. Employment policy encompasses a broad range of formally separate but related initiatives that seek to affect macroeconomic conditions and the operation of the labor market.[4] In the United States, policies in this
broad domain have exhibited considerable, often unexpected, innovation since
the 1930s. Nonetheless, over time, the scope of innovation narrowed, and by the

I would like to thank Sven Steinmo and Kathy Thelen for their helpful comments on this chapter.

1980s, proposals for government action to address employment problems were distinctly disadvantaged in policy debates.

What accounts for the pattern of periodic innovation set within a broader historical trajectory in which arguments favoring a government role in employment steadily lost ground? To answer this question I show how the interaction of ideas and politics over time created a pattern of "bounded innovation" in which some ideas became increasingly unlikely to influence policy. Central to this narrowing process was the creation of institutions, whose existence channeled the flow of ideas, created incentives for political actors, and helped to determine the political meaning of policy choices. These boundaries, I argue, handicapped ideas favoring government action when they came under attack in the late 1970s.

EXPLAINING THE AMERICAN PATTERN OF EMPLOYMENT POLICY

The questions raised by the distinctive pattern of innovation and boundaries in American employment policy call for an approach that can probe the relationships among policy areas often viewed as separate and one that can comprehend the historical sequences that sent employment policy off in particular channels. This task defines a broad focus of inquiry that is not often found in individual case studies of policy. But it raises concerns that are addressed by broad theories about American politics and by general models of policy-making. By examining what each of these approaches tells us about policy-making and what each leaves unsaid we can begin to build a research strategy that accounts for policy boundaries as well as the possibilities for innovation.

Values and power as policy explanations

Broad theories of American politics, which examine cultural norms or the power of social interests, highlight the restrictions on innovation posed by enduring features of the American regime. Values deeply embedded in American political culture are often called upon to explain the distinctive features of social and economic policy in the United States.[5] Two cultural traits in particular are credited with shaping American policy. The first is what Louis Hartz called "the liberal tradition in America" – an antistatist individualist strain running deep in the American political character; the second is a pervasive work ethic that prizes advancement through individual effort.[6]

Such broad cultural explanations are quite limited as explanations for policy because they are poorly equipped to explain variations in the shape and timing of particular policies. Although observers of American politics from Tocqueville on have been struck by the antistatism, individualism, and the work ethic that seem imprinted in American national character, the social and economic policies that bear on these values have changed substantially over time. The federal role in social welfare provision has grown dramatically over the past half century with the enactment of major policy initiatives. Likewise, the work ethic has found expression in diverse policies. At times it has served to justify support for full employment, in which jobs would be provided for all who want to work; at other times the work ethic has primarily found expression in support for "workfare" programs in which work is mandated as a condition for receiving welfare.[7] How and why values are expressed in particular ways remains unanswered in these accounts of American politics.

A second type of approach, power explanations, point to the influence of social interests in determining policy. One variant of this explanation identifies the disproportionate influence of business in American politics and policy; a second looks to the activities of political coalitions. These explanations provide more insight into policy variation but, like value approaches, they are poorly equipped to explain the appearance and type of new policy.

Explanations that highlight the power of business examine two main actors, business and labor. This perspective not only ignores the critical role often played by other groups, it also makes unwarranted assumptions about the nature of business and labor interests. Because it ties interests to the mode of production in such a broad way, it assumes a commonality of interests within business and labor and, conversely, it presumes antagonism between business and labor. In fact, businesses differ greatly both cross-nationally and within individual countries in the support they have lent to different kinds of employment measures; labor positions on these issues have likewise varied.[8] The assumption that business and labor are necessarily in conflict over employment policies is equally problematic. On such issues as Keynesianism, labor market policy, or industrial policy, where business or sectors of business stand to gain by government intervention, the assumption of zero-sum conflict among labor and business is misleading.

Economic sector or coalition arguments remedy some of these problems by dividing business and labor – along with other relevant economic groups, such as agriculture – into different sectors based on their economic interests.[9] Despite the more nuanced analyses they produce, these explanations also neglect important features of policy-making. By assuming that ideas enter politics on the shoulders of influential social groups, economic coalition arguments overlook the more independent role that new ideas can play in causing existing groups to rethink their interests and form alliances that would not be possible under an older system of ideas. In addition, they often fail to consider how political and policy-making institutions can affect a group's capacity to influence policy and shape the probability that diverse interests will form policy coalitions.[10]

These gaps in economic coalition arguments suggest that the role economic interests play in shaping policy is heavily mediated and that it is essential to understand the links between economic interests and political choices in order to make sense of policy. Highlighting the importance of these links does not mean that explanation should ignore the role economic interest plays, nor does it deny that policy outcomes may disproportionately benefit some groups and harm others. It does, however, suggest that power over policy cannot be assumed on the basis of statements by business executives or other economically powerful interests. Instead, policy explanations need to examine how political conflicts over policy lead some definitions of interest to win out over others. This requires understanding how different groups come to have particular conceptions of their policy interests and how the arena in which policy is debated affects the formation of alliances.

General theories of policy-making

General theories of policy-making, in contrast to broad theories of politics, say little about the boundaries of policy; instead they envision policy-making as a process with multiple determinants, without systematic restrictions. Rather than identifying key enduring features of American politics or culture, they seek to explain outcomes on the basis of characteristic modes of decision-making. These models often identify different factors as the central elements of decision-making and they have different visions of how these elements merge to produce policy. What they share, however, is a view of policy innovation that is not systematically constrained by deep-seated features of American politics or culture.

A recent influential approach to policy-making in the United States has been offered by John Kingdon.[11] Kingdon proposes a variant of the "garbage can" model of decision-making, in which several separate processes merge to produce policy.[12] He identifies three "streams" that must come together for a policy to find a place on the nation's agenda: problem recognition, generation of policy proposals, and political events. Each of these streams is largely independent of the other and their joining is fundamentally unpredictable. The emergence of new problems or significant political changes are the most frequent preconditions for merging the streams, but their joining often depends on the actions of skillful policy entrepreneurs.

Kingdon's model provides a way of thinking about the conditions under which innovation occurs, but because it is ahistorical, it is in many ways too fluid. The limits of this model are clearest in Kingdon's contention that problems, politics, and policy are fundamentally independent. On the contrary, a historical perspective would show that these streams are linked in important ways over time. Policies from an earlier period can affect each of these streams at a later time. The conception of what problems are and how they should be defined very often depends on previous policies, which establish some groups as authoritative voices in a particular field and make other perspectives less credible. Earlier policies also provide politicians and policy-makers with analogies that they use to judge future policy options.[13] Likewise, the range of appropriate solutions to a problem can be influenced by earlier policies, which direct research along particular lines by making funding and other resources available. Policies introduced at one time can also be a powerful influence on the politics at a later moment.

These examples of the way that problems, policies, and politics are linked over time are not meant to suggest that the past uniquely determines what is possible at a later time. Rather, they show how action taken at one time can make some future perceptions and decisions more plausible than others. An historical perspective is needed to understand the ways in which ideas and action may be channeled by earlier policies and politics.

The politics of bounded innovation

The approach I take aims to make sense of innovation as well as boundaries in American policy-making. This objective directs attention to the diverse links between ideas, political institutions, political actors, networks of experts, and social interests that are often overlooked in culture- or interest-based accounts of policy-making. But it also entails understanding how, over time, some avenues of policy become increasingly blocked if not entirely cut off. Central among the questions I ask are how do social phenomena become "policy problems" and how do particular understandings of problems emerge to guide policymaking? How do such understandings affect the way groups identify their policy interests, in the process facilitating some alliances and discouraging others?

Answering such questions requires an approach that is fundamentally historical, which looks for connections among policies over time. Such perspective is essential for understanding how opportunities for innovation arise and for assessing the range of policy possibilities open at any particular moment. Inherent in this approach is the notion that individual innovations are part of a "policy sequence" in which institutional development renders some interpretations of problems more persuasive and makes some prospective policies more politically viable than others.[14] Underlying the concept of a policy sequence is the notion of "path dependence": Decisions at one point in time can restrict future possibilities by sending policy off onto particular tracks, along which ideas and interests develop and institutions and strategies adapt.[15]

To understand how a sequence develops requires examining not only the direct antecedents of innovation but also policies formally classified in other arenas, which may nonetheless shape the problem itself, thinking about the problem, or the politics of the issue.[16] This calls for casting a broad eye over politics to understand how developments in different domains of politics and policy collide to create outcomes that cannot be readily anticipated or easily controlled by individual actors. Such collisions can become turning points in a sequence by creating opportunities for political actors seeking to promote new ideas and different visions of politics.[17]

The mode of bureaucratic recruitment, the procedures that govern advancement within the federal government, and the permeability of the federal government to social groups all facilitate consideration of innovative ideas in national policy-making. The American practice of recruiting "inners and outers," whose primary identification and prospects for career advancement lie in their professional expertise, provides a hospitable setting for introducing new ways of looking at problems. In contrast to systems where recruitment into government is governed by strict guidelines emphasizing conformity to established civil service norms, the American federal bureaucracy is routinely refreshed with ideas from outside government.[18] These features of American political institutions mean that a wide range of ideas have a chance of influencing American policy. Ideas that are formulated and advocated by preexisting interests as well as those devised by professional groups may find their way onto the policy agenda.

But because politicians in the United States have considerable freedom to consider and solicit a range of ideas, we must also examine the distinctive incentives that guide their choices. Two features of American politics offer clues to the conditions under which parties and presidents have evaluated policy choices. The first is the fragmented structure of national political institutions, which creates a wealth of opportunities for mobilizing opposition. The ease of mobilizing opposition encourages politicians to adopt a shortened time horizon and makes short-term coalitions the bread and butter of American policy-making. Such arrangements do not encourage attention to the long-term repercussions of policy. The second feature of American politics that affects politicians' evaluations of policy is the federal system, which can create formidable political and procedural barriers to implementing policy. The need to negotiate the different levels of the federal system affects the way political actors decide about how policy goals should be achieved or indeed whether they are possible at all.

The need to achieve results in the short term pushes parties and presidents to put together ad hoc coalitions around specific issues and to assemble broad public support sustained by rhetoric with wide but shallow and often vague appeal.[19] Although the support engendered by such appeals may be diffuse or ephemeral, it serves immediate political needs.[20] In this context, policies that depend on reforming existing institutions or building new institutional capacity are less attractive than those that funnel distributive benefits through existing institutions, those that bypass existing institutions altogether, or those that rely on private activity, since they may be more easily launched. Reliance on new channels or private actors to implement policy also helps to solve obstacles posed by the federal system. Because there is little incentive to consider the long-range repercussions of policy, tactics useful in passing a policy can actually undermine the emergence of long-term political coalitions and enduring institutions needed to sustain a policy direction.

Policy ideas may reach the national agenda and even be selected by politicians, but unless they build supportive alliances, they will be vulnerable to political attacks. Such support is often critical in allowing policy administrators to "learn from their mistakes" and modify policy accordingly. It also permits policy-makers to redesign policy to respond to new circumstances.

I argue that such alliances are the product of political processes, not preexisting preferences.[21] This view presumes that policy interests can be defined in different ways so that several distinct policies may be compatible with a group's interest: Potential group members do not always know their interests in a specific policy area; moreover, existing groups may be divided or ambivalent about their policy interests. This means that the process by which a group forms around support for a specific set of policy preferences cannot be taken for granted; instead questions must be asked about why one policy is favored over another.[22]

One of the most powerful factors determining how groups define their policy interests and which alliances they enter is the organization of political institutions. The aspects of the political system that aggregate interests, in particular the party system and legislature, are central in this regard. By channeling the way groups interact in politics and policy-making, these institutions greatly affect the possibilities for diverse groups to recognize common interests and construct political alliances and often determine whether such alliances are necessary.

Another factor affecting the way groups define their interests is the way a policy is packaged. Conceptualizing policy as part of a package helps to locate it within the broader framework of political conflict by identifying its relation to past policies and to other items currently on the national agenda. Such identifications can help sway definitions of interest. For example, the identification of the War on Poverty as a "black" program cut into white support by the late 1960s when urban riots replaced peaceful marches. Thinking about policy in such relational terms helps make sense of patterns of support and opposition since a single policy is unlikely to be judged simply on its own terms; rather, it will be considered as part of a constellation of policies that seem to be related. The way a policy is packaged plays an important role in maintaining the diffuse support or acceptance necessary to protect it from challenge.

Politicians seek to affect these processes of group interest identification and alliance formation, but a variety of strong inertial forces limit what they can do. Interests attached to established policies can obstruct later efforts to reorganize policy along new lines.[23] The political terms on which policies are first introduced may also block later efforts to mobilize support. For example, if social support has been initially won on the basis of the effectiveness of the policy, efforts to sustain support on different grounds, such as citizens' rights, will prove difficult. Likewise, initial decisions about implementation may affect later possibilities for sustaining a supportive alliance. Implementation problems can erode support for policy by giving force to arguments that unwanted side effects outweigh benefits, even if the policy is inherently desirable. At the extreme, poorly implemented policies can undermine support to the extent that the goal is deemed outside the realm of public policy altogether.[24]

Efforts of politicians to create support for policies are also limited by events they cannot control, such as social movements, economic changes, or international political developments. Such events, often only indirectly connected to a particular policy, can nonetheless have important ramifications for the positioning of that policy. By creating a new context, such events can change the meaning of a policy, linking it with a different set of issues and tying its fate to new forces.

As I examine the development of employment policy in the United States, I stress the role of institutions in guiding the development of ideas and interests. I show first how the institutions of American policy-making encouraged consideration of a range of ideas during the Depression but ultimately advantaged interests that preferred a narrow scope for government action in the area of employment. I then analyze how the new institutions for making economic policy created boundaries that shaped the later development of ideas and interests. Such adaptations, I argue, made it very difficult to build support for redirecting the government's role in employment. By the late 1970s, the apparent inability of policy-makers to reorient government action paved the way for the triumph of market-oriented approaches to employment problems.

SETTING BOUNDARIES ON EMPLOYMENT POLICY

One of the most significant innovations of the New Deal was the use of "proto-Keynesian" spending policies to combat unemployment.[25] These policies marked a fundamental challenge to earlier notions that unemployment was a voluntary phenomenon that governments could do little to affect. Their fate reveals much about how innovations occur in the American political system and about the forces that help to determine the shape they ultimately take.

Introducing innovation

Central to understanding the development of pro-spending ideas and their influence on policy during the 1930s is the organization of the American national institutions. When Franklin D. Roosevelt became president in 1933, executive authority to control finances was housed in the Bureau of the Budget, a small ineffectual agency established only a decade earlier.[26] The only overarching authority within the executive branch was the president, but he did not have the means to impose a single viewpoint on the federal bureaucracy, and Roosevelt, in any case, preferred a rather freewheeling competition of ideas within his own administration.[27] In fact, he exacerbated the fragmentation by setting up a wide variety of ad hoc advisory groups and emergency agencies with little reference to the existing structure of public administration.

Such fragmentation encouraged diverse policy views within the executive branch; the lack of centralized authority within the federal bureaucracy allowed like-minded policy advocates to create niches within the federal government and build networks across agency lines. Their ability to construct such niches was enhanced by a system of departmental recruitment and advancement that allowed agency heads considerable room to select and mold their staffs as they saw fit. The American civil service posed little obstacle to this style of recruitment: although long-fought-for reform had been enacted a decade earlier, the civil service was a relatively weak system regularly bypassed by New Deal agencies.[28]

Pro-spending ideas developed in just this way. Federal Reserve chairman Marriner Eccles, a maverick Utah banker, had brought with him to Washington in 1934 a set of highly unorthodox perspectives on economic recovery; unlike the mainstream of the banking and financial community, whose views reflected eastern interests, Eccles had little attachment to the sanctity of balanced budgets. Instead he argued that public deficits, deliberately incurred by government spending, would promote economic recovery by increasing purchasing power.[29]

Eccles pierced the conservative orientation of the Federal Reserve by bringing intellectual allies into the bureaucracy and bypassing established hierarchy.[30] He recruited as his assistant Lauchlin Currie, a former economics instructor at Harvard, who had been formulating proto-Keynesian ideas about deficits since 1930.[31] Eccles's advocacy of unorthodox economic views also began to attract allies from other government agencies, most notably Secretary of Agriculture Henry Wallace and Works Progress Administrator (WPA) and Roosevelt confidant, Harry Hopkins.

The discretion that agency heads enjoyed in recruiting staff and their relative autonomy within the administration were critical in allowing the spending strategy to emerge. Over time, the scattered voices that favored spending made contact, brought in like-minded allies, and converted those likely to be sympathetic to their arguments. As these networks grew stronger, so did the intellectual and practical arguments favoring their policy proposals.

The permeability and fragmentation of national institutions helps to explain how these ideas developed and won support within the administration, but they do not explain why such ideas that broke so sharply with conventional notions about balanced budgets became politically feasible. To make sense of this we must consider how political actors mediate the relationship between ideas and politics.

As Peter Hall and Desmond King point out in this volume, political parties can play a key role in linking ideas and politics; in nations with strong party systems, party competition spurs policy innovation. In the United States, however, parties are too diffuse as organizations to take up this role in a predictable or consistent manner.[32] As a result, individual presidents often have considerable leeway in defining issues and setting policy agendas. This presidential role is enhanced by the freewheeling relationship between politics and administration, which allows American presidents routinely to solicit ideas from different levels of the bureaucracy. Rarely do they restrict themselves to interaction with those at the apex, as is customary in systems that operate on more strict norms of hierarchy.[33]

The importance of the presidential role is evident in the decision to embrace spending strategies during the 1930s. This decision was not the product of a prior position worked out in party councils or mapped out by major bureaucratic actors. Instead, these were ideas developed on the outskirts of mainstream political and policy wisdom, which managed to catch the eye of important presidential advisers.

But even with a strong network arguing in favor of spending, Roosevelt would not likely turn to a course he perceived to be politically damaging. Although he doubted the wisdom of unbalanced budgets, spending had won Roosevelt spectacular political rewards. Dramatic gains for congressional Democrats in 1934 were followed by Roosevelt's landslide reelection two years later. In each case the outpouring of popular support owed much to the New Deal spending programs that made the federal – and particularly the presidential – presence felt more deeply in citizens' lives than ever before.

Thus, when the recession of 1937 showed no signs of abating, Roosevelt ultimately heeded the advice of the spenders in his administration. In late March of 1938 spending advocates converged under the direction of Hopkins to persuade the president to shift course.[34] Within a matter of days, the president decided to endorse a spending program to pull the nation out of the recession.[35]

The ideas behind this initial policy were later more fully developed into a form of "social Keynesianism," in which spending on social aims would be used to stimulate the economy. In the words of Alvin Hansen, the leading American Keynesian, this approach could resolve the "apparent conflict between the humanitarian and social aims of the New Deal and the dictates of 'sound economics.'"[36] American Keynesians predicated their approach on the idea that the United States was a "mature" economy with a tendency toward economic stagnation that would persist unless the government intervened to promote economic activity.[37]

The influence and apparent success of Keynesian economists during World War II suggested that their ideas would form the basis of postwar economic policies.[38] These favorable developments, however, did not lead to a smooth acceptance of Keynesian principles in the United States after the war. Although the proponents of these ideas were influencing policy, their ties to government were essentially ad hoc. The future of this new relationship between economists and government would depend on institutional changes after the war.

Barriers to institutionalizing innovation

Central to the fate of Keynesianism after the war was the fact that the systematic public spending advocated by most Keynesians could not be implemented through the existing institutional structure of the American government. The fragmentation of the executive branch would make it difficult for an administration to formulate and present to Congress a package of spending programs keyed to macroeconomic objectives. Such fragmentation weakened the executive in its interactions with Congress and exacerbated problems the executive might have in securing congressional approval in any case.

Because institutional reform was a prerequisite to institutionalizing social Keynesianism, the struggle over Keynesianism in the United States became a contest about institutional reform, and in particular about innovations that would create more hierarchical lines of authority within the executive branch and strengthen the executive vis-à-vis Congress. Because such reform required congressional approval, policy coalitions organized through Congress would play a central role in determining the fate of Keynesianism.

The debate over the Full Employment bill in 1945 and 1946 helps reveal why ideas so well positioned in the executive could not be institutionalized in the form first proposed. The bill was strongly influenced by the theories of the stagnationist Keynesians. These ideas, like those being considered in Britain at the same time, favored a strong role for the government in ensuring full employment. But in the United States, the approach was even more far-reaching because it envisioned the need for continual public investment to keep the economy afloat. To reach this goal the bill sought to centralize authority within the federal executive and enhance the executive's coordination capacities. At the same time, it committed the federal government to an essentially open-ended program of public spending.[39]

The main opposition in Congress came from business and agricultural groups, who feared that an intrusive and powerful federal government would upset the economic and political relationships that they viewed as essential. Agricultural interests and businesses each had prior experiences with New Deal policies that led them to oppose social Keynesianism. Not only was Keynesianism tied to the entire New Deal agenda, it was identified with the most liberal elements of the New Deal. The Works Progress Administration (WPA), which provided temporary work to the unemployed, and the Farm Security Administration, which aided poor farmers and sharecroppers, had shown the potentially disruptive effects that federal programs could have on local political and economic relationships.[40] In the business community, the chaotic administration of the National Recovery Administration (NRA) engendered an enduring bitterness that reinforced pre–New Deal antipathy to government involvement in the economy.[41]

For southern agricultural interests the stakes were especially high. The fusion of economic and political power in the South meant that the repercussions of losing control over labor were political as well as economic. Social Keynesianism, associated as it was with generous social welfare benefits and increased federal oversight of local activities, thus seemed to threaten an entire way of life organized around a racial caste system that rested on the social, political, and economic subordination of African Americans.

The alliance of business and agriculture was facilitated and rendered particularly potent by several features of the American political system that organized relationships among social interests, policy, and government. The limits on democracy in the South amplified its power in Congress.[42] Likewise, the rural bias of Congress and the loose organization of American political parties strengthened the coalition that opposed social Keynesianism.[43]

By contrast, interests supporting social Keynesian measures in general and the Full Employment bill in particular were handicapped by American political arrangements. The decentralized and nonprogrammatic nature of American parties gave Democratic supporters of the bill little leverage over opponents in the party. Southern Democrats could desert their party with little fear of reprisal. Late in the 1930s, Roosevelt had realized the problems that such intraparty dissension posed for extending the New Deal and sought to replace southern opponents in Congress with New Deal allies. The failure of this 1938 "purge" indicated the continuing strength of local party organizations and the elites that controlled them.[44] It also meant that political parties could not easily serve as sites for reformulating policy interests or enforcing compromises around policy.

The policy coalition of southern Democrats and midwestern Republicans in Congress and their interest group allies in business and agriculture defeated the Full Employment bill and managed to circumscribe sharply the reach of the 1946 Employment Act. The most visible change in the 1946 Employment Act was the omission of the slogan "full employment." Behind the change in language lay a quite different vision of the goals and conduct of economic policy. At the heart of the new conception was a much weaker public role than envisioned by the New Deal's social Keynesians.

Although the United States had been a pioneer in experimenting with economic policies that sought also to meet social objectives, the organization of politics and the sequence of policy innovation during the New Deal facilitated the emergence of a powerful opposition that blocked the institutionalization of social Keynesianism after the war.

INNOVATING WITHIN BOUNDARIES

The defeat of the Full Employment bill prompted advocates of Keynesian ideas to rethink the form their innovation should take. In the years after 1946, Keynesian ideas were reworked and disseminated in a prolonged process of "social learning." But the framework of the Employment Act constrained the directions in which the ideas, institutions, and interests relevant to employment policy developed. Networks of expertise emphasizing macroeconomic approaches to employment limited the scope of employment policy. Political actors shunned the task of building institutions in a domain that promised little immediate payoff. And, the key interests in employment policy, labor, and business elaborated alternative mechanisms rooted in the seniority system to govern employment issues.

As a consequence, employment policy began to exhibit several distinctive features: Social and economic policy were sharply divided, policy focused narrowly on the rate of unemployment, and little in the way of institution building occurred. These characteristics came to mark boundaries in American employment policy during the 1960s, for despite considerable innovation in that decade, new initiatives reinforced, rather than altered, these features of policy.

Reworking Keynesian ideas

To understand why employment policy remained within the boundaries set in the late 1940s despite innovation, we must examine how institutions relevant to employment policy helped to shape later possibilities. One of the most important ways they did this was by affecting the development and flow of ideas by encouraging research and thinking about problems along specific lines.

Much of the process by which Keynesian ideas were reworked can be understood by examining the institutional framework created by the Employment Act of 1946. The act did not write Keynesian principles into government activity the way the Full Employment bill had. Instead, systematic attention to economic matters would be assured by an annual presidential report to the Congress on the state of the economy. Presidential capacities to analyze the economy were enhanced by the establishment of a Council of Economic Advisers (CEA), a small body of advisers appointed by the president and mandated to serve him in an advisory capacity only. A companion body in Congress, the Joint Committee on the Economic Report of the President (later the Joint Economic Committee), would ensure congressional consideration of economic conditions.[45]

This set of institutions and mechanisms gave Keynesian ideas a tenuous foothold in the federal government. The most receptive entry point for such ideas was the Council of Economic Advisers because it had a mandate to monitor the whole economy and because it recruited academic economists, among whom Keynesian ideas were spreading quickly, into short-term government service. But the CEA could act only as an advocate for Keynesian ideas if the president appointed Keynesians to the council. Even then, the council would need substantial internal strength to win battles against opposing agencies within the executive branch if discretionary action, such as tax cuts, were to be accepted. The experience of the CEA under Truman and Eisenhower demonstrated that it would take time to build such influence.

Truman's appointees to the CEA were sympathetic to Keynesian ideas and made significant contributions to their development.[46] Nevertheless their impact on policy was small. As a new agency that had to compete with large, well-established departments including the Treasury, the Federal Reserve, and the Budget Bureau, the CEA had neither the authoritative position nor the institutional strength to control policy. The CEA's early years were spent trying to sort out its status: The relationship among the three members of the council had to be thrashed out, as did the council's relationship to the president.[47]

The other major innovation of the 1946 Employment Act, the Joint Economic Committee (JEC), was more successful in building support for Keynesian ideas. In the latter half of the 1950s, it played a key role in bringing Democrats, organized labor, and economists together around a Keynesian economic agenda.[48] Because the committee's Democratic majority was dominated by liberals, it could function with a set of shared understandings about economic goals and government action that was absent from the Democratic party as a whole. Yet, the JEC was a limited tool for disseminating and organizing broad support for Keynesian ideas. It could and did schedule hearings to publicize particular perspectives, but its lack of legislative function and staffing limitations restricted its reach.

The inadequacies of public vehicles for advancing and adapting Keynesian ideas allowed private groups to play an important role in reshaping and winning acceptance for Keynesian principles of economic management. The model for this type of activity and a key actor in the development of Keynesian ideas was the Committee for Economic Development (CED). Launched in 1942 by forward-looking business leaders concerned that business be prepared to help shape postwar policy, the CED was a small research organization that brought together social scientists and business leaders.

Even before the war was over, the CED began to rework Keynesianism so that its most objectionable features – the potential for capricious action by the federal government and out-of-control spending policies – were removed. Instead of spending, the CED advocated reliance on automatic stabilizers, variations in government revenues and expenditures that occurred in response to economic conditions without any deliberate government action. If discretionary action were undertaken, cutting taxes, not spending, was the route the CED approved.[49]

The committee's organizational form, a small, well-funded group of economists working with liberal business leaders, was an ideal setting for advocacy and development of innovative economic ideas. This type of forum was far more insulated from outside pressure and from shifts in the political winds than the public institutions responsible for forming economic policy. Because it was not immediately answerable to a broad business constituency, the committee could advocate policies that the majority of the business community opposed. Yet the committee's undisputed expertise in economic matters and its ties to important business interests allowed it to launch a vigorous educational campaign that helped businesses reinterpret their economic policy interests to embrace demand management; at the same time the CED made Keynesianism more palatable to business.[50]

If in private organizations Keynesian ideas were being reworked to make them more acceptable to business, within the academic discipline of economics they were being transformed into technical and theoretical problems. In the academy, economics sought to model itself on the natural sciences, with a considerably narrowed agenda that excluded concerns not readily handled by prevailing models of economic behavior.[51] Increasingly, economic questions were severed from the institutional considerations that had been present in the era of institutional economics before the New Deal and in the 1930s and 1940s, when economists worked with government administrators on administrative and political innovations relevant to policy. The dominant economic ideas about employment issues thus contracted and became more technical.

The Kennedy administration's decision in 1962 to support tax cuts as a means to stimulate the economy indicated both the power that ideas could still exercise and the way those ideas had been transformed since the 1940s. Although Kennedy did not endorse Keynesian ideas in his presidential campaign and opposed cutting taxes, his appointees to the CEA were drawn from the leading liberal Keynesian economists in the nation. His choice reflected the available pool of expertise: In 1960 economists who aligned with liberal Democrats were likely to be thoroughly steeped in Keynesian ideas.[52] The selection of CEA members also reflected the emergence of a consensus among liberal economists about the relationship between economic policy, social welfare goals, and expansion of the public sector. While more generous social policies and enhanced public capacities might be attractive, economic policies should not be held captive to such goals.

Led by the energetic and persuasive Walter Heller, the CEA played the role of economic educator and advocate within and outside the Kennedy administration. The council enjoyed unprecedented influence under Kennedy because of the substantial access that the president granted it and the encouragement he gave it to publicize its analysis through congressional testimony and public speeches.[53] It was also helped by the strength of the Keynesian consensus within the economics profession at the time. Heller could – and did – call upon a range of prominent economists from prestigious universities to reinforce his message.[54] His efforts ultimately paid off in 1962 when the president accepted the need for fiscal stimulus in the midst of an economic recession.

Tax cuts was the route selected. This choice reflected the doubts about the administration's ability to secure congressional approval for spending increases as well as the council's belief that tax cuts were the more efficient route.[55] The president received further encouragement to go with the tax cut strategy from the business community. The long educational project of the CED had paid off by the early 1960s in widespread business acceptance of federal deficits as a means of economic stimulus, although not all major business organizations supported cutting taxes to create those deficits. But for a president who worried about being branded antibusiness this broad approval likely helped to tip the balance in favor of the decision to act.[56]

Even so, there was considerable congressional resistance to enacting a tax cut in a period of rising deficits. The intensive educational activities of the CED and later of Kennedy's CEA had swayed opinion at the elite level but had not conquered the realm of popular economic discourse to which Congress was more closely attuned.[57] Not just southern conservatives, but many moderate Democrats, too, worried that cutting taxes would be economically irresponsible. In fact, congressional approval of the tax cut was not assured until after President Johnson had agreed to trim his 1965 budget request.[58] During the Kennedy administration, Democratic economists had created a new language with which to justify deficits; by promoting such concepts as the "full employment budget" they succeeded in blunting the influence of the balanced-budget ideology.[59] But continued congressional wariness raised questions about the depth of the nation's conversion.

Working with the institutional framework and the configuration of interests left by the Employment Act of 1946, Democratic politicians and their economic advisers had finally launched an activist fiscal policy twenty-six years after Roosevelt first proposed spending to stimulate the economy. In Andrew Shonfield's words, Americans had been the "intellectual leaders" and the "institutional laggards" in actively deploying Keynesian principles.[60] The institutional fragmentation that had allowed experimentation with Keynesian ideas during the Depression later prevented those same ideas from being institutionalized as government policy for many years. Only after a reworking of the ideas, the emergence of a strong consensus in the economics profession, and a long process of education did an administration propose deliberately to increase the deficit in order to stimulate the economy.

Limits to innovation

During the 1960s, Democratic politicians introduced a range of innovations relevant to employment policy under the umbrella of the War on Poverty. Although these policies extended federal activity related to employment, they did not challenge the framework established two decades earlier. As it developed, the War on Poverty revealed the limits of that framework: Efforts to expand the definition of the problem to include underemployment were stymied, the divisions between social and economic policies intensified, and little lasting institutional framework for expanding federal capacities to administer employment programs emerged. The imprint of the past was evident in the intellectual assumptions underpinning the War on Poverty as well as in the perspectives of political actors and the positions social groups took on employment issues in the coming decades.

Officially launched in 1964, the War on Poverty had its origins in a rather vague request several years earlier by President Kennedy to have his CEA look into the problem of poverty.[61] The program his advisers devised over the next two years encompassed a variety of remedial service and job readiness programs that targeted the lowest end of the labor market.[62] Underpinning this strategy was the belief that macroeconomic measures would produce ample opportunities for all who were prepared to take advantage of them. The CEA devoted little attention to the relationship between poverty and underemployment, and directed thinking away from the relationship between poverty and the structure and operation of labor markets, and toward the problems of individuals. As Henry Aaron has noted, "Perhaps the most striking characteristic of this view of the poverty cycle is the absence of any mention of the economic system within which it operates."[63]

The most innovative feature of the poverty program was the decentralized and participatory implementation framework. The federal government funneled monies directly to local communities, bypassing state and, initially at least, city authorities. The call for "maximum feasible participation" sparked the mobilization of communities to participate in administering the new programs.[64] Localities set up community action programs that created new participatory structures and oversaw the delivery of the varied services launched under the auspices of the War on Poverty.

The vagueness of the presidential directive and the dearth of academic material about poverty gave the Council of Economic Advisers considerable latitude in setting the terms for the new poverty program. The CEA's conception of the problem that policy should address – unemployment due to insufficient macroeconomic stimulation and lack of job readiness among the poor – dominated thinking about poverty and unemployment throughout the 1960s.

The influence of macroeconomists in setting the terms of the War on Poverty highlights the importance of established networks of expertise. The council's skepticism about manpower policy undermined efforts to enhance significantly the public role in job training during the 1960s. As the War on Poverty developed, efforts from within the Labor Department to expand the definition of the problem to include underemployment faced severe obstacles. Proponents of expanding policy had to fight against established theoretical perspectives as well as elaborate new criteria and categories for collecting and interpreting data. With few allies and mired in institutional rivalries, the advocates of a broader scope for employment policy did not succeed in changing established definitions.[65] Thus, although the organization of American national political institutions generally encourages consideration of a range of ideas in national policy-making, the creation of institutionally linked networks of expertise over time advantages some ideas over others.

By creating a separate realm of poverty policy, the architects of the War on Poverty in the CEA helped to reinforce the divisions between social and economic policy. Guided by a disciplinary perspective that devoted little attention to institutions, they did little to address problems of institution building or reform. It would have been difficult for the economists on the CEA to influence institutions in any case, since the CEA was a small agency without the capacity to implement policy.

The short-term perspective of politicians and, particularly the president's need to push policy through quickly, also help account for the problems of institution building in employment policy and for the strengthened divisions between social and economic policy. The decision to create a separate set of agencies to implement the War on Poverty – in the process bypassing such unresponsive federal-state bureaucracies as the United States Employment Service – allowed rapid implementation of new policies but at the same time it created obstacles for institutionalizing them. The institutional rivalries and political conflict that this route provoked placed poverty policies in constant political jeopardy. The approach embedded in the War on Poverty was far more suited to challenging existing institutions than to creating or reforming enduring institutions needed to administer employment policy.

The incentives of politicians also helps account for a distinguishing feature of the War on Poverty: its racial focus. Although the poverty program was initially and remained officially nonracial in character, the civil rights movement and later the urban riots created pressures to focus resources on African Americans. Community action agencies were pressed from below to increase the representation of blacks, and the Office of Economic Opportunity overseeing the program in Washington took on black empowerment as central to its mission.[66] And as riots began to shake northern cities, President Lyndon Johnson looked to the poverty program as a way to funnel resources into the affected black communities. The collision of the civil rights movement with employment policy gave the poverty program a racial identification that shaped its political meaning.

The positions relevant social groups took on employment policy ratified the direction laid out by intellectual networks and political choices. Most striking was the relative lack of interest expressed by business or organized labor in extending employment policy. Although organized labor supported proposals for job training, it never viewed these programs as essential to its own well-being. And, indeed, expansions and redirections of employment policy had little to offer labor or business. Alternative arrangements, secured during the New Deal and immediately after the war, governed promotion and pay. Most central were the seniority system and collective bargaining; such training as existed was an internal function of the firm.[67] So long as these arrangements worked satisfactorily, neither unions nor business had much incentive to support alternative conceptions of employment policy, especially if they threatened existing arrangements. In this way established institutions in the domain of labor relations affected later possibilities for employment policy.

The perspectives of black Americans on employment policy developed in response to a different set of considerations. The limited focus of the War on

Poverty and the failure of efforts to extend the reach of employment policy encouraged black leaders to make legal regulation – the affirmative action approach – the centerpiece of a black employment strategy. This approach, together with efforts to preserve the new jobs available to blacks in expanded federal bureaucracies, defined the most promising avenues of employment policy for African Americans.[68] Although black organizations vigorously supported broader approaches to employment when they reached the agenda, after the War on Poverty they focused on the legal realm, where black employment problems, cast as questions of rights, stood a better chance of being addressed.[69]

The War on Poverty was an extraordinary episode in American politics and policy, providing a hothouse environment for experimentation. But prominent features of the poverty program, as it developed, had troubling consequences: The focus on the individual problems of the poor served to direct attention away from the broader economic sources of poverty; suspicion of established agencies, however well-founded, undermined possibilities for reforming existing institutions; and the racial focus of the War on Poverty limited political possibilities for enhancing existing programs or even shifting their focus.

These features of policy in the 1960s were the product of different actors who were pressing against the perceived bounds of politics and established frameworks of policy understanding. The directions in which they pushed, however, were limited by their starting points. Thus, the CEA's approach to employment policy and poverty rested on its assumptions about macroeconomic policy-making; the president's enthusiasm for the poverty program stemmed from his efforts to overcome the institutional constraints on presidential policy-making.

Once in place, the political meaning and policy possibilities embodied in the War on Poverty were transformed by unexpected intersections with other events. The collision of the War on Poverty with the movement for black political empowerment was central to its political fate. The sequencing of policy innovation and the interaction of policy with unpredicted events deeply affected the politics of employment policy. After the War on Poverty, efforts to link poverty to employment problems faced new barriers. Policy had been carved up into two realms: a politics of economic policy and a politics of poverty; no broader politics of employment united them.

IDEAS, POLITICS, AND ADMINISTRATION IN AMERICAN POLICY-MAKING

During the 1970s the United States suffered the highest rates of unemployment since the Great Depression. At the same time the puzzling performance of the economy suggested that traditional Keynesian remedies no longer worked as they once had. In this uncertain setting three very different perspectives contended to shape American employment policy. The first called for a larger and qualitatively different government role that would involve planning or new forms of cooperation between business and labor. A second, adopted by the Carter administration, offered a blend of macroeconomic policy, jobs programs, and wage and price guidelines.

The third perspective, increasingly influential among economists and the new crop of think tanks that emerged in the 1970s, broke with the fundamental premises underlying policy for the past thirty years.[70] It argued that government action hampered the operation of the economy and asserted that the best employment policy was less government activity. Public spending and regulation, the major routes of policy development in the 1970s, were singled out as barriers to creating the economic prosperity that was the best remedy for employment problems.

The election of Ronald Reagan and the policy changes implemented during his first years in office signaled the victory of the pro-market approach. Although policy consistently fell short of the vigorous rhetoric of the Reagan administration – most notably on the subject of deficits – the character of the debate around employment qualitatively shifted during the 1980s. Debates were no longer centered around the question of *how* the government should intervene but *whether* the government should act. Moreover, the growth of federal responsibilities was curtailed as the task of coping with employment issues was increasingly placed on the shoulders of the states.[71]

To understand why the pro-market approach prevailed in the 1980s, we must reexamine the links that had been forged between ideas, politics, and administration in employment policy since the 1940s. The growing disjuncture among these components essential for innovation presented problems for those who wanted to extend the government role. It meant not only disrupting patterns of political-administrative interaction that had been developing for decades but also finding new ways to reorganize these elements without replicating the political and administrative problems of the past. Proponents of staying the course, on the other hand, had been weakened by a decade of puzzling economic performance. Those arguing for less government faced fewer administrative and political barriers than either alternative perspective.

Public philosophies and technical ideas

There are two distinct ways in which the word "ideas" is used in accounts of policy-making: The first meaning is captured by the concept of "public philosophy."[72] It expresses broad concepts that are tied to values and moral principles and that can be represented in political debate in symbols and rhetoric. A second usage of the word ideas refers to a more programmatic set of statements about cause and effect relationships attached to a method for influencing those relationships. The language expressing programmatic ideas is the technical or professionally rooted terminology of the expert.[73]

Although the two meanings of ideas shade into each other and on occasion interlock, it is useful to differentiate them because their influence on policy and politics is distinct. Public philosophies play a central role in organizing politics, but their capacity to direct policy is limited; without ties to programmatic ideas their influence is difficult to sustain. Likewise, programmatic ideas are most influential when they are bound to a public philosophy; but these ideas must also forge links with administration. Programmatic ideas developed without reference to administration may be technically strong but are likely to be politically impotent. The influence of ideas on politics is strongest when programmatic ideas, tied to administrative means, are joined with a public philosophy; unhinged, the influence of each becomes difficult to sustain.

In American employment policy, much of the period from the 1940s to 1980 was characterized by a dissociation of programmatic ideas and public philosophy. The social Keynesianism championed by Alvin Hansen had joined a set of programmatic, administratively rooted ideas with a broader vision about politics, most fully articulated by Roosevelt's 1944 Economic Bill of Rights. After its failure, ideas as public philosophy became increasingly disjointed from the technical policy ideas, and these ideas became increasingly divorced from administration. The growing distance of these two types of ideas and their separation from administration impoverished both.

Because programmatic ideas increasingly developed without political or administrative moorings, it became difficult for them to influence policy in any regular way. Although the expression of these ideas grew ever more sophisticated, their ability to chart new policy directions involving government action was narrowing. Research relevant to employment policy emphasized the movement of aggregate measures and microeconomic models, leaving untouched a middle ground concerned with sectors and institutions that the government was grappling to address.[74] In the absence of sufficient applicable research, purely political criteria held sway. This was particularly evident in the 1970s, in the federal responses to growing unemployment and inflation, ranging from wage and price guidelines to pork barrel public service employment.

The dissociation of the two kinds of ideas made public philosophy increasingly hollow. During the 1960s and 1970s, rhetorical appeals grew in importance but they were increasingly unanchored in programmatic content. The War on Poverty, for example, was declared with little effort to assemble support based on a rationale for the specific policies to be undertaken.[75] The difficulty in matching politics and programmatic ideas lay behind the exhaustion of New Deal liberalism and the crisis in public philosophy that characterized the 1970s.[76] Yet, as party ties attenuated, rhetoric and symbols bore a greater burden for organizing electoral politics.

Much of Ronald Reagan's early political success can be attributed to the way he fused a bold and appealing rhetoric to a set of programmatic ideas about how the economy worked. Although widely rejected by economists, supply-side economics resonated with the growing disillusion with government action among mainstream economists. Most important, however, supply-side economics appeared plausible, in part, because it was clearly "do-able" within the context of American politics and institutions. But the merging of programmatic ideas and public philosophy was more apparent than real for most policy areas during the Reagan administration. As the decade progressed, the disjuncture between rhetoric and government action on the economy grew. While the rhetoric remained firmly pro-market, policy was actually a disjointed blend of initiatives.[77] In this sense, the Reagan administration did not so much resolve as elide the problems of uniting philosophy with programmatic ideas about the economy.

The political problem of positive government in the United States

The experience of employment policy suggests that the development, access, and plausibility of ideas calling for new kinds of government capacities are handicapped by the difficulty of uniting politics, ideas, and administration in the United States.

Immediately after the war, some supporters of a broad, more encompassing employment policy worried about precisely this problem. The political scientist E. E. Schattschneider argued that national employment policy would be impossible without "responsible" programmatic parties. He urged that parties establish permanent research organizations that could fuse policy and politics in what he called "political planning." Stressing the inherently political nature of devising and mobilizing policy ideas, he warned that "parties simply cannot afford to rely on nonparty research and publicity to do the job."[78]

Yet, that is just what presidents and parties had to do in the United States. It meant that connections between politics, administration, and policy were forged in piecemeal and sporadic ways, when cooperation among technical experts, interests, and government agencies could be effected or when the president threw the weight of his office behind policy innovation. In some policy areas, including social security, this union was unproblematic; in others such as medical care, it experienced partial success.[79]

In employment policy, by contrast, the most important private interests, business and labor, had little interest in extending policy; the dominant experts paid little attention to administrative issues; and the relevant government agencies were either hostile or weak. Moreover, the president had little political interest in backing employment policy innovation so long as America remained economically strong and Keynesian policy appeared sufficient to manage unemployment. In this context the scope of employment policy remained limited and proposals for extending it were contested. Nothing in the political, intellectual, or administrative history of employment policy provided a foothold for reorienting the government's role during the 1970s, when it became clear that the older approach had broken down.

Where the difficulties of uniting politics, administration, and ideas are less severe, policies may be enacted more easily. The successes of deregulation and tax reform in the 1980s provide a telling counterexample to employment policy: In neither of these cases did ideas about reform have to contend with arguments about administrative feasibility or with opposition to building new government capacities.[80] In this context, technical ideas were able to influence policy more easily and were able to benefit from their attachment to an appealing rhetoric.

A number of analysts have portrayed the recent successes of tax reform and deregulation as evidence of the importance of ideas in policy-making.[81] In each case a strong consensus among experts allowed them to shape the terms of the policy debate and exert influence on the outcome. But what each of these instances of reform also has in common – and shares with the pro-market reforms in employment policy as well – is administrative simplicity. Ideas that create new forms of government activity face a more difficult task. Although they might also fashion an appealing rhetoric and find political support for such concepts as fairness or opportunity, their rhetorical claims remain unconvincing and support ephemeral if government's capacity to act is widely doubted. When there is a history of administrative failure, as in the case of employment policy, the rhetoric becomes even less likely to influence policy.

CONCLUSION

The organization of American policy-making institutions is unusually suited to seizing on new ideas to launch innovative activity. The permeability of the federal executive and its sprawling character allow small groups to develop and market their distinctive perspectives within the government. At the same time political leaders are not constrained much by party ties or narrowly established channels of advice. This gives them the freedom to solicit and consider a range of ideas. These arrangements account for the American government's periodic decisions to launch innovations that seem to "come from nowhere" and mark sharp breaks with the past.[82]

But the possibilities for such innovation are historically bounded. The development of institutions that unite networks of expertise and orient the policy concerns of private actors make it difficult to redirect the course of policy once it is under way. The creation of policy networks narrows the range of ideas likely to receive a hearing as it establishes authoritative voices and modes of discourse. American institutions also hinder efforts to shift course; the system of federalism combined with fragmented party politics makes it difficult to assemble sufficient political authority to redirect existing institutions.

In the case of employment policy, policy-makers whose response to changing economic circumstances remained within the established boundaries of policy left themselves open to attack by those arguing that government was, by definition, unable to address economic problems, including employment. The triumph of the pro-market perspective reconfirmed the American political system's capacity to innovate; at the same time, however, it highlighted the difficulties of extending the institutionally rooted boundaries of existing policy.

NOTES

1 Max Weber, "The Social Psychology of World Religions," in *From Max Weber: Essays in Sociology*, ed. H. H. Gerth and C. Wright Mills (New York: Oxford University Press, 1946), p. 280.
2 John Maynard Keynes, *The General Theory of Employment, Interest, and Money* (New York: Harcourt, Brace Jovanovich, 1964), p. 383.
3 Recent works that have begun to tackle these questions include the essays in Peter A. Hall, ed., *The Political Power of Economic Ideas* (Princeton, N.J.: Princeton University Press, 1989) esp. the concluding chapter by Peter A. Hall; Paul Quirk, "In Defense of the Politics of Ideas," *Journal of Politics* (Feb. 1988):31–41; Martha Derthick and Paul J. Quirk, *The Politics of Deregulation* (Washington D.C.: Brookings Institution, 1985), esp. ch. 7; and Robert B. Reich, ed., *The Power of Public Ideas* (Cambridge, Mass.: Ballinger, 1988). Students of international relations have been particularly interested in the role of ideas; see John S. Odell, *U.S. International Monetary Policy: Markets, Power, and Ideas as Sources of Change* (Princeton, N.J.: Princeton University Press, 1982) and Judith Goldstein, "The Impact of Ideas on Trade Policy: the Origins of U.S. Agricultural and Manufacturing Policies," *International Organization* 43 (Winter 1989):31–71.
4 For an overview definition of employment policy, see Isabel V. Sawhill, "Rethinking Employment Policy," pp. 9–36 in D. Lee Bawden and Felicity Skidmore, eds., *Rethinking Employment Policy* (Washington D.C.: The Urban Institute Press, 1989).
5 See Anthony King, "Ideas, Institutions and the Policies of Governments: a Comparative Analysis: Part III," *British Journal of Political Science* 3 (1973):409–23; Lawrence J. R. Herson, *The Politics of Ideas: Political Theory and American Public Policy* (Homewood, Ill.: The Dorsey Press, 1984).
6 On antistatism and individualism in American political culture, see Louis Hartz, *The Liberal Tradition in America* (New York, Harcourt, Brace and World, 1955); on the effects of such ideas on policy, see King, "Ideas, Institutions and the Policies of Governments," p. 419. On the work ethic see Daniel T. Rodgers, *The Work Ethic in Industrial America, 1850–1920* (Chicago: The University of Chicago Press, 1978) and David H. Freedman, "The Contemporary Work Ethic," pp. 119–35 in David H. Freedman, ed., *Employment Outlook and Insights* (Geneva: International Labour Office, 1979).
7 On variations in public support for various kinds of work programs over time see Robert Y. Shapiro, Kelly D. Patterson, Judith Russell, and John T. Young "The Polls–A Report: Employment and Social Welfare," *Public Opinion Quarterly* 51 (Summer 1987):268–81.
8 For an analysis that discusses variation in business attitudes in the United States, see Alan Barton, "Determinants of Economic Attitudes in the American Business Elite," *American Journal of Sociology* 91 (1985):54–87.
9 Peter Gourevitch, *Politics in Hard Times: Comparative Responses to International Economic Crises* (Ithaca, N.Y.: Cornell University Press, 1986); Thomas Ferguson, "From Normalcy to New Deal: Industrial Structure, Party Competition, and American Public Policy in the New Deal," *International Organization* 38 (Winter 1984):41–93.
10 Peter Gourevitch's analysis of support coalitions in *Politics in Hard Times* acknowl-

edges the importance of such mediating institutions while affirming the centrality of social interests. Contrast his analysis with that of Thomas Ferguson in "From Normalcy to New Deal." Ferguson presents a sophisticated rationale for the emergence of different sectoral interests but devotes little attention to how these interests get translated into policy.

11 John Kingdon, *Agendas, Alternatives, and Public Policies* (Boston: Little, Brown, 1984). See the discussion about the streams on pp. 20, 92–4 and the discussion about "first principles" on pp. 200–1.

12 Ibid., ch. 4; on the garbage can model, see Michael Cohen, James March, and Johan Olsen, "A Garbage Can Model of Organizational Choice," *Administrative Science Quarterly* 17 (March 1972):1–25.

13 On analogical reasoning in decision-making, see Ernest R. May, *"Lessons" of the Past: The Use and Misuse of History in American Foreign Policymaking* (New York: Oxford University Press, 1973); Richard E. Neustadt and Ernest R. May, *Thinking in Time: The Uses of History for Decision Makers* (New York: The Free Press, 1986).

14 On the notion of sequences, see Sidney Verba, "Sequences and Development," pp. 283–316 in Leonard Binder et al., eds. *Crises and Sequences in Political Development* (Princeton, N.J.: Princeton University Press, 1971). For a discussion of policy sequences applied to the case of housing, see Bruce Headey, *Housing Policy in the Developed Economy* (New York: St. Martin's Press, 1978).

15 See the discussion in Stephen D. Krasner, "Approaches to the State: Alternative Conceptions and Historical Dynamics," *Comparative Politics* 16 (Jan. 1984):223–46; Stephen D. Krasner, "Sovereignty: An Institutionalist Perspective," pp. 69–96 in James Caporaso, ed., *The Elusive State: International and Comparative Perspectives* (Beverly Hills, Calif.: Sage Publications, 1989); Edward G. Carmines and James A. Stimson, *Issue Evolution: Race and the Transformation of American Politics* (Princeton N.J.: Princeton University Press, 1989). On path dependence, see Paul A. David, "Clio and the Economics of QWERTY," *American Economic Review* 75 (May 1985):332–7.

16 For a discussion of the emergence and definitions of social problems that emphasizes relationships among different arenas, see Stephen Hilgartner and Charles L. Bosk, "The Rise and Fall of Social Problems: A Public Arenas Model," *American Journal of Sociology* 94 (July 1988):53–78.

17 These collisions are similar to the sharp changes that are envisioned by the theory of punctuated equilibrium. Developed by biologists Stephen J. Gould and Nils Eldredge, the theory has attracted interest by political scientists concerned with explaining change over time and those seeking to develop a nonutilitarian perspective on institutions. See Carmines and Stimson, *Issue Evolution;* and Krasner, "Sovereignty: An Institutionalist Perspective."

18 See the essays in G. Calvin MacKenzie, ed., *The In-&-Outers: Presidential Appointees and Transient Government in Washington* (Baltimore: Johns Hopkins University Press, 1987).

19 Fred I. Greenstein, "Change and Continuity in the Modern Presidency," in Anthony King, ed., *The New American Political System* (Washington D.C.: American Enterprise Institute, 1978), p. 65. On the use of rhetoric, see Jeffrey K. Tulis, *The Rhetorical Presidency* (Princeton, N.J.: Princeton University Press, 1987).

20 On the pressure for the president to move quickly (or "to move it or lose it"), see Paul Light, *The President's Agenda: Domestic Policy Choice from Kennedy to Carter with Notes on Ronald Reagan* (Baltimore: Johns Hopkins University Press, 1982).

21 On the need to investigate the sources of preferences, see Aaron Wildavsky, "Choosing Preferences by Constructing Institutions: A Cultural Theory of Preference Formation," *American Political Science Review* 81 (March 1987):3–21; James G. March

and Johan P. Olsen, "The New Institutionalism: Organizational Factors in Political Life," *American Political Science Review* 78 (Sept. 1984):734–49.

22 For an argument stressing the role of culture in interest construction, see Wildavsky, "Choosing Preferences by Constructing Institutions."

23 For a discussion of this process, see Gosta Esping-Andersen, *Politics against Markets* (Princeton, N.J.: Princeton University Press, 1986).

24 This process is similar to the notion of disappointment that Albert Hirschman uses to account for shifts between public and private activity. See his discussion in *Shifting Involvements: Private Interest and Public Action* (Princeton, N.J.: Princeton University Press, 1982).

25 Bradford A. Lee, "The Miscarriage of Necessity and Invention: Proto-Keynesianism and Democratic States in the 1930s," pp. 129–70 in Hall, *The Political Power of Economic Ideas.*

26 Larry Berman, *The Office of Management and Budget and the Presidency, 1921–1979* (Princeton, N.J.: Princeton University Press, 1979), pp. 3–9; Gerhard Colm, "Fiscal Policy and the Federal Budget," in Max F. Millikan, ed., *Income Stabilization for a Developing Democracy: A Study in the Politics and Economics of High Employment Without Inflation* (New Haven, Conn.: Yale University Press, 1953), pp. 227–32.

27 On Roosevelt's political style in this regard, see Richard E. Neustadt, *Presidential Power* (New York: Wiley, 1976), ch. 7.

28 Richard Polenberg, *Reorganizing Roosevelt's Government* (Cambridge, Mass.: Harvard University Press, 1966), p. 22.

29 May, *From New Deal to New Economics,* ch. 3.

30 Ibid., pp. 45–6.

31 Herbert Stein, *The Fiscal Revolution in America* (Chicago: University of Chicago Press, 1969), pp. 165–7; Alan Sweezy, "The Keynesians and Government Policy, 1933–1939," *American Economic Review* 62 (May 1972):117–18; and John Kenneth Galbraith, "How Keynes Came to America," in Andrea D. Williams, ed., *Economics, Peace, and Laughter* (Boston: Houghton Mifflin, 1971), pp. 47–8. On Currie's work, see Carol Carson, "The History of the United States National Income and Product Accounts: The Development of an Analytic Tool," *Review of Income and Wealth* (1975):165–6.

32 See Theodore Lowi, "Party, Policy and Constitution in America," in William Nisbet Chambers and Walter Dean Burnham, eds., *The American Party Systems: Stages of Political Development* (New York: Oxford University Press, 1975), pp. 238–76; David Mayhew, *Placing Parties in American Politics* (Princeton, N.J.: Princeton University Press, 1986), pp. 244–56, 327–31.

33 Peter A. Hall, "Policy Innovation and the Structure of the State: The Politics–Administration Nexus in France and Britain," *Annals* no. 466 (March 1983):43–59; on the relationship between the president and the bureaucracy, see Richard Nathan, *The Administrative Presidency* (New York: John Wiley and Sons, 1983).

34 See Stein, *The Fiscal Revolution in America,* p. 109; see also Collins, pp. 67–71.

35 For the details of the 1938 proposal, see Stein, *The Fiscal Revolution in America,* pp. 109–14, and Collins, *The Business Response to Keynes,* pp. 69–71.

36 Quoted in Ester Fano, "A 'Wastage of Men': Technological Progress and Unemployment in the United States" *Technology and Culture* 32 no. 2 (1991):288.

37 For a description of the stagnationist theory, see *The Business Response to Keynes,* pp. 10–11, 51; for early expositions of the theory, see Alvin Hansen, *Full Recovery or Stagnation?* (New York: Norton, 1938) and Hansen's 1938 presidential address before the American Economic Association, "Economic Progress and Declining Population Growth," *American Economic Review* 29 (1939):1–15.

38 Byrd L. Jones, "The Role of Keynesians in Wartime Policy and Postwar Planning, 1940–46," *American Economic Review* 62 (May 1972):125–33; Carson, "The History of the United States National Income and Product Accounts," pp. 173–7.

39 For an account of the bill's development see Stephen Kemp Bailey, *Congress Makes a Law* (New York: Columbia University Press, 1950).

40 On the Farm Security Administration, see Sidney Baldwin, *Poverty and Politics: The Rise and Decline of the Farm Security Administration* (Chapel Hill: The University of North Carolina Press, 1968), esp. ch. 9; on rural complaints about the WPA, see James T. Patterson, *Congressional Conservatism and the New Deal* (Lexington: University of Kentucky Press, 1967), p. 297.

41 On business's bitterness toward the federal government after the NRA experience, see the discussion in Donald R. Brand, *Corporatism and the Rule of Law* (Ithaca, N.Y.: Cornell University Pres⸱, 1988), chs. 5–8. On business antistatism more generally, see David Vogel, "Why Businessmen Distrust Their State: The Political Consciousness of American Corporate Executives," *British Journal of Political Science* 8 (Jan. 1978):45–78; on business attitudes in the 1920s, see James Prothro, *Dollar Decade: Business Ideas in the 1920s* (Baton Rouge: Louisiana State University Press, 1954).

42 See V. O. Key, *Southern Politics in State and Nation* (New York: Knopf, 1949), esp. pp. 302–10.

43 See Patterson, *Congressional Conservatism and the New Deal*, p. 333.

44 Sidney M. Milkis, "FDR and the Transcendence of Partisan Politics," *Political Science Quarterly* (Fall 1985):493.

45 For a description of the Employment Act, see Bailey, *Congress Makes a Law*, ch. 11.

46 On intellectual contributions see Walter Salant, "Some Intellectual Contributions of the Truman Council of Economic Advisers to Policy-Making," *History of Political Economy* 5 (Spring 1973):36–49. On the Truman Council more generally, see the account by his first CEA chairman in Edwin G. Nourse, *Economics in the Public Service* (New York: Harcourt Brace, 1953); Edward S. Flash, *Economic Advice and Presidential Leadership: The Council of Economic Advisers* (New York: Columbia University Press, 1965), chs. 2, 3; see the introductory essay and interview with Leon Keyserling, the second head of the CEA under Truman, in Erwin C. Hargrove and Samuel A. Morley, *The President and the Council of Economic Advisers: Interviews with CEA Chairmen* (Boulder, Colo.: Westview Press, 1984), ch. 1.

47 In addition to the sources cited in note 48, see William J. Barber, "The United States: Economists in a Pluralistic Polity," *History of Political Economy* 13 (1981):513–24.

48 On the congressional role in economic decision-making, see Victor Jones, "The Political Framework of Stabilization Policy," in Millikan, ed., *Income Stabilization for a Developing Democracy*, pp. 604–10; Alvin Hansen, "The Reports Prepared under the Employment Act," and Edwin Nourse, "Taking Root (First Decade of the Employment Act)," in Gerhard Colm, ed., *The Employment Act Past and Future: A Tenth Anniversary Symposium*, National Planning Association Special Report, no. 41 (Washington D.C.: National Planning Association, 1956), pp. 92–7 and 62–5.

49 It was work by the CED's Beardsley Ruml that made possible the tax cut route. In the early 1940s, Ruml devised the withholding plan that became the basis for the American tax system, allowing tax policy to be used for stabilization purposes. On Ruml and the CED's policies, see Stein, *The Fiscal Revolution in America*, pp. 220–40; Collins, *The Business Response to Keynes*, chs. 5, 6.

50 Collins, *The Business Response to Keynes*, ch. 6, presents an excellent account of the CED's extensive campaigns to educate business and government officials about its views on economic policy.

51 Ibid., pp. 6–7; on the economics profession in the United States and the acceptance of Keynesianism, see Marc Trachtenberg, "Keynes Triumphant: A Study in the So-

cial History of Ideas,'' *Knowledge and Society: Studies in the Sociology of Culture Past and Present* 4 (1983):17–86.
52 See the discussion in Stein, *The Fiscal Revolution in America*, pp. 372–84. According to Paul Samuelson, the lawyers in the Kennedy campaign had no clear notion about why they needed economists in the first place but ''wanted to be sure they weren't missing a trick.'' See his remarks in the Oral History Interview with Walter Heller, Kermit Gordon, James Tobin, Gardner Ackley, Paul Samuelson by Joseph Pechman Aug. 1, 1964, Fort Ritchie, Md., John F. Kennedy Library, p. 35.
53 Hargrove and Morley, *The President and the Council of Economic Advisers*, pp. 174, 181–2; Walter Heller, *New Dimensions of Political Economy* (Cambridge, Mass.: Harvard University Press, 1966), pp. 26–7.
54 Hargrove and Morley, *The President and the Council of Economic Advisers*, p. 202.
55 Walter Heller, ''Memorandum for the President Re: The Economics of the Second Stage Recovery Program,'' March 17, 1961, President's Office Files, File: Council of Economic Advisers, 1/61–3/61, John F. Kennedy Library; ''Minute on the President's Request for a Review of the Clark Community Facilities Bill and Allied Projects,'' June 15, 1961, File 6/1/61–6/15/61, Walter Heller Papers, John F. Kennedy Library. ''Recap of Issues on Tax Cuts and the Expenditure Alternative,'' Dec. 16, 1962, File: ''Council of Economic Advisers,'' Record Group 174, National Archives, p. 3; see also Hargrove and Morley, *The President and the Council of Economic Advisers*, pp. 196, 200–1.
56 On Kennedy's relationship with business, see Hobart Rowen, *The Free Enterprisers: Kennedy, Johnson, and the Business Establishment* (New York: G. P. Putnam, 1964), ch. 1; and Jim F. Heath, *John F. Kennedy and the Business Community* (Chicago: University of Chicago Press, 1969).
57 A 1962 public opinion poll showed that 72 percent of the general public opposed a tax cut if it meant an increase in the national debt. See Heath, *John F. Kennedy and the Business Community*, p. 115.
58 Hargrove and Morley, *The President and the Council of Economic Advisers*, pp. 205–10.
59 See the discussion in James D. Savage, *Balanced Budgets and American Politics* (Ithaca, N.Y.: Cornell University Press, 1988), pp. 175–9.
60 Andrew Shonfield, *Modern Capitalism* (London: Oxford University Press, 1965), p. 333.
61 James L. Sundquist, *Politics and Policy: The Eisenhower, Kennedy and Johnson Years* (Washington D.C.: Brookings Institution, 1968), p. 112.
62 For general accounts of the initiation of the War on Poverty, see Allen J. Matusow, *The Unraveling of America: A History of Liberalism in the 1960s* (New York: Harper & Row, 1984), ch. 4; Sundquist, *Politics and Policy*, ch. 4.
63 Henry J. Aaron, *Politics and the Professors* (Washington D.C.: Brookings Institution, 1978), p. 20.
64 Daniel P. Moynihan, *Maximum Feasible Misunderstanding: Community Action in the War on Poverty* (New York: Free Press, 1970).
65 On the efforts to establish a measure for underemployment, see the discussion in *The Manpower Report of the President, 1967, 1968*, pp. 73–8 and 34–6, respectively.
66 Paul E. Peterson and J. David Greenstone, ''Racial Change and Citizen Participation: The Mobilization of Low-Income Communities through Community Action,'' in Robert H. Haveman, ed., *A Decade of Federal Anti-Poverty Programs: Achievements, Failures and Lessons* (Madison: University of Wisconsin Press, 1977), pp. 248, 251–6.
67 See Peter B. Doeringer and Michael J. Piore, *Internal Labor Markets and Manpower Analysis* (Armonk, N.Y.: M. E. Sharpe, 1985).
68 On the War on Poverty and public employment of African Americans, see Michael

K. Brown and Steven P. Erie, "Blacks and the Legacy of the Great Society: The Economic and Political Impact of Federal Social Policy," *Public Policy* 29 (Summer 1981):299–330.

69 On the development of the affirmative action approach, see Hugh Davis Graham, *The Civil Rights Era: Origins and Development of National Policy* (New York: Oxford University Press, 1990), ch. 9.

70 On the political appeal of supply-side economics, see Herbert Stein, *Presidential Economics: The Making of Economic Policy from Roosevelt to Reagan and Beyond* (New York: Simon and Schuster, 1984), ch. 7.

71 This was evident in both changes in unemployment insurance policy and in the creation of a small new job training program by the Job Training Partnership Act. See W. Lee Hansen and James F. Byers, ed., *Unemployment Insurance: The Second Half Century* (Madison: The University of Wisconsin Press, 1990). For a discussion of JTPA, see Donald C. Baumer and Carl E. Van Horn, *The Politics of Unemployment* (Washington D.C.: Congressional Quarterly Press, 1985), ch. 6.

72 See the discussion of public philosophy in Samuel H. Beer, "In Search of a New Public Philosophy," pp. 5–44 in Anthony King, ed., *The New American Political System* (Washington D.C.: American Enterprise Institute, 1978).

73 Ideas of this sort are often the product of social research. See Carol H. Weiss, "Improving the Linkage between Social Research and Public Policy," pp. 23–81 in Laurence E. Lynn, Jr., ed., *Knowledge and Policy: The Uncertain Connection* (Washington D.C.: National Academy of Sciences, 1978).

74 See the strongly worded critique of John T. Dunlop, "Policy Decisions and Research in Economics and Industrial Relations," *Industrial and Labor Relations Review* 30 (April 1977):275–82. The call for more attention to institutions has been central to critiques of Keynesianism and neoclassical economics. See Leon Lindberg, "The Problems of Economic Theory in Explaining Economic Performance," *Annals* 459 (Jan. 1982):14–27 and Lester C. Thurow, *Dangerous Currents: The State of Economics* (New York: Vintage Books, 1983), esp. pp. 230–5.

75 See Tulis, *The Rhetorical Presidency*, p. 165.

76 See Beer, "In Search of a New Public Philosophy."

77 See Emma Rothschild, "The Real Reagan Economy," *The New York Review of Books* (June 30, 1988):46–54; see also Benjamin M. Friedman, *Day of Reckoning: The Consequences of American Economic Policy under Reagan and After* (New York: Random House, 1988).

78 E. E. Schattschneider, "Party Government and Employment Policy," *American Political Science Review* 39 (Dec. 1945):1154.

79 On social security, see Martha Derthick, *Policymaking for Social Security* (Washington D.C.: Brookings Institution, 1979); on the development of health policy, see Theodore Marmor, *The Politics of Medicare* (New York: Aldine, 1970).

80 On tax policy, see David R. Beam, Timothy J. Conlan, and Margaret T. Wrightson, "Solving the Riddle of Tax Reform: Party Competition and the Politics of Ideas," *Political Science Quarterly* 105 (Summer 1990):193–217; on deregulation, see Derthick and Quirk, *The Politics of Deregulation.*

81 See Beam, Conlan, and Wrightson, "Solving the Riddle of Tax Reform," and Derthick and Quirk, esp. ch. 7.

82 Beam et al. citing Joseph J. Minarik's observation that tax reform seemed to come from nowhere "to become the law of the land." See Beam, Conlan, and Wrightson, "Solving the Riddle of Tax Reform," p. 204.

8

The establishment of work–welfare programs in the United States and Britain: Politics, ideas, and institutions

DESMOND S. KING

THE INTEGRATION OF WORK AND WELFARE

In the postwar period both involuntary unemployment and poverty have been judged ills that society no longer wishes to tolerate. One factor shaping this preference for employment is memory of interwar mass unemployment and the resultant social and economic hardship. President Roosevelt's Committee on Economic Security, whose report informed the Social Security Act of 1935, advocated federal programs to provide an "assured income" for citizens deprived of earnings from unemployment, old age, fatal injury at work or illness.[1] The Beveridge plan enacted by the 1945–51 Labour administration in Britain was designed to establish basic social rights of citizenship including health care, child allowances, unemployment benefits, and education.[2]

The commitment to relieving poverty and unemployment has been uncontroversial until recently. Since the mid-1970s a combination of economic pressures (principally to reduce government spending and taxes) and political ideas (evolving conceptions about the purpose of welfare policy) have resulted in important debates and reforms in several advanced industrial countries. Two pertinent examples of these trends are the United States and Britain, whose welfare traditions share many features though they differ in important ways. The achievement of the 1980s, and the subject of this chapter, is the reforms to the systems of welfare and unemployment benefits in each country under the Reagan and Thatcher administrations, which created work–welfare programs.

Work–welfare programs require the recipients of welfare benefits (in the United States) or unemployment benefit (in the United Kingdom) to satisfy a work or

Funding for part of the research reported in this chapter was provided by the Nuffield Foundation and the Suntory-Toyota International Centre for Economics and Related Disciplines, LSE.

The author is grateful to the following for comments upon earlier drafts of this chapter: Peter Hall, Christopher Hood, Peter Katzenstein, John Keeler, Peter Lange, Lawrence Mead, Frank Longstreth, Jonas Pontusson, Bo Rothstein, Theda Skocpol, Sven Steinmo, Margaret Weir, Mark Wickham-Jones, Joel Wolfe, and Hal Wolman.

training requirement in exchange for receiving their benefits. The relevant legislation is Title II of the Family Support Act of 1988 in the United States, and in Britain the December 1988 Employment and Training program (ET) combined with complementary amendments to the social security law (Social Security Acts of 1988 and 1989) and employment law (Employment Act 1989). The United States and Britain adopted similar policies, in their emphasis on work or training requirements from welfare or unemployment benefit recipients. The programs modify prevailing assumptions about the welfare rights of citizens (though less so in the United States) and recognize the importance of skill acquisition (however modest) to labor market entry.

In the United States the perceived failure of the 1960s liberal welfare policies of the Johnson administration and the salience of the underclass created a welfare crisis to which the 1988 Act was a response.[3] Welfare was high on the Reagan administration's reform agenda. The problem of welfare was linked by some politicians, notably state governors, to that of skill shortage in the U.S. work force.[4] The most ambitious work–welfare program in the United States, ET Choices in Massachusetts, was designed with this trend in mind. In Britain the post-1979 growth in unemployment, exacerbated by the 1980–1 recession, posed a political challenge to the Thatcher administration, to which it responded in an initially piecemeal then comprehensive fashion. The growth of unemployment after the election of the Conservative administration, led by Mrs. Thatcher, compelled the government to act, despite its commitment to free market principles politically. In response initially short-term training measures were expanded into a comprehensive work–welfare program.

As all students of the political system in the United States acknowledge, efforts to legislate more commonly result in failure than success. Attempts to reform the welfare state established by the Social Security Act of 1935 proved abortive during the Nixon and Carter presidencies,[5] when policy-makers failed to construct sufficiently large coalitions to enact reform. However, fifty-three years after the Social Security Act, Congress initiated and President Reagan signed the Family Support Act, a piece of legislation heralded as a major reform of the welfare system by its principal architect Senator Daniel Patrick Moynihan.[6] The enshrinement of mandatory work requirements for welfare recipients (with various exemptions) is an important development. Although Title II (the JOBS program) is only one element of the Act, it was crucial for enactment and constitutes a transformation in how welfare benefits are conceived and how they should be related to the labor market. One editorial, titled "Real Welfare Reform, at Last," concluded that the Family Support Act "amounts to a revision of the social contract between the nation and the needy. Instead of maintaining poor children and their parents above the starvation level but in dependency, the Government will offer financial support plus education and training to help people move from welfare to work. . . . Education and job training, leading toward employment, are the heart of welfare reform."[7] These remarks capture the modification to the welfare system intended by the architects of the Family Support Act.

In Britain the prevailing commitment to universal social rights of citizenship and the separation between welfare institutions and labor-market policy makes their linkage in work–welfare novel. However, universal welfare has always been accompanied by some means testing, particularly for benefits for those suffering long-term unemployment. The 1988 Employment Training (ET) program not only introduces a comprehensive training program, but parallel changes to the social security law have made participation, especially for young people, in this program compulsory. To accomplish this change the government had to alter fundamentally the state organization responsible for training, the Manpower Services Commission (MSC, now called the Training Agency), established as a tripartite body in 1973. The government weakened and then abolished the MSC's tripartite membership and brought it under direct government control, and simultaneously tightened the eligibility criteria for receiving social security benefits.

INSTITUTIONAL AND POLICY LEGACIES

New institutional theorists provide robust explanations of cross-national policy differences and internal policy stability; In Peter Hall's words, "There are likely to be structural consistencies behind the persistence of distinctive national patterns of policy."[8] I argue that the new institutional assumption of internal policy stability is broadly correct since the work–welfare legislation in Britain and the United States was in each case diluted in ways consistent with existing institutional and policy legacies. It is necessary, however, to attend more closely to the ideas that informed these policies since both their mobilization and content reflect significantly each polity's institutions; and furthermore the imitation by British policy-makers of aspects of American policy necessitated modifying entrenched assumptions. Cross-national policy convergence is not normally expected by new institutional analysis, and this chapter explains an instance of such a pattern. In both administrations politicians were influenced by New Right[9] arguments. An analysis of how these ideas were adopted and pursued in policy by the Reagan and Thatcher administrations offers a means to understanding the role of ideas in policy. Advocates of New Right ideas marshaled economic and political arguments for a harsher regime for those receiving benefits,[10] but the realization of these arguments entailed their dilution in the United States and administrative reorganization in Britain.

Policy-making

The policy processes in the United States and Britain differ. In the United States the decentralized federal system facilitates the introduction of policy ideas through vertical access points (such as the states) and horizontal access points (such as interest groups lobbying in Congress). The difficulties of forming coalitions with a shared consensus favors proposals compatible with existing ideology and assumptions. Furthermore, policies with a small congressional coalition are vulnerable to presidential vetoes. In Britain, by contrast, the centralized state limits channels of access but accords a greater importance to agents of change and promoters of ideas if they succeed in influencing the government. The achievement of influence requires success in the party competition acted out at each election since it is parties who form governments and effect policy.

Although the U.S. party system is a two-party one, unlike Britain, the dispersion of power and independence of politicians within each party limits their role in initiating change. Presidents are limited to two terms and so their influence may recede in the second term though the power of veto persists. Conversely, the extraordinarily high success rates of incumbent House and Senate members moderates somewhat the electoral constraint though it does not eliminate it. In this system interest groups, including subfederal actors, enjoy direct access to policy-makers (in the Congress, executive, and bureaucracy) independently of political parties though the multiplicity of such groups may diminish their influence.[11]

Different actors initiate policy in the two countries. In the United States the president and Congress must work more or less together, though this cooperation is often strained. Negotiation and bargaining between the executive and legislature feature in all federal policy-making. In Britain governments legislate on the basis of their parliamentary majority. These configurations demonstrate how each polity's institutions shape the absorption and diffusion of policy ideas. In Britain the power held by a government through its parliamentary majority, especially of the magnitude enjoyed by the Conservatives after the 1983 and 1987 elections, makes the winning of agreement from other actors in the pursuit of policy less important.

The individual states have taken a leading role in policy-making in the United States and must be analyzed with other policy actors including the Congress, the executive, and, to a lesser extent, the federal bureaucracy. Through the National Governors' Association the states have mobilized to influence federal decision-making. The combined effects of Reagan's New Federalism initiative (which reduced federal funding) and the post-1970 professionalization of state governments[12] makes the states, by way of their governors, a consequential element of the national state. This policy role of the governors and states differs from earlier periods. An important stimulus for the New Deal legislation of Franklin Roosevelt and the active federal government during that period was the failure of the state and local governments to address the problems concentrated in their jurisdictions. According to Weir and Skocpol, ''By 1932 local and state governments were begging the federal government to take over the burden of dealing with the problems of their distressed constituents.''[13] By the 1980s the state and local governments were used to a powerful fiscal, judicial, and political federal presence in their affairs. However, in 1981 the Reagan administration pursued wide-ranging cuts in federal grants, many enacted in the Omnibus Budget Reconciliation Act of that year. Further cuts in the subsequent years of this administration forced the state to assume major policy-making roles if they wished to maintain or expand programs.

Under the dominance of Mrs. Thatcher the post–1979 Conservative administration provides a contrast with recent U.S. administrations. The British state is vastly more centralized – there is a central governing authority located in the government, directed by the prime minister – and the government's parliamentary majorities provide it with immense power to enact laws. Furthermore, at the height of her powers Prime Minister Thatcher consolidated the government's capacity to legislate. Institutionally, the British state is centralized[14] and party loyalty within Parliament ensures the government a majority. The eleven years of Conservative incumbency gave them an opportunity to modify the parameters of national public policy. The Conservatives also laid siege to the bureaucracy hiving off portions of the public sector as private sector units.

Welfare legacies

The move to work–welfare programs in the Family Support Act does not constitute a major policy break.[15] U.S. federal welfare policy has always been designed to avoid creating disincentives to labor-market participation.[16] This attitude has prevailed since Roosevelt's New Deal legislation and characterized the implementation of the AFDC program before 1965. Title II of the Family Support Act is in this tradition, building upon the WIN demo program established in the Omnibus Reconciliation Act of 1981.[17]

The principal amendment to the U.S. welfare system after Roosevelt occurred in the 1960s when a series of programs initiated by Presidents Kennedy and Johnson augmented its size and scope. Many of these programs were enacted under Johnson's War on Poverty and Great Society project aimed at eradicating poverty. Almost all of these programs expanded the noncontributory, usually means-tested programs and included expanded health coverage, child care, and education schemes such as Headstart. By the early 1980s there was a consensus among Republicans and conservatives that many of these programs had failed, a view consonant with the New Right influence upon the Reagan administration.[18] The main object of wrath was means-tested public assistance programs notably food stamps and Aid to Families with Dependent Children (AFDC). Table 8.1 reports some expenditure figures for welfare and education, while Table 8.2 records the growth in AFDC rolls.

The figures for public aid and AFDC constitute a relatively small percentage of the federal government's expenditure on welfare services, if social security is included, yet public discussion has focused disproportionately upon them. This

Table 8.1. *U.S. social welfare expenditures, 1960–1987*
(*per capita constant 1987 dollars*)

Year	Social insurance[a]	Public aid	Education
1960	383	82	350
1970	729	221	681
1980	1373	430	726
1985	1633	432	757
1986	1660	446	807
1987	1671	447	826

[a]Includes old-age, survivors, disability (i.e., social security), health insurance (i.e., Medicare), public employee retirement, railroad employee retirement, unemployment insurance, other railroad employee insurance, state temporary disability insurance, and workers' compensation. The first two groups – social security and Medicare – form the overwhelming bulk of this category.
Source: Statistical Abstract of the United States 1990 (Washington, D.C.: Bureau of the Census, 1991), p. 350.

skewed emphasis reflects institutional and cultural factors. Institutionally the universal basis of contributory programs such as social security, Medicare, and unemployment insurance has given them a near immunity from political attack whereas the selective noncontributory character of public assistance and AFDC programs limits their political support.[19] Furthermore, this institutional dichotomy has reified a popular distinction about legitimate public assistance to the disadvantaged and benefits for the undeserving. Hugh Heclo draws the distinction between welfare as self-sufficiency and welfare as mutual dependence. According to Heclo the former is a

conception of wellbeing that is supremely individualistic, for it has to do with the capacity of an individual to go his own way, to enjoy the fruits of his own labor . . . To paraphrase President Reagan in a recent Fourth of July speech, we Americans do not get together to celebrate Dependence Day.

. . . the second [conception] has to do with a social or group-oriented rationality. . . . This is not a question asking us to choose between rational individualism and all other behavior that is somehow irrational. It is . . . asking us to apply rational criterion to the self-in-group rather than to the self-in-isolation as the point of reference.[20]

It is quotidian that assumptions about the legitimate bases of social welfare assistance in the United States are consistent with Heclo's first category. This view limits the responsibility Americans extend toward the less fortunate, resulting in an unpreparedness to aid those they believe can help themselves. The trajectory for the work–welfare program lay in existing federal welfare measures as two recent commentators suggest: "In America . . . despite the New Deal and the

Table 8.2. *AFDC enrollments 1970–1988 (in thousands)*

| Fiscal year | Average monthly number of | | | |
	families	recipients	children	unemployed parent families
1960		3,100		
1965		4,300		
1969		6,100		
1970	1,909	7,429	5,494	78
1972	2,918	10,632	7,698	134
1974	3,170	10,845	7,824	95
1976	3,561	11,339	8,156	135
1978	3,528	10,663	7,475	127
1980	3,642	10,597	7,320	141
1982	3,569	10,431	6,975	232
1984	3,725	10,866	7,153	287
1986	3,747	10,995	7,294	253
1988	3,748	10,920	7,326	210

Source: Adapted from *Background Material and Data on Programs within the Jurisdiction of the Committee on Ways and Means,* Committee on Ways and Means, U.S. House of Representatives (Washington, D.C.: Government Printing Office, March 15, 1989), p. 559. Figures for 1960, 1965 and 1969: J. T. Patterson, *America's Struggle against Poverty* (Cambridge, Mass.: Harvard University Press, 1981), p. 171.

Great Society, commitment to State Welfare provision has always been tempered by scepticism about its side-effects and its implications. The strength of faith in market mechanisms and self-help has remained . . .''[21]

In their analysis of several opinion polls Erikson, Luttberg, and Tedin confirm this interpretation. They find consistent support for helping the less well off but within limits including an unwillingness to "support innovative social welfare programs":

As innovative suggestions turn toward such matters as guaranteeing each family a minimum income, mass opinion is clearly lagging behind the thinking of reformers and government leaders. One reason for this resistance is the widespread belief that people who receive financial assistance ought to work for their money, even if the work they do is of little use. Also, when government programs are perceived as benefiting only the lowest-income groups, few people see themselves as beneficiaries of these policies. As a result, the bulk of the public sometimes appear on the conservative side of social welfare controversies.[22]

Combined with the institutional structure of the U.S. welfare state and the U.S. polity, these attitudes undercut reform initiatives during both the Nixon and Carter administrations. Nixon's Family Assistance Plan was designed to give benefits to single- and two-parent families and to create a national uniform level of assistance. The plan failed to garner political support from either the Right (congressional opposition was led by Senator Russell Long of Louisiana) or the Left (most welfare rights groups opposed the plan). It was defeated twice in Congress.

The 1945–51 Attlee-led Labour administration implemented the Beveridge Plan in Britain thereby creating the postwar welfare state.[23] In 1945 a family allowance scheme was introduced together with national insurance for those injured at work. In 1946 national insurance for the sick, unemployed, widows, orphans, and retired, and for maternity were all reformed and the National Health Service founded. A national assistance scheme was implemented in 1948. These programs expanded prewar ones to create a universal welfare state in which the distinction between benefits claimed as rights and those administered at discretion was weakened though not eliminated. Beveridge emphasized creating a system in which those who had contributed should receive benefits without any means testing or stigma, though with some means-tested benefits for those individuals, through disability or caring for another for example, unable fully to participate in the labor-market–based contributory scheme. This proposal did not break with the assumptions of the first national insurance legislation enacted in 1911. It was undoubtedly a family-based scheme assuming a traditional domestic division of labor. However, neither family nor insurance benefits were ever set at a rate sufficiently high to erode poverty as Beveridge had intended.

The 1944 White Paper on Employment Policy committed postwar governments to the pursuit of full employment through a mixture of Keynesian macroeconomic policies.[24] Lipservice only was paid to the development of microeconomic mechanisms such as training programs in the pursuit of this objective, in part because employment was high until relatively recently (Table 8.3).[25] The insurance system to assist unemployed persons was administered through the social security laws enacted in the late 1940s. At their enactment it was assumed that unemployment was characteristically short-term. Unemployed persons who had contributed to the national insurance system while in work received unemployment benefits (UBs), a taxable benefit available for 52 weeks. Those lacking sufficient national insurance payments to receive UB applied for means-tested supplementary benefit (SB), the most important source of benefits for unemployed persons by the 1980s as unemployment grew dramatically.[26] Thus according to the Central Statistical Office in 1985 62 percent of the unemployed received SB benefits only, while 18 percent received UB with 8 percent receiving both[27] (Tables 8.4 and 8.5). Benefit rates are kept below wage levels to avoid any disincentive effect. Government training programs for young and long-term unemployed persons, whose expansion is discussed below, have also kept their payment levels linked to wages and close to benefit levels. The distinction between contributory, non–means-tested insurance and noncontributory means-tested assistance was advocated by Beveridge in his 1942 report and this separation

Table 8.3. *Unemployment in Britain, 1955–1991*

Year	Number of unemployed (thousands)	Unemployed as percentage of working population
1955	213.2	1.0
1960	345.8	1.5
1965	317.0	1.4
1969	543.8	2.4
1970	582.2	2.5
1971	751.3	3.3
1972	837.4	3.7
1973	595.6	2.6
1974	599.5	2.6
1975	940.9	4.0
1976	1,301.7	5.5
1977	1,402.7	5.8
1978	1,382.9	5.7
1979	1,295.7	5.4
1980	1,664.9	6.9
1981	2,520.4	10.7
1982	2,916.0	12.1
1983	3,104.7	11.7
1984	3,159.8	11.7
1985	3,271.2	11.8
1986	3,289.1	11.8
1987 Jan.	3,297.2	11.9
Sept.	2,870.2	10.3
1988 Jan.	2,722.2	9.5
Dec.	2,046.8	8.2
1989 March	1,960.2	6.9
1990 Jan. 11	1,687.0	5.9
April 12	1,626.6	5.7
July 12	1,623.6	5.7
Oct. 11	1,670.6	5.9
1991 Jan. 10	1,959.7	6.9

Source: Department of Employment Gazette various issues.

remains a defining feature of the British welfare state. High employment until the 1970s meant that the second category was of marginal importance.

With the growth of unemployment in the 1980s the government's desire to address the problem and concern that no malingerers receive benefits, manifest in regular diatribes against scroungers, stimulated efforts to compel participation in training programs or exclusion from benefits, a development manifest in work–welfare programs. According to one observer, "concern about 'scroungers' and

Table 8.4. *Trends in social security benefits*

Year	Total contributory benefit outlay (£ millions)	Total noncontributory benefit outlay (£ millions)
1982–3	18,593	12,476
1983–4	19,709	13,902
1984–5	20,777	15,613
1985–6	22,356	18,496
1986–7	23,983	19,231
1987–8	24,939	20,405
1988–9	25,693	21,600
1989–90	27,100	22,700

Source: The Government's Expenditure Plans 1988–89 to 1990–91, Vol II (London: Her Majesty's Stationery Office, Cmd. 288-II, 1991), table 15.1.

fear that people may 'settle down' on benefits has produced a variety of controls (financial and otherwise), which make the unemployed . . . the least generously treated of social security recipients."[28] This pattern accorded with earlier practices in the British welfare state. As the unemployment insurance system was expanded during the 1920s and 1930s so the government's obsession with excising the undeserving grew. Labor exchange administrators, responsible for distributing unemployment benefits, had concurrently to implement a work test to establish whether recipients were "genuinely seeking work but unable to obtain suitable employment."[29] This injunction politicized labor exchanges and unemployment benefits: "Between March 1921 and March 1932 nearly three million claims for benefit were refused because the claimant had failed to meet this condition."[30] In March 1930 the "genuinely seeking work" test was abolished but replaced with a means-tested benefit that still required administrators to establish that unemployment was involuntary. Consequently, even in a period of mass unemployment such as the 1930s the government interpreted hostility to malingerers as sufficient to require strict policing of benefit claimants. This position is reflected in strong public support for the health, old-age pensions, disability, and education aspects of the welfare state but weaker support for unemployed persons especially young and healthy ones considered capable of finding work.[31]

This review of the institutional and policy features of U.S. and British welfare states before the 1980s reveals three points.

First, the founding acts in each country (1935 in the United States and 1945–51 in Britain) occurred during periods of crisis when the scale of hardship (the 1930s) or the potential future risk (the postwar period) stimulated major policy.

Table 8.5. *Social security spending in real terms*

Year	DHSS social security (£ millions)
1978–9	32.0
1979–80	32.3
1980–1	33.0
1981–2	36.5
1982–3	38.7
1983–4	40.1
1984–5	41.6
1985–6	42.7
1986–7	44.4
1987–8	44.5
1988–9	44.5
1989–90	45.3
1990–1	46.1

Source: The Government's Expenditure Plans 1988–89 to 1990–91, Vol I (London: Her Majesty's Stationery Office, Cmd. 288-I, 1991), table 5.7.

In the United States the unemployment crisis of the Great Depression was sufficient to generate a political coalition for policy. In Britain the Labour Party was elected on a wave of euphoria with a mandate to improve economic and social standards. The electoral mandate and parliamentary control provided a window of opportunity to act and the Beveridge Plan, prepared during the war, constituted detailed proposals for policy.

Second, institutional features of the founding legislation persist. In the United States the dichotomy between contributory and noncontributory programs inherent in the Social Security Act of 1935 became the framework within which problems of welfare were debated, with the second type of program by far the weaker partner. In Britain the postwar welfare programs established a universal institution enjoying popular and wide political support, but they retained selective means testing for the weakest members of the labor market. In both countries work–welfare programs focused principally upon claimants within the means-tested category.

Third, public opinion in each country assumed particular forms. In the United States support for noncontributory programs was weaker than for contributory pension, health, and unemployment insurance schemes. The image of the "able-bodied beneficiary" dominated excoriation of welfare programs. In Britain widespread support for the education, health, disability, and old-age dimensions of the welfare state have always been tempered by an easily aroused fear of the lazy malingerer preferring benefits to work.

These institutional, policy, and attitudinal legacies constitute the framework within which the ideas of the New Right for reforming work–welfare in the United States and Britain were enacted during the 1980s. While important features of these reforms were consistent with existing patterns, their success required in Britain some modification to prevailing practice and orthodoxy. Explanation of how this modification occurs provides the basis for understanding the convergence in British and American work–welfare programs. Furthermore, an explanation of how policy ideas were successfully mobilized in each country is necessary to an explanation of these reforms. Some ideas were privileged, through filtering by the agents of mobilization (for example, state governors in the United States and the Conservative Party in Britain), the extant programs and attitudes of the policy-makers.

THE WORK–WELFARE REFORMS

The United States[32]

Institutionally, the American polity offers no clear point of policy initiation or leadership. There are competing sources of policy proposals, a feature that can induce innovation though more commonly thwarts legislation. Three actors were important to the Family Support reform.

First, President Reagan, located in the White House and representing a national constituency, signaled his support for an overhaul of the welfare system in his 1986 and 1987 State of the Union addresses, building upon the opportunity for state innovation created in the Omnibus Budget Reconciliation Act of 1981. In the 1986 address Reagan exploited remarks by Franklin D. Roosevelt to support his own conception of welfare reform: "Roosevelt "said welfare is 'a narcotic, a subtle destroyer of the human spirit.' And we must now escape the spider's web of dependency. Tonight, I am charging the White House domestic council to present by 1 December 1986 . . . a strategy for immediate action to meet the financial, educational, social and safety concerns of poor families."[33]

The president's initiative reflected political debates about welfare including the themes of "welfare dependence" from *Losing Ground*, Charles Murray's influential book,[34] and labor-market disincentives.[35] Reagan's statement received wide press coverage and indicated that welfare reform was a priority. His emphasis upon welfare dependency and labor market disincentives privileged one interpretation of the welfare debate. In his weekly radio address Reagan reiterated his themes: "the welfare tragedy has gone on too long. It is time to reshape our welfare system so that it can be judged by how many Americans it makes independent of welfare. . . . In 1964 the famous war on poverty was declared and a funny thing happened. Poverty, as measured by dependency, stopped shrinking and then actually began to grow worse. I guess you could say that poverty won the war."[36] By making welfare reform an integral part of his administration's agenda President Reagan contributed to the view that there was a serious problem. It provided an opportunity for him to propose and advance favored remedies.

The second force precipitating legislative reform was the state governors, organized through their bipartisan lobby group the National Governors' Association (NGA). As a matching program the states bore half the cost of administering the welfare system and their governors were eager to reduce this burden. They wanted a national public system of welfare. Several governors had instituted their own reforms, which, on the best evidence available (supplied by the Manpower Demonstration Research Corporation), were judged successful in reducing welfare rolls and constituted a model for national reform.

The different aims of the president and governors had to be reconciled in the draft legislation, a process illustrative of how ideas are affected by political institutions. President Reagan supported a work requirement for welfare recipients – and this preference influenced the whole legislative process – but was reluctant to commit additional funds for the transition costs deemed necessary by the governors for an effective program.

The third force involved the actions of members of Congress. Responding to Reagan and the governors, the House Subcommittee on Public Assistance and Unemployment Compensation held hearings on welfare reform as did Senator Moynihan's subcommittee on Social Security and Family Policy. "Working for welfare" was a salient theme in the hearings before each committee. This theme was discussed both liberally as a means of providing work opportunities and punitively as a mechanism of enforcing work requirements upon welfare recipients. Working for welfare was commonly invoked under the vague rubric of "workfare," a term used in differing ways.[37]

In the Senate the key actor pursuing welfare reform in the 100th Congress was Daniel Patrick Moynihan, Senator for New York. Reforming welfare became a single-minded passion for Moynihan, who was involved with both the earlier initiatives, and he was determined to make progress on this task in his capacity as subcommittee chairman. Moynihan's long association with welfare issues lent credibility to this reform initiative.[38]

In the House of Representatives member Gus Hawkins from California had been a prime mover in welfare reform for over a decade. His aims, however, resembled those of a European social democrat and they received little attention during the 1980s under the Reagan administration. Hawkins chaired the House Education and Labor Committee. It was the Public Assistance and Unemployment Compensation subcommittee of the Ways and Means Committee, however, at first chaired by Representative Harold Ford of Tennessee, that paralleled Moynihan's initiatives in the Senate. After his indictment by a grand jury on charges of bank and tax fraud, Ford was replaced by Thomas Downey of New York, an able and ambitious seven-term member of Congress.

The object of reform for Reagan, the governors, and the Congress was to combat the growth of large numbers of welfare-dependent single mothers receiving Aid to Families with Dependent Children (AFDC). It is this group that concerned both critics of the welfare system such as Charles Murray and President Reagan and supporters of a liberal European-style system. Moynihan considered the pre-1988 welfare system an income-maintenance system with a small work-training program component. The old system was not designed to assist people get off the welfare rolls and so the AFDC numbers had grown.[39] These reformers therefore sought an employment program with an income-maintenance element. Institutionally, if only one of these actors had initiated reform success was unlikely. The two major previous reform failures were both led by the White House, by Nixon and Carter, but did not have the same support in the Congress or with subfederal actors. The institutional separation of powers between the executive and legislative (maintained by the presidential veto) ensure that both influence policy.

The new work–welfare policy.   The committees in the House and Senate each formulated and pursued their own welfare reform bill. The House bill was introduced first, fully debated in committee, successfully reported out of committee, and voted upon the floor. Moynihan's major hurdle in the Senate was getting his bill out of the Finance Committee. It was reported as bipartisan. At this stage there were no participation rates – that is, any requirement for participation in work or training programs at stipulated percentages of those on welfare. It was reported out in April 1988 and came to the floor in June; as the debates began, the White House quickly expressed a desire to negotiate about the bill. Moynihan agreed to negotiate believing that the vote in the Senate would be insufficient to override a veto from the president. Policy leadership is shared institutionally between the executive and the legislature. The latter can rarely expect to proceed without some agreement or support from the former, and the presidential veto is a significant constraint on legislating. Thus the activism of both branches was important for the bill's prospects. The White House and members of the Finance Committee (Packard, Dole, Rockefeller, and Moynihan) reached an agreement that included participation rates – that is, specified rates of participation in work or training programs by welfare recipients for each state to satisfy. Failure to meet the required rates would result in a reduction or loss of federal funding. These work or training requirements could take one of four different forms.[40] In the end, there was little debate about the bill on the floor.

The House and Senate bills differed. The House bill emphasized education and training; it targeted those in need of remedial education and was to cost $7.2 billion over five years. The Senate bill was punitive, less generously funded, state-based, closer to the White House view and was to cost $2.7 billion. The main disagreement during the conference stage concerned mandating work–welfare. President Reagan's representatives were adamant about including this measure, threatening a presidential veto if the mandatory rule was excluded. It was included in the legislation.

The bill agreed by the conference committee was closer to the Senate bill than to the House bill. This outcome partly reflected the belief that it was the Senate bill that the president would sign. Also, the Senate bill had received greater support within its chamber than had the House bill. The passing of the conference bill reflected the work of Representative Downey and the determination of Senator Moynihan not to let this reform opportunity fail as had earlier attempts. Throughout, Moynihan and Downey had the support of the governors, and this support, combined with adroit negotiating, succeeded in pushing the Family Support bill forward. The power of the White House, however, is illustrated by the inclusion of a compulsory work–welfare role in the bill, despite the resistance of members of the Congress and the governors.

The ideas for reform. The diffuse nature of the U.S. political system offers numerous access points for ideas to be promoted. Within the political system ideas can be "tested" or first applied in state or local government and then advocated for federal laws. The example of state programs provided one source for the Family Support Bill. The second source of ideas were the proposals from welfare interest groups, particularly experts.

The ideas promoted by the NGA on the basis of their state experiments were most influential with the key members of the Congress including Moynihan and, belatedly, President Reagan. There were over twenty such programs including Massachusetts's Employment Training Choices (ET), California's Greater Avenues to Independence (GAIN), Georgia's Positive Employment and Community Help Program (PEACH), and programs in New York, Connecticut, West Virginia, and Illinois with equally appealing acronyms. These programs offered a means of breaking with the Great Society initiative and returning U.S. policy to its self-help, means-tested trajectory. The success of these programs was promoted by the governors and validated (though not uncritically) by welfare experts. These innovative state programs provided models for a federal scheme that could be modified to satisfy the New Right punitive ambitions of the White House.

The governors' ideas for federal reform were formulated by an executive committee of the NGA, chaired by Bill Clinton of Arkansas, which reported to the first of their twice yearly meetings in February 1987. Subtitled a "Job-Oriented Welfare Reform" the proposals envisaged welfare programs as providing work or training opportunities for their recipients.[41] The governors' objective was to reduce dependence by providing welfare recipients with the skills necessary to leave welfare and enter work: "The principal responsibility of government in the welfare contract is to provide education, job training and/or job placement services to all employable recipients. These services must be carefully structured so that they suit the employment needs of individual participants.''[42] Achieving a transition from welfare to work required the provision of "transition services," including child care facilities, health care benefits, and some transportation subsidy.[43]

Without federal participation the NGA believed a jobs-oriented welfare strategy would be unsuccessful.[44] The governors resisted a compulsory work–welfare system.[45] Despite initially opposing the governors, believing their proposals too liberal, President Reagan endorsed their welfare reform plans in a White House meeting on February 23. However, he stressed the inclusion of a work requirement in return for child, medical insurance, and other aid.[46] In the Congress Senator Moynihan frequently cited the governors' proposals as the primary source for his bill. The governors did not promote explicitly New Right views – that is, mandatory work or training requirements – and the states offered a range of practice in their programs. Thus, policy-makers could choose between, for example, the voluntary Massachusetts system or the compulsory Californian one. That a compulsory scheme was favored reflects the differential power of national policy-makers. The act finally passed gave less importance to education and training than the governors' proposals implied.

External experts' views were important for the welfare reform process. Several academic writers on welfare testified before congressional hearings, and their arguments about welfare dependency and citizenship as obligation featured in the welfare reform debates and proposals.

A crucial set of expertise was provided by the New York–based Manpower Demonstration Research Corporation (MDRC). Their evaluations of the Massachusetts's ET program and the programs in New York, New Jersey, and California provided evidence that work–welfare programs succeeded in reducing welfare rolls over the long run.[47] This evidence, presented before congressional hearings, demonstrated program effectiveness fiscally, a priority of all the reformers, and highlighted the existence of policy comparisons available as a model for the extension of work–welfare programs in a federal law. The evidence of MDRC research was used to support the propositions advanced by New Right advocates, but not the governors, for a stringent work–welfare regime and reversal of the Great Society welfare liberalism. The cogency of this evidence reveals perhaps the power of ideas in policy-making, particularly in the United States, where it is common to hold extensive hearings during the legislative process at which experts acquire an opportunity to present their findings. These ideas were thus filtered by the political institutions of the United States and accorded, by the White House and conservatives, a role in supporting a work–welfare regime that might not have been shared by the evaluators researching the state programs.

There was a second set of interest groups whose members' interests were affected by the proposed reform sought to protect their interests. Trades unions such as the AFL-CIO and the AFSCME feared the "displacement" of their union members from permanent jobs as a consequence of the community work experience program (CWEP) under the new act. Working with AFL-CIO, the AFSCME succeeded in lobbying for strong displacement language in the act.[48]

Representing state welfare administrators the American Public Welfare Association (APWA) broadly supported the Family Support Act. Its own recommendation for reform, issued in November 1986, influenced the proposals promulgated by the governors. The APWA had reservations about the mandatory element in Title II of the Family Support Act. The Association questioned both the adequacy of federal funds allocated for the JOBS program and the likely content of state programs. The Children's Defense Fund opposed the Family Support Act because it provided insufficient protection for children. Its views were incorporated in an umbrella group, the National Coalition on Women, Work and Welfare Reform, orchestrated by the Wider Opportunities for Women (WOW). The National Coalition wanted a work component in welfare policy but as part of a comprehensive training policy. It opposed mandatory work. The Coalition proposed a four-point strategy of which "education, employment, and training" was one key element.[49] Their views failed to influence policy; their proposals were rejected by policy-makers, who were not prepared to allocate resources on the scale required.

The National Alliance for Business (NAB) supported the work–welfare legislation for its contribution to alleviating the labor shortage, an argument promoted by several of the governors too, notably New Jersey's Thomas Kean. The National Association of Manufacturers (NAM) and the U.S. Chamber of Commerce also supported work–welfare programs, wanting more persons trained (by which they meant provided, where appropriate, with remedial education skills) to enter the work force.[50]

In sum, the Family Support Act of 1988 in the United States established a federal work–welfare program. The act amended Title IV of the Social Security Act of 1935 by introducing a condition for the receipt of benefits. This change alters the entitlement of the poor to public income maintenance formulated in the 1935 act. The receipt of benefits is now conditional upon participation in a work or training program for all parents. Each state had to establish (from October 1990 with a statewide coverage by October 1992) and maintain some sort of Jobs Opportunities and Basic Skills Training Program (JOBS). The states are obliged to coordinate with the Job Training Partnership Act (JTPA) program administrators in their state, forging a link between the major federal job training and federal welfare programs. The principal source for this reform was the experiments conducted by the states and validated by MDRC. The objections of welfare rights' groups and the NGA to a compulsory system were, however, disregarded by the White House.

Britain

The capacity of the Thatcher administration to respond to the crisis posed by unemployment was enhanced by the nature of the British state. Constitutionally and institutionally policy leadership is concentrated in the office of the government. This concentration does not mean that political judgments and bureaucratic expertise are unimportant influences upon the content or timing of policy or that existing policies can be automatically ended. It does mean that these latter influences are tempered by the priorities of politicians and that civil servants' policy role can be curtailed. Before the 1980s, it has been argued frequently, the civil service in Britain prevailed in public policy-making; this claim has been advanced by many Labour Party politicians.[51] Since 1979 it is the politicians who have assumed the leading role and they were more important to the establishment of work–welfare programs than their bureaucratic counterparts. The lengthy incumbency of one administration, its parliamentary majorities, and its deliberate shrinking of the number of civil servants and "hiving off" as autonomous units run on market sector criteria of some public sector activities have succeeded in reducing the influence of civil servants.[52] The Conservative administration elected in 1979 pitched many of its actions as direct challenges to the power of civil servants to the extent of dismantling or hiving off state activities to the private sector, through the Next Steps program.[53]

The power of politicians is illustrated by the government's shifting approach to the organization responsible for training, the Manpower Services Commission (MSC), whose programs were expanded in parallel with the growth in unemployment. The MSC was authorized in the Employment and Training Act of 1973,[54] operative in 1974.[55] While the decision to found the MSC reflected in part academic and international influence, the key motive was the short-term one of negotiations about pay in 1972–3. It was designed as a tripartite corporatist institution. There were three members each from employers and trades unions nominated by the Confederation of British Industry (CBI) and the Trades Union Council (TUC) respectively, two local authority representatives and an academic together with a chairman. Section 2 of the 1973 act directed the MSC "to make such arrangements as it considers appropriate for the purpose of assisting persons to select, train for, obtain and retain employment suitable for their ages and capacities and to obtain suitable employees."[56] The Commission was empowered to make arrangements for the provision of training by subcontracting and to make its facilities and programs available to others in receipt of fees.

The establishment of the MSC was not envisaged as a major policy innovation and until 1979 it remained a small organization. Its activities were not subject to detailed ministerial attention, nor did it play a pivotal role in national policy despite the ambitions of MSC officers.[57] However, unemployment quickly dominated the MSC's work. In 1981 the prime minister appointed David (now Lord) Young as Chairman of the MSC, a signal that this organization was intended to play a larger role in government policy. Young's first year in the job coincided with Norman Tebbit's occupancy of the Ministry of Employment. Young introduced new training programs directed at the young, the long-term unemployed, and middle-aged displaced workers. His successful incumbency made the MSC's policies the central institution in the government's attack on unemployment. Many of these programs, for example the Youth Training Scheme (YTS), were the subject of controversy as to their effectiveness in providing training rather than cheap and/or compulsory labor, and of conflict between the government and welfare rights' advocates and the unions.[58] The hostility of the unions, intensified by the post-1988 requirement that young people participate in YTS, was a thorn in the government's side, and the MSC in 1988 remained the final manifestation of corporatist tripartitism under the Conservatives. It was ripe for abolition, a decision taken in 1988 when it was renamed the Training Commission.

The Conservatives looked askance upon the MSC because of its tripartitism. They needed the MSC to implement a work–welfare program. The Confederation of British Industry (CBI) supported the 1988 ET training program, but it was opposed by the TUC. At their annual conference in 1988 the TUC resolved against participation in the new ET scheme, despite the efforts of the MSC and TUC leaders to win support, on pragmatic grounds, for the program.[59] The TUC's decision was quickly followed by one to redesignate the Training Commission a Training Agency with no trade union representation on its board. Tripartitism ended with this decision. New Right proponents opposed tripartite-based institutions intervening in the market. Its abolition was a pretext for ending the role of the TUC in influencing government policy, and a necessary step for the government's consolidation of control over training programs and policy. It was the final stage in restructuring this organization for the government's policy of creating work–welfare programs. Members of the commission had queried the last major training program, the New Job Training Scheme, and as a consequence responsibility for Job Centres and the Restart counseling scheme was shifted from the Commission to the Department of Employment.

Between 1979 and 1989 the government modified the social security system, including the benefits given to unemployed persons. These reforms were motivated by the political problem posed by the growing number of unemployed persons and the ideological desire to narrow eligibility. For income support the system is divided into two categories consistent with those introduced during the postwar period. First, there are contributory benefits based upon weekly payments into a national insurance fund while in work. In this category payees are entitled to unemployment benefit after three days out of work, if complex contributory conditions are satisfied, a benefit exhausted after fifty-two weeks. A further thirteen weeks of work is necessary to requalify. The strict policing laws noted above apply to applicants for unemployment benefit and include proof of involuntary unemployment, availability for work, nonrefusal to take a suitable opening or loss of work through the claimant's own fault. These regulations have been tightened recently (see below). Second, means-tested supplementary benefits have been replaced by income support, which now constitutes the main source of income maintenance for long-term unemployed adults. These benefits are distributed by complex means-testing criteria. The distinction advanced by Beveridge between contributory and noncontributory (and means-tested) benefits for unemployed persons persists though the rates and conditions of their allocation have been modified during the 1980s.[60]

Those receiving unemployment and social security benefits have gradually been linked to the government's training policy by quasimandatory requirements that they participate in training programs. Previously persons receiving benefits were under no requirement to participate in training programs, though they had to register as unemployed and demonstrate their "availability for work" at Restart interviews. The Social Security Act of 1985 empowered the Employment Secretary to designate training programs "approved training schemes," and under the act trainees who refused a reasonable offer of a place on an approved scheme can have their unemployment benefits reduced for six months.[61]

The new work–welfare policy.   The work–welfare program was established by implementing and dovetailing reforms in training and unemployment policy. In February 1988 the government issued a White Paper titled "Training for Employment" that set out a range of measures intended to tackle the perceived problems of unemployed persons.[62] The three issues of skills, motivations, and incentives dominated the White Paper and shaped the government's training proposals. These issues reflect both economic problems[63] and the charge that some claimants were not fulfilling the legal obligation actively to seek work[64] (which reflects an inadequate incentive system[65]).[66] The ambitious Employment Training program was launched in September 1988 combining the existing programs of the MSC (now called the Training Agency) and intending to create 600,000 training places of up to 12 months with an average participation of six months.[67]

In its White Paper (February 1988), the government proposed establishing a system in which advisers would formulate a "personal action plan" for all persons unemployed (an idea with U.S. counterparts). This task would be the responsibility of the Job Centres, which conduct Restart interviews. Since 1986 everyone on the unemployment register for more than six months is called to a Restart interview at which advice is given about government training programs. The interview is intended to determine claimants' availability for work. Failure to attend an interview can lead to the loss of benefits. If a claimant fails to attend the whole or part of a Restart Course (normally lasting a week) his or her claimant adviser can reduce his or her income support payment by up to 40 percent.[68]

The new work–welfare policy is apparent in the 1988 Employment Act, the 1988 Social Security Act, and the 1989 Social Security Act. In each act significant clauses overlap (a point noted repeatedly by the government's critics during the legislative process) suggesting a coherent policy. The Social Security Act

1988, considered during the 1987–8 parliamentary session, included a clause making participation in Youth Training Schemes (YTS) compulsory; refusal to participate (or leaving prematurely) would result in the withdrawal of benefits from the offending persons. The shift to compulsory participation in YTS schemes introduced by the Social Security Act 1988 was complemented by Part II of the Employment Act 1988, which disqualified persons from receiving unemployment benefits if they withdrew from a training scheme or were dropped for misconduct or declined a place on the scheme "without good cause." These developments are reinforced in the 1989 Social Security Act. At the committee stage in the House when the bill was discussed, considerable time was devoted to Clause 7 of the bill (which became section 10 in the act). To receive unemployment benefits under this clause, unemployed persons must produce evidence that they are "seeking employment actively."

The ideas for reform. How did the Thatcher administration derive the objectives it pursued in its work–welfare program? Briefly, it drew upon the proposals advanced by New Right pressure groups and imitated American programs.

It would be inaccurate to argue that the Conservative Party entering office in 1979 held a coherent conception of the work–welfare program that they wished to implement. The Conservatives did have definable New Right principles guiding their policy formulation that interacted with contingent political priorities and calculations. However in contemplating major reforms politicians must have detailed ideas and proposals available to them. In Britain these were provided by think tanks outside the state, including the Adam Smith Institute, Institute of Economic Affairs, Centre for Policy Studies and Social Affairs Unit (in the U.S. groups such as Heritage Foundation, Hoover Institute, and American Enterprise Institute played a comparable role).[69] They campaigned to advance New Right proposals and succeeded in winning over leading members of the Conservative Party close to the leader Mrs. Thatcher.[70] (In Chapter 4 Peter Hall explains how these groups also influenced the Conservatives' economic policy.) These groups criticized the universalism of the welfare system, citing the United States as a preferable model, and they promulgated the views of American scholars. They advocated narrowing eligibility for benefits, requiring some activity from the recipients of benefits and expanding means testing.[71]

The influence of New Right ideas and American practice can be illustrated from the parliamentary debates between the government and its Labour opposition during the bills' enactment.

New Right advocates wish to reduce the attractiveness of the welfare system and to extract an activity from recipients in exchange for their benefits, an aim first achieved in the Social Security Act of 1988. Persons collecting unemployment benefits must not merely be available for employment but should actively be seeking employment.[72] Young people must participate in a training scheme. The Opposition's characterization of this requirement in the Social Security Act of 1988 as "compulsory" was refuted during enactment by Michael Portillo, under-secretary of state for health and social security:

I entirely rebut the . . . repeated allegation about compulsion. It is true that we are with-drawing income support from 16- and 17-year-olds who have left school, are not in work and have not taken up a YTS place, but the choices for young people are still there. They can stay at school. They can go to college. They can, if they are lucky, take a job. Or they can take the YTS place that is on offer to them. I persist in saying therefore, that there is no compulsion. We are talking about the guaranteed option of a place on a YTS and the response of the Government and the taxpayer to that new situation.[73]

In an earlier contribution to the committee discussion the Labour MP from Derby South, Margaret Beckett, noted that "as long ago as 1982 the MSC expressed strong reservations about compelling people to go on YTS. . . . Once young people are compelled to take up places if only for economic reasons, every in-centive to improve the quality of the scheme is removed."[74] Internal MSC op-position to compulsory participation made it necessary to modify the status of this organization for it to be an effective institutional resource for the Conserva-tives' work–welfare ambitions.

During the Second Reading in the House of Lords, the government's minister, Lord Skelmersdale, dismissed his critics' worries: "YTS provides a guarantee of a good quality training place to all young people under 18. With such a guar-antee for the able bodied and a safety net for those who are not able to take up a place, there is no longer any reason to continue paying income support to the under-18s."[75] Thus, by the time of the Conservative Party's third electoral suc-cess in 1987, their legislation was gradually but ineluctably creating a work–welfare program.

The change to compulsory participation under the Employment Act of 1988 was also debated heatedly during the parliamentary readings and committee hear-ings.[76] Labour MP Michael Meacher argued that, "if the schemes are so good and the quality of training offered is so high and valuable, why not allow people to choose them? The Government have ignored the consensus. They have intro-duced legislation that will make YTS compulsory. What can young people do except join YTS?"[77] Responding to these criticisms, Norman Fowler, the sec-retary of state for employment, maintained that benefits would be withdrawn only on the basis of a "range of evidence. For example, [the claimant] may have refused three or four jobs and three or four places on a training programme. That is where the training programme argument is applicable. . . . The new pro-gramme is not compulsory in the way that it is argued that YTS is compul-sory."[78] The minister rejected the notion that Restart interviews constituted a form of compulsion.[79]

The clearest statement of the New Right influences shaping policy is provided by Nicholas Scott, the minister for social security, speaking to the Standing Committee about the 1989 Social Security Bill. Scott adopted the language of contract and duty familiar from the United States and promoted by the New

Right: ''The state . . . has the task of advising and guiding people towards available job opportunities. But surely the unemployed person has a duty, as his part of the contract, not to sit passively waiting for a job to turn up but to take active steps to seek work. That is the essence of the clause, and it is a thoroughly reasonable proposition.''[80] Scott emphasized this point later in the debate:

the principle at the heart of the clause is that the State rightly accepts a duty to provide benefits for the unemployed under an insurance scheme; if their unemployment is longer than the insurance period, to provide income support for those without other means; and to provide advice, guidance and encouragement for the unemployed. While it accepts the responsibility, as far as is compatible with broader economic aims, to create an environment of enterprise and job creation, the State is entitled in return to expect individuals to take the trouble actively to seek work. This is not . . . some monstrous imposition on the unemployed. It is a genuine effort to provide a path from the misery of unemployment towards self-respect and the ability of individuals to provide for themselves and their families.[81]

This statement is a coherent account of the New Right's conception of the contract between state and citizen in work–welfare. It has significant parallels to the debate raised by the Family Support Act, though the British conception is more legalistic than the U.S. version: Obligation is to the state in Britain and to society in the United States. The Conservatives turned to the U.S. model because its stress upon the contractual obligations of the citizen receiving public funds fitted their ideology and policy objectives.

Scott's parliamentary statement illustrates how influential New Right arguments were with members of the Conservative administration. Such ideas did not provide a blueprint for government legislation but they did influence the content of that legislation, a view with which Wikeley concurs: ''The emphasis on claimants actively seeking work can . . . be seen as a response of economic neo-liberalism to a tightening labour market. This reflects the 'moral hazard' argument as to the supposed disincentive effect of Unemployment Benefit.''[82] This ''moral hazard'' view was promoted by the 1981 established Social Affairs Unit and alluded to in the publications of the Institute of Economic Affairs.[83] Through access points, such as the prime minister's Downing Street Policy Unit, New Right interest groups were able to present and advocate their radical proposals for welfare policy, particularly a weakening of the benefit entitlement system. They continued to have that influence until Mrs. Thatcher's defeat as party leader in November 1990. The Conservatives were eager to hear these proposals both because of their ideological appeal and because of their need of ideas for legislation.

The implementation of the ET program borrows from American practice. Key responsibility is devolved to local Training and Employment Councils (TECs) and, in Scotland, Local Enterprise Councils (LECs), organizations composed of local business persons. These TECs are modeled on the U.S. system of Private Industry Councils (PICs) utilized in the Job Training Partnership Act (JTPA) program. Establishing TECs as instruments of policy has required the ending of the equal representative role of unions with business and the state.[84]

The Thatcher administration "learned" from the United States: Officials visited state programs and designed their long-term work–welfare scheme (ET) after these visits. Ideological sympathy between Reagan and Thatcher provided a rationale for the Conservatives's decision to imitate U.S. practices. British officials visited and studied West German and Swedish programs but opted for the U.S. model. The Massachusetts and California schemes were examined in detail by Department of Employment officials and by the secretary of state for employment. The extent of U.S. influence is indicated by the presence in the Department of Employment as "special adviser" to the secretary the former director of work–welfare training in Massachusetts.[85] The similarity between the content of the British and American work–welfare programs is most pronounced in measures for the long-term unemployed, welfare dependents, and in devolved administrative structure. The British ET's emphasis upon designing an "individual action plan" and providing counseling is similar to the Massachusetts program[86] and the Title II requirements of the Family Support Act. Despite the different origins of work–welfare in the two countries British policymakers borrowed liberally from the U.S. program.

In sum, the British Employment and Social Security Acts of 1988 and the Social Security Act of 1989 introduce significant changes to young and long-term unemployed persons' eligibility for social security benefits and participation in training programs. They dovetailed with the ET program introduced in 1988. Since July 1990 training courses became compulsory for those unemployed for two years or more and who reject offers of help at their Restart interview.[87] Whether or not the changes amount to a compulsory system they do constitute a new emphasis on the government's part regarding participation by the unemployed in some sort of work–welfare scheme.

CONCLUSION

Returning to the institutional, policy, and attitude legacies introduced earlier in this essay, it is notable that both the U.S. and British reforms were largely consistent with prevailing patterns. The U.S. reform introduces a punitive element into the receipt of welfare benefits, but this innovation sits comfortably with attitudes toward welfare recipients and with the institutional dichotomy between contributory and noncontributory beneficiaries established in 1935. In Britain the implementation of work–welfare programs initially focused upon those receiving means-tested unemployment assistance, but its scope has been broadened to include beneficiaries of unemployment benefit for relatively short periods. Policymakers in both countries designed these policies for the weakest members of the benefit system, but in Britain, at least, that universe is an enlarging one. The welfare institutional legacy affected the character of work–welfare programs adopted in each country. The labor-market implications of these policies differs. In the United States the Family Support Act reform has a social significance, irrelevant in Britain, to alter the circumstances of poor, in many cases black, families. In its most generous interpretation it is intended to provide routes for these families to social and economic integration. In Britain, the work–welfare programs have a much closer affinity with traditional labor-market disciplines, vividly illustrated in the modern incarnation of the 1920s' maxim "genuinely seeking work" as "actively seeking work." Despite policy convergence between the United States and Britain the programs still reflect each system.

In both the United States and Britain a version of New Right ideas triumphed in the policy outcome, but this success occurred in different ways reflecting each polity's institutions. The latter diluted and metamorphosed policy proposals. In the United States work–welfare programs became a practical basis for federal policy because of their success in a number of state experiments. It was the governors who originated and tested these ideas, a pattern that illustrates the states' contemporary role as policy innovators. However, when the NGA promoted and Congress acted to legislate federal programs, they labored under the constraint of congressional-presidential relations and of a presidential veto. This constraint was significant because the president favored a harsh work–welfare system and insisted upon the inclusion of a mandatory participation clause in the final legislation. Thus New Right ideas were successful in the United States despite the opposition of the governors and many members of the Congress because the key actor, in this legislation, held sufficient power to advance his preference. The institutional dispersion of power in the United States shaped the version of work–welfare established. The ideas were not static but shaped by the political institutions within which legislation was drafted.

In Britain the Conservative government implemented work–welfare schemes by a twofold strategy. First, it diluted the MSC's training brief, though its budget was expanded, to suit its New Right–inspired conservative ends. This task required modifying the MSC and ending union influence upon policy. For the Conservatives the MSC constituted an institutional resource that they usurped for their policy ends and remolded to their preferred nontripartite structure. Second, the government tightened the criteria under which social security benefits are administered, changes confined initially to those receiving the politically weak noncontributory means-tested benefits but subsequently expanding this regime to cover all recipients of unemployment benefits.

In Britain New Right ideas enjoyed success because of their influence with the Conservatives. The Tory Party's affiliation with New Right groups began while they were in opposition in the late 1970s. The party's role in advancing New Right principles in public policy, including the version of work–welfare developed, indicates how the British party system can facilitate change. The incentives created by a principally two-party system encourage a party in opposition to devise policies critical of the incumbent party. This incentive was heightened by the stagflation of the mid-1970s, which discredited Keynesianism. Peter Hall identifies a similar process in his contribution to this volume (Chapter 4) when he notes that, "on the one hand, the two party system gives the party that is out of office strong incentives to propose innovative lines of policy so as to develop a distinct profile in the eyes of the electorate and a basis from which to mount an effective critique of the incumbent party. On the other hand, once in office, the system of responsible cabinet government concentrates power effectively enough to permit a new government to implement a distinctive pattern of policy."[88]

The Conservatives were able to formulate their work–welfare program by successfully exploiting the crisis posed by unemployment and harvesting the benefits of parliamentary majorities, lengthy incumbency, and a weakened MSC. The 1979 election became comparable to the 1945 election of the Labour Party in that circumstances were propitious for new policy. Repeated electoral success and perceived problems allowed the Conservatives to remold the distribution of unemployment benefits by linking them to training programs. These factors are crucial to understanding how New Right ideas were marshaled in work–welfare policy and how the Conservative Party played an important role in inducing political change. It is improbable that a Labour administration would have opted for a similar work–welfare scheme, though the problem of unemployment could not have been ignored by this party either.[89] The Conservatives acted as a conduit for selecting and translating New Right ideas into policy; these ideas became the equivalent of the Beveridge Plan used for the postwar welfare system. The Conservatives seized the opportunity presented by the crisis of unemployment to advance the New Right principles that had informed their electoral campaigns in 1983 and 1987.[90]

Political parties and politicians link ideas, political institutions, and policy. Ideas are translated into a language and slogans appropriate for political decision-making, a process that often results in metamorphosis of the original notions. Parties, interest groups, and politicians play a crucial role in this "translation." Institutional arrangements undoubtedly structure decision-making in the way Peter Hall's influential analysis suggests,[91] but to explain how the ideological innovations represented by work–welfare programs became policy in Britain requires attention to ideas and politics too.[92]

NOTES

1 Committee on Economic Security, "Report to the President," Jan. 1935, Franklin D. Roosevelt Library Official File 1086, Folder: Committee on Economic Security 1935–40, p. 7.
2 Sir William Beveridge, *Social Insurance and Allied Services* (London: Her Majesty's Stationery Office, Cmd. 6404, 1942). On the social rights of citizenship see T. H. Marshall, *Class, Citizenship and Social Development* (New York: Doubleday, 1984) and D. S. King and J. Waldron, "Citizenship, Social Citizenship and the Defence of Welfare Provision," *British Journal of Political Science* (1988):415–43.

3 See R. Segalman and D. Marsland, *Cradle to Grave* (London: Macmillan in association with the Social Affairs Unit, 1989).

4 Some commentators stressed the absence of work discipline and not work skills. The 1987 government-commissioned study "Workforce 2000" emphasized the impending skills crisis among American workers used to routinized tasks requiring minimal literacy and numeracy. Hudson Institute, *Workforce 2000* (Indianapolis: Hudson Institute, 1987).

5 Major initiatives to reform welfare occurred under the Nixon and Carter presidencies. For details, see L. Mead, *Beyond Entitlement* (New York: Free Press; London: Collier Macmillan, 1985), ch. 5.

6 This judgment was not shared by all observers of the reform. See Sanford F. Schram, "Reinforcing the Work Ethic by Negative Example: A Critical Analysis of the Family Support Act of 1988," paper presented to the annual meetings of the American Political Science Association, Aug. 30–Sept. 2, 1990.

7 *The New York Times*, October 1, 1988, p. 1. See also D. S. King, "Citizenship as Obligation in the United States: the 1988 Welfare Reform," in M. Moran and U. Vogel, *The Frontiers of Citizenship* (London: Macmillan, 1991).

8 Peter Hall, *Governing the Economy* (New York: Oxford University Press, 1986), p. 18. See also P. Lange and G. Garrett, "The Politics of Growth: Strategic Interaction and Economic Performance in the Advanced Industrial Democracies, 1974–1980," *Journal of Politics* 47 (1985):792–827, M. Weir and T. Skocpol, "State Structures and the Possibilities for 'Keynesian' Responses to the Great Depression in Sweden, Britain and the United States," in Peter B. Evans, Dietrich Rueschemeyer, and Theda Skocpol, eds., *Bringing the State Back In* (Cambridge: Cambridge University Press, 1985), and Sven Steinmo, "Political Institutions and Tax Policy in the United States, Sweden and Britain," *World Politics* (July 1989):500–35.

9 The term New Right is used in the British sense to refer to the neoliberal ideology associated with the Reagan and Thatcher administrations. For discussions and definitions, see D. Green, *The New Right* (Brighton: Wheatsheaf, 1987; published in the United States as *The New Conservatism*), K. Hoover and R. Plant, *Conservative Capitalism* (London: Routledge, 1988), D. S. King, *The New Right: Politics, Markets and Citizenship* (Chicago: Dorsey; London: Macmillan, 1987) and G. Peele, *Revival and Reaction* (Oxford: Clarendon Press, 1984).

10 See R. Segalman and D. Marsland, *Cradle to Grave* (London: Macmillan, in association with the Social Affairs Unit, 1989), p. 118 for an account of "welfare dependency."

11 See Robert H. Salisbury, "The Paradox of Interest Groups in Washington – More Groups, Less Clout," in A. King, ed., *The New American Political System*, 2d version (Washington D.C.: American Enterprise Institute, 1990).

12 On the role of the states and the governors since 1980, see D. S. King, "The Changing Federal Balance," in G. Peele, B. Cain, and C. Bailey, eds., *Developments in U.S. Politics* (London: Macmillan, 1992) and P. R. Piccigallo, "Taking the Lead: The States' Expanding Role in Domestic Policymaking," *Journal of American Studies* (1988):417–42. Between 1979 and 1988 full-time professional staff in the state legislatures grew from 8,346 to 13,755, an increase of 64.8 percent.

13 Weir and Skocpol, "State Structures . . ." p. 134. and M. Weir, "Ideas and Politics: The Acceptance of Keynesianism in Britain and the United States," in Peter Hall, ed., *The Political Power of Economic Ideas* (Princeton, N.J.: Princeton University Press, 1989), pp. 53–86.

14 As prime minister, Margaret Thatcher made extensive use of ad hoc cabinet committees that reviewed and drafted policy proposals before they were discussed in full

cabinet. This process strengthened her position and weakened the cabinet's role in policy-making.

15 For discussions of the origins of the U.S. welfare state, see Theda Skocpol and John Ikenberry, "The Political Formation of the American Welfare State in Historical and Comparative Perspective," *Comparative Social Research* 6 (1983):87–148, and E. Amenta and T. Skocpol, "Taking Exception: Explaining the Distinctiveness of American Public Policies in the Last Century," in F. G. Castles, ed., *The Comparative History of Public Policy* (Oxford: Polity Press, 1989), pp. 292–333.

16 This view is expressed by Frances Fox Piven and Richard A. Cloward, *Regulating the Poor: The Functions of Public Welfare* (New York: Random House, 1971).

17 Work–welfare programs such as WIN existed from the mid-1960s, but underfunding limited their implementation.

18 See contributions by neoconservatives to *The Public Interest* during the 1970s and 1980s; see also N. Glazer, *The Limits of Social Policy* (Cambridge, Mass.: Harvard University Press, 1988). The failure of the Great Society programs was a consensus view among Republicans and conservative policy-makers; it was disputed by other scholars and politicians. Unfortunately the latter group have failed to promote their view successfully.

19 The significance of the distinction between contributory and noncontributory programs is a familiar one and many analysts have noted it. See, for example, "Political Formation of the American Welfare State," p. 141, where Skocpol and Ikenberry write that social security "has come to be anchored politically in a broad voting constituency – perhaps the broadest that exists for any American public program – and it is defended by congressional representatives, 'conservative' and 'liberal' alike, anxious to service the needs of well-organized constituents."

20 Hugh Heclo, "General Welfare and Two American Political Traditions," *Political Science Quarterly* 101 (1986):182, 183. See also J. Donald Moon, "The Moral Basis of the Democratic Welfare State," in Amy Gutmann, ed., *Democracy and the Welfare State* (Princeton, N.J.: Princeton University Press, 1988).

21 Segalman and Marsland, *Cradle to Grave*, p. 116. See also D. S. King "Citizenship as Obligation in the U.S.," in M. Moran and U. Vogel, eds., *The Frontiers of Citizenship* (London: Macmillan, 1991). For an analysis of how work–welfare programs fit with conservative conceptions of the link between state benefits and the work discipline in Britain and the United States, see D. S. King and Hugh Ward, "Working for Benefits: Rational Choice and the Rise of Work–Welfare Programmes," *Political Studies* 40 (Sept. 1992).

22 Robert S. Erikson, Norman R. Luttbeg, and Kent L. Tedin, *American Public Opinion* (New York: Macmillan, 1988), p. 59.

23 W. Beveridge, *Social Insurance and Allied Services* (London: Her Majesty's Stationery Office, Cmd. 6404, 1942).

24 Cmd. 6527, 1944 White Paper on Employment Policy. Parliamentary Papers 1943–4, vol. VIII.

25 For discussions, see D. S. King and B. Rothstein, "Institutional Choices and Labour Market Policy: A British–Swedish Comparison," *Comparative Political Studies* 26 (in press).

26 The measure of unemployment has been changed on innumerable occasions during the 1980s and government critics argue that the standard measure now underrepresents the accurate picture.

27 Central Statistical Office, *Social Trends 1987* (London: Her Majesty's Stationery Office, 1987).

28 Jane Keithley, "United Kingdom," in John Dixon and Robert P. Scheurell, *Social Welfare in Developed Market Countries* (London: Routledge, 1989), p. 336.
29 Unemployment Insurance (no. 2) Act of 1924.
30 Alan Deacon, *In Search of the Scrounger,* Occasional Papers on Social Administration no. 60 (London: G. Bell & Sons, 1976), p. 9.
31 See R. Jowell and S. Witherspoon, *British Social Attitudes: the 1985 Report* (Aldershot: Gower, 1985); N. Bosanquet, "Interim Report: Public Spending and the Welfare State," in R. Jowell, S. Witherspoon, and L. Brook, eds., *British Social Attitudes: The 1986 Report* (Aldershot: Gower, 1986) and P. Taylor-Gooby, *Public Opinion, Ideology and State Welfare* (London: Routledge, 1985). For criticisms of these polls and alternative views, see R. Harris and A. Seldon, *Welfare without the State: A Quarter-Century of Suppressed Choice,* Hobart Paperback No. 26 (London: Institute of Economic Affairs, 1987).
32 The discussion in this section is based upon over fifty interviews conducted in Washington, D.C. after the passage of the Family Support Act. Interviewees included congressional aides of the principal policy-makers, interest-group representatives, and federal bureaucrats.
33 *Public Papers of the Presidents of the United States: Ronald Reagan Book 1,* Jan.–June 1986 (Washington, D.C.: U.S. Government Printing Office, 1988), p. 1281. Reagan continued thus: "I am talking about real and lasting emancipation because the success of welfare should be judged by how many of its recipients become independent of welfare."
34 C. Murray, *Losing Ground* (New York: Basic Books, 1984).
35 Mead's arguments about the obligations of citizenship were also implicit. Lawrence Mead, *Beyond Entitlement* (New York: Basic Books, 1985).
36 *The New York Times,* Feb. 16, 1986, p. 1.
37 Representative of these hearings is the one before the Subcommittee on Trade, Productivity, and Economic Growth of the Joint Economic Committee in April 1986 titled "Workfare versus Welfare." Testimonies about workfare were both positive and negative (which referred to mandatory work requirements – usually Community Work Experience Programs – for AFDC recipients). Morton Sklar, a former director of Jobs Watch, contended that "workfare is a variant of public service jobs with one important difference: it is nowhere near as good because it is not a job; it is working off of benefits." Lawrence Mead presented contrary testimony, arguing: "A merely voluntary training program will not have enough impact on the long-term poor to really solve the problem that they pose for American society. Although we must offer training and investment in human capital, there must be a definite obligation to participate to go along with it." Hearing before the Subcommittee on Trade, Productivity, and Economic Growth of the Joint Economic Committee, Congress (99th Cong., 2d Sess. April 23, 1986), pp. 4, 37.
38 For a detailed discussion of Moynihan's role in various welfare reforms, see N. Lemann, *The Promised Land* (New York: Alfred Knopf, 1991).
39 See *Background Material and Data on Programs within the Jurisdiction of the Committee on Ways and Means,* Committee on Ways and Means, U.S. House of Representatives, March 15, 1989 (Washington D.C.: U.S. Government Printing Office, 1989.).
40 For details of the Family Support Act, see King "Citizenship as Obligation in the United States."
41 "Public assistance programs must . . . provide incentives and opportunities for individuals to get the training they need and to seek jobs. It is our aim to create a system where it is always better to work than to be on public assistance. . . . The Governors

recommend that all employable welfare recipients must participate in an education, job training or placement program and accept a suitable job when it is offered." National Governors' Association, "Job-Oriented Welfare Reform" (Washington, D.C.: NGA, Feb. 1987), pp. 1–2.

The same document reported also that the "Governors' aim in proposing a welfare reform plan is to turn what is now primarily a payments system with a minor work component into a system that is first and foremost a jobs system, backed up by an income-assistance component. The major obligation of the individual in the public-assistance contracts we propose is to prepare for and seek, accept, and retain a job."

42 NGA, "Job-Oriented Welfare Reform," p. 2.

43 Child and health care facilities have to be provided during the initial period of work (for between 6 and 12 months) or the incentive to participate will not be sufficient: "Parents cannot be expected to give up welfare if the loss of Medicaid jeopardizes access to health care for their families. Once a participant has found a job, support services should be provided for a transition period." NGA, "Job-Oriented Welfare Reform," p. 3.

44 The governors did not advocate a uniform federal system: "We oppose federal requirements that tell us how to implement job-related services. There is no one solution to the challenge of employability and job placement" (NGA, "Job-Oriented Welfare Reform," p. 4). The governors' preference for subnational flexibility in the implementation of work–welfare schemes reflects their desire to guard state independence jealously. It illustrates also how the states come to perform an innovative role in the federal system.

45 Central to the governors' analysis of the problems of welfare and prescriptions for reform is a conception of the interrelationship between welfare dependency and work opportunities. This perceived linkage was new to the welfare debate. See National Governors' Association, *Making America Work: Bringing Down the Barriers* (Washington, D.C.: NGA, 1987), p. vi.

46 The governors' proposals, formally launched on February 24, received wide national coverage, particularly in the print medium with editorials in the *Chicago-Tribune, Boston Globe, Los Angeles Times,* and *New York Times.* These commentaries emphasized the work requirement element of the reforms and the language of social contract in which it was presented. Typical of these views is *The Washington Post*'s editorial (Feb. 26, 1986): "The governors' proposal comes in the form of a contract. Welfare recipients promise to seek jobs, and the government promises to provide them with the necessary support. The president likes the first part of this but not the second, because it will cost money. On the issue of work, the liberals have disarmingly adopted the conservative vocabulary. As the government's side of the new bargain, the governors and other reformers are proposing a major increase in education, and training funds for welfare mothers, day care, a continuation of health insurance."

47 See, e.g., J. Quint and C. Guy, *Interim Findings from the Illinois Win Demonstration Program in Cook County* (New York: MDRC, June 1986) and D. Freidlander et al., *West Virginia: Final Report of the Community Work Experience Program* (New York: MDRC, 1986). For a discussion of the MDRC reports, see F. Block and J. Noakes, "The Politics of New-Style Workfare," *Socialist Review* (1988):31–58. While positive, the MDRC results demonstrated fairly marginal success rates, a result that the Corporation's reports stressed.

48 State and local governments are prohibited from replacing regular employees with workfare workers; and a grievance procedure was established for ensuring compliance with the displacement requirement.

49 The Coalition sought training programs that imparted useful (that is, marketable) skills

targeted to known labor-market needs at above minimum wage level. *Changing Welfare: An Investment in Women and Children in Poverty: The Proposal of the National Coalition on Women, Work and Welfare Reform* (Washington D.C.: Wider Opportunities for Women, April 1987).

50 Neither lobbied Congress about the Family Support Act, but the U.S. Chamber of Commerce issued a number of publications during the 1980s stressing the education and training deficiencies of the U.S. work force. See U.S. Chamber of Commerce publications including *Business and Education: Partners for the Future* (Washington, D.C.: U.S. Chamber of Commerce, 1985).

51 See P. Hennessy, *Whitehall* (London: Secker and Warburg, 1989), B. Castle, *The Castle Diaries 1984–70* (London: Weidenfeld, 1984), and R. Crossman, *The Diaries of a Cabinet Minister* (London: Hamish Hamilton, 1976).

52 See P. Dunleavy, "Explaining the Privatisation Boom: Public Choice versus Radical Approaches," *Public Administration* 64 (1986):13–34, and "Government at the Centre," in P. Dunleavy, A. Gamble, and G. Peele, eds., *Developments in British Politics, 3* (London: Macmillan, 1990).

53 For an account of the Next Steps program see House of Commons Treasury and Civil Service Committee Fifth Report, "Developments in the Next Steps Programme 1988–89," July 19, 1989, and Eighth Report, "Civil Service Management Reform: The Next Steps," Vol. 1, July 25, 1988. There are of course disadvantages to a lengthy incumbency: a government can lose a sense of direction. However, between 1979 and 1989 the Conservatives had not confronted this problem. Radical change does not always require lengthy incumbency, as the 1945–51 Labour administration's record demonstrates.

54 Before the founding of the MSC the only training organization was the twenty-four Industrial Training Boards (ITBs) established under the Industrial Training Act of 1964. For an overview of industrial training in Britain, see A. Brown and D. S. King, "Economic Change and Labour Market Policy: Corporatist and Dualist Tendencies in Britain and Sweden," *West European Politics* 11 (1988):75–91. In 1972 a consultative paper titled "Training for the Future" was issued, followed in November of that year by the decision to establish a Commission for Training Policy.

55 The MSC was established after the Fulton Committee of Inquiry review of the civil service. The Fulton Committee expressed a preference for units separate from departments. Fulton Committee, *Report of the Committee on the Civil Service 1966–68* (London: Her Majesty's Stationery Office, Cmd. 3638, 1968), ch. 5, paras. 147 and 150.

56 *Employment and Training Act 1973*, p. 3.

57 Manpower Services Commission, *Annual Report* 1975, p. 3: the MSC envisages a role in national economic policy similar to the Swedish Labor Market Board. However, short-term concern with unemployment dominated. In April 1975 Chancellor of the Exchequer Denis Healey allocated an additional £20 million to the MSC, with a further £30 million earmarked for 1976–7, to expand its training for the unemployed. Redundant workers, apprentices, and people with disabilities were the intended targets for this additional money. The MSC's first annual report argued for training programs and employment services to be included in national economic strategy. *Department of Employment Gazette*, April 1975, p. 328.

58 See D. Lee, "The transformation of training and the transformation of work in Britain," in S. Wood, ed., *The Transformation of Work* (London: Unwin Hyman, 1989); D. Finn, *Training without Jobs* (London: Macmillan, 1987); and D. S. King, "The Conservatives and Training Policy: From Tripartitism to Neoliberalism," *Political Studies* 41 (March, 1993).

59 The biggest union, the Transport and General Workers' Union (TGWU), led by Ron Todd, decided in March 1988 to oppose the new training scheme (*Financial Times, March 11, 1988*). The TGWU set four conditions for giving its support: including employee protection; trade union involvement; the scheme being voluntary; and paying those in it the rate for the job. Ron Todd said, "The ET scheme is about lack of choice. It is about putting unemployed people into low-skilled, low-paid placements" (*Financial Times*, Sept. 8, 1988). The TGWU was joined in opposition by the Scottish TUC, GMB union, and local authority unions NALGO and NUPE (*Financial Times*, June 11, 1988).

60 For technical discussion of these and other changes, such as for housing, disability, and family credit, see M. Hill, *Social Security Policy in Britain* (Aldershot: Edward Elgar, 1990), chs. 5, 6, Albert Weale, "Social Policy," in Dunleavy, Gamble, and Peele, eds., *Developments in British Politics, 3*, and N. Wikeley, "Unemployment Benefit, the State, and the Labour Market," *Journal of Law and Society* 16 (1989).

61 Early concern from the trade union movement that ET would be so designated did not materialize.

62 White Paper, "Training for Employment" (London: Her Majesty's Stationery Office, Cmd. 316, Feb. 1988).

63 According to the White Paper, "Human resources are now one of the keys to international competitive success. Britain must develop and bring back into productive use the skills and capacities of the unemployed." Ibid, p. 18.

64 "We must ensure that resources are not wasted and in particular that they are not devoted to those who are not entitled to unemployment benefits who are actually in jobs but claiming benefits as if they were unemployed. It is an obligation on all Governments to take whatever steps are necessary to make sure that the social security system is not abused." Ibid., p. 33.

65 "The Government will seek to ensure that unemployed people are aware that they will be financially better off in employment." Ibid., p. 38.

66 In their determination to achieve universal participation Bill Clay, Labour MP, characterized these changes as amounting to "workfare." Parliamentary Debates (Hansard) Official Report Standing Committee F, Jan. 21, 1988, cols. 624–5.

67 The success or failure of this new ET is disputed, with many critics contending that the anticipated monthly number of places have not been filled and that the creation of 82 TECs is too ambitious. By February 1989 the government cut the number of ET places by 10 percent because of lack of demand and early dropouts (*Financial Times*, Feb. 14, 1989); only 137,000 trainees had signed instead of the 600,000 (at 45,000 per month) planned in September 1988. In London the number of ET places has been cut by one-third ("ET in London" and "ET: There Are Alternatives," Centre for Alternative Industrial and Technological Systems, London, May 1989). Only thirteen large companies, compared to 135 in the YTS, are participating on a national basis in ET (*Financial Times*, June 20, 1989). Labour Party claims that "ET was spurned" by large companies and that business did not support ET were rejected by Fowler in the House of Commons. Fowler described ET as "an enormous achievement." In criticism the Labour shadow cabinet employment spokesman, Michael Meacher, "said ET was 'posed to collapse.' It had filled only 187,000 of its 450,000 target places and the dropout rate had accelerated from 36% in January to 75% in April" (*Financial Times*, July 6, 1989). On October 25, 1989, the employment secretary announced that forty applications to establish TECs had been received of which thirty-one were in the development phase (*Financial Times*, Oct. 26, 1989). After a slow start seventy-six TECs had been established by July 1990, six short of the number planned. However, the Association of British Chambers of Commerce has expressed skepticism about the ability of TECs to implement government aims. The most serious criticism came in a

House of Commons Employment Committee Report (June 1990), which concluded
that if ET was to achieve its aims then its budget needed to be expanded substantially.

68 Amendment to Regulation 22 of the 1987 Income Support (General) Regulations effective from December 17, 1990.

69 See Hoover and Plant, *Conservative Capitalism;* King, *The New Right;* and Peele, *Revival and Reaction.*

70 See William Keegan, *Mrs Thatcher's Economic Experiment* (Harmondsworth: Penguin, 1984).

71 See D. Anderson, D. Marsland, and J. Lait, *Breaking the Spell of the Welfare State* (London: Social Affairs Unit, 1981) and G. Gilder, *Wealth and Poverty* (London: Buchan and Enright, 1981).

72 The first amendment to Clause 7 of the 1988 Social Security bill proposed by Labour MP Paul Flynn required the secretary of state for employment to prepare a report on the "genuinely seeking work" condition operative between 1924 and 1930, a marker of the character of the ensuing debate and its historic connotations. Flynn explained the purpose of the amendment thus: "to try to persuade the Government to accept the clear lesson of history and the lesson from the 1920s to 1930 of the turmoil, confusion, unhappiness, humiliation, and futility of a similar clause in that unhappy and bewildering decade." Parliamentary Debates (Hansard) Official Report House of Commons Standing Committee F "Social Security Bill," Jan. 31, 1989, col. 159. For a discussion of the earlier law, see TUC, "Administering Unemployment Insurance" (London: TUC, 1929).

73 Parliamentary Debates (Hansard) Official Report House of Commons Standing Committee E, Dec. 1, 1987, col. 313. Norman Fowler, Secretary of State for Employment, also denied the compulsory component (*Financial Times,* March 24, 1988). The MSC was opposed to making any scheme compulsory and its working party's report concludes: "The programme must be voluntary. The programme must attract participants by what it offers and the best attraction is demonstrated by high-quality outcomes and, for as many participants as possible, a job" (*Financial Times,* Jan. 6, 1988). This view was not shared by the Training Commission's (part-time) chairman Bryan Wolfson, appointed in October 1988, who said that "workfare" could not be ruled out as a policy option (*The Independent,* Aug. 24, 1988).

74 Parliamentary Debates (Hansard) Official Report House of Commons Standing Committee E, Nov. 26, 1987, col. 239.

75 Parliamentary Debates (Hansard) Official Report House of Lords, Jan. 25, 1988, vol. 492, col. 460.

76 Bill Clay, MP, noted: "We know that there will be a debate about compulsion and that the Government will deny that there is compulsion. Because of Restart, there is a considerable degree of compulsion, even before the Government's new workfare plus scheme." Parliamentary Debates (Hansard) Official Report House of Commons Standing Committee F, Jan. 21, 1988, col. 628.

77 Parliamentary Debates (Hansard) Official Report House of Commons Standing Committee F, Jan. 21, 1988, cols. 632, 633, 634. Ms. Clare Short reiterated Meacher's argument: "The new availability for work test . . . asks what wage level is expected, and compares not with the wage level that a person has had previously but with the current wage level in that area." Ibid., col. 638.

78 Parliamentary Debates (Hansard) Official Report House of Commons Standing Committee F, Jan. 21, 1988, col. 639.

79 For comments see Michael Meacher, Parliamentary Debates (Hansard) Official Report House of Commons Standing Committee F, Jan. 21, 1988, col. 643.

80 Parliamentary Debates (Hansard) Official Report House of Commons, Jan. 26, 1989, col. 134. One MP, Mrs. Beckett, intervened during the minister's speech with the

following observation: "The lesson of history and of the amendment is that whatever the test may be designed to do, in practice, the test – both in its original form and in its new form – did humiliate and will humiliate people and cause enormous hardship. . . . The test is not linked to whether work is available. The test is designed to examine people's efforts without considering whether those efforts are utterly pointless. That caused humiliation and resentment in the 1920s and it will do so again in the 1990s." (col. 134)

81 Parliamentary Debates (Hansard) Official Report House of Commons, Jan. 31, 1989, col. 164.

82 N. Wikeley, "Unemployment Benefit, the State, and the Labor Market," *Journal of Law and Society* 16 (1989):291–309, on p. 304.

83 See H. Parker, *The Moral Hazards of Social Benefits* (London: IEA, 1982) and A. Seldon, *Whither the Welfare State* (London: IEA, 1981).

84 D. S. King, "The Conservatives and Training Policy: From Tripartitism to Neoliberalism," *Political Studies* 41 (March 1993).

85 Cay Stratton who was assistant secretary of economic affairs for employment and training in Massachusetts (interview by the author, Nov. 23, 1988).

86 It should be noted that the Massachusetts program is voluntary.

87 See *Working Brief* (London: Unemployment Unit), July 1990.

88 Peter Hall, "The Movement from Keynesianism to Monetarism: Institutional Analysis and British Economic Policy in the 1970s," unpublished manuscript, p. 40. Two caveats should immediately be added to Hall's argument. First, despite being in opposition for over ten years, the Labour Party has failed to behave in the predicted way – that is, to develop new programs – though it has certainly tried. Second, the postwar period in Britain was characterized by relative agreement between the two parties about public policy with neither developing innovative ideas while in opposition.

89 Monetarist policy was introduced first by the Labour government in 1976 acting under pressure from the IMF, to whom the government had successfully applied for a loan. This decision suggests that the policy-making scope for any administration at that time was limited. Similar constraints may have applied to unemployment policy.

90 A recent article in *The Independent on Sunday* (July 8, 1990) outlines how the next likely Conservative Party manifesto will be informed by the ideas of New Right think tanks. The paper reported that the "Prime Minister had lunch with representatives of two think tanks which have played a significant role in shaping the free market Thatcherism of the 1980s: the Adam Smith Institute and the Institute of Economic Affairs. . . . Five days later Mrs Thatcher took Whitehall by surprise when she treated the Conservative Women's Conference in London to a 'stream of consciousness' agenda of fourth-term policies."

91 P. Hall, *Governing the Economy*.

92 See discussion in Joel Wolfe, "State Power and Ideology in Britain: Mrs Thatcher's Privatization Programme," *Political Studies* 39 (1991):237–52.

Index

Printed in the United States
1126000004B/87